Best Racehorses of 2020

Volume 1

European Group 1 Winners

Dr SIEGLINDE McGEE

Set in 10.5 pt Garamond
Sleipnir Press

ISBN 978-1-8384331-0-9

Cover: Ghaiyyath was the world's top-rated horse of 2020. The son of classic stars Dubawi and Nightime was bred in Ireland by Dermot Weld's Springbank Way Stud and bought by Godolphin for €1,100,000 at the 2015 Goffs November Foal Sale. The multiple Group 1 star was trained in England by Charlie Appleby and has now joined the Darley stallion team at Kildangan Stud in Co Kildare.
Photo: Healy Racing

Every effort has been made to ensure that the information in this book is accurate and up to date. Assessments of each horse reviewed are the personal opinion of the author, based on decades of experience examining the pedigrees, racing and stud careers of thoroughbreds.

ABOUT THE AUTHOR

Sieglinde discovered horse racing by chance on Grand National day 1982 and was instantly hooked, reading and watching everything she could about it. She started writing on the subject in the summer of 1983, began keeping personal databases on racing and pedigrees the following year, and got her first job in racing five years after that, doing course wires (tipping) and bloodstock sales reports for *The Sporting Life*, maintaining a small pedigree database, and producing press releases for a major stud. She has been widely published on racing and pedigrees over the past three decades, wrote and produced her own 'Timeform Annual-style' books for several years in the 1990s and has been writing for *The Irish Field* since the spring of 2000.

While still in secondary school, a well-known member of the British racing press joked that "with databases that detailed, you should almost be doing a degree in it!" So, she did, many years later, and in 2005, was conferred with a doctorate from Trinity College Dublin for a thesis titled *Behavioural Reactivity and Ensuing Temperamental Traits in Young Thoroughbred Racehorses (Equus caballus)*, the culmination of four years of postgraduate research.

Sieglinde is also a graduate of Dublin City University and of the world-famous Thoroughbred Breeding Course at the Irish National Stud. She taught in Trinity College Dublin and for Oscail (in DCU) for several years, has presented at academic conferences and given guest lectures.

OTHER BOOKS BY THE AUTHOR

Racing & bloodstock:

Best Racehorses of 2020 – Volume 2: Great Britain & Ireland's Group 2 & Group 3 Winners – print-on-demand paperback via Amazon

European Group 1 Winners of 2019 – print-on-demand paperback & eBook via Amazon

New Sires of 2019 – print-on-demand paperback & eBook via Amazon

Freshman Sires of 2019 – print-on-demand paperback via Amazon

European Group 1 Winners of 2018 – print-on-demand paperback
& eBook via Amazon

Others include:
Key Research & Study Skills in Psychology (SAGE, 2010) – hardback,
paperback & eBook

Thank you for reading *Best Racehorses of 2020 – Volume 1:
European Group 1 Winners.*

If you enjoy this book, please spread the word
and perhaps leave a review on Amazon, Goodreads or another
book-review site.

Even a single line will do.

Reviews help authors!

CONTENTS

INTRODUCTION

The year 2020 was one for the history books and not just because of the races that ran and the horses that won them. It was a pandemic year, and as we get ready for the 2021 season it is still not known if or when any sense of the old normality will return. The Covid-19 virus, whose effect can be mild, moderate, long-term debilitating or lethal to those unlucky enough to catch it, is in its third wave in some parts of the world, a second wave in others. To date, over 106 million people have been confirmed as infected, with in excess of 2.3 million dead, and hundreds of thousands of new cases of infection are reported globally every day. And just as newly developed vaccines are being steadily rolled out there are reports that one of the most easily transportable ones is as little as ten per cent effective against a particular rapidly spreading strain. We all hope that we are near the end of this plague, but there could still be a long way to go.

The opening months of the 2020 season were unlike no other. Initially run behind closed doors, racing in Germany was suspended on March 16th, France halted its action from March 17th and Ireland's racing shutdown from March 25th. National Hunt racing's Cheltenham Festival went ahead as usual from March 10th to 13th but all further racing in Great Britain was then suspended from March 18th. The multi-million-dollar Dubai World Cup day at Meydan in the United Arab Emirates, due to be held on March 28th, was called off just six days before, and horses who had shipped over to compete made it out before a local lockdown. Many US tracks also shut down, as did racing in other jurisdictions, while Hong Kong, Japan, Australia, and New Zealand continued without spectators. For the northern hemisphere's flat sector, it would mean rescheduling of the early-season trials and classics, but for the National Hunt sector it meant the loss of the Grand National meeting at Aintree—which had been due to feature Tiger Roll's bid for a third victory in the feature event—plus both the Irish Grand National festival meeting at Fairyhouse and the Punchestown Festival.

The British Horseracing Authority (BHA) announced that the first four classics of the English season would be postponed to an as-yet unknown date. Soon afterwards, Ascot racecourse issued a statement that should the Royal Ascot festival go ahead on its scheduled dates in June then it would take place behind closed doors. At this point, both Horse Racing Ireland and France Galop remained hopeful that their countries' classic would go ahead on their usual dates.

The William Haggas-trained geldings Addeybb and Young Rascal were among those who had been overseas as the lockdowns spread, the pair having travelled to Australia with some big targets in mind. Both ran their races, with the former landing both the Group 1 Ranvet Stakes at Rosehill and Group 1 Longines Queen Elizabeth Stakes at Randwick and the latter taking a Group 3 contest at the first-named venue. The latter top-level win came hours after the Irish Taoiseach, Leo Varadkar, announced that Ireland's lockdown would be extended to May 5th.

In mid-April it was proposed to move the English mile classics to early June and the Derby and Oaks to July. Germany's racing officials hoped to be able to have a return to action as early as May 4th, and then the French announced plans to reopen their racing behind closed doors from May 11th, with no foreign-based horses or riders permitted entry until the end of that month. The answer to the question of whether or not foreign runners would be allowed was not yet available, so there was no guarantee that any could line-up for the rescheduled classics, which would be moved to a month later than their usual spot in the calendar. The French mile classics would run on June 1st, the Prix Saint-Alary and Prix Ganay on June 14th, the Prix du Jockey Club and Prix de Diane on July 7th, the Prix d'Ispahan on July 19th and for three-year-olds only, with the Grand Prix de Paris replacing the Prix Niel's slot in mid-September.

Also, in April, there was some speculation as to whether any restrictions on the ability of jurisdictions to accept international entries for their races would necessarily lead to a reduction in the pattern status of those races. Races that are restricted to horses who have been born in a specific country or only to horses trained in a particular region or nation have local pattern status only, for example, the Local Grade 1 of Canada's premier classic, the Queen's Plate, a race that counts only as listed status internationally. Thankfully, this remained no more than a short-lived discussion point.

The picture was clearer with regard to racecourse attendances by spectators. In Ireland, for example, this would be under restrictions until at least September, which meant that the Galway Festival, a famous week-long event with no pattern races but several top National Hunt handicaps, and which typically takes place around the same time as the Glorious Goodwood festival, would be without the massive crowds normally associated with it. In the end, the general public was still unable to attend a meeting in the country by the end of the year, whereas spectators were permitted on only a few days in Britain. The virus levels increased in the autumn and winter, necessitating further lockdowns.

Competition in France returned as planned, there was a flurry of stakes and pattern races, but just days later the region of Ile-de-France was one of those designated a 'red zone' and so racing was stopped again at ParisLongchamp, Chantilly, and a number of other tracks. The country's first classics of the year would instead be held at Deauville. Meanwhile, revised schedules for Ireland and Great Britain were being finalised, the latter despite an absence of any official confirmation that the sport would resume as hoped on June 1st. The Irish Derby and Irish Oaks would remain on their originally set day but the Guineas races would be held on June 12th and 13th, with the Tattersalls Gold Cup moving to July. That race is usually for older horses only, but for 2020 it would be open to three-year-olds too.

Entries were made and declarations finalised for the proposed opening of the British flat season, in the expectation that the go-ahead would come in time, and that clearance was finally given on Saturday, May 30th, two days before a ten-race card at Newcastle was set to launch. A cap of twelve runners per race was one of the safety measures put in place. It had also been revealed that many of the major races would have their prize money cut due to the developing financial impact of the pandemic.

The first three weeks in June provided a feast of Group 1 and other pattern racing. The opening classics in France went ahead on the 1st, the Coronation Cup, 2000 Guineas and 1000 Guineas held at Newmarket on the 5th, 6th and 7th, the Irish 2,000

Guineas and Irish 1,000 Guineas the following Friday and Saturday, and then on to Royal Ascot where the running order was reorganised to create distance between the initial mile classics and the top three-year-old races, and to give as many two-year-old as possible the chance to qualify for a berth. Those initial few weeks were flooded with five- and six-furlong races for juveniles, with trainers given an opportunity to nominate the horse they'd rather not have balloted. With numbers restricted, qualification for Royal Ascot's juvenile contests would be based on wins and places obtained on the track before then, with unraced horses down the list but ahead of unplaced ones.

There was also a flurry of such contests held in France from late May, and that country's freshman sire Goken (by Kendargent) made a quick impression by notching up five individual winners before the start of June. Adaay (by Kodiac), Dariyan (by Shamardal) and Twilight Son (by Kyllachy) all had a winner apiece on the continent too before racing began again in Britain or Ireland.

Finally, things were rolling, yet always under a cloud of doubt as to how much of a full season could take place. Victor Ludorum (by Shamardal), an undefeated top-level star at two but beaten on his seasonal reappearance before the lockdown, won the Group 1 Emirates Poule d'Essai des Poulains (French 2000 Guineas) on June 1st, Dream And Do (by Siyouni) had her nose in front on the line in the Group 1 Emirates Poule d'Essai des Pouliches (French 1000 Guineas) about 35 minutes later—both at Deauville—followed just over half an hour after that by Fearless King's (by Kingman) narrow victory against the previously undefeated juvenile champion Rubaiyat in the Group 2 Mehl-Mülhens-Rennen (German 2000 Guineas) at Cologne.

It was strange to see well-known classic trials taking place after the classics with which they are associated. The move of the Tattersalls Gold Cup to a July slot resulted in it being a stronger race than typical—it's a pity it cannot remain in that temporary slot—and the only Group 1 race that was lost in the reshuffle was the Newbury's one-mile Lockinge Stakes.

By the end of the year, after an almost complete if somewhat rejigged pattern-race schedule, sixty-nine horses had won a Group

1 race in Europe and/or been a British- or Irish-trained winner of such a race in another continent, accumulating a combined haul of ninety-two top-level contests.

Multiple Group 1 winners

Seventeen horses won more than once at the top level in 2020, six of them winning three Group/Grade 1 contests.

Ghaiyyath (by Dubawi) finished the year as the highest-rated horse in the world (130) and Godolphin's five-year-old got his major wins in the Coronation Cup at Newmarket, Coral-Eclipse Stakes at Sandown and Juddmonte International Stakes at York. He was runner-up to Magical (by Galileo) in the Irish Champion Stakes, and that prize was the third Group 1 of the season for the Aidan O'Brien-trained mare. Her other big wins came in the Pretty Polly Stakes and Tattersalls Gold Cup, great reward for the change of heart over her intended retirement at the end of 2019. Her team-mate Love (by Galileo) lit up the classic scene with impressive wins in the 1000 Guineas and Oaks, to which she added another easy success in the Yorkshire Oaks. Ghaiyyath and Magical have been retired to stud, but Love is due back in action in 2021.

Like Ghaiyyath, Barney Roy (by Excelebration) is a Godolphin runner for the Charlie Appleby stable. He was classic-placed a mile Group 1 star at three but withdrawn from stud after being found to be sterile. The five-year-old gelding is now an effective middle-distance performer and he landed the Jebel Hatta, Grosser Dallmayr-Preis - Bayersiches Zuchtrennen, and Grosser Preis von Baden. Addeybb (by Pivotal) is also a gelding and although known to be a capable sort before last season, he was a revelation in 2020. The standard of middle-distance racing in Australia is a few pounds below what it is in Europe, so he perhaps did not get the credit he deserved for his Group 1 double there at the start of the year. However, it is doubtful that anyone questions his merit now following his victory in the Champion Stakes at Ascot in October.

Tarnawa was the other triple top-level winner. She is owned and bred by H H the Aga Khan, trained by Dermot Weld and won all four of her starts. She had been purposely given an autumn campaign and is reportedly going to have another one in 2021, geared towards a potential Prix de l'Arc de Triomphe bid. Following an impressive Group 3 success at Cork on her reappearance in early August, she won the Prix Vermeille, Prix de l'Opera and Breeders' Cup Turf. The latter was a popular result in part because it was a long-overdue first Breeders' Cup victory for Weld, one of the all-time great trainers. It was also a striking double for Weld: training a Breeders' Cup champion and breeding the number-one horse in the world. Ghaiyyath was bred by his Springbank Way Stud.

The eleven dual Group 1 winners consisted of five fillies, five colts/entires and one gelding. Battaash (by Dark Angel; King's Stand Stakes, Nunthorpe Stakes) was the latter, whereas the other males were Mogul (by Galileo; Grand Prix de Paris, Hong Kong Vase), Palace Pier (by Kingman; St James's Palace Stakes, Prix Jacques le Marois), Persian King (by Kingman; Prix d'Ispahan, Prix du Moulin de Longchamp), Sottsass (by Siyouni; Prix Ganay, Prix de l'Arc de Triomphe) and Stradivarius (by Sea The Stars; Gold Cup, Goodwood Cup).

The fillies who won twice at the top level were Audarya (by Wootton Bassett; Prix Jean Romanet, Breeders' Cup Filly & Mare Turf), Fancy Blue (by Deep Impact; Prix de Diane, Nassau Stakes), Glass Slippers (by Dream Ahead; Flying Five Stakes, Breeders' Cup Turf Sprint), Nazeef (by Invincible Spirit; Falmouth Stakes, Sun Chariot Stakes), and Wonderful Tonight (by Le Havre; Prix de Royallieu, British Champions Fillies & Mares Stakes).

Breeders

Three breeders were responsible for three or more Group 1 winners and although the identity of the top two finishers on that table will come as no surprise to anyone, the third would have been considerably longer odds at the start of the year and yet is one of the most influential people in European racing.

Coolmore Stud bred five in their own name, four of them classic stars and one a two-year-old. Shale (by Galileo; Moyglare Stud Stakes) is the latter and she appeals as a leading classic prospect for 2021. Love (by Galileo; 1000 Guineas, Oaks,

Yorkshire Oaks) was the highest-rated of the older quartet and is due to be back in action in 2021. Fancy Blue (by Deep Impact) won both the Prix de Diane (French Oaks) and Nassau Stakes, Peaceful (by Galileo) won the Irish 1,000 Guineas, and Serpentine (by Galileo) slipped the field at Epsom to win the Derby in style.

Godolphin's quartet included two of their three unbeaten juvenile Group 1-winning sons of Shamardal (by Giant's Causeway) from 2019: Pinatubo (Prix Jean Prat) and Victor Ludorum (Poule d'Essai des Poulains). They also bred the Dubawi (by Dubai Millennium) pair Lord North (Prince of Wales's Stakes) and Space Blues (Prix Maurice de Gheest).

The great Irish trainer Jim Bolger helped make Ahonoora and Galileo into the sires they became, and he had an outstanding year as a breeder, which included a Group 1 double in the space of a few minutes on the afternoon of Saturday, October 24th. Gear Up (by Teofilo) won the Criterium de Saint-Cloud for the Mark Johnston stable, followed almost immediately by Mac Swiney (by New Approach) taking the Vertem Futurity Trophy Stakes at Doncaster. That colt is trained by Bolger, who also bred Teofilo (by Galileo) and trained him through his undefeated career on the track, and he also trained Derby star New Approach (by Galileo). Twilight Payment (by Teofilo) brought up the treble, the former Bolger trainee winning the Melbourne Cup for the Joseph O'Brien stable.

Five other breeders had a pair of Group 1 winners. Juddmonte Farms was represented by Enable (by Nathaniel; King George VI and Queen Elizabeth Stakes) and Siskin (by First Defence; Irish 2,000 Guineas), Lynch Bages Ltd supplied the classic winners Even So (by Camelot; Irish Oaks) and Santiago (by Authorized; Irish Derby), Rabbah Bloodstock Ltd struck with Addeybb (by Pivotal; Ranvet Stakes, Queen Elizabeth Stakes, Champion Stakes) and Hello Youmzain (by Kodiac; Diamond Jubilee Stakes), Shadwell Estate Company Ltd bred and raced Nazeef (by Invincible Spirit; Falmouth Stakes, Sun Chariot Stakes) and Tawkeel (by Teofilo; Prix Saint-Alary), whereas Aidan and Anne-Marie O'Brien's Whisperview Trading Ltd produced Order of Australia (by Australia; Breeders' Cup Mile) and Thunder Moon (by Zoffany; National Stakes).

Trainers

A total of thirty-one trainers representing five countries had a European or European-trained Group/Grade 1 winner in 2020. The breakdown is shown in Table 1 below. Of the ninety-two races won, nine were held outside of Europe: four in the United States of America, three in Australia and one each in Hong Kong and the United Arab Emirates.

Table 1: Distribution of the European and European-trained
Group 1 winners of 2020

Trained In	Trainers	Horses	Wins
France	6	12	14
Germany	2	3	3
Great Britain	13	28	41
Ireland	9	25	33
United States of America	1	1	1
TOTAL	31	69	92

Ireland's Aidan O'Brien led the way again, this time with ten horses who notched up fifteen Group/Grade 1 wins, down marginally from eleven winners of sixteen races the previous year. The stable won classics with Love (by Galileo; 1000 Guineas, Oaks, plus the Yorkshire Oaks), Peaceful (by Galileo; Irish 1,000 Guineas), Santiago (by Authorized; Irish Derby) and Serpentine (by Galileo; Derby). Their three-year-olds also included Mogul (by Galileo; Grand Prix de Paris, Hong Kong Vase) and Order of Australia (by Australia; Breeders' Cup Mile), their older horses featured Circus Maximus (by Galileo; Queen Anne Stakes) and Magical (by Galileo; Pretty Polly Stakes, Tattersalls Gold Cup, Irish Champion Stakes), whereas both St Mark's Basilica (by Siyouni; Dewhurst Stakes) and Van Gogh (by American Pharoah; Criterium International) struck in the two-year-old division.

England's John Gosden had seven winners of ten races, an excellent haul yet down on the previous year's seventeen races with seven horses. Enable (by Nathaniel; King George VI and Queen Elizabeth Stakes) and Stradivarius (by Sea The Stars; Gold Cup, Goodwood Cup) led the way again, and the stable's older horses also included Lord North (by Dubawi; Prince of Wales's Stakes) and Nazeef (by Invincible Spirit; Falmouth Stakes, Sun

Chariot Stakes). Mishriff (by Make Believe; Prix du Jockey Club) and Miss Yoda (by Sea The Stars; Preis der Diana) won classics, whereas Palace Pier (by Kingman; St James's Palace Stakes, Prix Jacques le Marois) shone in the milers' division.

Three trainers had four Group/Grade 1 winners: Charlie Appleby (England), Francis-Henri Graffard (France) and Joseph O'Brien (Ireland). Appleby notched up eight races for the Godolphin team, striking gold with Barney Roy (by Excelebration; Jebel Hatta, Grosser Dallmayr-Preis - Bayersiches Zuchtrennen, Grosser Preis von Baden), Pinatubo (by Shamardal; Prix Jean Prat), Space Blues (by Dubawi; Prix Maurice de Gheest) and the top-rated horse in the world for 2020: Ghaiyyath (by Dubawi; Coronation Cup, Coral-Eclipse Stakes, Juddmonte International Stakes). Graffard landed a classic with the subsequent Arc runner-up In Swoop (by Adlerflug; Deutsches Derby), sent The Revenant (by Dubawi; Queen Elizabeth II Stakes) to big-race success at Ascot in October and won top-level races in France with four-year-old filly Watch Me (by Olympic Glory; Prix Rothschild) and three-year-old colt Wooded (by Wootton Bassett; Prix de l'Abbaye de Longchamp). O'Brien also won a classic, taking the St Leger with Galileo Chrome (by Australia), he had two of the leading two-year-olds of the season in Pretty Gorgeous (by Lawman; Fillies' Mile) and Thunder Moon (by Zoffany; National Stakes), and he notched up his second Melbourne Cup success, this time with Twilight Payment (by Teofilo).

Thirteen trainers sent out two Group/Grade 1 winners. They represented four countries and are grouped below by where they are based.

The four trainers in Ireland were: Jessica Harrington – Alpine Star (by Sea The Moon; Coronation Stakes) and Lucky Vega (by Lope de Vega; Phoenix Stakes); Ger Lyons – Even So (by Camelot; Irish Oaks) and Siskin (by First Defence; Irish 2,000 Guineas); Donnacha O'Brien – Fancy Blue (by Deep Impact; Prix de Diane, Nassau Stakes) and Shale (by Galileo; Moyglare Stud Stakes); and Dermot Weld – Search For A Song (by Galileo; Irish St Leger) and Tarnawa (by Shamardal; Prix Vermeille, Prix de l'Opera, Breeders' Cup Turf).

There were five in Great Britain: Andrew Balding – Alcohol Free (by No Nay Never; Cheveley Park Stakes) and Kameko (by Kitten's Joy; 2000 Guineas); Clive Cox – Golden Horde (by Lethal Force; Commonwealth Cup) and Supremacy (by Mehmas; Middle Park Stakes); William, Haggas – Addeybb (by Pivotal; Ranvet Stakes, Queen Elizabeth Stakes, Champion Stakes) and One Master (by Fastnet Rock; Prix de la Foret); Mark, Johnston – Gear Up (by Teofilo; Criterium de Saint-Cloud) and Subjectivist (by Teofilo; Prix Royal-Oak); and Kevin Ryan – Glass Slippers (by Dream Ahead; Flying Five Stakes, Breeders' Cup Turf Sprint) and Hello Youmzain (by Kodiac; Diamond Jubilee Stakes).

Three French trainers were represented by a pair of Group 1 winners, namely André Fabre – Persian King (by Kingman; Prix d'Ispahan, Prix du Moulin de Longchamp) and Victor Ludorum (by Shamardal; Poule d'Essai des Poulains); Frederic Rossi – Dream And Do (by Siyouni; Poule d'Essai des Pouliches) and Sealiway (by Galiway; Prix Jean-Luc Lagardere - Grand Criterium); and Jean-Claude Rouget – Sottsass (by Siyouni; Prix Ganay, Prix de l'Arc de Triomphe) and Tawkeel (by Teofilo; Prix Saint-Alary). Henk Grewe was the sole German trainer to make this list and he won with the fillies Donjah (by Teofilo; Preis von Europa) and Sunny Queen (by Camelot; Grosser Preis von Bayern).

Owners

The identity of the most successful owner depends on how you handle the various Coolmore partnerships. Taken as single entities, there is tie between Godolphin and the combination of Michael Tabor, Derrick Smith and Mrs J. Magnier, both having had five Group/Grade 1 winners. That becomes six for Godolphin if you add in their part-owned Persian King (with Ballymore Thoroughbreds Ltd) but jumps to thirteen for Coolmore if you combine all of the horses owned by their various partners.

Tabor, Smith & Magnier had Fancy Blue (by Deep Impact; Prix de Diane, Nassau Stakes), Love (by Galileo; 1000 Guineas, Oaks, Yorkshire Oaks), Mogul (by Galileo; Grand Prix de Paris, Hong Kong Vase), Peaceful (by Galileo; Irish 1,000 Guineas) and

Santiago (by Authorized; Irish Derby). Tabor, Smith, Magnier & Mrs David Nagle is the partnership that owns Van Gogh (by American Pharoah; Criterium International). Smith, Magnier & Tabor owns Shale (by Galileo; Moyglare Stud Stakes) and St Mark's Basilica (by Siyouni; Dewhurst Stakes), and if you add Anne-Marie O'Brien to that sequence of names then you add in Order of Australia (by Australia; Breeders' Cup Mile). Reorder them to Magnier, Tabor & Smith and you have the partnership that owns Derby winner Serpentine (by Galileo), and that grouping was a part-owner, with Flaxman Stables, of Circus Maximus (Queen Anne Stakes). Mrs J Magnier and Mrs Paul Shanahan own the Irish Oaks scorer Even So (by Camelot), whereas Magical (by Galileo; Pretty Polly Stakes, Tattersalls Gold Cup, Irish Champion Stakes) raced solely in Smith's name.

Godolphin's solo five were Barney Roy (by Excelebration; Jebel Hatta, Grosser Dallmayr-Preis - Bayersiches Zuchtrennen, Grosser Preis von Baden), Ghaiyyath (by Dubawi; Coronation Cup, Coral-Eclipse Stakes, Juddmonte International Stakes), Pinatubo (by Shamardal; Prix Jean Prat), Space Blues (by Dubawi; Prix Maurice de Gheest) and Victor Ludorum (by Shamardal; Poule d'Essai des Poulains). Hamdan Al Maktoum had four this time around: Battaash (by Dark Angel; King's Stand Stakes, Nunthorpe Stakes), Mohaather (by Showcasing; Sussex Stakes), Nazeef (by Invincible Spirit; Falmouth Stakes, Sun Chariot Stakes) and Tawkeel (by Teofilo; Prix Saint-Alary), whereas Khalid Abdullah, with Enable (by Nathaniel; King George VI and Queen Elizabeth Stakes) and Siskin (by First Defence; Irish 2,000 Guineas), was the only other owner with more than a single winner.

Sires

Prolific champion Galileo (by Sadler's Wells) was the leading sire of Group 1 winners again, although with 'only' eight this time compared to ten the previous year. There was a lot of talk about the world record number of Group 1 winners in a stallion's career after Peaceful won the Irish 1,000 Guineas, but she was not the record-breaker. That honour went to Magic Wand when she won the Mackinnon Stakes in November 2019, thereby becoming

Group 1 winner number eighty-four for the great Coolmore sire. Some name Fairy King Prawn among Danehill's top-level winners, others show Scintillation as being eligible for the list, but neither is correct—their top wins were all local Group 1-level only, and that is merely listed status as per the International Cataloguing Standards.

As Weatherbys' data show, Danehill had eighty-three Group/Grade 1 winners, not eighty-four. Peaceful, in becoming number eighty-five for her sire, merely extended the record that had been set months before. Galileo's other Group 1 winners in 2020 were Circus Maximus (Queen Anne Stakes), Love (1000 Guineas, Oaks, Yorkshire Oaks), Magical (Pretty Polly Stakes, Tattersalls Gold Cup, Irish Champion Stakes), Mogul (Grand Prix de Paris, Hong Kong Vase), Search For A Song (Irish St Leger), Serpentine (Derby), and Shale (Moyglare Stud Stakes).

Kildangan Stud stallion Teofilo (by Galileo), who is on the verge of becoming the first son of his great sire to reach 100 stakes winners, finished in second place despite not having a top-level winner in either Ireland or Great Britain. Donjah (Preis von Europa) struck in Germany, Gear Up (Criterium de Saint-Cloud), Subjectivist (Prix Royal-Oak) and Tawkeel (Prix Saint-Alary) won in France, and Twilight Payment landed the Melbourne Cup in Australia.

Dubawi's (by Dubai Millennium) quartet was headlined by the world's top-rated horse of the year, Ghaiyyath (Coronation Cup, Coral-Eclipse Stakes, Juddmonte International Stakes) and completed by Lord North (Prince of Wales's Stakes), Space Blues (Prix Maurice de Gheest) and The Revenant (Queen Elizabeth II Stakes). Shamardal (by Giant's Causeway) and Siyouni (by Pivotal) came next on three apiece. The late Kildangan Stud ace struck with Pinatubo (Prix Jean Prat), Tarnawa (Prix Vermeille, Prix de l'Opera, Breeders' Cup Turf) and Victor Ludorum (Poule d'Essai des Poulains), whereas Haras de Bonneval's Siyouni was represented by Dream And Do (Poule d'Essai des Pouliches), Sottsass (Prix Ganay, Prix de l'Arc de Triomphe) and St Mark's Basilica (Dewhurst Stakes).

Nine stallions had a pair of Group/Grade 1 winners. Adlerflug (by In The Wings) had two of Europe's leading middle-distance three-year-olds via In Swoop (Deutsches Derby) and Torquator Tasso (Grosser Preis von Baden). Australia (by Galileo), Camelot (by Montjeu) and Sea The Stars (by Cape Cross) also had a classic winner plus one other. For Australia they were Galileo Chrome (St Leger) and Order of Australia (Breeders' Cup Mile), Camelot had Even So (Irish Oaks) and Sunny Queen (Grosser Preis von Bayern), and Sea The Stars was represented by Miss Yoda (Preis der Diana) and Stradivarius (Gold Cup, Goodwood Cup). Kingman (by Invincible Spirit) had two of the best milers of the year: Palace Pier (St James's Palace Stakes; Prix Jacques le Marois) and Persian King (Prix d'Ispahan, Prix du Moulin de Longchamp). Dream Ahead (by Diktat), sire of Dream of Dreams (Sprint Cup Stakes) and Glass Slippers (Flying Five Stakes, Breeders' Cup Turf Sprint), and Kodiac (by Danehill), sire of Campanelle (Prix Morny) and Hello Youmzain (Diamond Jubilee Stakes), had sprinters, whereas both Pivotal (by Polar Falcon) and Wootton Bassett (by Iffraaj) struck with both a sprinter and a middle-distance horse. Pivotal's pair were Glen Shiel (British Champions Sprint Stakes) and Addeybb (Ranvet Stakes, Queen Elizabeth Stakes, Champion Stakes), whereas Wootton Bassett's were Wooded (Prix de l'Abbaye de Longchamp) and Audarya (Prix Jean Romanet, Breeders' Cup Filly & Mare Turf).

Group 1-winning broodmares
Five Group 1-winning fillies of past seasons were represented by a European Group 1 winner in 2020: Halfway To Heaven, Homecoming Queen, Imagine, Iota, and Nightime.

Halfway To Heaven (by Pivotal) was bred by Trevor Stewart and bought by Coolmore for €450,000 at the 2006 edition of the Goffs Million Sale (now Orby Sale). She notched up four wins and four placings from nine starts for the Aidan O'Brien stable, the former featuring the Group 1 Irish 1,000 Guineas, Group 1 Nassau Stakes and Group 1 Sun Chariot Stakes and her best placings being when third in both the Group 1 Poule d'Essai des Pouliches (French 1000 Guineas) and Group 1 Matron Stakes. She has been bred to Galileo (by Sadler's Wells) every year since she retired to stud and, so far, has had two outstanding daughters. Rhododendron won the Group 1 Lockinge Stakes, Group 1 Prix de l'Opera and Group 1 Fillies' Mile and was runner-up in each of the Grade 1 Breeders' Cup Filly & Mare Turf, Group 1 Oaks and Group 1 1000 Guineas. That star had a Deep Impact (by Sunday Silence) colt in 2020 and was then bred to Dubawi (by Dubai Millennium).

Magical is the year-younger full sister. She was due to go to stud last year as a four-time Group 1 star booked to visit No Nay Never (by Scat Daddy), but there was a change of plans. She remained in training as a five-year-old and added three more Group 1 wins to her name: the Pretty Polly Stakes, plus a second edition of both the Tattersalls Gold Cup and Irish Champion Stakes. Her victory in the latter made her just the second horse to have taken that prize twice: Dylan Thomas was the other one. She is now part of Coolmore's broodmare band and arrived there with career totals of a dozen wins, including seven Group 1s, and over £4,875,000 in prize money.

Halfway To Heaven had a full brother to her celebrity daughters in 2019, and her 2010-born son Flying The Flag, a ten-furlong Group 3 scorer, went to stud in South Africa. She is out of the Group 2 King's Stand Stakes winner Cassandra Go (by Indian Ridge) and her many blacktype relations include her dam's classic-placed, pattern-winning half-brother Verglas (by Highest Honor). He stood at Haras de la Haie Neuve in France, shuttled to Australia and eventually took up long-term residence at the Irish National Stud, and his tally of Group 1 winners would have been larger were it not for his death at the age of just seventeen.

Homecoming Queen (by Holy Roman Emperor) was bred by Tower Bloodstock, and she achieved four wins and three placings from sixteen starts. She won a one-mile listed contest by four and a half lengths on yielding-to-soft at the Curragh as a two-year-old, narrowly landed the seven-furlong Group 3 Leopardstown 1000 Guineas Trial Stakes on her second start at three and then put up a performance-of-a-lifetime display at Newmarket to take the Group 1 1000 Guineas by nine lengths. She is a half-sister to the unbeaten juvenile filly champion Queen's Logic (by Grand Lodge), who is the dam of the Group 2-winning sprinter Lady of The Desert (by Rahy) and grandam of the juvenile Group 2 sprint winner Queen Kindly (by Frankel). She is also a half-sister to Serpentine's (by Galileo; Derby winner in 2020) classic-placed dam Remember When and can be described as being a three-parts sister to Dylan Thomas (by Danehill). That six-time Group 1-star's tally included the Irish Derby, the Prix de l'Arc de Triomphe, the King George VI and Queen Elizabeth Stakes and two editions of the Irish Champion Stakes. He has sired several Group 1 winners.

Shale (by Galileo), who is closely related to Serpentine, is a daughter of Homecoming Queen and she is trained by Donnacha O'Brien. She won three of her six starts in 2020. She beat Pretty Gorgeous in both the Group 3 Silver Flash Stakes and Group 1 Moyglare Stud Stakes, chased home that same rival in the Group 2 Debutante Stakes and will probably renew that rivalry on the classic scene this coming season. Homecoming Queen's first two foals, both also by Galileo, were blacktype placed. Now owned by Katsumi Yoshida of Northern Farm, the mare had a full brother to Shale in 2019, was bred to Saxon Warrior (by Deep Impact) and then sent to Japan where she had a filly on March 20th, 2020.

Imagine (by Sadler's Wells) was one of the shining lights of the 2001 season. The eleventh foal of the unraced Doff The Derby (by Master Derby), a mare who was a half-sister to the dam of the 'Iron Lady' Triptych (by Riverman), she had spent most of her career racing over seven furlongs, much of that as two-year-old, but, as you might expect of a half-sister to the Timeform 139-rated superstar Generous (by Caerleon), she improved considerably when stepped up in trip. First, she beat Crystal Music by two lengths in the Group 1 Irish 1,000 Guineas at the Curragh and then defeated Flight of Fancy by a length and a quarter to take the Group 1 Oaks at Epsom. She was not seen in action again. The wonderful Triptych was sadly denied a broodmare career when, pregnant in her first season, she lost her life in a freak accident. Imagine, on the other hand, has had a long and successful stud life.

The ill-fated juvenile Group 1 winner Horatio Nelson (by Danehill), who broke down over a furlong from home in the Derby, was her first foal. He was followed by the Group 1-placed Red Rock Canyon (by Rock of Gibraltar) and Group 2 Rockfel Stakes scorer Kitty Matcham (by Rock of Gibraltar). Then came

Viscount Nelson (by Giant's Causeway), a Group 2 Al Fahidi Fort winner who was placed in the Group 1 Irish 2,000 Guineas and Group 1 Coral-Eclipse Stakes before going to stud in Chile. His full brother Point Piper was a Grade 3-winning miler in the USA, and now the mare has Van Gogh (by American Pharoah) to represent her. He represents the second crop of his US Triple Crown-winning sire and gave the stallion his second top-level winner when landing the Group 1 Criterium International by four lengths over a mile on heavy ground at Saint-Cloud in late October. Imagine foaled a full sister to Van Gogh in March 2019.

Gestüt Schlenderhan's homebred **Iota** (by Tiger Hill) has established herself among the elite broodmares in her native Germany. She was trained by Peter Schiergen, raced in Germany, England and Canada and had her finest hour on the track when taking the Group 1 Preis der Diana (German Oaks) by four lengths on soft ground at Hamburg in June 2005. She is out of Iora (by Konigsstuhl), which makes her a half-sister to the Group 1-placed stakes winner Ioannina (by Rainbow Quest) and to Illo (by Tertullian), a ten-and-a-half-furlong Group 3 scorer and twelve-furlong listed scorer in Germany who went on to finish a four-and-three-quarter-length fourth to the great Black Caviar in the Group 1 C.F. Orr Stakes over seven furlongs at Caulfield. The granddaughter of Danehill (by Danzig) has produced the pattern-placed middle-distance filly Igraine (by Galileo) and that one's stakes-placed full brother Iniciar, but when bred to Adlerflug (by In The Wings), the Group 1-winning distant relation to Galileo (by Sadler's Wells) and Sea The Stars (by Cape Cross), she has come up with two Group 1 stars.

Ito won the Group 1 Grosser Preis von Bayern by four lengths at Munich in November 2015. He is also a dual Group 2 scorer, he stands at Gestüt Erftmühle and his eldest are now three-year-olds. In Swoop is even better and that Francis-Henri Graffard-trained colt could be one of Europe's leading middle-distance horses again in 2021. The lightly raced bay beat the subsequent Group 1 scorer Torquator Tasso by three-quarters of a length to win the Group 1 Deutsches Derby in July, chased home Mogul in the Group 1 Grand Prix de Paris at ParisLongchamp two months later and then failed by only a neck to catch Sottsass when storming home in the Group 1 Prix de l'Arc de Triomphe on heavy ground at that same venue in October. Iota's new three-year-old is a Gavin Hernon-trained filly named Iffy (by Australia), she returned to Adlerflug in 2018 and 2019 and was bred to Highland Reel (by Galileo) in 2020.

As a student on the Irish National Stud's famous Thoroughbred Breeding Course back in 1995, I could scarcely have imagined that the Bluebird (by Storm Bird) mare I was so fond of would go on to become the direct ancestor of three Group 1 stars, one of them a Horse of the Year, but that's exactly what Ridge Pool did. Her track career was cut short by a broken pelvis, she died after only a few seasons at stud, but the sweet-natured mare who liked to use me as a scratching post, to deposit half-eaten feed in my pocket and who often served as the live model during practicals, produced the stakes winner Caumshinaun (by Indian Ridge). The late Marguerite Weld sent Caumshinaun to the dual Derby star Galileo (by Sadler's Wells) in his maiden season at stud and the result was the runaway Group 1 Irish 1,000 Guineas heroine **Nightime**, dam of the Grade 1 winner Zhukova (by Fastnet Rock) and her champion half-brother Ghaiyyath (by Dubawi).

Zhukova was trained by Mrs Weld's son Dermot, she won seven of her thirteen starts and was a six-length winner of the Grade 1 Man O' War Stakes over eleven furlongs at Belmont Park. She also won listed races at Galway, Cork and the Curragh, beat US Army Ranger in the Group 3 Enterprise Stakes over twelve furlongs at Leopardstown and trounced Pretty Perfect by seven and a half lengths in the Group 3 Blue Wind Stakes over a quarter of a mile less at Naas. Her first two foals, both in February 2019 and February 2020, are sons of Dubawi (by Dubai Millennium), which makes them three-parts brothers to Ghaiyyath. He burst onto the international scene in 2019 when winning the Group 1 Grosser Preis von Baden by fourteen lengths and he has now joined the team at Kildangan Stud following a triple Group 1-winning season that saw him top the World's Best Racehorse Rankings for 2020 on a mark of 130. He won a pattern race at Meydan then impressed in the Group 1 Coronation Cup, Group 1 Coral-Eclipse Stakes and Group 1 Juddmonte International before chasing home Magical in the Group 1 Irish Champion Stakes.

Ghaiyyath, bred by the Welds' Springbank Way Stud, was sold as a foal in Goffs for €1,100,000. Zhukova was bought by Godolphin as a broodmare prospect in Newmarket, for 3,700,000 guineas, after completing her racing career. Nightime's current three-year-old New Kingdom (by Dubawi) was sold for 700,000 guineas as a foal and her 2019-born full brother to Ghaiyyath made €1,200,000 in Goffs as a weanling, also to race for Godolphin. She had a Kingman (by Invincible Spirit) colt in 2020 and was then bred back to Dubawi.

Broodmare Sires

Only nine broodmare sires were represented by two or more Group/Grade 1 winners in 2020, down one from the previous year, and following a quieter season than has become usual for Cheveley Park Stud's veteran Pivotal (by Polar Falcon), Galileo (by Sadler's Wells) topped this ranking. He had only three in 2018, five in 2019 and five again last season. The latest batch were Barney Roy (by Excelebration), Ghaiyyath (by Dubawi), Sottsass (by Siyouni), St Mark's Basilica (by Siyouni) and Watch Me (by Olympic Glory).

Pivotal shared second place with Danehill (by Danzig) and Sadler's Wells (by Northern Dancer), the three tied on four winners apiece. Magical (by Galileo) again led the way for Pivotal; his other three were Golden Horde (by Lethal Force), Love (by Galileo) and One Master (by Fastnet Rock). Danehill's daughters were responsible for Even So (by Camelot), Mogul (by Galileo), Order of Australia (by Australia) and Search For A Song (by Galileo), whereas it was mares by Sadler's Wells who gave us Enable (by Nathaniel), Fancy Blue (by Deep Impact), Thunder Moon (by Zoffany) and Van Gogh (by American Pharoah).

Cape Cross (by Green Desert), one of three broodmare sires of three Group 1 scorers, was represented by Lucky Vega (by Lope de Vega), Santiago (by Authorized) and Tarnawa (by Shamardal). The others on three were: Danehill Dancer (by Danehill) via Circus Maximus (by Galileo), Serpentine (by Galileo) and Subjectivist (by Teofilo), and Oasis Dream (by Green Desert) with Siskin (by First Defence), Tawkeel (by Teofilo) and Twilight Payment (by Teofilo). Dansili (by Danehill) and Tiger Hill (by Danehill) were the pair with two apiece. The former struck with the contrasting duo Dream of Dreams (by Dream Ahead) and Galileo Chrome (by Australia), whereas Tiger Hill's two were In Swoop (by Adlerflug) and Princess Zoe (by Jukebox Jury).

Galileo's great sire, Sadler's Wells, was a three-parts brother to Nureyev (by Northern Dancer), the grandsire of Pivotal. Aside from that male lineage, the only sire line that got a look-in among those with two or more Group 1 winners was that of Danzig (by Northern Dancer), represented as usual by his two powerful branches: Danehill and Green Desert. We need something different to emerge in the coming years.

Auctions

Thirty-two of the sixty-nine Group/Grade 1 stars featured in this book were sold at least once in a public auction ring, excluding vendor buy-backs. Four of those were sold twice, each of them having changed hands as both a foal and yearling. Three were sold only as foals (Alcohol Free, Dream of Dreams, Ghaiyyath), two were sold as five-year-olds in training (Glen Shiel, Twilight Payment), and the rest—including the four who were sold twice (Barney Roy, Champers Elysees, Lucky Vega, Pretty Gorgeous)—were sold as yearlings.

Prix Marcel Boussac winner Tiger Tanaka (by Clodovil) was the cheapest and the only Group 1 winner purchased for a four-figured sum. The €6,500 buy happened at the Tattersalls Ireland September Yearling Sale in 2019. At the other end of the scale, Goffs sold Ghaiyyath (by Dubawi) for €1,100,000 as a foal in 2015, whereas both Mogul (by Galileo) and St Mark's Basilica (by Siyouni) made seven-figure prices at Tattersalls' Book 1 Sale, 3,400,000 guineas (2018) and 1,300,000 guineas (2019) respectively. The lowest and highest prices for Group 1 winners from the various sales companies are shown in Table 2.

The auctions at which the thirty-two Group 1 winners were sold are listed in Table 3. Further details are provided in an index at the back of the book, including who they are, who consigned them to the sales and who bought them on the day.

Table 2: Lowest and highest prices of Group 1 winners of 2020 who were sold by the various sales companies

Company	sold	lowest	highest
Arqana	6	€55,000	€340,000
BBAG	4	€24,000	€280,000
Doncaster Bloodstock Sales (DBS)	1	£70,000	£70,000
Goffs	5	€40,000	€1,100,000
Goffs UK	3	£45,000	£65,000
Keeneland	1	$90,000	$90,000
Tattersalls	12	30,000gns	3,400,000gns
Tattersalls Ireland	2	€6,500	€28,000

Table 3: Auctions at which Group 1 winners of 2020 were sold, showing the number sold plus the lowest and highest price at each venue

Auction	Sold	lowest	highest
Ireland			
Goffs Horses-in-Training	1	€200,000	€200,000
Goffs November Foals	3	€40,000	€1,100,000
Goffs Orby	2	€52,000	€175,000
Tattersalls Ireland November Flat	1	€12,500	€12,500
Tattersalls Ireland September Yearling	1	€6,500	€6,500
Auction	**Sold**	**lowest**	**highest**
Tattersalls Ireland September Yearling Part 2	1	€28,000	€28,000
Great Britain			
DBS Premier Yearling	1	£70,000	£70,000
Goffs UK Premier Yearling	2	£65,000	£65,000
Goffs UK Spring Horses-in-Training	1	£45,000	£45,000
Tattersalls October Book 1	5	190,000gns	3,400,00gns
Tattersalls October Book 2	5	50,000gns	200,00gns
Tattersalls December Foals	2	30,000gns	37,000gns
France			
Arqana Deauville August	3	€40,000	€340,000
Arqana Deauville October	2	€90,000	€125,000
Arqana December Sale	1	€55,000	€55,000
BBAG October Yearling	1	€24,000	€24,000
BBAG September Yearling	3	€35,000	€280,000
United States of America			
Keeneland September Yearling	1	$90,000	$90,000

Earliest career win

Many seem obsessed with the idea of early two-year-old speed, but of the sixty-nine Group 1 winners featured in this book, not a single one won a juvenile contest before the start of May. Perhaps there could have been one this year if the 2020 campaign in Ireland and Great Britain had not been confined to a single two-year-old contest run before the beginning of June. The subsequent Group 3 scorer Poetic Flare beat the subsequent listed winner Lipizzaner by half a length in that March 23rd contest at Naas. However, six did get their first win in the month of May, the earliest being Pinatubo's debut success over six furlongs on the Tapeta at Wolverhampton on the 10th, in 2019. Siskin scored at Naas a day later and Sealiway, in 2020, on May 12th.

In contrast, seven of the sixty-nine did not get their first win until November of their two-year-old season: Mishriff (6th), Space Blues (7th), Stradivarius (7th), Watch Me (10th), Glen Shiel (12th), Wonderful Tonight (22nd) and Enable (28th). Another sixteen of them did not win at all at two—including the sprinter Oxted (three-year-old; April 28th)—and some hadn't even raced at that age. The latest to get off the mark was Order of Australia who, strange as it may seem, did not get his maiden success until September 18th, 2020, less than two months before landing the Grade 1 Breeders' Cup Mile. Early two-year-old form isn't necessary to make a top-class racehorse.

Month of birth

Those with an early foaling date have a physical advantage over those born later in the season, an effect that reduces over time but can be pronounced in two-year-old races and the eight-to-twelve-furlong classics. Only four of the sixty-nine Group 1 winners here were born in the month of January: Tiger Tanaka (20th), Peaceful (22nd), Barney Roy (29th) and Tawkeel (29th). Most were born in February (N=21) or March (N=23), as you might expect, with a slightly smaller number arriving in the month of April (N=17). This is a small sample size and the differences between the three most populous months are not significant.

Those horses born in the month of May are the result of coverings that took place either in the end of the previous May or in June, a period of the season in which many breeders are hesitant about having their mares bred. Although there were two classic stars among the later-foaled ones in 2019, plus a top two-year-old, this time all but one of the late foals was successful as an older horse. The other one was a leading juvenile. The four Group 1 winners from last season who had a May foaling date were: Thunder Moon (1st; National Stakes), Twilight Payment (6th; Melbourne Cup), Glen Shiel (7th; British Champions Sprint Stakes) and Magical (18th; Pretty Polly Stakes, Tattersalls Gold Cup, Irish Champion Stakes).

Note on suffixes in names

Readers may notice that some horses have not been given a suffix with their names in the pedigree charts or in the various indexes. This is not an error or omission. The suffix indicates the country in which the horse was born, but those who were born in Ireland or Great Britain did not get suffixes until 1988. Therefore, horses born in those countries before that year do not have one as part of their official name. Some older Canadian-bred horses (pre-1967) do not have them either. There is at least one database out there that seems to have put a GB by default after the name of all horses without a suffix; this is an error. There is also another well-known racing website that has replaced many, if not all, of the GB suffixes with UK, whereas a well-known Australian one has all the IREs as IRL and the GBs as GBR; these are also incorrect. The latter has also changed NZ to NZL and GER to DEU, which may add further confusion for any readers from that region of the world.

To quote the International Federation of Horseracing Authorities (IFHA), "The suffix between brackets is taken from the International Code of Suffixes ... and constitutes part of the animal's registered name."

Having come across various sources that change the suffixes in horses' names to suit their own style, I have been reminded again of just how important those usually three-letter codes can be. Change it and you could be taking about a completely different horse; they are, in effect, like a surname. An example I give when talking to a class about the issue is that of Eva Luna. To which horse are they referring if someone tells you that their horse comes from the family of Eva Luna? There are five horses of that name registered with Weatherbys and if it's the talented one you want then you are probably choosing between the two who were born in 1992.

Eva Luna (USA) was a daughter of Alleged (by Hoist The Flag) and the Oaks-placed Media Luna (by Star Appeal) and, as one might expect with such a pedigree, she showed stamina on the track and passed it on at stud. The Juddmonte Farms homebred won the Group 3 Park Hill Stakes and Listed Galtres Stakes, she is the dam of the Group 1 St Leger winner Brian Boru (by Sadler's Wells), his classic-placed Group 2-winning closer-than-half-brother Sea Moon (by Beat Hollow), and the Group 2 Prix de Royallieu winner Moon Search (by Rainbow Quest). She is also the grandam of the Group 1 Derby and Group 1 Prix de l'Arc de Triomphe star Workforce (by King's Best).

The other one born that same year was Eva Luna (IRE), a Jim Bolger trainee who was one of the top juvenile fillies of the crop. She won the Group 1 Phoenix Stakes, Group 3 Railway Stakes and Listed Silver Flash Stakes, she was third in the Group 1 Moyglare Stud Stakes, and she comes from a prolific blacktype family. The daughter of Double Schwartz (by Double Form) and Guess Again (by Stradavinsky) is inbred 3x3 to Fanghorn (by Crocket), a classic-placed mare from whom a string of notable winners descends. This Eva Luna disappointed as a broodmare, but she is the grandam of the Group 2 Flying Childers Stakes winner Beacon (by Paco Boy) and the Dişi Tay Deneme (Turkish 1000 Guineas, a local Group 1 only) scorer Luna Lovegood (by Kaneko) and ancestor of a couple of other high-profile Turkish horses.

The stallion Acclamation is another current example. In this part of the world, we are most likely referring to Acclamation (GB), the 1999-born son of Royal Applause (by Waajib) and Princess Athena (by Ahonoora) who was a high-class sprinter before going on to become a Group 1-producing sire for Rathbarry Stud. He has also earned a good reputation as a sire of stallions. However, if you are in North America then chances are you are talking about Acclamation (USA), the 2006-born son of

Unusual Heat (by Nureyev) and Winning In Style (by Silveyville). He was an Eclipse Award winner in 2011, won the Grade 1 Pacific Classic Stakes, two editions of the Grade 1 Eddie Read Stakes and three back-to-back runnings of the Grade 1 Charles Whittingham Handicap, and he stands in California where he has sired several six-figured earners and some blacktype horses.

Conclusion

The 2020 season was certainly different in how we, as spectators, were able to view it, with the Covid-19 situation restricting or eliminating attendances, but how lucky that we live in an age where so much racing from around the world is available for viewing, live or via soon-posted replays. Think of what we would have missed last year were it not for such technology. Such disruption looks set to continue until the summer of 2021, if not into the autumn—it depends on how quickly each country can roll out its vaccination programme and begin easing and lifting restrictions, and on how effective those vaccines are against new strains—but, fingers crossed, by the time the flat season of 2022 comes around we should all be able to attend as much racing as we can manage. That is something to look forward to with enthusiasm.

So too is the array of talent that will be back in action this coming season, both established stars and less exposed but promising contenders. The major horse racing authorities managed to host an almost complete schedule of blacktype action in 2020, remarkable given the circumstances, and high praise is due to all who made it happen. Among Group 1 races, for example, only the Lockinge Stakes was missing from the British schedule.

Sieglinde McGee
February 15th, 2021

ADDEYBB (IRE)

One hopes that the top finishers in open or male-only Group 1 races will identify future stallion prospects, but on British Champions Day 2020 they failed to do so. Geldings finished one-two in the Sprint, a gelding beat a seemingly well-exposed stakes-winning four-year-old colt in the Queen Elizabeth II Stakes, and then another pair of geldings came home first and second in the Qipco Champion Stakes. What these races did do, from a stallion perspective, was provide further advertisements for two of the top sires in Europe. Dubawi's (by Dubai Millennium) son The Revenant won the mile feature but both the six- and ten-furlong events went to sons of Pivotal (by Polar Falcon). And, for good measure, the Cheveley Park Stud's long-time flag bearer also supplied Brando, the former Group 1 star whom Glen Shiel pipped in the Sprint's photo.

A track record setter at two and Group 1-winning sprinter at three, the powerfully built chestnut has just turned twenty-eight and was retired from covering duties shortly before this book went to print. He reportedly got fifteen of his thirty mares in foal in 2020, and his tally of more than 150 stakes winners includes thirty-two who have won at least once at the highest level. His prominence in pedigrees is guaranteed for many years to come thanks to the exploits of his descendants at stud. His stallion sons include the retired Kyllachy and the notable teenagers Farhh and Siyouni. The latter had an outstanding year in 2020, with Group 1 wins for Dream And Do, Sottsass, and St Mark's Basilica in addition to Canadian Grade 1 success for Etoile. The Haras de Bonneval resident is established as one of Europe's most sought-after sires.

It remains to be seen how far Pivotal's male line will endure. Kyllachy's sprint star Twilight Son has made an encouraging start with his first crop, now aged three, and his Dragon Pulse has proved capable of getting the occasional blacktype horse among a long list of winners. Farhh's early sons King of Change and Far Above will only be starting their stallion careers in 2021, whereas of those by Siyouni, City Light and Le Brivido have their first foals arriving now and Sottsass is one of the newest members of the

Coolmore Stud team. Pivotal's daughters, on the other hand, are greatly prized jewels and he has consistently been among Europe's leading broodmare sires of Group 1 winners in recent years.

Addeybb will obviously play no part in extending his sire's considerable influence but he is a wonderful advertisement for him. The William Haggas-trained chestnut has won eleven of his twenty career starts, earned almost £2 million in prize money and, in 2020, went from being a Group 1-placed Group 2 scorer perceived to be just below the top level to becoming a triple winner at it.

He began his latest campaign in Australia in March, just as Europe was in the process of locking down due to the Covid-19 pandemic, and he was fortunate enough to encounter underfoot conditions to his liking. It was good-to-soft for his first start and soft for the second, he landed the Group 1 Ranvet Stakes by half a length and followed-up three weeks later with a two-and-three-quarter-length score in the Group 1 Longines Queen Elizabeth Stakes, both races over ten furlongs, with the first at Rosehill and the second at Randwick. Verry Elleegant, the top-class mare who chased him home both times, went on to pip 2019's Derby winner Anthony Van Dyck by a head in the Group 1 Stella Artois Caulfield Cup just hours before Addeybb's finest hour in Europe.

There must have been some concerns that the gelding might be unable to travel home, but he made it back and lined-up at the Royal Ascot meeting in mid-June. The going this time was described as good, as it was when he won a one-mile handicap there in July of his three-year-old season and having hit the front briefly around a furlong from home, he had no answer for the strong finish of the John Gosden-trained Lord North, who stormed home for a three-and-three-quarter-length victory in the hands of James Doyle. With Barney Roy another length and a quarter back in third, geldings had filled the top three placings in one of Europe's top mile-and-a-quarter tests.

Although geldings winning at the highest level has been a very long-established feature of racing in some other jurisdictions, for example Australia and the United States of America, their presence in European Group 1s is comparatively recent. It was in part the exploits of the notable pair Teleprompter and Bedtime in the 1980s who led to change here and they made history in July 1986 when being the first of their kind to be permitted to take part in a top-level race in England: they finished third and sixth in the Group 1 Eclipse Stakes at Sandown, this being the year that the great Dancing Brave won the prize from the 'Iron Lady', Triptych. Now, of course, it's commonplace, although geldings are still barred from the classics—true classics are Group 1s and for three-year-olds only—from the best two-year-old races and from many other major events, including the Prix de l'Arc de Triomphe.

Japan, who crossed the line half a length behind Barney Roy at Ascot, was the first colt home in Prince of Wales's Stakes, a nose ahead of Bangkok (also a colt) and with the four-year-old filly Mehdaayih a neck away in sixth. Addeybb's rivals on his next appearance consisted of two colts and four geldings, although that's not uncommon for a listed contest. This time he gave seven pounds and a three-quarter-length beating to 2019 Group 1 scorer Lord Glitters—not the same force in 2020 as in the previous year—to take the Doonside Cup at Ayr, that ten-furlong contest run on ground described as good-to-soft, again showing his turn of foot. This was the same one-two as in 2018's Lincoln Handicap at Doncaster, a race in which the subsequent stakes winner Mitchum Swagger finished third and the multiple pattern-placed stakes winner Gabrial, who had pipped the subsequent top-level scorer Mondialiste in the 2015 edition of that heritage handicap, took fourth.

Several former rivals were again in opposition on his final start of the year, the Group 1 Qipco Champion Stakes, in what was a competitive though not vintage edition of the ten-furlong feature. Twelve months previously he had split the star fillies Magical and Deirdre in the same race, the margins three-quarters of a length and two and a quarter lengths. That race had been thought to be the career finale of the Aidan O'Brien-trained winner but instead of retiring to the paddocks and keeping a date with No Nay Never, she returned to action as a five-year-old and added three wins and a second from four more starts, all of them in Group 1s. The most recent of those had seen her reverse York placings with Ghaiyyath in the Irish Champion Stakes at Leopardstown and so she was the favourite to add her name to the short but select list of dual Champion Stakes stars.

Lord North and Japan were also in the line-up, although both disappointed and finished in rear, as were the talented geldings Desert Encounter and Extra Elusive, the former, now aged eight, not the force of old, and the latter, a five-year-old, having struck up a partnership with Hollie Doyle to win a pair of Group 3s on the run-up to Ascot. They finished fifth and sixth respectively. The classic generation was represented by two classic winners plus one classic-placed Group 2 scorer, and the line-up was completed by the notably talented French gelding Skalleti, a five-year-old for whom future Group 1 success may still await.

Older horses dominated the placings. The shock Derby winner Serpentine, this time ridden by William Buick, went to the front after a furlong and tried to make all as he had done with Emmet McNamara at Epsom, but he had to settle for fourth, passing the line three and a half lengths adrift of a spot in the frame. Pyledriver, the St Leger-placed King Edward VII Stakes and Great Voltigeur Stakes winner, came home seventh but half a length ahead of Mishriff for whom this was an even more disappointing effort. The John Gosden-trained bay had easily won all three of his European starts in 2020 including the Group 1 Prix du Jockey Club (French Derby) and Group 2 Prix Guillaume d'Ornano and it is hoped that he can bounce back from this and have a successful four-year-old campaign.

The destination of the top prize, however, was in little doubt inside the final quarter mile as Addeybb, who had led at the start and then tracked Serpentine for most of the journey, was back in front and going well. Skalleti and Magical kept on in the closing stages but were never going to catch him. They finished half a length apart at the line but the grey was two and a quarter lengths behind Addeybb. It was good to see him get a top-level success in Europe, just reward for a lengthy career of proven talent and consistency and confirmation of his position as a genuine Group 1 performer. That may seem an odd remark to make of a horse hitting the top for a third time in the year, but it is fair to say that the middle-distance division in Australia is not always as strong as it is here. Although he had beaten a proven top-class performer in both his races there, it was perhaps important, in terms of how he is assessed and remembered for posterity, that he landed a top win in Europe too. He was entered for the big international meeting at Sha Tin in Hong Kong in December but, in mid-November, his trainer indicated that he would bypass that meeting and likely head to Australia after Christmas in a bid to get his seven-year-old season off to a Group 1 start.

Addeybb, who was gelded before his debut fourth in a seven-furlong Newbury maiden in mid-May of his three-year-old season, won a maiden and two handicaps that year, kicked off his four-year-old campaign with the aforementioned Lincoln success and then stepped straight into pattern company. He looked full of promise when beating Stormy Antarctic by almost three lengths in the Group 2 bet365 Mile at Sandown but disappointed when only eighth to Rhododendron in the Group 1 Lockinge Stakes, was off the track until finishing well-beaten behind Roaring Lion in the Group 1 Queen Elizabeth II Stakes and then took third place in a ten-furlong listed contest on the Polytrack at Lingfield that November, a race for which he had been favourite.

The only time he finished out of the frame in five starts during 2019 was when fourth to Forest Ranger in the Group 2 Huxley Stakes that May, but he trounced Magic Wand by two and a half lengths in the Listed Wolferton Stakes over ten furlongs at Ascot in June, chased home Elarqam in the Group 2 York Stakes six weeks later and then landed the Group 3 Rose of Lancaster Stakes on heavy ground at Haydock before his outstanding end-of-season effort against Magical. He finished 2020 on an official handicap figure of 125.

There are two sides to every horse's pedigree, of course, and, as you might expect of a mare bred to one of Europe's top stallions, the distaff side of the page is one that gave Addeybb every chance of becoming a horse of note. What is striking at first glance is that he stays farther than might have been expected given that he is by a top sprinter and out of a relation to the Group 2-winning sprinter Nicholas (by Danzig). But a closer look makes it clear that ten furlongs always had a good chance of being this trip.

Nicholas's sibling is the mile listed scorer and Group 3 Royal Whip Stakes third Arbusha, the dam of a pair of minor stakes-winning juveniles in the USA. Their three-parts sister Gdansk Victory (by Danzig Connection) was a nine-furlong Curragh handicap scorer on soft ground for the Jim Bolger stable, and that one later became the dam of Rose Petal (by Majestic Light), a five-time winner, also for the Bolger team, from nine to ten furlongs and whose sole piece of blacktype came when finishing third to On Call and Ebadiyla in the Listed Ballycullen Stakes over fourteen furlongs at Leopardstown. It should be noted that a Danzig Connection (by Danzig) or Majestic Light (by His Majesty) would be less likely to be a sprinter/miler than would many by Pivotal. The same is true of Motivator (by Montjeu), the sire of Addeybb's multiple winning half-brother Blue Tiger's Eye, who has been successful at up to eleven furlongs, but when their dam, Bush Cat (by Kingmambo), was bred to Iffraaj (by Zafonic), a stallion more usually associated with speed at up to a mile, the result was a multiple middle-distance flat winner who went on to win over hurdles. Indeed, Bush Cat also stayed farther than might have been expected as, having been a seven-furlong maiden winner at Folkestone as a juvenile, she was running on at the finish when fourth in the Listed Cheshire Oaks over an extended eleven furlongs on fast ground at Chester the following May.

Of course, Arbusha's siblings also include the Irish winner Danlu (by Danzig), a mare best known for the exploits of her star son, Strategic Choice (by Alleged). He was by a dual Arc hero famed for his stamina influence as a sire and grandsire, his top middle-distance wins featured the Group 1 Gran Premio di Milano, Group 2 Grand Prix de Deauville and Group 3 John Porter Stakes, and when he stepped up in trip to 14 furlongs, he added the Group 1 Irish St Leger. He later achieved some success as a National Hunt stallion.

If you take another step back then you will find that Lulu Mon Amour, the third dam of Addeybb, was a winning daughter of the US classic star and influential stallion Tom Rolfe (by Ribot) and of a mare called Sister Shu (by Nashua). That non-winner was also responsible for the US Grade 3 winner and successful Brazilian stallion Shudanz (by Danzig Connection) and the Grade 2-placed stakes winner and minor European blacktype sire Nordance (by Danzig), but the exploits of her siblings, ancestors and other relations were more significant. Her full sister Shuvee was a top winner at two, three, four and five years of age, a multiple US champion who is in that country's Hall of Fame, and that great mare's full sister Nalee was both a highly talented racehorse and notable as being the dam of 1976's Group 1 Irish St Leger winner Meneval (by Le Fabuleux).

They were all out of Levee (by Hill Prince) who, like Shuvee, included the Coaching Club American Oaks and Beldame Stakes among her top wins, and that US Broodmare of the Year was, in turn, one of the notable daughters of Claiborne Farm's outstanding broodmare Bourtai (by Stimulus). That made her a full sister to 1957's US three-year-old filly champion Bayou and a half-sister to the prolific and high-class performer Delta (by Nasrullah), both of whom were notably successful at stud, and a granddaughter of 1930's Alabama Stakes winner Escutcheon (by Sir Gallahad).

We're now in remote territory so far as relationship to Addeybb goes, given that a direct ancestor in the fifth generation—Levee is his fifth dam—contributes around 3.125% (modern genetic analysis shows that this can be a little more or can be less) to the current animal. But it is a famous family whose various branches also extend to standout performers such as Ekraar (by Red Ransom), Fair Mix (by Linamix), Pleascach (by Teofilo), Sacahuista (by Raja Baba), and Spain (by Thunder Gulch), all of them successful at the highest level at least once and with no real connection to 2020's triple Group 1 star.

Addeybb, a 200,000-guinea Tattersalls October Book 2 graduate bred by Rabbah Bloodstock Ltd, is a proven top-class performer who has been seen to best effect when there is some ease in the ground. It has been said that international travel may again be on his agenda in 2021, and it would be no surprise to see him strike at the top level again before he eventually retires from the track. He has been entered for a potential repeat bid for the Group 1 Queen Elizabeth Stakes over ten furlongs at Randwick on April 10th.

SUMMARY DETAILS
Bred: Rabbah Bloodstock Ltd

Owned: Sheikh Ahmed Al Maktoum
Trained: William Haggas
Country: England
Race record: -41131-11003-41212-11211-
Career highlights: 11 wins inc Qipco Champion Stakes (Gr1), Longines Queen Elizabeth Stakes (Gr1), Ranvet Stakes (Gr1), bet365 Mile (Gr2), Rose of Lancaster Stakes (Gr3), Jordan Electrics Doonside Cup Stakes (L), Wolferton Stakes (L), 2nd Prince of Wales's Stakes (Gr1), Qipco Champion Stakes (Gr1), Sky Bet York Stakes (Gr2), 3rd Betway Churchill Stakes (L)

ADDEYBB (IRE) – 2014 chestnut gelding

Pivotal (GB)	Polar Falcon (USA)	Nureyev (USA)
		Marie d'Argonne (FR)
	Fearless Revival	Cozzene (USA)
		Stufida
Bush Cat (USA)	Kingmambo (USA)	Mr Prospector (USA)
		Miesque (USA)
	Arbusha (USA)	Danzig (USA)
		Lulu Mon Amour (USA)

ALCOHOL FREE (IRE)

Jeff Smith is no stranger to seeing his famous purple and blue colours carried to success at the highest levels, and his roll of honour includes standouts such as Lochsong, Lochangel and Arabian Queen. Each of that trio was also bred by him at Littleton Stud. Lochangel won the Nunthorpe Stakes, just one of the Group 1 prizes that her great dam Lochsong landed in a glittering career on the track, whereas Arabian Queen sprang a 50/1 shock when narrowly beating Golden Horn in the Juddmonte International Stakes at York. That previously Group 1-placed Group 2 scorer is out of Smith's homebred dual Group 2 Lancashire Oaks heroine Barshiba.

In 2020, he added to his big-race haul when Alcohol Free won the Group 1 Juddmonte Cheveley Park Stakes at Newmarket in late September, but this Andrew Balding-trained bay is not homebred. In fact, Smith bought her for €40,000 at the Goffs November Foal Sale where she was consigned by her breeder, Churchtown House Stud. That price looked potentially good value given the exploits of her young sire that year, and it looks even better now that the filly has established herself as one of the leading members of that cohort.

She represents the third crop of Coolmore Stud's talented sprinter and rising star No Nay Never (by Scat Daddy), her appearance in the auction ring came two months after the stallion's first-crop son Ten Sovereigns completed an unbeaten juvenile season with victory in the Group 1 Middle Park Stakes, and the stallion's global tally currently stands at twenty-six stakes winners. They include the Chilean classic heroine Brooke, the Group 1-placed Group 2 scorers Arizona, Nay Lady Nay, and Wichita, Group 2 winner and young British-based stallion Land Force, and seven others who have been successful at pattern level. His fee was quadrupled to €100,000 in 2019, after his first-crop success, it soared again to €175,000 in 2020, and the quality of mares he has received in those years increased to match the cost.

Alcohol Free made her racecourse debut at Newbury in mid-August where, having hit the front a furlong from home, she ran on well to beat a pair of more experienced rivals by one and three-quarter lengths and a head over six furlongs on ground described as good-to-soft. She went to Salisbury three weeks later and caught the eye with an excellent effort in the Group 3 Shadwell Dick Poole Fillies' Stakes on good ground, failing by just three-quarters of a length to beat Happy Romance and with a two-length gap back to the third, Scarlet Bear. The winner was running for the sixth time, had been fifth in the Group 2 Queen Mary Stakes and won both the Weatherbys Super Sprint and the Goffs UK Premier Yearlings Stakes. Neither of that latter pair of races is a blacktype contest, but they are competitive events that attract big fields in the hunt for good prize money.

The pair met again in the Cheveley Park Stakes but this time the less exposed filly came out on top. The Group 2 Lowther Stakes winner Miss Amulet set off in front, Alcohol Free edged into the lead after quarter of a mile, and although the Group 3 Firth of Clyde Stakes scorer Umm Kulthum took on the pair of them from two out, that daughter of Kodiac had to settle for third at the line, a head behind the Irish raider and a further half a length adrift of Alcohol Free. Happy Romance was another length and a quarter back in fourth, with the Group 3 Albany Stakes and Group 2 Duchess of Cambridge Stakes heroine Dandalla losing her unbeaten record in fifth, another three and a quarter lengths behind.

The juvenile division of 2020 was not as strong as it has been in some prior seasons and so it remains to be seen just how many of its current divisional leaders can hold or improve on their position in the rankings by this time next year. It is possible that the brightest stars of the 2018 foal crop may be maidens, one-time winners or even unraced at this point. However, there is every reason to hope that Alcohol Free can progress and hold her own in stronger company. She has run only three times so far, her siblings include Alexander James (by Camelot), who was a stakes winner in France as a three-year-old, and her dam, Plying (by Hard Spun), won three times at that age.

The distance over which she may be effective in 2021 is an obvious question and one for which we won't have an answer until she steps up in trip. Progeny of her sire and maternal grandsire are proven in sprints, at a mile and over middle distances, but it is possible that Alcohol Free may be more of a Commonwealth Cup or Prix Jean Prat contender than a Guineas one. Her dam's next two foals, a now two-year-old Starspangledbanner (by Choisir) filly who made 130,000 guineas in Newmarket in late November and yearling son of Dandy Man (by Mozart) who made €80,000 at the rescheduled Goffs November Foal Sale in December, will probably prove to be sprinters given how offspring of their sire typically fare, and the better horses in the first few generations of the family tend to show speed at up to seven furlongs.

Grandam Nasaieb (by Fairy King) got her blacktype when finishing third in the Listed National Stakes at Sandown as a two-year-old and that mare's nine successful offspring include Kissing Lights (by Machiavellian), a filly who was third in both the Group 2 Flying Childers Stakes and Group 3 Princess Margaret Stakes. Her tally also included Luminous Gold (by Fantastic Light), a triple sprint handicap winner whose progeny feature the Group 3 Prestige Stakes third Zifena (by Zamindar), triple six-furlong scorer Waddat (by Kodiac) and three-time seven-furlong winner Aventius (by Zoffany).

If you go back another step on the page then you will find that Nasaieb is a half-sister to the talented seven-furlong horse Raise A Grand (by Grand Lodge) and that his dam, Atyaaf (by Irish River), was a half-sister to the seven-furlong listed winner and Group 2 Gimcrack Stakes third Weldnaas (by Diesis). Fourth dam Bank On Love (by Gallant Romeo) was an unraced full sister to 1982's Group 2 Richmond Stakes winner Gallant Special.

This is a branch of the famous family of standouts such as Assatis (by Topsider), Dance Number (by Northern Dancer), Numbered Account (by Buckpasser), Private Account (by Damascus) and Woodman (by Mr Prospector), but it is a speed one rather than a more classic-distance-oriented line and so, although it is not impossible that she will stay the trip and could even prove to be well suited by the mile, it may be that Alcohol Free will find the final furlong of the 1000 Guineas a stretch too far. She also holds an entry in the Group 1 Emirates Poule d'Essai des Pouliches, and if an early-season trial was to cast doubt on her stamina then perhaps that could be the better classic option given how the style of French racing can often turn top races more into a test of speed than stamina. Whatever her distance, she remains a bright prospect both on the track and eventually at stud.

SUMMARY DETAILS

Bred: Churchtown House Stud
Owned: Jeff C Smith
Trained: Andrew Balding
Country: England
Race record: 121-
Career highlights: 2 wins inc Juddmonte Cheveley Park Stakes (Gr1), 2nd Shadwell Dick Poole Fillies' Stakes (Gr3)

ALCOHOL FREE (IRE) – 2018 bay filly

No Nay Never (USA)	Scat Daddy (USA)	Johannesburg (USA)
		Love Style (USA)
	Cat's Eye Witness (USA)	Elusive Quality (USA)
		Comical Cat (USA)
Plying (USA)	Hard Spun (USA)	Danzig (USA)
		Turkish Tryst (USA)
	Nasaieb (IRE)	Fairy King (USA)
		Atyaaf (USA)

ALPINE STAR (IRE)

The Group 1 and other pattern events are often where we look when trying to pinpoint the star broodmares of the future but sometimes those who go on to have considerable influence were of lesser note on the track. Pasadoble (by Prove Out), for example, notched up a record of four wins and a place from ten starts, her best results being victories in the Listed Prix de la Calonne at Deauville and the Listed Prix de Liancourt at Longchamp. Her fourth dam, Now What (by Chance Play), had been the US juvenile filly champion of 1939, but neither her own dam nor grandam had ever raced and her third dam was a minor winner of one race from five starts. However, they had made their name at stud instead, and Pasadoble would go on to outperform them all.

She went to the paddocks as a mare of potential, a stakes-winning half-sister to the Grade 1 Brooklyn Handicap scorer and Grade 1 Jockey Club Gold Cup runner-up Silver Supreme (by Al Hattab) and out of a half-sister to the excellent Comtesse de Loir (by Val de Loir). That Group 1 Prix Saint-Alary winner had been placed in two editions of the Group 1 Prix de l'Arc de Triomphe, runner-up in the Group 1 Prix de Diane (French Oaks) and placed in the Group 1 Prix Vermeille, Group 1 Prix Ganay, Grade 1 Canadian International and Group 1 Criterium des Pouliches. Comtesse de Loir had a stakes-placed daughter before Pasadoble's first foal arrived and that Nureyev (by Northern Dancer) filly was a few months old when Comtesse de Loir's daughter Heron Cove (by Bold Bidder) won the Grade 2 Long Island Handicap.

The Nureyev filly, bred and raced by Stavros Niarchos, became one of five winners from Pasadoble's ten foals. Her stakes-winning full sister Massaraat would become the ancestor of talented horses such as Old Persian (by Dubawi), Permian (by Teofilo) and Silkwood (by Singspiel), her unraced half-sister Yogya (by Riverman) would become the dam of the triple Group 1 mile star Six Perfections (by Celtic Swing) and ancestor of several horses of note, but their achievements pale in comparison to hers. Miesque was one of the greats of the Turf, a brilliant miler who would become a broodmare of considerable influence, and Alpine Star is one of her many notable descendants.

The Niarchos Family homebred began her career in the seven-furlong Leopardstown maiden won by Love in July 2019, finishing third as the previously twice-raced Ballydoyle filly made all to score by a head from the Ger Lyons-trained newcomer Soul Search. Alpine Star was a further length and a half behind, and given what this trio achieved, it was among the best juvenile fillies' maidens of the year. The winner is 2020's champion three-year-old filly, the runner-up is a multiple pattern-placed maiden winner and the third a classic-placed Group 1 scorer. The fourth, Petite Mustique, won a maiden next time out and is the filly who Alpine Star short-headed in the Group 2 Debutante Stakes; she did not race again after that.

Alpine Star's maiden win came at Galway, where she trounced the subsequent Group 1 Irish Derby winner Santiago by three and a quarter lengths, and that was three weeks before her Group 2 success, which came on yielding ground. Soul Search was three-quarters of a length back in third, with Love another two lengths behind in fifth. Both the Group 1 Prix Marcel Boussac and Group 1 Fillies' Mile looked like potential targets and, looking further ahead, there was plenty of talk of the winner being a potential Oaks filly for 2020 rather than a mile prospect.

That was a little surprising given the distaff side of her family. She struck me more as a likely miler with the potential to be equally effective at ten furlongs and, given her sire, with a chance of staying twelve furlongs too. But perhaps the exploits of her second-crop sire, Sea The Moon (by Sea The Stars), who had famously won the Group 1 Deutsches Derby by eleven lengths, was influencing perception. Yes, she was doing her best work in the later stages of the Debutante Stakes. However, needing the full seven furlongs and looking ready for a mile in late summer of one's two-year-old season does not automatically mean the horse will be a middle-distance one. If backed up by a stout pedigree then yes, the odds are fairly good that you have a middle-distance prospect on your hands, but if there is a lot of mile pace close on the page then the Oaks trip may be doable while a little farther than ideal.

Alpine Star was not seen out again that year and the Group 1 Coronation Stakes at Royal Ascot in June was the next opportunity to see her in action. This is a race that her brilliant half-sister Alpha Centauri (by Mastercraftsman) won by six lengths in 2018, and she upheld the family's honour with an impressive performance of her own. She was being nudged along by Frankie Dettori around half-way, looked briefly like she might be stuck for room, was asked for her effort a quarter of a mile from home, hit the front about a furlong later and stormed clear to beat the previous season's Grade 1 Breeders' Cup Juvenile Fillies' Turf heroine Sharing by four and a quarter lengths. The Group 1 Fillies' Mile winner and Group 1 1000 Guineas third Quadrilateral crossed the line another length and three-quarters back in third. Dettori expressed doubt, in post-race interviews, as to Alpine Star's ability to stay twelve furlongs but was certain that ten would be no problem for her.

The ground at Chantilly weeks later was good-to-soft, as it had been at Ascot, and a notably competitive edition of the ten-and-a-half-furlong Group 1 Prix de Diane Longines produced a four-way finish. Alpine Star, this time ridden by Stephane Pasquier, tried to make all, and although headed a furlong from home she fought back and was only a short neck down at the line. Fancy Blue landed the top prize, Peaceful was another head back in third, Raabihah was the same margin behind in fourth and there was a two-and-a-half-length gap back to Magic Attitude in fifth. The latter would later move to North America and easily win the Grade 1 Belmont Oaks Invitational Stakes over half a furlong less on firm ground.

Pasquier was again in the saddle when the filly took on the colts and older horses in the Group 1 Prix du Haras de Fresnay-le-Buffard Jacques le Marois over a mile ground at Deauville the following month. This time they settled in third as Pretreville set the pace. She came under pressure three furlongs from home, made her move a furlong and a half later but was always going to have to settle for second place after Palace Pier moved to the front shortly afterwards. That said, he only won by three-quarters of a length and the pair pulled another five lengths clear of the third-placed Circus Maximus, himself a multiple Group 1-star. Persian

King and Romanised disappointed in fourth and fifth. The ground at Deauville was described on the *Racing Post*'s website as being heavy but it was given as "collant", which is holding (between very soft and heavy) on France-Galop's site; "lourd" means heavy ground.

Alpine Star was entered in the Group 1 Qipco Champion Stakes but was instead last seen in action at ParisLongchamp two weeks before that race for what was a competitive edition of the Group 1 Prix de l'Opera Longines. It did look briefly like the Jessica Harrington-trained chestnut might take the prize, but the Aga Khan's homebred four-year-old Tarnawa stayed on strongly in the closing stages and got the verdict by a short neck, making it a one-two for Ireland. That daughter of Shamardal (by Giant's Causeway) is trained by Dermot Weld. Audarya and Tawkeel, both featured elsewhere in this volume, were the next two home, finishing three-quarters of a length and the same behind the runner-up, while fifth place went to Ambition, the Group 2 winner whom Audarya had pipped by a neck in the Group 1 Prix Jean Romanet over the same trip at Deauville in August. Each of the first four finishers had previously been a Group 1 winner.

As noted above, Alpine Star is a Sea The Moon-sired half-sister to Alpha Centauri, and that makes her a fascinating prospect in the years to come. She is among eleven stakes winners for her Lanwades Stud-based sire to date, a tally that includes the Group 1-placed Group 2 scorer Quest The Moon, fellow German Group 2 (and triple Group 3) winner Wonderful Moon, and the pattern winners Hamariyna, Noble Moon, and Privilegiado. The latter, who took the Group 3 Oslo Cup at Ovrevoll at the end of June, was runner-up in the Swedish Derby and won both the Listed Norsk Derby and the Norsk St Leger in 2019, storming home by fifteen and a half lengths in Norway's premier classic. The stallion's tally also includes several pattern-placed stakes winners, notably Tickle Me Green, the listed scorer and Group 2 Prix de la Nonette runner-up who was sixth to Tarnawa in the Group 1 Prix de l'Opera. It is a promising start to his stallion career.

Alpha Centauri, of course, won the Group 1 Irish 1000 Guineas, Group 1 Coronation Stakes, Group 1 Falmouth Stakes and Group 1 Prix Jacques le Marois before losing out to Laurens in the Group 1 Matron Stakes at Leopardstown, a career-ending injury sustained in the closing stages a likely contributor to that defeat. She is now at stud and had a Galileo (by Sadler's Wells) colt foal in 2020.

Their dam, Alpha Lupi (by Rahy), has a two-year-old full sister and yearling full brother to Alpha Centauri waiting in the wings, whereas Etoile Filante (by So You Think), the filly she had between her two Group 1 stars, produced a Mastercraftsman (by Danehill Dancer) filly in mid-January of 2020. Their older half-brother Tenth Star (by Dansili), on the other hand, was a four-length winner of a seven-furlong listed contest at Leopardstown as a two-year-old, chased home Daddy Long Legs in the Group 2 Royal Lodge Stakes, finished third in the Group 3 Tyros Stakes and went to stud in India where his first foals arrived in 2017.

Alpha Lupi did not race but there is no surprise that she has become a notably successful broodmare and potentially one of long-term influence. That is because she is a daughter of East of The Moon (by Private Account), the classic-winning half-sister to the classic star and leading international sire Kingmambo (by Mr Prospector), who sired twenty-four Group/Grade 1 winners, and she is a granddaughter of Miesque. Several of her siblings also deserve a mention even though their achievements fall some way behind that of her own and her illustrious relations.

She is a full sister to the stakes-placed multiple ten-and-a-half-furlong winner Helike, who sired a handful of Australian-bred stakes winners, and a half-sister to both the Group 3 Prix d'Arenberg-scorer Moon Driver (by Mr Prospector) and the stakes-placed Canda (by Storm Cat). The latter is arguably of most interest as she produced two talented sons and she has a daughter who has been doing well at stud.

Evasive (by Elusive Quality) won the Group 3 Horris Hill Stakes at two, finished sixth to Sea The Stars in the 2000 Guineas and missed out on a Group 1 placing when fourth to Mastercraftsman in the St James's Palace Stakes. He has sired winners from his early crops in France, including the pattern-winning sprinter Trois Mille, and he has completed two seasons in Norway. His half-brother Autocratic (by Dubawi) won the Group 3 Brigadier Gerard Stakes when trained by Sir Michael

Stoute, had his name changed to Captain Cook when he moved to Australia and won a Group 3 handicap at Moonee Valley in 2019 for the Chris Waller stable. Stoute also trained their half-sister Cantal (by Pivotal), and although she retired to stud as a seventy-eight-rated seven-furlong Lingfield Polytrack maiden winner who was placed a couple of times on turf, she has made an excellent start to her second career. Her first foal, Munawer (by Dutch Art), has won twice, his full sister, Perfection, won two listed sprints and was runner-up three times in Group 3 contests, and the mare's fourth foal is the talented Molatham (by Night of Thunder). A stakes winner at two and Group 3 Jersey Stakes winner in 2020, he is among those reviewed in *Volume 2: UK & Ireland's Group 2 & Group 3 Winners*.

Miesque's descendants also include the Group/Grade 1 winners Amanee (by Pivotal), Loves Only You (by Deep Impact), Karakontie (by Bernstein; first foals in 2017, five stakes winners to date), Real Steel (by Deep Impact; Shadai Stallion Station, first foals in 2020), Rumplestiltskin (by Danehill), Study of Man (by Deep Impact; Lanwades Stud, first foals in 2021), Tapestry (by Galileo), and various others who have won at listed or pattern level, including the Group 1 sire Miesque's Son (by Mr Prospector), and she has a long list of sons, some of them with no blacktype as racehorses, who are standing at stud around the world.

Alpine Star is a beautifully bred, Group 1-winning filly who held an official rating of 119 after her final start of the year. She is due to remain in training as a four-year-old, and it will be fascinating to see what the future holds for her, both on the track and, when the time comes, at stud. It would be fascinating to see how she might fare over a mile and a half, but there would surely be more good prizes to be won with her at a mile and ten furlongs too.

She also has the now rare quality of having an outcross pedigree. The term is often misused to refer to something akin to "represents a different sire line to". However, it applies to a horse who shows no duplicated ancestors within the first five generations of their pedigree; one cannot "be an outcross for" someone or something because the outcross is the individual itself. Alpine Star can make this claim, and yet given that the names who appear on her chart include representatives of the most successful and popular lines, it would be a challenge to ensure that any of her offspring would also be outcrosses. There is a perception among some that inbreeding increases the chance of producing a good horse, but when you look only at the success stories and have as your sample pool a collection of horses who are almost entirely inbred somewhere within those first five generations, in part due to a lack of choice, then it becomes a self-fulfilling prophecy. There are far more horses of limited-to-little racing talent who show supposedly desirable duplications in their pedigree than ones who have been racehorses of note.

SUMMARY DETAILS
Bred: Niarchos Family
Owned: Niarchos Family
Trained: Jessica Harrington
Country: Ireland
Race record: 311-1222-
Career highlights: 3 wins inc Coronation Stakes (Gr1), Debutante Stakes (Gr2), 2nd Prix de l'Opera Longines (Gr1), Prix de Diane Longines (Gr1), Prix du Haras de Fresnay-le-Buffard Jacques le Marois (Gr1)

ALPINE STAR (IRE) – 2017 chestnut filly

Sea The Moon (GER)	Sea The Stars (IRE)	Cape Cross (IRE)
		Urban Sea (USA)
	Sanwa (IRE)	Monsun (GER)
		Sacarina (GB)
Alpha Lupi (IRE)	Rahy (USA)	Blushing Groom (FR)
		Glorious Song (CAN)
	East of The Moon (USA)	Private Account (USA)
		Miesque (USA)

AUDARYA (FR)

Wootton Bassett (by Iffraaj), an unbeaten Group 1 scorer at two, began his stallion career for just €6,000 at Haras d'Etreham in France in 2012, that figure leapt to €20,000 in 2017 thanks to the exploits of his classic and multiple Group 1-winning son Almanzor, and now he is about to embark on a new phase of his career. He stood for €40,000 in 2019 and 2020 and his final French-bred crop are arriving now as he settles into his first season as a member of the Coolmore Stud team in Ireland. The owners of the no-doubt elite book of mares he will receive this year will have to pay a fee of €100,000. Last season proved he was no one-hit-wonder as his string of stakes winners featured the Group 1 winners Audarya and Wooded, juvenile Group 2 scorer Chindit, US Grade 2 winner Tamahere, dual classic-placed pattern victor The Summit and classic-placed stakes winner Speak of The Devil, among others. He had only seventeen stakes winners in total to his name as he turned thirteen years old in at the start of 2021 but this tally can be expected to soar over the coming seasons as his more expensively produced crops and his Coolmore-conceived crops reach the track.

Audarya was a surprise winner the first time she struck at the highest level, 48/1 to put it in terms of her starting price, but she confirmed her raised profile with an excellent effort in the Group 1 Prix de l'Opera Longines a few weeks later. Her initial top-level success came at Deauville in late August when, having hit the front over a furlong from home, she stayed on well to hold off the challenge of the regally related Ambition by a neck in the Darley Prix Jean Romanet. The pair finished four lengths clear of the third, Romanciere. This was a considerable step up on anything she had achieved before and she had made the trip to France as a formerly 101-rated filly whose mark had dropped to 99 following two unplaced finishes in listed contests and a Newcastle handicap success under ten stone. The latter plus her final two runs of the year were over ten furlongs, her two listed-race disappointments were over a mile, but she had previously won a Goodwood handicap and been runner-up in a Saint-Cloud listed contest over that shorter trip. That said, her two poor efforts were on her initial two outings of 2020, the first of those coming after an eight-and-a-half-month absence from the track.

The ground was soft at Deauville but heavy at ParisLongchamp on the first Sunday in October, the only time she has encountered such underfoot conditions on the track. It did not appear to inconvenience her and, having again raced keenly, she kept on well in the closing stages to finish third in what was a notably competitive edition of the race. The Irish three-year-old Alpine Star had looked briefly like she might be about to add this prize to her earlier runaway Group 1 Coronation Stakes success but the Jessica Harrington-trained chestnut was caught in the final few yards by the year-older Tarnawa, an Aga Khan homebred trained by Dermot Weld. Audarya was three-quarters of a length behind with a similar gap back to the previously undefeated Group 1 Prix Saint-Alary heroine Tawkeel in fourth and old rival Ambition a length and a quarter adrift in fifth.

Conditions were quite different at Keeneland in early November when she sprang a mild surprise (12/1) in the Grade 1 Maker's Mark Breeders' Cup Filly & Mare Turf over nine and a half furlongs. The ground was described as firm and having settled mid-field with jockey Pierre-Charles Boudot, she stayed on strongly from around a furlong and a half from home. The top-class US mare Rushing Fall, who was favourite for the race, had gone to the front just before that point and she looked like holding on for victory, but Audarya caught her inside the final half furlong and hit the line a neck in front. The strong-finishing Harvey's Lil Goil was a head back in third, with Lady Prancealot an additional three-quarters of a length behind in fourth. The European runners Cayenne Pepper (tenth), Peaceful (eleventh) and Terebellum (thirteenth) were further back. The winner's time for the race was a new course record.

It will be interesting to see what the future holds now for Audarya as she has a pedigree that could see her excel as a broodmare. In addition to being the daughter of a rising star in the stallion ranks, the €125,000 Arqana Deauville October Yearling Sale graduate is considerably the better of two winners from the first two foals of Green Bananas (by Green Tune), a mare who won four times at up to twelve and a half furlongs in

France and whose most recent coverings have been of somewhat lower profile. Her 2018 colt, who died as a yearling, and her 2019 filly Mourjana, are by the stakes-placed triple mile winner Polarix (by Linamix) whose fee was just €1,200. The mare was bred back to him in 2019 and then catalogued for but withdrawn from the Arqana Breeding Stock Sale in Deauville in December, in foal to Renat. Who is that stallion? He is an Invincible Spirit (by Green Desert) half-brother to No Nay Never (by Scat Daddy) who was injured on his only run as a two-year-old and was exported to Tunisia for stallion duties. The foal is due to arrive in February 2021 and it will be fascinating to see how it turns out.

Audarya's grandam, Anabaa Republic (by Anabaa), was Group 3-placed over twelve and a half furlongs at Deauville and that Haras D'Ecouves homebred—the stud also bred Audarya—is out of Gigawatt (by Double Bed), a winning full sister to the leading international performer Jim And Tonic. He was a multiple pattern winner and a runner-up in the Group 1 Prix Maurice de Gheest in his native France, runner-up in the Group 1 Lockinge Stakes in England, landed the Group 2 Dubai Duty Free at Nad Al Sheba in Dubai, and won both the Group 1 Hong Kong International Cup and Group 2 Queen Elizabeth II Cup at Sha Tin in Hong Kong. He was twice runner-up in the Singapore Airlines International Cup at Kranji in Singapore, was only beaten by a head when runner-up in the Grade 1 Woodbine Mile in Canada, and when the François Doumen-trained gelding finally retired, at the end of his eight-year-old season, he had notched up a total of 13 wins and 17 placings and over £3.1 million in prize money.

His full brothers Spice of Life and Double Tonic notched up eight wins between them, with the latter earning minor blacktype when finishing third in a listed contest at Chantilly, whereas their winning full brother Jimble compiled a useful record as a National Hunt stallion. Their winning full sister Jimkana, on the other hand, did her bit for the family by producing two horses of particular note at stud. Petit Calva (by Desert King) won listed races at six and eight furlongs in France, she chased home Grey Lilas in the Group 3 Prix de la Grotte over the latter trip at Longchamp, and her progeny include the pattern-placed mile stakes winner Rosay (by Raven's Pass). Mauralakana, two years younger than Petit

Calva, notched up eleven wins and over $1.6 million in prize money, her tally featuring the Grade 1 Beverly D Stakes, Grade 2 New York Stakes and Grade 2 Sheepshead Bay Handicap, those races over nine and a half furlongs, ten furlongs and eleven furlongs respectively. She had been a leading juvenile when trained in France, winning the Group 3 Prix de Cabourg over six furlongs, finishing fourth to Silca's Sister in the Group 1 Prix Morny and third to the ill-fated Horatio Nelson in the Group 1 Prix Jean-Luc Lagardere over seven. She was also a seven-furlong listed scorer at Maisons-Laffitte first time out at three and finished fifth and sixth respectively in the two French fillies' classics before making the move across the Atlantic.

Alison Swinburn's dual top-level winner Audarya, now aged five, is among an array of top-class performers due to return to action in 2021. The older horses' division could be an exciting one this coming season.

SUMMARY DETAILS

Bred: Haras D'Ecouves
Owned: Mrs A M Swinburn
Trained: James Fanshawe
Country: England
Race record: 2-221012-001131-
Career highlights: 5 wins inc Maker's Mark Breeders' Cup Filly & Mare Turf (Gr1), Darley Prix Jean Romanet (Gr1), 2nd Prix Coronation (L), 3rd Prix de l'Opera Longines (Gr1)

AUDARYA (FR) – 2016 bay filly

Wootton Bassett (GB)	Iffraaj (GB)	Zafonic (USA)
		Pastorale (GB)
	Balladonia (GB)	Primo Dominie
		Susquehanna Days (USA)
Green Bananas (FR)	Green Tune (USA)	Green Dancer (USA)
		Soundings (USA)
	Anabaa Republic (FR)	Anabaa (USA)
		Gigawatt (FR)

BARNEY ROY (GB)

There has been a surprising number of high-profile males in recent years who have been found to have low fertility or be sterile when tried at stud and, unfortunately, Barney Roy is one of the latter. Like Kingsgate Native, G Force, Reckless Abandon, Kementari and others, he was gelded and resumed training. And unlike many horses who make a return to action, he has proved himself to be at least as good as he was before his initial retirement.

Phase one of his career was as a member of the Richard Hannon stable and he looked a bright prospect when easily winning a one-mile maiden at Haydock on his only start at two. He followed that with a two-length defeat of Dream Castle in the Group 3 Greenham Stakes at Newbury, chased home Churchill in the Group 1 2000 Guineas, then beat Lancaster Bomber by a length to take the Group 1 St James's Palace Stakes at Royal Ascot. Ulysses pipped him by a nose in the Group 1 Coral-Eclipse Stakes at Sandown and by two and a quarter lengths in the Group 1 Juddmonte International Stakes at York, and Barney Roy's addition to the team at Dalham Hall Stud came about after one last start, a disappointing ninth-place finish in the first edition of the Group 1 Champion Stakes won by Cracksman.

He joined the Charlie Appleby stable for the second phase of his racing career but ran just three times as a five-year-old. He was a neck runner-up to Zaaki in a one-mile listed contest at Ascot, a half-length winner of a similar contest at ParisLongchamp and then only fifth to Lord Glitters in the Group 1 Queen Anne Stakes at Ascot. However, when he returned to action seven and a half months later, now aged six, he showed signs of his old talent. He beat Dream Castle by two and a quarter lengths to take the Group 2 Al Rashidiya over nine furlongs at Meydan in late January, followed that with a near two-length defeat of Magic Lily in the Group 1 Jebel Hatta over the same course and distance in early March and then finished third to Lord North and Addeybb in the Group 1 Prince of Wales's Stakes at Ascot in June. The margins there were three and three-quarter lengths and one and a quarter lengths, he appeared outclassed by the front pair and, although hanging left, kept on in the closing stages to hold off Japan, Bangkok and Mehdaayih for the minor placing.

Barney Roy's next three outings were all in Germany and, having been a top miler in his youth, these performances proved that he was now a highly effective middle-distance performer. He hit the front inside the last half furlong of ten-furlong Group 1 Grosser Dallmayr-Preis - Bayersiches Zuchtrennen at Munich in late July and held off Quest The Moon to take the prize by a neck. The Irish raider Patrick Sarsfield stayed on to finish third, another length and a quarter behind, and the classic-placed Group 2-winning filly Durance was fourth. The ground there was good, as it had been on each of his previous starts of the year, but it was soft at Cologne the following month when he stepped up to twelve furlongs for the first time. He still had every chance over a furlong out but could not get to the front and had to settle for fourth as the four-year-old fillies Donjah and Dame Malliot were split by three-year-old colt Kaspar. The margins were a neck, half a length and three-quarters of a length, with the previous year's Group 1 Deutsches Derby winner Laccario, running for the first time of the year, among those further behind.

The first two from that race plus old rivals Quest The Moon and Durance were among the seven who took on Barney Roy in the Group 1 Longines Grosser Preis von Baden in mid-September but none hit the frame on this occasion. The gelding went to the front over a furlong and a half from home and stayed on well, proving that twelve furlongs is within his range, to take the race by a length and a quarter from Communique. Torquator Tasso, who was runner-up to In Swoop in the Group 1 Deutsches Derby on his previous start and would win the Group 1 Grosser Preis von Berlin next time out, was a neck back in third, with the same gap back to Donjah, who was a head in front of Durance. This was the winner's final run of the year.

Barney Roy, who made 30,000 guineas in Newmarket as a foal and £70,000 in Doncaster as a yearling, was bred by Eliza Park International Pty Ltd, he is a half-brother to three winners, including the stakes-placed mile scorer Wisdom Mind (by Dark Angel), and he was the first foal out of Alina (by Galileo). His half-brother Noble Dynasty (by Dubawi), who cost Godolphin

3,600,000 guineas from Book 1 of 2019's Tattersalls October Yearling Sale, has made two starts so far for the Charlie Appleby stable, finishing a neck runner-up in a six-furlong Newmarket maiden in early June and then winning a seven-furlong novice race on the Polytrack at Kempton in late October, and remains a promising prospect for the coming season. He was bred by Sun Kingdom Pty Ltd and holds an entry in the Group 1 Tattersalls Irish 2,000 Guineas.

Alina did not show much talent in a short track career in France, but she is a daughter of the prolific and talented Cheyenne Star (by Mujahid), which makes Barney Roy inbred 4x4 to Danzig (by Northern Dancer), among other duplications within the first five generations of his pedigree. That filly won the Group 3 Brownstown Stakes at Leopardstown, the Group 3 Ridgewood Pearl Stakes at the Curragh and listed contests at Naas and Dundalk, she was placed in a string of blacktype contests too and was effective from six furlongs to a mile.

Four of Cheyenne Star's siblings also became blacktype producers at stud, two of them of particular note. One-time scorer Silent Secret (by Dubai Destination) had a promising prospect in Sparkle'n'joy (by Sepoy), who won the Listed Ingabelle Stakes at Leopardstown as a juvenile, but sadly that filly died young. The unraced Boa Estrela (by Intikhab), on the other hand, did her part for the family by coming up with one of the most popular Irish-trained horses of recent years: Gordon Lord Byron (by Byron).

The Tom Hogan-trained grandson of Green Desert (by Danzig) ran 108 times in a glittering international career that saw him win the Group 1 Sprint Cup and Group 2 British Champions Sprint Stakes in England, the Group 1 Prix de la Foret in France, the Group 1 George Ryder Stakes in Australia, and the Group 2 Greenlands Stakes in Ireland. He also raced in the United Arab Emirates, in Qatar and in the Czech Republic, and his 16 wins and 32 placings helped him to accumulate almost £2 million in prize money. He has even been the subject of a film. Not bad for a €2,000 Goffs Foal Sale graduate who lost his action and was pulled up on his racecourse debut as a two-year-old!

The unraced Be Released (by Three Valleys) is the most notable of his siblings and that's because of what her daughter did in 2020. Bebeautiful (by Le Havre) made a winning debut for the Frederic Rossi stable over ten furlongs on the Polytrack at Cagnes-sur-Mer in January, followed up over the course and distance just over three weeks later and then, a month after that, added the Listed Prix Rose de Mai over nine and a half furlongs at Deauville, also on Polytrack. She has since moved to Australia where she joined the Chris Waller team.

Charita (by Lycius), the third dam of Barney Roy, also had ability and the better of her two wins came in a one-mile listed contest at Naas as a four-year-old, trained by Liam Browne. Her half-brother Stanott (by Mukaddamah) was also best at that trip, and although trained in England by Luca Cumani, he landed the Group 2 Premio Emilio Turati and was runner-up in the Group 1 Premio Vittorio di Capua in Italy.

Barney Roy will presumably be back in action this year and, although now seven, there is every reason to hope that he can add further good prizes to his tally. He is the standout performer for his sire, the former Coolmore Stud-based star miler Excelebration (by Exceed And Excel), and the stallion's other representatives in 2020 were headed by the Joseph O'Brien-trained high-class sprinter Speak In Colours, who is reviewed in *Volume 2: UK & Ireland's Group 2 & Group 3 Winners.*

SUMMARY DETAILS

Bred: Eliza Park International Pty Ltd
Owned: Godolphin
Trained: Charlie Appleby
Country: England
Race record: 1-121230-201-113141-
Career highlights: 8 wins inc 148th Longines Grosser Preis von Baden (Gr1), Grosser Dallmayr-Preis - Bayerisches Zuchtrennen (Gr1), Jebel Hatta sponsored by Emirates Airline (Gr1), St James's Palace Stakes (Gr1), Al Rashidiya sponsored by Hamdan Bin Mohammed Cruise Terminal (Gr2), JLT Greenham Stakes (Gr3), Prix de Montretout (L), 2nd Coral-Eclipse Stakes (Gr1), Qipco 2000 Guineas Stakes (Gr1), Ascot Shop Paradise Stakes (L), 3rd Prince of Wales's Stakes (Gr1), Juddmonte International Stakes (Gr1)

BARNEY ROY (GB) – 2014 bay gelding

Excelebration (IRE)	Exceed And Excel (AUS)	Danehill (USA)
		Patrona (USA)
	Sun Shower (IRE)	Indian Ridge
		Miss Kemble (GB)
Alina (IRE)	Galileo (IRE)	Sadler's Wells (USA)
		Urban Sea (USA)
	Cheyenne Star (IRE)	Mujahid (USA)
		Charita (IRE)

BATTAASH (IRE)

Battaash ran fewer times in 2020 than he had done in any previous season, but his brilliance was still there at the age of six, and even if he's not quite so good as a seven-year-old it will still take a seriously talented horse to beat him when he's having a good day. The gelding is one of the very best sprinters of recent decades and he was Timeform's top-rated runner of the year. His figure of 136 placed him ahead of Ghaiyyath (133), Palace Pier (132) and Stradivarius (130) at the top of their table. He also topped 2019's rankings on the same mark, having been rated 133 by that organisation in 2018. However, the official handicap figures always seem to downplay the strength of the sprinting division and having hit a peak BHA figure of 127 after his 2018 victory in the Group 2 King George Stakes, he was on 123 for most of 2019, started 2020 on 126 and remained on that until after his Group 1 Nunthorpe Stakes in August, returned to a mark of 123. Ghaiyyath, on 130, was the world's top-rated racehorse on the official handicap.

Battaash is a five-furlong specialist and he made his seasonal reappearance in the Group 1 King's Stand Stakes at Royal Ascot in June. The ground was described as good-to-soft, the opposition featured the previous year's Group 1 Prix de l'Abbaye heroine Glass Slippers as well as a string of mostly Group 3-type horses, and the Charlie Hills-trained bay was never in any danger. He made all, went clear over a furlong out and came home two and a quarter lengths and a short head clear of his stablemate Equilateral and three-year-old filly Liberty Beach, comfortably breaking fifty-nine seconds despite the ease underfoot. Glass Slippers disappointed in fifth.

That talented four-year-old put up a much better performance at Goodwood just over a month later but although she beat rank outsider Ornate by a neck, with a four-length gap back to Liberty Beach, who was a further length and a half in front of the Group 3 Pavilion Stakes winner Dubai Station, she was no match for Battaash. He carried a five-pound penalty for his Ascot success, took over the lead from the French raider Ken Colt after a couple of furlongs and galloped to a two-and-a-quarter-length victory.

This was his fourth consecutive win in the Group 2 King George Qatar Stakes and, on a good-to-firm surface, he smashed the track record, clocking a time of 55.62 seconds.

York was the obvious next stop, for yet another crack at the Group 1 Coolmore Nunthorpe Stakes. He finished fourth to Marsha in the race as a three-year-old, fourth to Alpha Delphini at four, but had made it third time lucky with an impressive three-and-three-quarter-length defeat of Soldier's Call in the 2019 edition, breaking the track record. The calibre of opposition he faced in 2020 was not as strong as some of the rivals he'd encountered at the venue in those previous years, with the three-year-olds A'Ali and Art Power looking the biggest dangers. Neither of those talented colts made the frame, both running below form. Instead, it was well-exposed listed-race winners Que Amoro and Moss Gill, trained by Michael Dods and James Bethell respectively, who chased him home, the margins just one length and two lengths, with an additional half a length back to A'Ali. The two placed horses are very much flattered by their proximity to Battaash that day, but the runner-up has given her future paddocks value a tremendous boost given how a Nunthorpe placing will look on her page.

The Group 1 Prix de l'Abbaye de Longchamp was to be his next target, but with the ground coming up heavy he bypassed the race. A potential Breeders' Cup Turf Sprint challenge had been suggested after his Goodwood victory, but it was announced in mid-October that he would not be travelling to Keeneland either. His season was over after just three starts, but he will be back in action in 2021. He has now earned over £1.75 million in prize money, and his prior racing record was reviewed in *European Group 1 Winners of 2019*.

Battaash was bred by Paul McCartan of Ballyphilip Stud in Ireland and he is a 200,000-guinea graduate of the Tattersalls October Book 2 Yearling Sale. One of seven Group 1 stars among sixty-eight stakes winners by Yeomanstown Stud's excellent stallion Dark Angel (by Acclamation), he is the first foal of an unplaced mare called Anna Law (by Lawman). The contrast between him and his only other sibling to race, so far, could hardly be more striking. Littlelordconford (by Intikhab) has shown little ability in eight races, his best placing being fourth off a mark of forty-six in a selling handicap at Brighton in July 2018.

The mare's third foal is Valletta Gold (by Gutaifan), an unraced four-year-old filly who cost 180,000 guineas from the Book 1 catalogue in Tattersalls, whereas number four is Battaash's now three-year-old full sister Altaayshah, who cost 800,000 guineas in Newmarket as a yearling and is listed as being trained by Charles Hills. Anna Law had a Dark Angel colt foal on February 7th last year.

Although lacking talent on the track, Anna Law always had the potential to produce at least one talented performer at stud because she is a well-bred mare. In addition to being by the classic sire Lawman (by Invincible Spirit), she has four blacktype-earning siblings, the best of whom is the Group 2 Champagne Stakes winner and Group 1 July Cup third Etlaala (by Selkirk). Portelet (by Night Shift), her dam, won four times and has a stakes-placed half-sister in Rozel (by Wolfhound), and she is a granddaughter of Noirmant (by Dominion), an unraced half-sister to the Group 1-winning stayer Braashee (by Sadler's Wells). That Prix Royal-Oak scorer had a quicker full brother of note in the multiple US Grade 3 victor Adam Smith, his half-sister Ghariba (by Final Straw) won the Group 3 Nell Gwyn Stakes and finished fourth in the 1000 Guineas, and others who descend from their listed-placed dam, Krakow (by Malinowski), include the Group 1-placed pattern winners Fantastic View (by Distant View) and High Standing (by High Yield).

Anna Law's siblings also include Bird Key (by Cadeaux Genereux) who, although unraced, has made a significant contribution to the family's reputation. Tasleet (by Showcasing) is the best of her offspring, to date, he stands at Nunnery Stud and his second-crop foals are arriving now. While Battaash is a five-furlong specialist, his 'cousin' Tasleet excelled over six and stayed seven. He won the Group 2 Duke of York Stakes and Group 3 Greenham Stakes, was runner-up in each of the Group 1 Diamond Jubilee Stakes (to The Tin Man), Group 1 British Champions Sprint Stakes (to Librisa Breeze) and Group 1 Sprint Cup (to Harry Angel), and he earned placings in several other top sprints from two to four years. This young representative of the

Oasis Dream branch of Green Desert's (by Danzig) line is a promising prospect who could figure prominently among the leading freshman sires of 2022.

Battaash, obviously, has no possible stud career ahead of him, but what is a loss to the breeding industry is a gain for the racing side as, all being well, we will get the chance to enjoy seeing this wonderful sprinter in action for at least one more season.

SUMMARY DETAILS
Bred: Ballyphilip Stud
Owned: Hamdan Al Maktoum
Trained: Charles Hills
Country: England
Race record: 10333-11141-12144-12110-111-
Career highlights: 13 wins inc Coolmore Nunthorpe Stakes (Gr1-twice), King's Stand Stakes (Gr1), Prix de l'Abbaye de Longchamp Longines (Gr1), King George Qatar Stakes (Gr2-four times), Armstrong Aggregates Temple Stakes (Gr2-twice), Coral Charge (Gr3), Randox Health Scurry Stakes (L), 2nd King's Stand Stakes (Gr1-twice), 3rd Newmarket Academy Godolphin Beacon Project Cornwallis Stakes (Gr3)

BATTAASH (IRE) – 2014 bay gelding

Dark Angel (IRE)	Acclamation (GB)	Royal Applause (GB)
		Princess Athena
	Midnight Angel (GB)	Machiavellian (USA)
		Night At Sea
Anna Law (IRE)	Lawman (FR)	Invincible Spirit (IRE)
		Laramie (USA)
	Portelet (GB)	Night Shift (USA)
		Noirmant

CAMPANELLE (IRE)

The number of American-trained horses that race in Europe is still quite small but it has been increasing in recent years and many of them have represented the Wesley Ward stable. Ward has had particular success with two-year-olds and Campanelle was his star runner in 2020. She kicked off her career with a three-and-a-half-length debut success over five furlongs on firm ground at Gulfstream Park at the end of May, flew to England to win the Group 2 Queen Mary Stakes at the Royal Ascot meeting and later travelled to France where she added the Group 1 Darley Prix Morny. Rather than return to Europe for a crack at the Group 1 Juddmonte Cheveley Park Stakes in the autumn, she stayed at home for a Breeders' Cup challenge.

The condensed and abbreviated start to the European flat season made the early juvenile pattern events a little harder to assess and some surprises an inevitability. Most of the runners had just one outing behind them, and not always a winning one at that, and it was possible that the form of the earliest ones, particularly those at Ascot, might not stand up in the following weeks and months. Campanelle showed plenty of speed and potential when taking the Queen Mary Stakes, hitting the front inside the final furlong and keeping on well to beat the maiden winner Sacred by three-quarters of a length. They finished two and a half lengths clear of Caroline Dale, a 100/1 shot who had been runner-up in a six-furlong contest on the Polytrack at Lingfield on her only prior start. The fourth, Sardinia Sunset, had also been placed on her sole run and that had been when chasing home Sacred at Newmarket, where Queen Mary fifth Happy Romance had been sixth.

As it turned out, the 2020 edition of this prestigious juvenile fillies' race featured plenty who would go on to make the frame in blacktype contests throughout the season. Sacred was also a runner-up in the Group 2 Lowther Stakes and short-headed in the Group 2 Flying Childers Stakes. Caroline Dale's three subsequent runs were a win at Windsor followed by third-place finishes in the Group 3 Princess Margaret Stakes and Listed St Hugh's Stakes. Sardinia Sunset won the Listed Marygate Fillies' Stakes next time out and Happy Romance, whose season is detailed in *Volume 2:*

UK & Ireland's Group 2 & Group 3 Winners, became one of the biggest earners of the year among her age group.

Looking back through the rest of the field, Scarlet Bear (sixth) picked up two Group 3 placings, Grammata (seventh) and Mamba Wamba (eighth) became stakes-placed maiden winners, Dickiedooda (tenth) won a listed race at Cork on her next start, Star of Emaraaty (eleventh at 200/1) went on to Group 3 success, Wings of A Dove (fourteenth) picked up a listed-race placing, and Royal Approval (seventeenth), the stable companion of the winner, went on to take a six-furlong Grade 3 contest at Belmont Park in October.

The ground at Ascot had been good but it was soft at Deauville in late August when Campanelle won the Prix Morny. The field had split into two groups, with the filly leading the larger one towards the centre of the track and the shock Group 2 Coventry Stakes winner Nando Parrado leading Listed Windsor Castle Stakes and Group 2 July Stakes scorer Tactical along the stands' rail. She was never headed and she galloped home strongly to a two-length victory. Nando Parrado took second, a neck in front of the once-raced winner Rhythm Master, with Acapulco Gold and Tactical the next two home, following at margins of one and a quarter lengths and three-quarters of a length.

She was not seen out again until early November when she stepped up to a mile for the Grade 1 Breeders' Cup Juvenile Fillies Turf on good ground at Keeneland. Aunt Pearl, a Brad Cox-trained daughter of Lope de Vega (by Shamardal), made all to win by an unchallenged two and a half lengths, chased by the strong-finishing Mother Earth. That Aidan O'Brien filly caught the Ken Condon-trained Miss Amulet near the line, beating her by a neck, and there was a further gap of two lengths back to Campanelle in fourth. She had come under pressure a quarter of a mile from home and had nothing more to give in the final half furlong, just managing to hold fourth place by a head from Plum Ali, who led a closely bunched group that included the Jessica Harrington-trained Group 1 Moyglare Stud Stakes third Oodnadatta (ninth).

Campanelle is one of five Group 1 stars among a total of sixty-five stakes for Tally-Ho Stud's veteran stallion Kodiac (by Danehill), the Group 3-placed closer-than-half-brother to the leading international sire Invincible Spirit (by Green Desert). He and his sibling were sprinters, but they are out of the Group 1 Prix de Diane (French Oaks) heroine Rafha (by Kris) and from a family that features talent over a wide range of distances, hence the lack of surprise that both are capable of getting their best winners across a spectrum. The top middle-distance horse Best Solution is a notable example for Kodiac, albeit a rare such one for him. Most of his offspring tend to show their best in sprints or around a mile.

His latest star, a 190,000-guinea Tattersalls Book 1 graduate bred by Tally-Ho Stud, is a half-sister to Suwaan (by Exceed And Excel), a dual winner who finished well-beaten on his only attempt beyond five furlongs, but also to Qafilah (by Arcano), a five-time US-based winner who has earned a low six-figure sum in prize money and stays a mile. Their dam, Janina, won the Listed Marygate Fillies' Stakes over five furlongs at York as a juvenile, and she is a daughter of the Group 1 Prix de l'Abbaye de Longchamp star Namid (by Indian Ridge) and of Lady Dominatrix (by Danehill Dancer), a Group 3-winning sprinter who was runner-up in the Group 2 Flying Five at the Curragh.

Third dam Spout House (by Flash of Steel) was placed over seven and twelve furlongs on the flat and finished a close fourth in a bumper (two-mile flat race for future hurdlers and chasers), fifth dam Lowna (by Princely Gift) won the five-furlong Molecomb Stakes as a two-year-old in 1967, and the various blacktype horses who appear under that distant generation of the family and its branches include a mixture of sprinters, milers and middle-distance horses, albeit all of them too remotely connected to Campanelle to have any impact on her prospects. Another notable feature of the pedigree is that the filly is inbred 2x4 to Danehill (by Danzig), 4x5 Northern Dancer (by Nearctic), 5x5 to Natalma (by Native Dancer), 3x5 to Kris and 4x5 to Kris's sire Sharpen Up (by Atan).

What is in the first three generations of a pedigree is most important in assessing potential, just as you would look to your parents, grandparents and maybe great-grandparents, but no further back, if seeking an explanation for why you have your own particular talents or aptitudes. And the picture that Campanelle's pedigree paints is one of a sprinter who might (like Qafilah) also get a mile. The odds appear to be tilted in favour of the Commonwealth Cup being more suitable for her than a Guineas or Coronation Stakes—she holds an entry in the Group 1 Tattersalls Irish 1,000 Guineas and the Group 1 Emirates Poule d'Essai des Pouliches—but it is not impossible that she will stay or even excel at the mile. Campanelle's end-of-year rating of 113 placed her joint-top of the juvenile fillies' division, tied with Pretty Gorgeous and Shale for the title of champion two-year-old filly.

SUMMARY DETAILS
Bred: Tally-Ho Stud
Owned: Stonestreet Stables LLC
Trained: Wesley Ward
Country: United States of America
Race record: 1114-
Career highlights: 3 wins inc Darley Prix Morny - Finale des Darley Series (Gr1), Queen Mary Stakes (Gr2)

CAMPANELLE (IRE) – 2018 bay filly

Kodiac (GB)	Danehill (USA)	Danzig (USA)
		Razyana (USA)
	Rafha	Kris
		Eljazzi
Janina (GB)	Namid (GB)	Indian Ridge
		Dawnsio (IRE)
	Lady Dominatrix (IRE)	Danehill Dancer (IRE)
		Spout House (IRE)

CHAMPERS ELYSEES (IRE)

There are so many ways in which 2020 was an unusual year and, from a racing perspective, one of those was the number of horses who soared through the ranks from low-to-moderate handicap figures up to highly regarded Group 2 and even Group 1 stars.

Baron Samedi, for example, showed little in three starts at two and was unplaced in his first two races at three, was gelded, narrowly won a ten-furlong Cork handicap off a mark of sixty-five and then ran up a sequence that culminated in victory in the Group 2 Prix du Conseil de Paris at ParisLongchamp in late October, an eleven-furlong test for which he was sent off favourite. That victory came two months exactly after his first win and he went to the start rated forty pounds higher than he'd started his spree. He is trained by Joseph O'Brien. Then there's the hugely popular Princess Zoe who left Germany after her four-year-old season, joined the Tony Mullins stable in Ireland, began her latest season with a second-place finish at Navan off a mark of sixty-four. She ran away with an amateur riders' handicap at the Curragh, followed up with two valuable handicaps at the Galway Festival, a listed race success at the same venue and then that memorable Group 1 Prix du Cadran success at ParisLongchamp on the first Sunday in October, giving her trainer and her apprentice jockey, Joey Sheridan, a first winner at the highest level. A forty-five-pound increase in rating in three and a half months.

Glen Shiel's twenty-one-pound jump from ninety-six-rated handicapper to 117-rated Group 1 sprint star and that of Subjectivist from a ninety-four-rated handicapper to 111-rated Group 1-winning stayer, are also impressive and yet pale in comparison to that pair, and Champers Elysees is a similar example; her rapid rise through the ranks was by 'only' twenty-nine pounds. The gelding is trained in England by Archie Watson, the colt by Mark Johnston in the same country, and the filly in Ireland by Johnny Murtagh.

Champers Elysees showed some ability in five starts as a juvenile, winning over six furlongs at the Curragh, finishing a close sixth the valuable Tattersalls Ireland Super Auction Sale Stakes at the same venue, and being placed in her other three races, notably when runner-up in the Birdcatcher Nursery at Naas that October. She started her three-year-old campaign rated eighty-six—winning a seven-furlong handicap on good-to-firm at the Curragh in mid-June—and finished it as a Group 1 winner rated 115. Her second start of the year was in a seven-furlong listed contest on yielding ground at Galway in late July and she followed that seven-length score with Group 3 success at Gowran Park.

That race was the Coolmore Stud No Nay Never Fairy Bridge Stakes over seven and a half furlongs, the ground was described as being soft-to-heavy, and it did not look like a strong line-up for the grade. Champers Elysees landed the prize by half a length from the second most highly rated horse in the field, Pearls Galore, with the eighty-six-rated Parent's Prayer another five lengths adrift in third. There was, however, the potential for each of the first three to improve, so it could look a little stronger in time. The runner-up, who had been unplaced in two starts in France as a juvenile was now trained in Co Tipperary by Paddy Twomey. She had won a Limerick maiden and Cork handicap easily on her only two prior outings in Ireland although disappointed on her only subsequent outing after Gowran Park. Maiden winner Parent's Prayer, on the other hand, had been making just her fourth start when running in the Group 3 test. She had one more race before the end of the year and it was an impressive effort, taking the Listed Irish Stallion Farms EBF Garnet Stakes by three lengths over a mile at Naas in mid-October.

Just ten days after her first pattern success, Champers Elysees was back in action, this time up in trip and grade for the Group 1 Coolmore America 'Justify' Matron Stakes at Leopardstown on the opening day of Irish Champions Weekend. The line-up featured the classic stars Fancy Blue and Peaceful, Group 1 scorer Albigna and several other pattern winners, but Champers Elysees put up the performance of her life. In what was a strongly run race, Colin Keane settled her off the pace, they hit the front inside the final furlong and came home a length and a quarter clear of Irish 1,000 Guineas winner Peaceful. It was a popular result. Prix de Diane (French Oaks) and Nassau Stakes heroine Fancy Blue was another length and a half back in third, a head in front of the winner's stable companion Know It All.

Both the Group 1 Kingdom of Bahrain Sun Chariot Stakes at Newmarket and the Grade 1 Breeders' Cup Mile at Keeneland were now potential targets. Although she had won on it before, it was unfortunate that the ground came up heavy at Newmarket at the start of October. She was sent off favourite for the Sun Chariot Stakes, again with Keane in the saddle, but encountered all sorts of trouble in running and, under the circumstances, did well to finish fourth. Nazeef, who hit the front a furlong out, won the race by a length and a half from Half Light, with the disappointing classic-placed filly Cloak of Spirits a neck back in third, half a length in front of Champers Elysees. Terebellum was another length and a quarter away in fifth, followed by Lady Bowthorpe, Feliciana de Vega, and the previous year's winner, Billesdon Brook. It was her final run of the year.

Champers Elysees was bred by Karl Bowen, she made just €12,500 when sold in Fairyhouse as a foal and was snapped up by Johnny Murtagh for €28,000 from Part 2 of the Tattersalls Ireland September Yearling Sale. The Fitzwilliam Racing syndicate took her on and kept her when she failed to meet her reserve at the Goffs Autumn Sale shortly after her Birdcatcher second. That paid off in the end as not only did she notch up her sequence, but her total earnings on the track were around €240,000 before noted Japanese owner-breeder Teruya Yoshida bought her, and it was in his famous yellow, black and red colours that she ran at Newmarket.

She comes from the fourth crop of the Ballyhane Stud stallion Elzaam (by Redoute's Choice), a sprinter who won a listed contest at Newbury as a three-year-old having been placed in the Group 2 Coventry Stakes, Group 2 July Stakes and Group 3 Horris Hill Stakes at two. He is a full brother to a Group 3 winner, out of a half-sister to US juvenile Grade 1 scorer Point Ashley (by Point Given), and he can boast the Group 1 Champion Stakes heroine Hurry Harriet (by Yrrah Jr) as his fourth dam. His star daughter is one of four stakes winners for him and he also has eight other offspring who have been blacktype placed at least once.

La Cuvee (by Mark of Esteem), who showed little ability in seven starts and ended her track career on an official rating of forty-five, is also the dam of Daddies Girl, a full sister to Champers Elysees who has won five times in England from five to almost eight and a half furlongs. That one was had been a €7,500 Goffs foal and £5,500 private sale at the Goffs UK Premier Yearling Sale, she hit a career peak handicap mark of ninety-two, retired on eighty-nine and earned over £71,000 in a thirty-two-race career for the Rod Millman stable.

The mare's fifth foal is a now three-year-old Alhebayeb (by Dark Angel) gelding named Performance Plus, who finished last of fourteen over six furlongs at Naas in early August, and she had a colt by the champion freshman sire Mehmas (by Acclamation) in March 2019. She is a daughter of Premiere Cuvee (by Formidable), who won Germany's top sprint, the Group 3 Goldene Peitsche, and that makes La Cuvee a half-sister to two one-mile stakes winners. Cask (by Be My Chief) ran six times for the John Gosden stable, earning blacktype on three occasions and getting the better of her two wins in a listed handicap on firm ground at Ascot. She Bat (by Batshoof), on the other hand, landed a Group 3 contest over the trip in Italy before going on to produce a ten-furlong listed scorer at stud. Premiere Cuvee is also notable as being a three-parts sister to the mile listed winner Fizzed (by Efisio) and to Swizzle (by Efisio), the unraced dam of the Group 3 Premio Parioli (Italian 2000 Guineas) scorer Al Rep (by Trade Fair). There are plenty of other talented horses in the family too, including a Group 1-siring stallion.

Clicquot (by Bold Lad), the four-time winning third dam of Champers Elysees, was a half-sister to a listed-race winner in France but, more notably, also to three fillies who went on to make some eye-catching contributions at stud. Babycham Sparkle (by So Blessed), for example, gave us the Group 3 Palace House Stakes winner Deep Finesse (by Reprimand) and is the grandam of the Group 1-winning miler and moderately successful blacktype sire Dick Turpin (by Arakan). More Fizz's (by Morston) three blacktype earners are headed by the Group 2 Gimcrack Stakes winner and Group 1 Middle Park Stakes third River Falls (by Aragon), she is the grandam of the pattern-placed, stakes-winning juvenile sprinter Needles And Pins (by Fasliyev) and third dam of the Group 3 Oh So Sharp Stakes scorer Alsindi (by Acclamation). And then there's Musical Essence (by Song), the mare who gave us Monsieur Bond (by Danehill Dancer).

He won the Group 2 Duke of York Stakes over six furlongs, was a seven-length winner of the Group 3 Gladness Stakes over seven, was runner-up to subsequent Group 1 star Zafeen in the Group 2 Mill Reef Stakes at two, fourth to Somnus in the Group 1 Prix de la Foret, and began his stallion career at Whitsbury Manor Stud. He transferred to Norton Grove Stud after five seasons, remained there until his death in 2019, and his offspring include the Group 1-winning sprinters Gilt Edge Girl and Move In Time.

The amount of blacktype to be found within the first few generations of the pedigree, and within its branches, augurs well for Champers Elysees's eventual future at stud, and the presence of Monsieur Bond in the family offers hope that a future high-class son of hers could be capable of success in a stallion role. She is to remain in training with the Murtagh stable in 2021 before, presumably, heading to Japan as a broodmare prospect, so there is every reason to hope that there is plenty more to come in her life story.

SUMMARY DETAILS

Bred: Karl Bowen
Owned: Fitzwilliam Racing (now Teruya Yoshida)
Trained: Johnny Murtagh
Country: Ireland
Race record: 32012-11114-
Career highlights: 5 wins inc Coolmore America 'Justify' Matron Stakes (Gr1), Coolmore Stud No Nay Never Fairy Bridge Stakes (Gr3), Colm Quinn BMW Irish EBF Corrib Fillies Stakes (L)

CHAMPERS ELYSEES (IRE) – 2017 bay filly

Elzaam (AUS)	Redoute's Choice (AUS)	Danehill (USA)
		Shantha's Choice (AUS)
	Mambo In Freeport (USA)	Kingmambo (USA)
		Golden Thatch (USA)
La Cuvee	Mark of Esteem (IRE)	Darshaan
		Homage
	Premiere Cuvee	Formidable (USA)
		Clicquot

CIRCUS MAXIMUS (IRE)

The pedigree and racing record of Circus Maximus were reviewed in detail in *European Group 1 Winners of 2019* and to the former aspect the only real update is the sire record of Munnings (by Speightstown), one of his remote relations under a branch of the fourth generation of his family. That triple seven-furlong Grade 2 scorer was placed in Grade 1 contests at seven, eight, and nine furlongs, he stands at Ashford Stud in Kentucky, and although nothing he has done can directly impact 2020's Group 1 Queen Anne Stakes winner, his achievements at stud add to the already strong evidence that a stallion from this famous distaff line can get winners at all levels at stud. The eldest progeny of Munnings have just turned nine, his offspring have won over 1,100 races around the world and his forty-six stakes winners include the Grade 1 scorers El Deal and I'm A Chatterbox, as well as the multiple Grade 2 winners Finite, Om, and Venetian Harbor, the latter pair of whom are also those who have been Grade 1-placed at least once. His fee has risen to $40,000 for 2021.

Triple Group 1-winning miler Circus Maximus is the only surviving son of the late Duntle (by Danehill Dancer), who won the Group 2 Duke of Cambridge Stakes, was placed in the Group 1 Prix Rothschild and Group 1 Sun Chariot Stakes and was unlucky not to have a Group 1 victory to her name. She finished first past the post in the Group 1 Matron Stakes at Leopardstown, short-heading Chachamaidee and closely pursued by the talented pair Emulous and Laugh Out Loud. However, the placings of the front two were reversed following a stewards' enquiry. Luck passed her by at stud too as she died young.

Her son has also thoroughly earned a shot at stud, and although he was never flashy and his strike-rate of wins to runs was not as eye-catching as that of some, he frequently exhibited a toughness that belied the unfortunate reputation that some still associate with a horse who wears headgear. That willingness to battle is an admirable trait, one for which the flashier Giant's Causeway, for example, exhibited to great effect, and in a talented horse with a top-class pedigree it could be a valuable extra to pass on to his future sons and daughters.

A pattern-placed winner at two and dual mile Group 1 star at three, his latest season started out well with a game head defeat of Terebellum over the aforementioned Ascot mile, run this time on ground described as good-to-soft. It is a little surprising that this remained his only success of the year. The front pair finished three lengths clear of their closest pursuer, Marie's Diamond, who finished a head and a length in front of Roseman and Accidental Agent. The fourth would go on to make The Revenant fight in the Group 1 Queen Elizabeth II Stakes at the venue in the autumn.

Circus Maximus went to the front early in the Group 1 Qatar Sussex Stakes at Goodwood a month later and tried to make all from there, but although keeping on well in the closing stages he had to give best to Mohaather who hit the line three-quarters of a length in front. The classic-winning three-year-olds Siskin and Kameko were third and fourth, the former just half a length behind the Ballydoyle colt, and the latter another two lengths back following a troubled passage. There was a further gap of the same amount back to the 2000 Guineas runner-up Wichita in fifth. The ground was good there but came up heavy at Deauville the following month, a surface he had not encountered since winning his maiden at Gowran Park as a two-year-old. Pretreville made the pace, chased by Circus Maximus, but this time he was unable to quicken as the early leader dropped back towards the rear and both Palace Pier and Alpine Star moved forward. That pair fought it out and five lengths pulled clear, the colt beating the filly by three-quarters of a length. Persian King finished an additional three lengths back in fourth, two and a half lengths in front of Romanised.

It was also soft when he finished unplaced behind The Revenant in the aforementioned Queen Elizabeth II Stakes at Ascot two months later. All of his best form is on good-to-soft and good, and both his Breeders' Cup fourth in 2019 and runner-up spot in 2020 were on firm, so the run can be excused.

There was good ground at ParisLongchamp in early September when he was part of a strong six-horse line-up for the Group 1 Prix du Moulin de Longchamp, and he set off in front to make it a good test. He perhaps overdid it a little though as he weakened with a furlong to run, but still had enough to finish a length and a head in front of Siskin and Victor Ludorum, with the slow-starting Romanised another five lengths adrift. However, both Persian King, who had raced keenly and chased him throughout most of the race, and Pinatubo had swept past him, the former having gone clear from over a furlong out and the latter staying on strongly to the end. The margins were one and three-quarter lengths and six lengths.

He was perhaps unlucky not to have won the Grade 1 Breeders' Cup Mile next time. One of three Ballydoyle runners in the race, he was partnered by Ryan Moore, settled in midfield, was asked for his effort a quarter of a mile from home but then encountered some traffic trouble. He was switched to the outside to make his final challenge and then stayed on strongly, failing by just a neck to beat his stablemate Order of Australia and with the third Ballydoyle runner, Lope Y Fernandez, staying on strongly to take the minor placing, another three-quarters of a length behind. All three were running on Lasix. It was his start and so he retired to Coolmore Stud with a record of five wins and six placings from seventeen starts, a three-time Group 1-winning miler by one of the all-time great stallions. He earned just under £1.5 million in prize money but even with an introductory fee of €20,000 won't be long in earning that much and more in stud fees. His racing and pedigree profile suggests that his better two-year-olds will appear in the autumn and that his best results will come with three-year-olds and older horses in the seven-to-fourteen-furlong range. He is a potential classic sire who, depending on the input from the mares, could also get some Cup horses.

SUMMARY DETAILS
Bred: Flaxman Stables Ireland Ltd
Owned: Flaxman Stables, Mrs John Magnier, Michael Tabor & Derrick Smith
Trained: Aidan O'Brien
Country: Ireland
Race record: 0134-1012014-123302-
Career highlights: 5 wins inc Queen Anne Stakes (Gr1), Prix du Moulin de Longchamp (Gr1), St James's Palace Stakes (Gr1), Homeserve Dee Stakes (L), 2nd FanDuel Breeders' Cup Mile

presented by Permanently Disabled Jockey Fund (Gr1), Qatar Sussex Stakes (Gr1-twice), 3rd Prix du Moulin de Longchamp (Gr1), Prix du Haras de Fresnay-le-Buffard Jacques le Marois (Gr1), Masar Godolphin Autumn Stakes (Gr3)

CIRCUS MAXIMUS (IRE) – 2016 bay colt

Galileo (IRE)	Sadler's Wells (USA)	Northern Dancer
		Fairy Bridge
	Urban Sea (USA)	Miswaki (USA)
		Allegretta
Duntle (IRE)	Danehill Dancer (IRE)	Danehill (USA)
		Mira Adonde (USA)
	Lady Angola (USA)	Lord At War (ARG)
		Benguela (USA)

DONJAH (GER)

Teofilo (by Galileo) had an excellent year and Donjah was one of his five European-trained Group 1 stars. The Kildangan Stud horse has long been established as one of the best stallion sons of his great sire and yet almost seems underrated. The just-turned seventeen-year-old has been represented by twenty-one individual Group 1 winners among an overall total of ninety-four blacktype scorers. They are typically milers and middle-distance horses with some notable juveniles and some stayers among them. He has had classic winners, two of his earliest sons to go to stud (Havana Gold, Kermadec) have got a first-crop Group 1 scorer on the board, and he is also the broodmare sire of pattern winners, including a juvenile top-level winner of 2020. Perhaps what he needs is a flashy son who will light up the track as a racehorse and later as a sire of them.

Donjah, of course, is a filly and she is one with the potential to do as well at stud as she has performed on the track. She was an easy winner of both her starts at two, including a six-length score in an eight-and-a-half-furlong Group 3 contest on good ground at Krefeld that November. Although only sixth to Diamanta in the Group 1 Preis der Diana (German Oaks) on her seasonal reappearance at three, only beaten by a total of three and a quarter lengths, she picked up a Group 2 win and two Group 1 placings from four subsequent outings that year. The win came in Italy where, on heavy ground, she took the Group 2 Gran Premio del Jockey Club by four and a half lengths. She disappointed as favourite next time when only fifth to Nancho in the Group 1 Grosser Preis von Bayern on soft ground at Munich, but her earlier runs at Baden-Baden and Cologne are the ones that enhanced her CV.

Take out the winner and she would likely have made headlines for her performance in the Group 1 Longines Grosser Preis von Baden because she beat Laccario and Colomano by four and a quarter lengths and four and a half lengths on good ground. The first of those had been the big-race favourite after running up a sequence of four wins that culminated in the Group 1 Deutsches Derby, and the latter a former Group 2 scorer with a string of placings and fourths in top events to his name. However, despite this good effort, Donjah was only the runner-up, her achievement dwarfed by the stunning fourteen-length victory of Ghaiyyath. Three weeks later, and with Colomano her closest pursuer, albeit four lengths adrift, she finished a slightly disappointing third to Aspetar in the Group 1 Preis von Europa.

Donjah ran four times in 2020, kicking off her campaign with a fourth-place finish to Satomi in the Group 2 Grosser Hansa-Preis over twelve furlongs on good-to-soft at Hamburg. She got her Group 1 win a month later on soft ground at Cologne. Notable international performer Barney Roy and the recent Group 2 Princess of Wales's Stakes winner Dame Malliot were expected to take the majority of the spoils, but they had to settle for third and fourth, the filly finishing three-quarters of a length in front of the gelding. Dame Malliot had tried to make all, but although she fought to the line, she passed the post a neck and half a length behind Donjah and Kaspar. The winner had stayed on strongly inside the final furlong and got to the front just before the line.

She was back in action a month later when part of a quality eight-horse line-up for the Group 1 Longines Grosser Preis von Baden on good-to-soft at Baden-Baden. This time it was the Mark Johnston-trained Communique who tried to make all and it was Barney Roy who stayed on best in the closing stages to secure victory, scoring by a length and a quarter, but it was close for the lesser prize money. Torquator Tasso, who had been runner-up to In Swoop in the Deutsches Derby two months before and would go on to Group 1 success at Hoppegarten in October, moved into third place in the final half furlong and held off the staying-on Donjah by a neck. She, in turn, was a head in front of Durance, with Quest The Moon leading home Kaspar and then a gap back to Satomi. Sadly, her final run was disappointing. Held up near the back of the field in the Grade 1 Longines Breeders' Cup Turf on firm ground at Keeneland in early November, she stumbled badly about halfway through the race, dropped back and never made an impression after that. Her racing days were likely over as her next scheduled appearance was in the Arqana Breeding Stock Sale at Deauville in December.

The Henk Grewe-trained Donjah, a €100,000 graduate of the Baden-Baden September Yearling sale, was bred by Gestüt Karlshof and her many blacktype relations include a colt who was a good winner in England during 2020. She has two stakes-placed siblings, including Swedish Derby third Tiglath (by Footstepsinthesand), and she is out of Dyanamore (by Mt Livermore), a stakes-placed daughter of the US listed scorer Dynatrol (by Dynaformer). That mare notched up three wins and nineteen placings from forty-five starts, she is a daughter of the multiple stakes winner Coast Patrol (by Cornish Prince) and her siblings include Emy Coasting (by El Gran Senor), a dual track winner who has excelled at stud in Germany.

That mare's double-digit tally of winning offspring includes several who have earned blacktype. Ever Strong's (by Lomitas) ten wins include the Group 3 Baden-Wurttemberg Trophy over ten furlongs, Easy Way (by Dashing Blade) was first past the post in the Group 2 Maurice Lacroix Trophy over six furlongs as a two-year-old but was demoted to second in the stewards' room, and Early Wings (by Winged Love) and Empire Hurricane (by Hurricane Run) were blacktype-placed over a mile at two. However, the unfortunate Empire Storm (by Storming Home) was the best of the siblings. He was a Group 3 scorer over a mile in Germany, many of his twenty-three placings were in listed or pattern company, featuring the runners-up spot in the Group 2 Al Maktoum Challenge R1, but he suffered a fatal injury when heading back out to Dubai shortly after turning nine. Emy Coasting is also responsible for Earthly Paradise (by Dashing Blade), the winning dam of the pattern-placed, stakes-winning stayer Earlsalsa (by Kingsalsa), of the dual ten-furlong listed scorer Emily of Tinsdal (by Librettist) and of the Group 1 Deutsches Derby runner-up and triple twelve-furlong Group 1 star Earl of Tinsdal (by Black Sam Bellamy). He stands at Gestüt Helenenhof and his first foals arrived in 2017.

The connection to the British horse alluded to above comes through Change My Heart (by El Gran Senor), a full sister to Emy Coasting. Her sole win came in Japan as a three-year-old, she has produced four winners from five foals, and her listed- and Grade 3-placed daughter Diavla (by Bahri) has become a broodmare of note. She too is the dam of four winners but they include Souviens Toi (by Dalakhani), an Italian listed scorer who was also stakes placed at Pontefract, Goodwood and Windsor and whose son Thunderous (by Night of Thunder) landed the Group 2 Dante Stakes at York in July. That Mark Johnston-trained bay won all three of his starts as a juvenile, including a seven-furlong listed contest at Newbury, and his only defeat so far is when he was runner-up in the Listed Fairway Stakes at Newmarket in June. He has not been seen out since York. Diavla's other progeny include Whippy Cream (by Dansili), a non-winner who picked up third place to Charity Line in the Group 2 Oaks d'Italia of 2013.

With a racing record and pedigree credentials like these, Donjah clearly has a lot of potential as a broodmare. She was offered for sale at the Arqana December mare sale on December 5th but was led out unsold at €720,000.

SUMMARY DETAILS
Bred: Gestüt Karlshof
Owned: Darius Racing
Trained: Henk Grewe
Country: Germany
Race record: 11-02310-4140-
Career highlights: 4 wins inc 58th Preis von Europa (Gr1), Gran Premio del Jockey Club (Gr2), Grosser Preis des Olympischen Dorfes In Berlin Von 1936 - Herzog Von Ratibor-Rennen (Gr3), 2nd 147th Grosser Preis von Baden (Gr1), 3rd 57th Preis von Europa (Gr1)

DONJAH (GER) – 2016 bay filly

Teofilo (IRE)	Galileo (IRE)	Sadler's Wells (USA)
		Urban Sea (USA)
	Speirbhean (IRE)	Danehill (USA)
		Saviour (USA)
Dyanamore (USA)	Mt. Livermore (USA)	Blushing Groom (FR)
		Flama Ardiente (USA)
	Dynatrol (USA)	Dynaformer (USA)
		Coast Patrol (USA)

DREAM AND DO (IRE)

Haras de Bonneval stallion Siyouni (by Pivotal) had an outstanding year. His classic-winning son Sottsass returned as a four-year-old to add the Group 1 Prix Ganay and Group 1 Prix de l'Arc de Triomphe, two-year-old St Mark's Basilica landed both the Group 1 Dewhurst Stakes for the Ballydoyle team and the European champion juvenile colt title, Etoile won the Grade 1 E. P. Taylor Stakes at Woodbine in Canada, and Dream And Do gave her sire a fourth career classic winner when landing the Group 1 Emirates Poule d'Essai des Pouliches on good-to-soft ground at Deauville at the start of June.

Both the date and the venue moved from their usual slots due to the Covid-19 situation, and her victory was by a nose from Speak of The Devil, just holding on following a battle and having been in front from a furlong out. The pair finished two lengths clear of Mageva, with an additional head back to the race favourite, Tropbeau, in fourth. It was that latter filly who had beaten her by half a length when the pair were first and second in the Group 3 Prix de la Grotte on very soft ground at ParisLongchamp three weeks before, a first defeat for the subsequent classic heroine since her runner-up spot to Savarin on her debut at Deauville the previous August.

She had run three times between those two races, all of them in the autumn of her two-year-old season and all wins. She had followed a mile maiden success on fast ground at Marseille Borely with a two-length conditions win over seven furlongs on soft ground at Maisons-Laffitte before beating Les Hogues by a neck to take the Group 3 Prix Miesque over that same course and distance, on heavy ground in late October. The pair finished three and a half lengths clear of their closest pursuer, Yogomi, and the aforementioned Mageva was among those further behind that day.

She had failed to meet her reserve when led out at €80,000 at the Arqana Deauville August yearling sale in 2018, but it was announced shortly after her classic success that she had been sold to Katsumi Yoshida. The plan was that she would remain in the Frederic Rossi stable before eventually retiring to Northern Farm in Japan to begin her stud career. The private deal was brokered by Emmanuel de Seroux of Navrick International. Before that, she had raced in the colours of her breeders, Haras Du Logis Saint Germain. Sadly, we did not see her in action again. France Galop's website shows her as having left France in December.

Dream And Do is the first foal of Venetias Dream (by Librettist), a mare who was placed twice over six furlongs on Polytrack when based in England. She was sold for just 1,000 guineas at the Tattersalls February Sale in 2013, was exported to Libya and won twice, and there was no reason to think that she might find her way back to this part of the world again. However, she reappeared in a British auction ring at the 2016 Tattersalls December Mare Sale and this time changed hands for 80,000 guineas. Being in-foal to Siyouni was attractive but the considerable increase in her perceived value was largely down to the big update on her page. A few months after her initial sale, her dam's half-sister L'Enjoleuse (by Montjeu) had a new blacktype addition to the family, a colt who finished third in the Group 1 Prix Jean-Luc Lagardere - Grand Criterium. He was Charm Spirit (by Invincible Spirit), who went on to finish fifth to Night of Thunder in a vintage edition of the 2000 Guineas at Newmarket before reeling off a four-timer headlined by a Group 1 treble in the Prix Jean Prat, Prix du Moulin de Longchamp and Queen Elizabeth II Stakes, earning a Timeform rating of 127.

Charm Spirit has been switching between Tweenhills Farm & Stud and Haras de Bonneval, he shuttles to southern hemisphere, and has moved to Haras du Logis Saint Germain for 2021, now standing for just €7,000, down from a career-high price of €27,500. He has sired nine stakes winners to date. They include the New Zealand-bred Group 2 winners Aretha and Fascino, pattern winner and Group 1 New Zealand Derby third Scorpz, British and Scandinavian pattern scorer Kick On, and juvenile Group 3 winner Yourtimeisnow. As for Venetias Dream, her second is a now three-year-old filly named Keepthedreamalive (by The Gurkha) and that one was followed by a son of Gleneagles (by Galileo).

Machaera (by Machiavellian) is the grandam of Dream And Do and that unraced half-sister to the Group 2-winning sprinters Snaadee (by Danzig) and Russian Bond (by Danzig) can also count the Group 3 scorer Cristofori (by Fappiano) and the broodmare Sombreffe (by Polish Precedent) among her siblings. The latter is best known as being the dam of the classic-placed middle-distance Group 1 winner Ransom O'War (by Red Ransom) and she is also the grandam of the New Zealand-bred Group 1-placed stakes winners Star of The Seas (by Thorn Park) and Spieth (by Thorn Park).

Third dam Somfas (by What A Pleasure) was a winning daughter of the prolific and hugely influential Ciboulette (by Chop Chop) whose sons include the leading sire Night Shift (by Northern Dancer). The mare's other descendants feature the Group 1 star and Australian juvenile filly champion Hasna (by Snippets), leading US juvenile Chapel Royal (by Montbrook), Group 3 Supreme Stakes winner and Group 1 Prix de la Foret third Inzar (by Warning), and the Australian-bred Group 1-placed Group 2 winner Gypsy Diamond (by Not A Single Doubt). And that's before you even glance at the record of her most famous daughter. That celebrity is the champion racehorse and 'blue hen' broodmare Fanfreluche (by Northern Dancer). Her Group/Grade 1-winning descendants around the world include Aube Indienne (by Bluebird), Combatant (by Scat Daddy), Encosta de Lago (by Fairy King; leading sire), Erupt (by Dubawi), Flying Spur (by Danehill; leading sire), Hi Happy (by Pure Prize), Hispanidad (by Pure Prize), Holy Roman Emperor (by Danehill; leading sire), I Am A Star (by I Am Invincible), L'Enjoleur (by Buckpasser), La Voyageuse (by Tentam), Majestic Roi (by Street Cry), Medaille d'Or (by Secretariat), Medici (by Sir Cat), Pear Tart (by Dehere), Russian Revolution (by Snitzel), and Sherwood Forest (by Fastnet Rock).

Most of those horses are so remotely connected to Dream And Do as to have no bearing on anything she has achieved, but when you have a classic winning relation to a star miler and who comes from a branch of such a powerful family, it is hard not to think about the possibility that one or more future Group 1 stars may be able to count her as their dam or direct ancestor.

SUMMARY DETAILS
Bred: Haras Du Logis Saint Germain

Owned: Haras Du Logis Saint Germain
Trained: Frederic Rossi
Country: France
Race record: 2111-21-
Career highlights: 4 wins inc Emirates Poule d'Essai des Pouliches (Gr1), Prix Miesque (Gr3), 2nd Prix de la Grotte (Gr3)

DREAM AND DO (IRE) – 2017 bay filly

Siyouni (FR)	Pivotal (GB)	Polar Falcon (USA)
		Fearless Revival
	Sichilla (IRE)	Danehill (USA)
		Slipstream Queen (USA)
Venetias Dream (IRE)	Librettist (USA)	Danzig (USA)
		Mysterial (USA)
	Machaera (GB)	Machiavellian (USA)
		Somfas (USA)

DREAM OF DREAMS (IRE)

Sir Michael Stoute has long been recognised as one of the world's great racehorse trainers, a prolific supplier of classic and other superstars over many years. He has also had a tremendous record with horses who took more time, ones who, for whatever reason, did not hit their peak until four, five or even six years of age. Dream of Dreams is such a horse.

The chestnut showed ability from the start of his career and developed an eye-catching blacktype profile that saw him win a pair of listed races, earn placings in a string of pattern contests and achieve a peak handicap mark of 119. Despite some outstanding efforts, he failed to make the breakthrough at pattern level. In 2019, he was a head runner-up to Blue Point in the Group 1 Diamond Jubilee Stakes at Royal Ascot, whereas the previous autumn he missed out by a neck in the Group 3 Bengough Stakes at the same track. Whether or not being gelded in October 2019 made the difference or it was just natural maturity, or even some other factor, cannot be known for certain, but Dream of Dreams finally had his breakthrough season in 2020 and added his name to the long list of Stoute-trained older horses that have won at the highest level.

His seasonal reappearance came at Ascot in June when, staying on strongly in the closing stages, he just failed to catch Hello Youmzain in the Group 1 Diamond Jubilee Stakes. The sadly ill-fated Sceptical was a neck back in third, with further gaps of one and a quarter lengths, the same, and half a length back to Khaadem, Speak In Colours and One Master. His form had tailed off after his fine runner-up spot in that race twelve months before, but not this time. The three horses officially rated closest to him failed to produce their running in the Group 2 Unibet Hungerford Stakes at Newbury in mid-August, but the manner in which Dream of Dreams disposed of the field was impressive. Neither the seven-furlong trip not the good-to-soft ground inconvenienced him in any way and, always going easily, he hit the front a quarter of a mile from home, was shaken up by Oisin Murphy and then stormed clear of the field, crossing the line with seven lengths to spare over Breathtaking Look. That capable mare finished four and a half lengths clear of the third, Symbolize.

This performance exuded Group 1 potential but time was running out and soft ground becoming more frequent. He had won a listed contest on soft ground at Doncaster as a three-year-old and been runner-up in a couple of Group 3s on it at four, so he could clearly handle easy underfoot conditions. It was also what prevailed on his final two outings of 2020. Murphy was again in the saddle when he landed the biggest win of his career, the Group 1 Betfair Sprint Cup Stakes at Haydock in early September. The thirteen-strong field featured prior top-level scorers Golden Horde, Hello Youmzain, The Tin Man and Brando as well as an array of promising, improving or established talent, but from the moment he went to the front inside the final furlong, Dream of Dreams had the race won. Both he and the surprise one-and-a-quarter-length runner-up Glen Shiel had proven ability to stay farther than this six-furlong trip. Golden Horde was a neck back in third, followed home by Art Power, Hello Youmzain, The Tin Man, and Lope Y Fernandez. The front pair had also raced on the near side while Golden Horde and most of those who followed him home had raced in a separate group.

The BHA raised his rating to 120 after Newbury and kept it at that level to the end of the year, even after his unplaced finish in the Group 1 Qipco British Champions Sprint Stakes at Ascot in mid-October. Dream of Dreams had again been sent off as the favourite, this time in a line-up that included prior Group 1 stars Brando, One Master, Oxted, and The Tin Man as well as the talented sprinters such as Art Power, Happy Power, and Speak In Colours and the unbeaten three-year-old Starman. However, although travelling well a quarter of a mile from home, he weakened in the final furlong and passed the post in eighth place, four lengths behind the winner, his old rival Glen Shiel, perhaps having done too much in the early stages of the race.

A 37,000-guinea Tattersalls December Foal Sale graduate bred by Prostock Ltd, Dream of Dreams is the latest Group 1 winner by the former juvenile and sprint star Dream Ahead (by Diktat). The Timeform 133-rated champion spent five years at Ballylinch Stud in Ireland, moved to Haras de Grandcamp in 2017 and has supplied a total of twenty-nine stakes winners. Those include the classic-placed mile Group 1 winner Al Wukair and the Group 1-winning sprinters Donjuan Triumphant and Glass Slippers, and the first pair are also standing in France. Al Wukair is at Haras du Bouquetot and will have his first two-year-olds in action in 2021, whereas the first foals by Haras de la Barbottiere stallion Donjuan Triumphant are arriving now. Glass Slippers, a dual top-level winner in 2020, is featured elsewhere in this volume.

His newest top-level star is the best of three blacktype horses out of an unraced mare named Vasilia (by Dansili), the other pair being the Group 3 Solario Stakes runner-up and Group 2 Superlative Stakes third Silverheels (by Verglas) and the speedy stakes-placed filly Lasilia (by Acclamation). The latter is also notable as being the dam of Brassica (by Australia), a Beverley winner who picked up blacktype in 2019 and 2020 by finishing third in a pair of listed races for the Sir Mark Prescott stable. She stays ten furlongs. Vasilia is also responsible for Cadelisa (by Dream Ahead), who has won four times from six furlongs to a mile, and for the prolific gelding Fiftyshadesfreed (by Verglas) who stays ten furlongs and missed out on blacktype in 2020 when finishing fourth to Kick On in a one-mile listed contest at Ovrevoll in Norway in early October.

Dream of Dreams has no possibility of a stallion career ahead of him but one of his dam's most talented relations is a freshman sire of 2021 and a likely candidate to feature prominently in that end-of-year table.

The mare's Timeform 119-rated half-sister Jwala (by Oasis Dream) sadly died just a few months after her Group 1 Nunthorpe Stakes victory, but their older sibling Airwave (by Air Express), the juvenile filly champion in England in 2002, has been a tremendous success at stud. Her top win at two was in the Group 1 Cheveley Park Stakes, she went on to add the Group 2 Temple Stakes at Sandown, she was placed in the Group 1 Golden Jubilee Stakes, the Group 1 July Cup and Group 1 Sprint Cup, and having later moved from the Henry Candy stable to join the team at Ballydoyle, won the Group 2 Ridgewood Pearl Stakes over a mile at the Curragh.

Airwave is the dam of the mile listed scorer Orator (by Galileo), of nine-and-a-half-furlong Group 3 winner Aloof (by Galileo) and of the speedy Meow (by Storm Cat), a lightly raced filly who narrowly won a five-furlong listed contest on fast ground at the Curragh a couple of months after failing by just a neck to beat Maqaasid in the Group 2 Queen Mary Stakes at Ascot. Since then, Meow has become a broodmare of rare value as, in addition to the Group 3 scorer Blenheim Palace (by Galileo) and 2017's juvenile filly champion Clemmie (by Galileo), who won the Group 1 Cheveley Park Stakes, she is the dam of the dual juvenile Group 1 star and dual Guineas hero Churchill (by Galileo). Timeform-rated 120p at two and 126 at three, the now seven-year-old is a popular member of the team at Coolmore Stud, one widely expected to become a sire of note. In 2020, he had twenty-two yearlings that were sold (excluding vendor buy-backs) for at least £100,000, with a top price of 350,000 guineas for a filly out of Date With Destiny—the only horse sired by the brilliant but ill-fated George Washington (by Danehill)—and a string of others who fetched £50,000 and upwards.

Dream of Dreams looks set to return to action this coming season, and if he is even close to his best then there should be more good prizes to be won with him before he eventually retires from the track.

SUMMARY DETAILS
Bred: Prostock Ltd
Owned: Saeed Suhail
Trained: Sir Michael Stoute
Country: England
Race record: 213P22-20101-00032220-112000-2110-
Career highlights: 7 wins inc Betfair Sprint Cup Stakes (Gr1), Unibet Hungerford Stakes (Gr2), Weatherbys Hamilton Stakes (L), Betfred Mobile Wentworth Stakes (L), 2nd Diamond Jubilee Stakes (Gr1-twice), Ladysford Stud Hungerford Stakes (Gr2), John Guest Racing Bengough Stakes (Gr3), Weatherbys Racing Bank Supreme Stakes (Gr3), coral.co.uk Rockingham Stakes (L), 3rd GAIN Railway Stakes (Gr2), bet365 Hackwood Stakes (Gr3)

DREAM OF DREAMS (IRE) – 2014 chestnut gelding

Dream Ahead (USA)	Diktat (GB)	Warning
		Arvola (GB)
	Land of Dreams (GB)	Cadeaux Genereux
		Sahara Star (GB)
Vasilia (GB)	Dansili (GB)	Danehill (USA)
		Hasili (IRE)
	Kangra Valley (GB)	Indian Ridge
		Thorner Lane

ENABLE (GB)

The year 2020 was not anything like the world expected. It was one of the Covid-19 pandemic and of record-breaking fire seasons, of death and destruction, lockdowns, social restrictions, political unrest, businesses and sporting seasons shut down or curtailed, the Olympic Games postponed and still at risk of cancellation, the aviation and hospitality industries near collapse. But for the horse racing sector there was a glimmer of hope that it might still produce a truly special moment when, following two easy wins, Enable was confirmed to be on course for another bid for an unprecedented third victory in the Group 1 Qatar Prix de l'Arc de Triomphe at ParisLongchamp in October.

The great mare had chased home Ghaiyyath while bidding for a second victory in the Group 1 Coral-Eclipse Stakes at Sandown on her reappearance in early July, trounced the previous year's Group 1 Irish Derby winner, Sovereign, by five and a half lengths in a three-runner edition of the Group 1 King George VI and Queen Elizabeth Stakes at Ascot, and then dismissed a bunch of vastly inferior rivals by seven lengths and more in the Group 3 Unibet September Stakes on the Polytrack at Kempton. She was clearly at the top of her game and, aside from staying healthy and avoiding trouble in running, it seemed that all she needed to go out in a blaze of glory with that unique treble was for the weather to remain favourable.

It was soft when she won her first Arc, beating Cloth of Stars by two and a half lengths at Chantilly for a fifth Group 1 win in a row in her remarkable three-year-old season, good at ParisLongchamp when she held on to beat the sadly ill-fated Sea of Class by a neck, but very soft at that venue on the day of her third attempt. Having gone to the front in a manner that elicited a tremendous roar of excitement from the crowds, she got tired in the ground and could not repel the challenge of Waldgeist who denied her hat-trick bid by a length and three-quarters. He was no longer in training, having completed a busy first season as a stallion at Ballylinch Stud in Ireland.

Sottsass was back, his first try at the distance since finishing third the previous year. He'd notched up a Group 1 win from four starts and been a two-length fourth to Magical in the Group 1 Qipco Irish Champion Stakes in mid-September. The line-up also featured the classic and Group 1 star Persian King, coming into the race after an impressive Group 1 score at a mile. The top Japanese mare Deirdre, who looked a bit out of her depth on this occasion, the highly regarded three-year-old filly Raabihah, who had been second and fourth in her two Group 1 attempts so far, and the French-trained Group 1 Deutsches Derby winner In Swoop were also in the field. So too was Enable's outstanding stable team-mate Stradivarius, one of the great stayers of the modern era but with much better twelve-furlong pace than most in his division.

Unfortunately, the rains came, the ground was even worse than in the previous year, trainer John Gosden expressed his concerns that she faced likely defeat in the conditions, and that was what came to pass. It was clear from a quarter of a mile from home that the treble was not going to happen, and it was sad to see her unable to do anything as five locally trained runners finished ahead of her. Sottsass held off In Swoop to win by a neck, Persian King, who had tried to make all, finished one and three-quarter lengths back in third, a head in front of Gold Trip who was two lengths clear of Raabihah. Enable crossed the line another two lengths adrift, half a length in front of Stradivarius for whom the ground was also too deep.

There was some speculation in the days that followed that perhaps she might run one more time, so she could go out with a win instead of such a defeat. The Group 1 British Champions Filly & Mare Turf was suggested in some media and online sources as a more likely candidate than the shorter Group 1 Qipco Champion Stakes, but in the end, it was all just talk. Her connections made the announcement that the racing phase of her career had come to an end and she would now join her owner-breeder's powerful broodmare band.

Enable won fifteen of her nineteen starts in five seasons, eleven of those wins coming at the highest level. She is one of a handful of horses to have won the Prix de l'Arc de Triomphe twice, she is the only horse to have won the King George VI and Queen Elizabeth Stakes three times, she is one of only three female horses ever to have won the Eclipse Stakes (Pebbles and Kooyonga are the other two), she won two classics, and a Breeders' Cup Turf, and she earned a remarkable £10,724,320 in prize money. Her Timeform rating of 134 as a three-year-old is one of the highest ever awarded by that organisation to a female horse; they rated her 129 at four, 131 at five and 125 at six. She was, quite simply, an outstanding racehorse, one against whom fillies and mares of the future will be compared and, more often than not, fall short.

Her achievements on the track from two to five years of age have been discussed in detail in the 2018 and 2019 editions of this annual, as has the powerful family that her pedigree represents. It remains, therefore, to consider what her future may hold as a broodmare. Many top-class and brilliant racemares have disappointed at stud, some even failing to produce a single stakes or pattern winner. However, with the pedigree and connections behind Enable, there is every reason to hope that at least one or two of her offspring will excel and that, perhaps, she can become a mare of long-term influence.

Kingman (by Invincible Spirit) is the stallion who has been chosen as her first mate. He is not, as some have said, an outcross for her given that, like her, he has both Northern Dancer (by Nearctic) and Mill Reef (by Never Bend) in the first five generations of his pedigree. An outcross means zero duplicated ancestors within the first five generations. However, he is about as close to one as can be found among potentially suitable sires. No foal she produces will ever be free of inbreeding, her own 3x2 cross to Sadler's Wells (by Northern Dancer) makes that impossible, but it seems likely that introducing further lines of that former Coolmore colossus will be avoided. A Kingman foal out of Enable will be inbred 5x5x4 to Northern Dancer, 5x5 to Mill Reef, 4x3 to Sadler's Wells, with the latter coming solely from the distaff side. If it has pattern or classic potential then it may win at seven furlongs and/or a mile at two, could possibly be a Guineas-type who quickly moves up to ten and even twelve furlongs, or it could bypass the mile at three and go straight into the middle-distance division. If it's a filly then she would have considerable future broodmare potential regardless of how her track days might turn out.

Kingman was a brilliant miler, his dam Zenda (by Zamindar) is a classic-winning half-sister to the sprint champion and influential sire Oasis Dream (by Green Desert), and his other Group 1-winning relations include Wemyss Bight (by Dancing Brave) and Beat Hollow (by Sadler's Wells). All of this made him a likely candidate to get his best winners in the broad six-to-twelve-furlong range. He stands at his owner-breeder's Banstead Manor Stud and his first three crops of racing age have thus far yielded twenty-nine stakes winners. Of those, Palace Pier and Persian King are multiple Group 1 stars, Domestic Spending has won once at the highest level in California, whereas Calyx (Coolmore Stud, first foals in 2021), Fearless King (Mehl-Mülhens-Rennen [German 2000 Guineas] in 2020) and Headman (Prix Guillaume d'Ornano, Prix Eugene Adam) have won at Group 2 level. It is a highly promising start for a stallion who has the potential to develop a long-term career at the top, and he looks like an excellent choice, especially as Headman's grandam is a full sister to Concentric (by Sadler's Wells), the dam of Enable.

That mare is the Group 2 Prix de Royallieu winner and Group 1 Prix de Diane (French Oaks) runner-up Dance Route, and in addition to her grandson Headman (standing his first season at stud in France in 2021) and his US Grade 2-winning half-brother Projected (by Showcasing), she is notable as being the dam of the dual Arc and dual Breeders' Cup-placed five-time Group/Grade 1 scorer Flintshire (by Dansili) who stands at Hill 'N' Dale Farm in Kentucky. His yearlings made up to $50,000 in 2020, his first-crop winners include Siskin's younger half-sister Talacre, who got off the mark over a mile at Gowran Park in September, and it is likely to be 2021 and beyond before we see what his progeny are capable of. Indeed, it would be interesting to see how he might fare if ever moving to a European stud, one focusing on the flat of course.

There have been a few other updates to the pedigree since it was reviewed in detail in prior editions. Enable's half-sister Portrush (by Frankel) was runner-up over ten furlongs at Newbury in June and then won over the same trip at Yarmouth a month later; those have been her only starts to date. She also has a promising half-brother, the John Gosden-trained Derab (by Sea The Stars), and that Group 1 Investec Derby entrant chased home La Barrosa in a seven-furlong maiden at Ascot in early September, his only run. The winner took a Group 3 contest next time and then finished fifth in heavy ground in the Group 1 Criterium International at Saint-Cloud.

Concentric's 2019 foal, born on February 27th, is a full brother to Enable, and she is booked back to Nathaniel (by Galileo) for 2021. In addition to being the sire of the great mare, that Newsells Park Stud stallion is also responsible for the Italian Group 1 winner God Given, French classic heroine Channel and nineteen other stakes winners.

Of potential note also, Enable's multiple graded-placed half-sister Contribution has a three-year-old son named Destinado (by Lope de Vega), had a Dubawi (by Dubai Millennium) filly in 2019 and a daughter of Golden Horn (by Cape Cross) twelve months later, whereas Birdwood (by Oasis Dream), a sibling owned by Newsells Park Stud, has a 2018 Lope de Vega filly named Bello Quies, her now two-year-old is a son of Frankel (by Galileo) and she had a Shamardal (by Giant's Causeway) colt in 2020. And then there's Entitle (by Dansili), a pattern-placed half-sister to Enable, who is booked to visit Sea The Stars (by Cape Cross) in 2021. Headman's dam, Deliberate (by King's Best) is booked to Siyouni (by Pivotal).

Presuming a long and healthy life for her, it will many years before we know where Enable, forever to be remembered as one of the greats of the Turf, will fit in with regard to her impact on the breed. She has everything going for her and it is hoped that her place at stud will be up there with giants such as Dahlia and Miesque, racing superstars who excelled in their second career and, in the case of the latter, wielded a considerable and wide-ranging influence. Her presence on the track will be missed.

SUMMARY DETAILS
Bred: Juddmonte Farms Ltd
Owned: Khalid Abdullah
Trained: John Gosden

Country: England
Race record: 1-3111111-111-1112-2110-
Career highlights: 15 wins inc Qatar Prix de l'Arc de Triomphe (Gr1-twice), King George VI and Queen Elizabeth Qipco Stakes (Gr1-three times), Coral-Eclipse Stakes (Gr1), Longines Breeders' Cup Turf (Gr1), Investec Oaks (Gr1), Darley Irish Oaks (Gr1), Darley Yorkshire Oaks (Gr1-twice), September Stakes (Gr3-twice), Arkle Finance Cheshire Oaks (L), 2nd Qatar Prix de l'Arc de Triomphe (Gr1), Coral-Eclipse Stakes (Gr1)

ENABLE (GB) – 2014 bay mare

Nathaniel (IRE)	Galileo (IRE)	**Sadler's Wells (USA)**
		Urban Sea (USA)
	Magnificient Style (USA)	Silver Hawk (USA)
		Mia Karina (USA)
Concentric (GB)	**Sadler's Wells (USA)**	Northern Dancer
		Fairy Bridge
	Apogee (GB)	Shirley Heights
		Bourbon Girl

EVEN SO (IRE)

Coolmore Stud's multiple classic star Camelot (by Montjeu), who came so close to landing the Triple Crown in 2012, wasted no time establishing his credentials as a stallion. His eldest offspring have finished their five-year-old season, he doesn't yet have a flashy star to his name, but he has had thirty-three blacktype scorers, seven of whom have won at the highest level, three of them in classics. His best representatives have been good or very good rather than showing a tendency towards brilliance, but it's early days yet and he has made an excellent start.

His Irish Derby-winning son Latrobe won only a Group 3 contest at four, was unplaced in two starts at five and is taking up a role as a National Hunt stallion in France in 2021, but the long list of other Camelot-sired blacktype earners in 2020 includes four who hit the top. Russian Camelot, a 120,000-guinea Tattersalls Book 1 graduate bred by the partnership of Lynch Bages and Camas Park Stud, achieved the remarkable feat of landing the Group 1 TAB South Australian Derby over twelve and a half furlongs at Morphettville in early May despite being over half a year younger than his rivals. He has since won the Group 1 Underwood Stakes over ten furlongs, been runner-up in the Group 1 Neds Stakes over the same trip and the Group 1 Makybe Diva Stakes over a mile, and he finished third in the Group 1 Ladbrokes Cox Plate at Moonee Valley in late October. That race was won by a four-year-old colt having his first start as an Australian-trained runner but well-known in Europe: Sir Dragonet. The Group 3 Chester Vase winner, who was fifth in the Group 1 Derby, fourth in the Group 1 St Leger Stakes and, one his final start for the Aidan O'Brien team, runner-up in the Group 1 Tattersalls Gold Cup, is also a son of Camelot. Group 1 Allianz - Grosser Preis von Bayern scorer Sunny Queen, who is discussed elsewhere in this volume, was number four.

Even So, on the other hand, was the stallion's third top-level star of 2020, and although she was unplaced on her two subsequent outings, both of them Group 1 contests, the Ger Lyons-trained bay won the Group 1 Juddmonte Irish Oaks at the Curragh in July, beating Cayenne Pepper by two lengths. This came a fortnight after her narrow defeat of Laburnum in a ten-furlong listed contest on ground described as yielding-to-soft at Naas. She had been third in the Group 3 Lodge Park Stud Irish EBF Park Express Stakes over a mile at that same on her seasonal reappearance in March and, between those two performances, finished a four-length fifth to Peaceful in the Group 1 Tattersalls Irish 1,000 Guineas.

Her only runs as a two-year-old were in maidens at Tipperary and Gowran Park, the latter she won by three and three-quarter lengths while going a mile on soft ground. Her two unplaced runs in her latest autumn were behind Tarnawa in the Group 1 Qatar Prix Vermeille at ParisLongchamp and behind Wonderful Tonight in the Group 1 Qipco British Champions Fillies & Mares Stakes at Ascot, both over twelve furlongs and the latter on soft ground.

Even So has a pedigree that entitles her to achieve anything, on the track and at stud, and she will be a fascinating addition to the broodmare ranks. Her dam, Breeze Hill (by Danehill), is bred to be equine royalty yet showed little in six starts, rated just seventy-eight when sold for 150,000 guineas in Newmarket and exported to Australia. She won a race there over ten and a half furlongs, her first seven foals were born in the southern hemisphere and include a couple of winners, and then she was sold again, this time for A$100,000 at the 2012 Australian Easter Broodmare Sale, and she returned to Ireland. Her first two Irish-bred foals are the winners Latin Beat (by Galileo) and Miss Latin (by Galileo), Even So is her third and she had a daughter of Footstepsinthesand (by Giant's Causeway) in mid-April 2019.

It is an unusual move to bring a horse back like that, especially if they have not done anything of note, but not really a surprise in this case given the mare's relationship to two Epsom classic stars, a Guineas winner and a host of other top-class performers. Breeze Hill is out of Rose of Jericho (by Alleged), which makes her a half-sister to Derby, Dewhurst and Irish Champion Stakes winner Dr Devious (by Ahonoora). Her close relation Dancing Rain (by Danehill Dancer and out of her half-sister Rain Flower, by Indian Ridge) won both the Group 1 Oaks at Epsom and the Group 1 Preis der Diana (German Oaks) before going on to success at stud, whereas Sumora (by Danehill), who could be described as being her three-parts sister, is responsible for Maybe (by Galileo), the classic-placed, Group 1-winning dam of Saxon Warrior (by Deep Impact). He won the Group 1 Racing Post Trophy and Group 2 Beresford Stakes at two, added the Group 1 2000 Guineas at three, was placed in each of the Group 1 Coral-Eclipse Stakes, Group 1 Irish Champion Stakes and Group 1 Irish Derby, and is a very popular young Coolmore Stud stallion whose first foals arrived in 2020.

Dr Devious sired winners at all levels although with fewer pattern scorers than one would have hoped, whereas his sprinting half-brother Archway (by Thatching) got several Group 1 winners in Australia including the Melbourne Cup-placed, South Australian Oaks-winner She's Archie. Their siblings Royal Court (by Sadler's Wells) and Shinko King (by Fairy King) were also blacktype winners, making Even So's dam Breeze Hill a half-sister to four track performers of note, but their half-sister Rose of Suzuka (by Fairy King) also deserves mention. She is the dam of Suzuka Phoenix (by Sunday Silence), a Group 1-winning sprinter in Japan who was also a Group 1-placed pattern winner at a mile. His offspring include the mile Group 1 scorer Meiner Ho O.

As for Dancing Rain, the stud success alluded to above consists of the talented full-siblings Jalmoud (by New Approach) and Magic Lily. The first-named has been a listed-race winner in France and placed in the Group 1 Grand Prix de Paris and Group 2 Prix Eugene Adam, whereas Magic Lily's excellent season booked her spot in *Volume 2: UK & Ireland's Group 2 & Group 3 Winners*. The Charlie Appleby-trained mare, who was off the track for a long time after finishing third in the Group 1 Fillies' Mile at two, was a Group 1-placed dual Group 2 scorer at Meydan early in the year.

Pedigree credentials like these combined with the opportunities that will no doubt be afforded to her as a classic-winning daughter of Camelot give Even So the potential to become a Group 1-producer, and that makes her a fascinating addition to the broodmare ranks. With regard to inbreeding, she has a 4x4x4 duplication to Northern Dancer (by Nearctic) and an eye-catching 4x2 cross to Danehill (by Danzig).

SUMMARY DETAILS

Bred: Lynch Bages Ltd
Owned: Mrs John Magnier & Mrs Paul Shanahan
Trained: Ger Lyons
Country: Ireland
Race record: 31-301100-
Career highlights: 3 wins inc Juddmonte Irish Oaks (Gr1), Irish Stallion Farms EBF Naas Oaks Trial (L), 3rd Lodge Park Stud Irish EBF Park Express Stakes (Gr3)

EVEN SO (IRE) – 2017 bay filly

		Sadler's Wells (USA)
Camelot (GB)	Montjeu (IRE)	
		Floripedes (FR)
	Tarfah (USA)	Kingmambo (USA)
		Fickle (GB)
Breeze Hill (IRE)	Danehill (USA)	Danzig (USA)
		Razyana (USA)
	Rose of Jericho (USA)	Alleged (USA)
		Rose Red (USA)

FANCY BLUE (IRE)

Deep Impact (by Sunday Silence) was one of the greatest racehorses ever trained in Japan and, like his sire, who was a US champion, he went on to become a phenomenally successful stallion. The multiple champion sire was only seventeen when he died and given how long the top horses race for in Japan, it is still early days yet to know how he will fare in the long-term as a sire of stallions. His classic-winning son Kizuna, a second-crop sire in Japan in 2020 and awaiting his first top-level winner, finished twelfth in the overall general sires' championship title race, which is a promising start. Deep Impact has also made a notable contribution in Europe, one that has the potential to become a force in future years.

Beauty Parlour gave him a first European classic winner when she landed the Group 1 Poule d'Essai des Pouliches (French 1000 Guineas) in 2012. She was then a runner-up in the Group 1 Prix de Diane (French Oaks) and her winning offspring include the British-bred but multiple US graded-placed stakes winner Blowout (by Dansili). Four years later, A Shin Hikari spent a short time in Europe, beat Dariyan by ten lengths in the Group 1 Prix d'Ispahan and returned home for stallion duties; he was a freshman sire in 2020. In 2018, Saxon Warrior landed the Group 1 2000 Guineas at Newmarket shortly before Study of Man won the Group 1 Prix du Jockey Club (French Derby) at Chantilly: two more European classic stars for their sire and, of potential long-term significance, two popular young stallions too. Saxon Warrior covered 165 mares in his first season at Coolmore Stud and at least that many again in his second one, whereas Study of Man covered seventy-one mares in his first book at Lanwades Stud in 2020.

There have been a few other blacktype horses in Europe for Deep Impact and they include Fancy Blue. She advertised her potential in 2019 when winning both her starts in Ireland, officially listed as being trained by Aidan O'Brien, although her education was being overseen by his son Donnacha. The younger O'Brien retired from the saddle to become an officially licensed trainer and, thanks to that filly, became a classic-winning one in his maiden season.

She kicked off her campaign in the Group 1 Tattersalls Irish 1,000 Guineas at the Curragh in mid-June and although losing her unbeaten record, she showed considerable potential when chasing home two-length winner Peaceful on fast ground, ridden by Declan McDonogh. So Wonderful and New York Girl were the next two home, a head and the same behind, with Even So another length and a half away in fifth, a neck in front of Albigna. The ground was on the soft side of good at Chantilly three weeks later for what was a notably competitive edition of the Group 1 Prix de Diane Longines. Alpine Star set out to try to make all, Fancy Blue put her head in front over a furlong out and a battle ensued, joined by Peaceful and the highly regarded French filly Raahibah. It was a one-two-three for Ireland, Fancy Blue, Alpine Star, Peaceful separated by margins of a short neck, a head and a head, and their closest pursuer, the subsequent Grade 1 Belmont Oaks Invitational Stakes heroine Magic Attitude, was another two and a half lengths behind. With Covid-19 restrictions affecting available jockey selections, the mount here had gone to the outstanding French rider Pierre-Charles Boudot.

Fancy Blue was dropped in distance by just over half a furlong for the Group 1 Qatar Nassau Stakes at Goodwood twenty-five days later: the race was run over thirteen yards short of the full ten furlongs. This time Ryan Moore was in the saddle. They did not break as quickly as some of the others but were soon tracking the pace-setting Magic Wand. That five-year-old remained in front until Fancy Blue put her head in front, and while the mare soon weakened and dropped to fifth, her younger rival kept on well to the line, just holding off the strong late challenge of the Jessica Harrington-trained One Voice. There was only a neck between that pair at the line, with Nazeef another two and three-quarter lengths back in third, a half-length and a length in front of Queen Power and Magic Wand.

Stated plans for the winner included one of two possible targets to be held during Irish Champions Weekend followed by either the Prix de l'Opera or Prix de l'Arc de Triomphe and then, perhaps, either the Breeders' Cup or "something in Japan". However, fate intervened and she had only one more race before an injury forced her retirement. It was the Group 1 Coolmore

America 'Justify' Matron Stakes over a mile at Leopardstown on the opening day of Irish Champions Weekend and although sent off the favourite and staying on well in the closing stages, she had to settle for third, just grabbing that placing in the final strides from Know It All. It was that filly's stable companion Champers Elysees who landed the spoils from Peaceful, the margins a length and a quarter and one and a half lengths.

It had been intended that her next start would be in the Group 1 Prix de l'Opera Longines at ParisLongchamp on the first Sunday in October. Heavy rain made it another year when the ground was very soft on the Saturday, turning to heavy overnight before Sunday's elite action, but Fancy Blue's absence was not due to the underfoot conditions. News broke on the eve of the two-day meeting that a potential contamination issue had come to light with one of the top horse-food brands, and although some of the horses involved tested negative and were cleared to race that weekend, a number tested positive. These included all of the intended Ballydoyle runners on Sunday's card in Paris plus those trained by Joseph O'Brien and Donnacha O'Brien. Sadly, it was a few days later the filly sustained the career-ending tendon injury.

Fancy Blue has tremendous potential as a broodmare because not only is she by one of the world's leading sires, but she is out of a full sister to High Chaparral (by Sadler's Wells). That dual Derby and dual Breeders' Cup star achieved a considerable of amount of success at stud, especially in the southern hemisphere where he was a champion sire. His northern hemisphere Group/Grade 1 winners included Toronado, Wigmore Hall, Redwood, and Lucky Lion, whereas those who stuck at the highest level in Australia and/or New Zealand, both bred here and there, featured Ace High, Contributor, Descarado, Dundeel, Monaco Consul, Rekindling (trained in Ireland), and Shoot Out. Of course, his outstanding son So You Think was a multiple Group 1 star in both Europe and Australia, and both that celebrity and Dundeel already have several Group 1-winning offspring to their name.

Chenchikova, the winning dam of Fancy Blue, is also a full sister to the Group 2 Dante Stakes winner and Grade 1 Secretariat Stakes runner-up Black Bear Island, whereas her stakes-placed half-sister Treasure The Lady (by Indian Ridge) is the grandam of the Group 3 scorer Love Locket (by No Nay Never; see *Volume 2: UK & Ireland's Group 2 & Group 3 Winners*). The unraced Mora Bai (by Indian Ridge), another of Chenchikova's half-sisters, has done her part for the family by producing David Livingston (by Galileo) and Hunting Horn (by Camelot), both of them top-level-placed Group 2 winners. The former, who went to stud in India, won the Group 2 Beresford Stakes, Group 3 Rose of Lancaster Stakes and was third in the Group 1 National Stakes. Hunting Horn, who is taking up stallion duties at Castlefield Stud in Ireland in 2021, was a twelve-and-a-half-furlong Group 2 winner in Australia, took the Group 3 Hampton Court Stakes over ten furlongs at the Royal Ascot meeting in England, and has been placed in the Grade 1 Belmont Derby Invitational Stakes in the USA, in the Group 2 Prix Niel in France and in the valuable Listed H.H. The Amir Trophy (local Group 1 status only) in Qatar.

All of this would be more than enough to advertise the potential that Fancy Blue has as a broodmare but there is more that deserves a mention too. For example, her siblings include the smart two-year-old Smuggler's Cove (by Fastnet Rock), who won a listed race and finished third in the Group 1 Dewhurst Stakes, and the talented stayer Casterton (by Fastnet Rock), a listed scorer at ParisLongchamp and Deauville who finished third in the Group 3 Prix de Lutece at Saint-Cloud. Her unraced grandam, on the other hand, is a mare called Kasora (by Darshaan) and, being a daughter of the Arc-placed Group 2 Prix de Mallaret heroine Kozana (by Kris), she was a half-sister to several blacktype horses, notably the listed scorer and Group 2 Pretty Polly Stakes third Khanata (by Riverman) and also Kotama (by Shahrastani), the stakes-winning grandam of the smart fourteen-furlong filly Art Eyes (by Halling). Fourth dam Koblenza (by Hugh Lupus) won the Poule d'Essai des Pouliches in 1969.

There is also the potential for more updates to come to the page from among Fancy Blue's younger siblings, all of them fillies, as Chenchikova had daughters of Caravaggio (by Scat Daddy) and Saxon Warrior (by Deep Impact) in 2019 and 2020. Her 2018 foal and €220,000 Arqana Deauville August yearling sale graduate,

Miss Chess (by Zoffany), has been placed once in three starts for the Ed Vaughan stable.

Of course, there will also be updates in the coming years via her progeny and it was not a surprise to hear that Fancy Blue is due to be among the first book of mares that French import and long-time Haras d'Etreham resident Wootton Bassett (by Iffraaj) will cover at Coolmore Stud. A foal from that cross would be inbred 5x4 to Northern Dancer (by Nearctic) and 5x5 to Special (by Forli) as Nureyev appears in the top half of the chart and his three-parts brother Sadler's Wells in the bottom, but it would have no other duplications within the first five generations of the pedigree. Deep Impact's early pattern winners as a broodmare sire include Kiseki, a son of Kingmambo's (by Mr Prospector) grandson Rulership (by King Kamehameha). Wootton Bassett, of course, represents the Gone West branch of the Mr Prospector (by Raise a Native) line, so there is a vague similarity between how 2017's Kikuka Sho (Japanese St Leger) winner and Fancy Blue's potential first-born will be bred.

SUMMARY DETAILS

Bred: Coolmore
Owned: Michael Tabor, Derrick Smith & Mrs John Magnier
Trained: Donnacha O'Brien
Country: Ireland
Race record: 11-2113-
Career highlights: 4 wins inc Qatar Nassau Stakes (Gr1), Prix de Diane Longines (Gr1), Staffordstown Stud Stakes (L), 2nd Tattersalls Irish 1,000 Guineas (Gr1), 3rd Coolmore America 'Justify' Matron Stakes (Gr1)

FANCY BLUE (IRE) – 2017 bay filly

Deep Impact (JPN)	Sunday Silence (USA)	Halo (USA)
		Wishing Well (USA)
	Wind In Her Hair (IRE)	Alzao (USA)
		Burghclere
Chenchikova (IRE)	Sadler's Wells (USA)	Northern Dancer
		Fairy Bridge (USA)
	Kasora (IRE)	Darshaan
		Kozana

GALILEO CHROME (IRE)

Some families seem to come up with one or more notable runners pretty much every year. The one that consists of the distaff line and branches from Alruccaba (by Crystal Palace) is a prime example. An Aga Khan-bred winner from four starts and who was a direct descendant of the famous and influential juvenile and sprint champion Mumtaz Mahal (by The Tetrarch), she made her name as a broodmare for Kirsten Rausing. The grey produced eight winners, some of them blacktype horses, and the Group 1 Pertemps St Leger scorer Galileo Chrome is the latest top-level winner who can claim her as a direct ancestor within the first four generations of his pedigree.

Alruccaba's non-winning daughter Jude (by Darshaan) is the dam of the Group 1 Irish 1,000 Guineas winner Yesterday (by Sadler's Wells) and the classic-placed juvenile Group 1 scorer Quarter Moon (by Sadler's Wells), and she is the grandam of Diamondsandrubies (by Fastnet Rock) whose victories included the Group 1 Pretty Polly Stakes. Her Group 3 Doncaster Cup-winning daughter Alleluia (by Caerleon) is responsible for the Group 1 Prix Royal-Oak heroine Allegretto (by Galileo), and her Group 1-placed stakes winner Alouette (by Darshaan) is the mare who gave us the multiple Group 1 stars Albanova (by Alzao) and Alborada (by Alzao). It is through her daughter Last Second (by Alzao) that we have 2020's classic star.

So-named because Faisal Salman made it to the ring in Goffs at the last second to buy her at the Orby Sale, where she cost 120,000 Irish guineas, she won the Group 2 Nassau Stakes and Group 2 Sun Chariot Stakes and was runner-up in the Group 1 Coronation Stakes before going on to an influential career at stud. Her star son Aussie Rules (by Danehill) won the Group 1 Poule d'Essai des Poulains (French 2000 Guineas) and Grade 1 Shadwell Turf Mile Stakes, stood at Coolmore Stud and Lanwades Stud but, sadly, died at the age of 13. The one-mile Group 1 heroine Fiesolana was the best of his stakes-winning offspring.

His half-sister Approach (by Darshaan) was a ten-furlong listed scorer in England before going on to be Grade 2-placed over nine and a half furlongs at Keeneland, and in addition to the

Group 2 winner and Group 1 Irish Derby runner-up Midas Touch (by Galileo), she is responsible for Coronet (by Dubawi), a dual top-level star whose record and pedigree were examined in *European Group 1 Winners of 2019*. Approach's full sister Intrigued was placed in two listed races in England and, like her dam and grandam, has achieved a very high strike-rate of winners to foals born, a tally that includes blacktype horses. Her son Private Secretary (by Kingman) won the same listed race at Goodwood in 2019 that his half-brother Michelangelo (by Galileo) took seven years before, although that older sibling went on to be placed a further three times in stakes company, notably when third in the Group 1 St Leger Stakes at Doncaster.

Intrigued's eight winners also include Curious Mind (by Danehill). She did not make her debut until late December of her three-year-old year, a one-mile Southwell maiden that she won by a length and a half, and her only other appearance came ten months later when she trailed home last of fourteen in a ten-furlong Newbury handicap. She failed to meet her reserve at the Tattersalls December Mare Sale shortly afterwards, was put in foal to Makfi (by Dubawi), sold privately for €75,000 at the Arqana December Sale and was exported to Tunisia where she had a daughter named Florencia. The mare then returned to Europe, was bred to Coolmore Stud's young Derby winner Australia (by Galileo) in May 2016, and the result of that union was Galileo Chrome. He is a great-grandson of Last Second and so has Alruccaba as his fourth dam. His dam had an Australia filly in 2019 and, twelve months later to the day, a son of the brilliant sprinter Dream Ahead (by Diktat).

The Joseph O'Brien-trained Galileo Chrome was an eight-and-a-half-length fifth of thirteen in a one-mile maiden on soft ground at Leopardstown on his only start at two but got off the mark next time, over ten furlongs on fast ground at the Curragh in mid-June of 2020. He followed that with a six-length score over the same trip at Leopardstown, added a five-length win in the Listed Irish Stallion Farms EBF Yeats Stakes over thirteen furlongs on soft at Navan in late August and so went to Doncaster as a leading contender for the world's oldest classic. Regular partner Shane Crosse missed the ride there due to a positive Covid-19 test, Tom

Marquand got the call-up, and having hit the front over a furlong from home, the colt kept on gamely to the line to hold off Berkshire Rocco by a neck. Pyledriver and Santiago were a length and a short head behind in third and fourth, with a two-and-three-quarter-length gap back to Hukum in fifth. The subsequent Group 1 scorer Subjectivist was among those further behind.

Galileo Chrome is a second-crop son of his sire and gave the stallion his first Group 1 winner. Indeed, the victory came during what was an eye-catching couple of days for Australia, as not only did this colt win a classic but it came the afternoon before the classic-placed three-year-old Cayenne Pepper won the Group 2 Moyglare 'Jewels' Blandford Stakes over ten furlongs at the Curragh on the second day of Irish Champions Weekend. That Jessica Harrington-trained chestnut, a pattern winner at two, had chased home Even So in the Group 1 Irish Oaks in July. Oodnadatta's third-place finish in the Group 1 Moyglare Stud Stakes was also a notable result for the stallion that day. Two months later, Order of Australia provided another big day when landing the Grade 1 Breeders' Cup Mile at Keeneland, leading home a one-two-three for horses trained at Ballydoyle.

Australia's overall total stands at seventeen stakes winners from his first three crops of racing age and they also include pattern success for Leo de Fury, Buckhurst, Epona Plays and Patrick Sarsfield. Each of them, plus Cayenne Pepper, is covered in *Volume 2: UK & Ireland's Group 2 and Group 3 Winners*. His prior pattern scorers include Broome, the Group 1-placed colt who finished a close fourth to Anthony Van Dyck in the Group 1 Derby at Epsom, and Sir Ron Priestley, the colt who chased home Logician in the Group 1 St Leger Stakes. Already in 2021, shortly before this book went to print, Australia has struck again, this time via his Chad Brown-trained four-year-old daughter Counterparty Risk who won an eight-and-a-half-furlong Grade 3 contest at Tampa Bay Downs. After what was not as high-profile a start as would have been hoped for the stallion, he now has two contrasting top-level winners to his name and there is no reason to think that they will remain his only ones. Indeed, it would not be a surprise to see his results pick up considerably over the coming seasons.

Galileo Chrome also held an entry in a two-mile Group 3 contest at the Curragh in late September although he was not seen out again, so it seemed likely that a Cup campaign awaited him in 2021 rather than a drop back to middle-distances. Whatever his distance though, he had the potential to be a leading player again this coming season. However, in a surprise announcement made in early December, he was retired from the track. He has now taken up a stallion position at Starfield Stud in Co Westmeath. That nascent operation has been building a roster of flat stallions, to which sprinter Far Above (by Farhh) is the most recent addition, but Galileo Chrome is to stand as a National Hunt stallion. Being a classic-winning grandson of Galileo, he should prove popular in his new role.

SUMMARY DETAILS
Bred: Mohamed Ali Meddeb
Owned: Galileo Chrome Partnership
Trained: Joseph O'Brien
Country: Ireland
Race record: 0-1111-
Career highlights: 4 wins inc Pertemps St Leger Stakes (Gr1), Irish Stallion Farms EBF Yeats Stakes (L)

GALILEO CHROME (IRE) – 2017 bay colt

Australia (GB)	Galileo (IRE)	Sadler's Wells (USA)
		Urban Sea (USA)
	Ouija Board (GB)	Cape Cross (IRE)
		Selection Board
Curious Mind (GB)	Dansili (GB)	Danehill (USA)
		Hasili (IRE)
	Intrigued (GB)	Darshaan
		Last Second (IRE)

GEAR UP (IRE)

The afternoon of October 24th was a remarkable one for Jim Bolger. Long renowned as being one of the world's great trainers, he has also made a considerable contribution as a breeder of racehorses and, in the space of a few minutes, he added two more Group 1 winners to his tally in the latter role. Mac Swiney, who he also trains, won the Group 1 Vertem Futurity Trophy Stakes at Doncaster just after the Mark Johnston-trained Gear Up landed the Group 1 Criterium de Saint-Cloud in France. Not even an hour had passed before Bolger struck again, this time with Flying Visit, a colt he bred and trained, in the Group 3 Eyrefield Stakes at Leopardstown.

He sold Gear Up for €52,000 at the 2019 Goffs Orby Sale, via his Redmondstown Stud. That makes the colt yet another high-profile winner that Johnston picked up for a five-figure sum. In an era when the elite yearlings fetch often substantial six-figure prices and occasionally more than a million, the number of more cheaply bought horses with whom he wins pattern events speaks volumes for his remarkable skill in judging a horse's potential.

Gear Up made a winning debut over seven furlongs at York in late July, followed-up over that course and distance in the Group 3 Tattersalls Acomb Stakes, where he won by margins of half a length, three lengths and a head from Spycatcher, Broxi and Royal Scimitar. He then stepped up in trip for the Group 2 Juddmonte Royal Lodge Stakes over a mile at Newmarket. The ground was good on all three occasions. Listed scorer Cobh tried to make all in the Royal Lodge but was headed over a furlong out as New Mandate and Ontario went past. The latter, who had been a one-length third to Mac Swiney in the Group 2 Futurity Stakes at the Curragh on his previous start, put a length and a quarter between himself and Cobh at the line but was still three-quarters of a length down on New Mandate. That Ralph Beckett-trained gelding had come into the race seeking a hat-trick following nursery and listed success at Sandown and Doncaster respectively. Gear Up was fourth, a half-length behind Cobh.

His final start of the year was over ten furlongs in France and it left his connections dreaming of a potential Derby bid in 2021.

The ground was heavy and the opposition included both the Group 1-winning filly Tiger Tanaka and the unbeaten and highly regarded Makaloun but Gear Up made almost all the running and held off every challenge, passing the post a short neck in front of the André Fabre-trained maiden winner Botanik. Makaloun and Tiger Tanaka were one and three-quarter lengths and a nose back in third and fourth, with the Aidan O'Brien-trained maiden winner Bolshoi Ballet another neck behind in fifth.

Gear Up is the sixth foal of the non-winning mare Gearanai (by Toccet) and his four winning siblings include a talented full brother in Guaranteed. He won the Group 3 Eyrefield Stakes at two and a ten-furlong listed contest at three, and he was a three-quarter-length runner-up to Latrobe in the Group 3 Ballyroan Stakes over twelve furlongs, among other useful efforts. Their grandam, Plaintiff (by Seeking The Gold), won once from eight starts and has produced several successful offspring, notably Argentine seven-furlong Grade 3 winner Plainswoman (by Zensational), the prolific US winner A.P. Eddie (by A.P. Indy) and the smart Russian middle-distance filly and subsequent broodmare Insayt (by Vindication). Plaintiff's unraced daughters Tiffed (by Seattle Slew) and Sanaara (by Anabaa) also joined Bolger's broodmare band and the latter mare is the first with a blacktype horse: Group 3 Anglesey Stakes and Group 3 Tyros Stakes runner-up Theobald (by Teofilo).

Four-time Grade 1 star Dispute (by Danzig) is the third dam of Gear Up. A direct descendant of the US champion filly Misty Morn (by Princequillo), who was the dam of the US juvenile champions Bold Lad (by Bold Ruler) and Successor (by Bold Ruler), she was one of three Grade 1 winners out of the Grade 1-placed listed winner Resolver (by Reviewer), and her top-level victories came in the Kentucky Oaks, Beldame Stakes, Gazelle Stakes and Spinster Stakes, all over nine furlongs. Her full brother Adjudicating won the Grade 1 Champagne Stakes and Grade 1 Cowdin Stakes and was a blacktype sire in Japan without making an impact, whereas half-brother Time For A Change (by Damascus), who won the Grade 1 Flamingo Stakes but died aged fifteen, sired juvenile champion Fly So Free and dual Grade 1 star Technology among over forty stakes winners. Being a representative of this family would also make Gear Up and interesting stallion prospect, should he get that chance someday.

Gear Up is one of twenty-one Group 1 winners among an overall total of ninety-four stakes winners by the Kildangan Stud stallion Teofilo (by Galileo), an unbeaten juvenile champion whom Bolger also bred and trained. He has sired Group 1 two-year-old winners, classic stars, milers, middle-distance horses and even stayers, two of those being Melbourne Cup winners, and he has had at least one top-level winner in each of Australia, England, France, Germany, Hong Kong, Ireland, and the United Arab Emirates. Of his stallion sons, both Havana Gold and Kermadec have a Group 1 winner to their name from their early runners, whereas his daughters' offspring include the aforementioned Group 1 winner Mac Swiney (by New Approach) and Group 3 scorer Flying Visit (by Pride of Dubai).

Gear Up is a well-bred horse who could achieve anything on the track and it would be no surprise to see him take high rank in the middle-distance division in 2021. He is due to begin his season in the Group 2 Dante Stakes at York, and in addition to the Derby, his entries include the Group 1 Grand Prix de Paris.

SUMMARY DETAILS
Bred: J S Bolger
Owned: Teme Valley 2
Trained: Mark Johnston
Country: England
Race record: 1141-
Career highlights: 3 wins inc Criterium de Saint-Cloud (Gr1), Tattersalls Acomb Stakes (Gr3)

GEAR UP (IRE) – 2018 bay colt

Teofilo (IRE)	Galileo (IRE)	Sadler's Wells (USA)
		Urban Sea (USA)
	Speirbhean (IRE)	Danehill (USA)
		Saviour (USA)
Gearanai (USA)	Toccet (USA)	Awesome Again (CAN)
		Cozzene's Angel (USA)
	Plaintiff (USA)	Seeking The Gold (USA)
		Dispute (USA)

GHAIYYATH (IRE)

Although long-established as one of the world's elite sires, it is still somewhat early for Dubawi (by Dubai Millennium) as a sire of stallion sons. Most of them are in nascent stages of their stud careers, and Ghaiyyath is joining them in 2021, but there are three who have had a few crops on the track and achieved some notable results.

The Group 1-winning miler Poet's Voice died young and although it is fair to say that he did not live up to early hopes and expectations, he has sired over twenty stakes winners of whom two have won at the highest level: Trap For Fools in Australia and Poet's Word in England. The former is a gelding and the latter covered one book as a flat sire before being moved to the National Hunt division. His tally also includes horses who have won Group 2 and Group 3 classics in Germany and Italy, whereas the Jessica Harrington-trained filly One Voice was a dual Group 1-placed pattern-winning three-year-old in 2020 (see Volume 2).

Classic-winning miler Night of Thunder, who stands at Kildangan Stud, is awaiting his first top-level winner but has four Group 2 scorers and six Group 3 winners among an overall total of nineteen blacktype winners from his first two global crops of racing age. Makfi, on the other hand, has had five Group 1 winners to date among an overall tally of thirty-four stakes winners and they include New Zealand Horse of the Year Bonneval and classic-winning miler Make Believe, the latter a Ballylinch Stud stallion and classic sire with his first three-year-olds in 2020. Makfi is now in Japan.

There is also a potential stallion of note among those who have had just a single crop of juveniles in action: New Bay. The Group 1 Prix du Jockey Club (French Derby) winner stands at Ballylinch Stud in Ireland and was among the leading freshman sires of 2020. His four blacktype earners featured the Group 2 Royal Lodge Stakes winner New Mandate and the unbeaten Group 3 Oh So Sharp Stakes heroine Saffron Beach, results made more eye-catching by the fact that his two-year-old career had consisted of a single run: a second-place finish in a one-mile conditions race on the Polytrack at Chantilly in late November.

Like those other sons of Dubawi, Ghaiyyath was a top-class racehorse. He was also the top-rated racehorse in the world in 2020, heading the final classifications on a mark of 130. He is also one who at times exhibited brilliance reminiscent of his Timeform 140-rated grandsire, Dubai Millennium (by Seeking The Gold). Unlike those other top sons noted above, he is a star at ten and twelve furlongs. He won twice over a mile at two including a Group 3 contest at Newmarket, but a setback led to him missing the classics and having just one start at three. It was a three-length Group 3 success over ten furlongs in France. Timeform had him on a rating of 119p at that point but raised him to 129 by the end of his four-year-old campaign; his official handicap mark was 126. That four-race season featured his famous fourteen-length defeat of Donjah in the Group 1 Grosser Preis von Baden over twelve furlongs on good ground at Baden-Baden that September.

His five-year-old campaign was his busiest one, with five starts, and it saw his Timeform form figure rise to 133, making him Europe's top-rated middle-distance horse of the year, ranked behind only Battaash across all divisions. He kicked off with an eight-and-a-half-length defeat of Spotify in the Group 3 Dubai Millennium Stakes over ten furlongs at Meydan in February, which suggested that the ultra-valuable Group 1 Dubai World Cup could be his for the taking. Sadly, the UAE season was cut short due to the Covid-19 situation, the big finale cancelled, so he was next seen in action at Newmarket in early June for the rescheduled Group 1 Hurworth Bloodstock Coronation Cup Stakes. This was his only run at twelve furlongs in 2020. He set off in front, was clear after half a mile and then held off all challengers, none of whom looked like catching him. His final margins of victory were two and a half lengths and the same, with the sadly ill-fated Anthony Van Dyck chasing him home followed by Stradivarius. There was another four-and-a-quarter-length gap back to the fourth, Broome, and Ghaiyyath's performance set a new course record for the distance.

He went to Sandown a month later and again making all and clocking a quick time, added the Group 1 Coral-Eclipse to his tally. It was a comfortable success, his margin of victory two and a quarter lengths, and although Enable had stayed on strongly in the final furlong, making her seasonal debut, she never looked like catching him. She had to settle for second, a head and one and a half lengths in front of the Ballydoyle pair Japan and Magic Wand. York was the winner's next stop and the Group 1 Juddmonte International Stakes attracted a small but select line-up. Only the triple pattern winner Rose of Kildare, who would be placed in Group 2 company on her only subsequent outing of the year, had not won at the highest level, and she did well, considering that she was out of her depth, finishing a seven-and-three-quarter-length last of five. Ghaiyyath, racing towards the centre of the track, set off in front and was not only never headed, but never looked in any danger of defeat. Kameko briefly threatened to beat Magical for second place in their battle at the rails, but the Guineas winner weakened in the closing stages. The mare stayed on to be a three-length runner-up in the race, while her younger rival came home a further two lengths adrift in fourth having lost the minor placing to Lord North, who, despite losing his right-fore shoe, moved three-quarters of a length in front of him near the line.

Ghaiyyath was expected to complete a ten-furlong Group 1 hat-trick at Leopardstown several weeks later where he was sent off the odds-on favourite to beat five rivals in the Irish Champion Stakes. This time it was the Group 2 scorers Armory and Leo De Fury who were the only non-top-level winners in the field. The latter of that pair was always in rear and made no impression at any stage of the race. William Buick sent his mount to the front as usual, but this time they didn't have it all their own way. Seamie Heffernan moved Magical forward to keep close to the leader from halfway, pressed him strongly from a quarter of a mile from home, hit the front inside the final furlong and kept on well for victory. Magical, who hit the line three-quarters of a length in front, joined Dylan Thomas in the history books as a dual winner of the race. Armory finished another length and a quarter back in third, just holding off Sottsass by the narrowest of margins and with a further four-and-a-half-length gap back to Japan in fifth.

Ghaiyyath's performance in Dublin was clearly below his best and it was disappointing that he didn't get another chance to dazzle before retiring. The €1,100,000 he cost in Goffs as a foal is a testament to both his looks and his pedigree and he looks certain to be among the busiest stallions in Ireland this year. There has long been evidence of talent in the family, but it took a massive leap forward when the late Marguerite Weld made the decision to send her mile listed-race scorer Caumshinaun (by Indian Ridge), a mare whose five wins included sprint handicaps at Leopardstown and the Curragh, to a young middle-distance horse standing his first season at stud. Her first foal had been a daughter of the sprinter Mujadil (by Storm Bird). That filly, Mermaid Island, would go on to become a stakes-placed winner and, later in Australia, a blacktype producer. Sending Caumshinaun to a dual Derby winner for her second covering was quite a change in direction. Galileo's first-season fee was IR£50,000; the resulting foal was the runaway Group 1 Irish 1,000 Guineas heroine Nightime.

She won her classic on her third start, by six lengths on heavy ground, but sadly disappointed on her only subsequent outings, both in Group 1 company on good-to-firm underfoot conditions. Her first foal was a daughter of Holy Roman Emperor (by Danehill) that fetched €75,000 in Goffs as a yearling, her second was the stakes-placed Sleeping Beauty (by Oasis Dream), number three was a son of Raven's Pass (by Elusive Quality) who fetched 800,000 guineas in Tattersalls' Book 1 sale in Newmarket, and her fourth was Zhukova. That daughter of Fastnet Rock (by Danehill) won the Group 3 Blue Wind Stakes, Group 3 Kilternan Stakes and listed races at the Curragh, Galway and Cork, but she also added her name to the list of international top-level winners trained by Dermot Weld when landing the Grade 1 Man o' War Stakes over eleven furlongs at Belmont Park as a five-year-old, scoring by six lengths on ground described as yielding. Zhukova had failed to meet her reserve in Newmarket as a yearling but was snapped up by Godolphin as a broodmare prospect at that venue four years later, retiring to stud with a 3,700,000-guinea price tag.

The progeny of Nightime have continued to excel in the auction ring and, since Ghaiyyath and Zhukova took their turn, there has been a pair of full brothers to her star son, both also purchased by Godolphin. New Kingdom, who is now a three-year-old, is a 700,000-guinea graduate of the December Foal Sale in Newmarket and the unraced chestnut is also trained by Charlie

Appleby. His year-younger full brother made €1,200,000 in Goffs at the same age. The mare had a son of Kingman (by Invincible Spirit) in early April of 2020 and was bred back to Dubawi. Zhukova has also met with Dubawi, producing colts by him in 2019 and 2020, and she was among the small but select final book covered by the late Shamardal (by Giant's Causeway).

Four-time Group 1 star Ghaiyyath, Horse of the Year for 2020, has joined the team at Kildangan Stud in Ireland, standing for a fee of €30,000. He looks sure to be very popular in his new role. He was an autumn Group 3 winner as a juvenile, which augurs well for his prospects of siring some notable late-season two-year-olds, but his best results are likely to come with his three-year-olds and older horses, mostly in the mile-to-twelve-furlong range, thereby making him a potential classic sire. It will be fascinating to see how his second career turns out.

SUMMARY DETAILS
Bred: Springbank Way Stud
Owned: Godolphin
Trained: Charlie Appleby
Country: England
Race record: 311-1-1310-11112-
Career highlights: 9 wins inc Juddmonte International Stakes (Gr1), Coral-Eclipse (Gr1), Hurworth Bloodstock Coronation Cup Stakes (Gr1), 147th Longines Grosser Preis von Baden (Gr1), Prix d'Harcourt (Gr2), Dubai Millennium Stakes sponsored by Jaguar (Gr3), Prix du Prince d'Orange (Gr3), Masar Godolphin Autumn Stakes (Gr3), 2nd Irish Champion Stakes (Gr1), 3rd Prix Ganay (Gr1)

GHAIYYATH (IRE) – 2015 bay horse

Dubawi (IRE)	Dubai Millennium (GB)	Seeking The Gold (USA)
		Colorado Dancer
	Zomaradah (GB)	Deploy
		Jawaher (IRE)
Nightime (IRE)	Galileo (IRE)	Sadler's Wells (USA)
		Urban Sea (USA)
	Caumshinaun (IRE)	Indian Ridge
		Ridge Pool (IRE)

GLASS SLIPPERS (GB)

The European record at the Breeders' Cup has been mixed in recent seasons, but it was excellent in 2020 with eleven horses making the frame over the two days of action including four who brought home a top prize. The Kevin Ryan-trained Glass Slippers was one of that quartet and also has the distinction of having been the first European-trained horse to take the Grade 1 Breeders' Cup Turf Sprint.

A winner at Beverley and Chester from five starts at two, the Bearstone Stud homebred's three-year-old campaign got off to a slow start, a pair of unplaced runs in blacktype company followed by second place in a five-furlong listed contest at Ayr and fourth to Royal Intervention in a York Group 3. The transformation began just over three weeks later when she picked up a short-head success in a listed race at Deauville, the six-furlong trip the longest she has tackled aside from her five-and-a-half-furlong victory at Keeneland in November. Deauville was followed by a narrow win in the Group 3 Prix du Petit Couvert, three weeks before she announced herself on the Group 1 scene with a three-length victory in the Prix de l'Abbaye de Longchamp. That was on very soft ground, her prior blacktype successes had been on good ground and her first juvenile win had been on good-to-firm.

She finished that year on a Timeform rating of 124, the figure by which she will be described in the years to come, although her official rating was only 116 as a three-year-old and that was eased to 114 despite what she achieved in 2020. She was only fifth to Battaash in the Group 1 King's Stand Stakes on her seasonal reappearance in mid-June, chased home that same star in the Group 2 King George Stakes at Goodwood at the end of July and then beat Keep Busy by half a length to take the Group 1 Derrinstown Stud Flying Five Stakes at the Curragh during Irish Champions Weekend. It looks impressive on her CV, but it is fair to say that this was not a strong edition of that sprint: the 103-rated (official handicap) runner-up was followed by 106-rated Sonaiyla, then 105-rated Maid In India, the margins between each placing also being half a length. The more high-profile runners—Make A Challenge (fifth), Equilateral (sixth), Liberty Beach (seventh), Que Amoro (twelfth), and A'Ali (last of fourteen)—all performed below expectations.

Three of her rivals from the Irish race re-opposed at ParisLongchamp in early October, with Liberty Beach (third) and Keep Busy (fifth) faring best on the heavy ground, coming home a short neck and one and three-quarter lengths behind her. However, although hitting the front briefly a quarter of a mile out, she was soon headed by the French-trained three-year-old Wooded who, after a battle, hit the line a neck in front. This was soon revealed to have been the colt's final race before taking up stallion duties at Haras de Bouquetot. He had the benefit of a stands'-rail draw, whereas she had been drawn wide and it is possible that with a better starting position the result may have been closer or even different.

The heavy ground that day was in striking contrast to the underfoot conditions at Keeneland a month later. This looked like a tougher task, and although a bit tight for room at one point, she found a gap about a furlong out, hit the front inside the final half furlong and held off the strong late challenge of the long-shot and former Canadian Grade 1 winner Wet Your Whistle to add her name to the Breeders' Cup roll of honour. Dual Grade 2 scorer and the big-race favourite, Leinster, was another half a length back in third, a head and one length in front of Extravagant Kid and Got Stormy. The latter, who came into the race off the back of a pair of Grade 3 wins, was running her third consecutive race as a sprinter having previously been a Breeders' Cup-placed dual mile Grade 1 star. The winner ran on Lasix.

The pedigree of Glass Slippers was reviewed in some detail in last year's edition. She is one of four Group 1 winners for the juvenile and sprint champion Dream Ahead (by Diktat), the Haras de Grandcamp stallion who spent his first five seasons at Ballylinch Stud in Ireland. The Timeform 133-rated grandson of Warning (by Known Fact) has had a total of twenty-nine stakes winners so far and his representatives in 2020 also included the Group 1 Sprint Cup winner Dream of Dreams and mile Group 2 scorer Dark Vision. She is the best of several multiple winners out of Night Gypsy (by Mind Games) and that winning full sister to the juvenile listed scorer and blacktype producer On The Brink is also responsible for the Group 3-placed seven-furlong listed winner Electric Feel (by Firebreak).

Glass Slippers will make an exciting broodmare prospect when the time comes for her to go to stud, but that time has not yet arrived. She has reportedly done well over the winter, strengthened up further, and is to return to training as a five-year-old. It will be good to see her back in action again in the top sprints. She has been a top five-furlong performer in the past two seasons, but the way in which she won over an extra half furlong at Keeneland raises the possibility that a return to six furlongs, the distance over which she won a listed contest in France in 2019, could be on the cards at some point, and that would bring in races such as the Group 1 July Cup, Group 1 Sprint Cup and Group 1 British Champions Sprint Stakes as potential targets, in addition to the obvious five-furlongs ones.

SUMMARY DETAILS

Bred: Bearstone Stud Ltd
Owned: Bearstone Stud Ltd
Trained: Kevin Ryan
Country: England
Race record: 30110-0024111-02121-
Career highlights: 7 wins inc Breeders' Cup Turf Sprint (Gr1), Derrinstown Stud Flying Five Stakes (Gr1), Prix de l'Abbaye de Longchamp Longines (Gr1), Qatar Prix du Petit Couvert (Gr3), Prix Club Hipico Santiago - Prix Moonlight Cloud (L), 2nd Prix de l'Abbaye de Longchamp Longines (Gr1), King George Qatar Stakes (Gr2), British Stallion Studs EBF Land O'Burns Fillies' Stakes (L)

GLASS SLIPPERS (GB) – 2016 bay filly

		Warning
	Diktat (GB)	Arvola (GB)
Dream Ahead (USA)		Cadeaux Genereux
	Land of Dreams (GB)	Sahara Star (GB)
		Puissance
	Mind Games (GB)	Aryaf (CAN)
Night Gypsy (GB)		Fairy King (USA)
	Ocean Grove (IRE)	Leyete Gulf (IRE)

GLEN SHIEL (GB)

A change in approach with Glen Shiel proved to be a revelation in 2020 and one cannot help but wonder how he might be viewed had his career started a bit differently.

Two of his most famous relations achieved Group 1 success over twelve furlongs, one of that pair also won the Group 1 Gold Cup at Ascot, and another of them scored at the highest level at both eight and ten furlongs. The latter horse is by the outstanding Cheveley Park Stud stallion Pivotal (by Polar Falcon), the Group 1-winning sprinter whose progeny have excelled in sprints, around a mile and over middle distances, and so is Glen Shiel. It was no surprise, therefore, to see him begin his career over seven and a half furlongs as a two-year-old, and he won that Saint-Cloud newcomers' race on heavy ground in mid-November by one and three-quarter lengths.

He raced from eight to ten furlongs throughout his three-year-old season, the André Fabre-trained chestnut winning twice, including a nine-furlong listed contest on very soft ground at Chantilly, and coming within a head of adding further listed success over ten furlongs at Compiegne. This was evidence of ability but with no indication of Group 1 potential. He was gelded, ran four times without success at nine and ten furlongs as a four-year-old and changed hands for just £45,000 at the Goffs UK Spring Horses-in-Training Sale in Doncaster the following May. The former Godolphin horse was now a member of the Archie Watson stable and, for the 2019 season, he continued in a similar vein.

He was well-beaten over ten furlongs at Chelmsford on his first start for his new connections, chased home a four-length winner in an optional claiming handicap over a mile on heavy ground at Goodwood, finished a good fourth in the valuable Balmoral Handicap over the same trip at Ascot, also on heavy, but then finished unplaced in a nine-furlong conditions race in France and a ten-furlong handicap at Lingfield. His rating was now ninety-six, a good figure for a heritage/premier handicapper yet below the level required to be a proper stakes horse. Only the most optimistic of dreamers would have imagined he could become a Group 1 star in 2020.

He is the son of a sprinter and out of an eight-and-a-half-furlong pattern-winning daughter of another sprinter of note, and it turns out that it's their speed influences he inherited and not the middle-distance tendency shown by some of his well-known relations.

He dropped to seven furlongs for his seasonal reappearance at Newcastle in early January and took that handicap by a length and a quarter. He was beaten in three subsequent tries at that distance but had been a runner-up on his six-furlong debut, also at Newcastle, and since the end of June not only remained at that shorter trip but proved himself to be among the best at it in Europe. He made all to beat Tabdeed (gave three pounds) by two lengths in a Newcastle handicap that day and then chased home Royal Crusade in the Group 3 Qatar Prix de Ris-Orangis on good ground at Deauville, after which his handicap mark rose to 106. He went up another two pounds in the order of merit after easily giving weight and a two-and-a-quarter-length beating to Danzeno in a conditions race on the Tapeta back at Newcastle just days before travelling to Ireland for his first pattern success. Oisin Orr took the ride at the Curragh and the pair got to the front just yards from the post, beating Sonaiyla, Forever In Dreams and Speak In Colours (gave five pounds) by a neck, a head and a short head. His official handicap mark remained on 108 after that but jumped by eight pounds after his next run.

Hollie Doyle, who has ridden Glen Shiel more often on the track than any other jockey, was back in the plate for his final two runs of the year, both races over six furlongs on soft ground in England. Thirteen went to post for the Group 1 Betfair Sprint Cup Stakes at Haydock and they split into two groups, one racing on the near side of the track and the other on the far side. Those hoping to see a future stallion prospect land the spoils would have been disappointed to see a pair of transformed six-year-old geldings finish one-two, but there were some candidates among those who finished behind that day. Dream of Dreams, who had been sent off as the favourite, hit the front inside the final furlong and powered home to a one-and-a-quarter-length victory from

Glen Shiel, with the Group 1 Commonwealth Cup winner Golden Horde, who had led the far-side group throughout, a neck back in third. The promising Art Power was another length behind in fourth, chased home by Hello Youmzain, The Tin Man, and Lope Y Fernandez. Of those just outside the frame, only The Tin Man had also raced in the far-side group, running second there throughout the race. Both Golden Horde and Hello Youmzain, prior winners at the highest level, are now at stud in France.

Dream of Dreams was expected to follow up in the Group 1 Qipco British Champions Sprint Stakes at Ascot the following month but having looked set for victory a quarter of a mile from home, he weakened and finished eighth. Instead, this was Glen Shiel's day and it was very close. He broke well, set off in front, fought back when headed by the July Cup-star Oxted a furlong out and although that rival tired and was passed by four horses in the final half furlong, Glen Shiel kept going to the line. He and the strong-finishing veteran Brando flashed past the post together, closely followed by One Master, Art Power and Oxted, just a length covering the quintet. It took a few moments for the result to be called, but the six-year-old Pivotal gelding had pipped the eight-year-old one by a nose, a notable result either way for the stallion. Both Glen Shiel and his immensely talented young rider had secured their first Group 1 win. He was raised to his end-of-year mark of 117.

In addition to being a Darley-bred son of one of the most influential British stallions of the modern era, Glen Shiel is the sixth of seven foals out of Gonfilia (by Big Shuffle), a Group 3 Princess Elizabeth Stakes winner who could also count listed wins at Goodwood, Redcar and Maisons-Laffitte in her tally. Her son Signs In The Sand (by Cape Cross) was placed in the Group 3 Sirenia Stakes as a two-year-old, whereas her youngest is an unraced now three-year-old filly named Greta Hellstrom (by Pivotal) whom Godolphin placed with the André Fabre stable.

The mare's full brother Gonlargo was a Group 3 scorer over nine furlongs in Germany, where their sire has been a multiple champion at stud, and he was three times runner-up in Group 2 contests including to Sumitas in the Mehl-Mülhens-Rennen (German 2000 Guineas). Two of their stakes-winning siblings are by the more stamina-laden Lando (by Acatenango) and, of those, Gonbarda is by far the more notable. She won the Group 1 Deutschlandpreis and Group 1 Preis von Europa, was runner-up in the Group 1 Grosser Preis von Baden and has produced two sons of particular note by Pivotal. Racing History is the younger of the pair and the Group 3 Winter Hill Stakes winner has been placed in both the Group 1 Grosser Preis von Bayern and Group 1 Grosser Preis von Berlin. Farhh is the older brother and his dam's first foal.

Champion older miler in Europe in 2013, Farhh won the Group 1 Lockinge Stakes and was runner-up in the Group 1 Sussex Stakes and Group 1 Prix du Moulin de Longchamp over that trip, but he also won the Group 1 Champion Stakes, was runner-up in the Group 1 Juddmonte International Stakes and Group 1 Coral-Eclipse, third in the Group 1 Prince of Wales's Stakes and rated 131 by Timeform. The top-class eight-to-ten-furlong horse went to Dalham Hall Stud with a racing and pedigree profile that made him likely to get his best results with autumn juveniles plus horses effective across the full classic range. He has had smaller crops than many of his cohorts—there are only thirty-one registered foals in his 2020 crop, he covered over seventh-three mares last year and his fee is listed as private for 2021—but he has achieved some eye-catching results. Both his 2000 Guineas-placed mile Group 1 star King of Change (Derrinstown Stud) and his pattern-winning sprinter Far Above (Starfield Stud) are new sires for 2021, his Group 2-winning middle-distance son Nocturnal Fox (Windmill View Stud) went to stud in 2020 and his stakes-winning offspring also feature the Group 2 Duke of Cambridge Stakes heroine Move Swiftly and the Derby and Gold Cup-placed dual pattern-winning stayer Dee Ex Bee.

Gonfalon (by Slip Anchor), the unraced grandam of Glen Shiel and Farhh, was out of the Group 2 Schwarzgold-Rennen (German 1000 Guineas) winner and Group 2 Preis der Diana (German Oaks) third Grimpola (by Windwurf) and that made her a half-sister to two broodmares of note. Goonda (by Darshaan) is the dam of the juvenile six-furlong Group 2 scorer Global Dream (by Seattle Dancer) and mile Group 3 winner Global Thrill (by Big

Shuffle) and her descendants include Patrick Sarsfield (by Australia), a Group 1-placed middle-distance Group 3 winner in 2020 for the Joseph O'Brien team (see *Volume 2*). Gryada (by Shirley Heights), on the other hand, was placed in the Group 3 Premio Dormello as a two-year-old, became the dam of Fame And Glory (by Montjeu) and the grandam of Legatissimo (by Danehill Dancer), among others of note.

Fame And Glory died early in his career as a National Hunt stallion for the Coolmore team but the indications are that a percentage of those among the large crops he left behind are going to propel him to prominence in the sires' championship title race over the next few years. Legatissimo, of course, won the Group 1 1000 Guineas, Group 1 Nassau Stakes and Group 1 Matron Stakes, was runner-up in each of the Group 1 Oaks, Group 1 Pretty Polly Stakes and Grade 1 Breeders' Cup Filly and Mare Turf and is a member of Coolmore's powerful broodmare band. Her first two progeny, born in 2019 and 2020, are January-foaled daughters of the great Galileo (by Sadler's Wells) and she was bred back to the prolific champion sire last season.

It is a pity, with family connections like these, that there can be no stallion career for Glen Shiel, something that could have been on the cards had his considerable prowess as a sprinter been manifest earlier in his career. But his status means that, instead, he is likely to be back in action on the track this coming season. It will be fascinating to see if he holds his newfound level of form or can even improve further, and it would not be a surprise to see him strike again at the highest level.

SUMMARY DETAILS
Bred: Darley
Owned: Hambleton Racing XXXVI & Partner
Trained: Archie Watson
Country: England
Race record: 1-412041-2002-02400-13020121121-
Career highlights: 8 wins inc Qipco British Champions Sprint Stakes (Gr1), Rathasker Stud Phoenix Sprint Stakes (Gr3), Prix Le Fabuleux (L), 2nd Betfair Sprint Cup Stakes (Gr1), Qatar Prix

de Ris-Orangis (Gr3), Grand Prix de Compiegne - 6eme Etape du Defi du Galop (L), Prix Ridgway (L)

GLEN SHIEL (GB) – 2014 chestnut gelding

Pivotal (GB)	Polar Falcon (USA)	Nureyev (USA)
		Marie d'Argonne (FR)
	Fearless Revival	Cozzene (USA)
		Stufida
Gonfilia (GER)	Big Shuffle (USA)	Super Concorde (USA)
		Raise Your Skirts (USA)
	Gonfalon (GB)	Slip Anchor
		Grimpola (GER)

GOLDEN HORDE (IRE)

The Group 1 Commonwealth Cup has been a valuable addition to the racing calendar and although the 2020 renewal was not as strong as some previous editions, its winner demonstrated his merit as a top-level performer both before and after the race. It was to be his final win before going to stud, but he notched up two Group 1 placings from three starts, adding to an excellent juvenile season when he had been a dual Group 1-placed Group 2 winner.

The Clive Cox-trained Golden Horde was bred by James Cloney of Cn Farm Ltd and snapped up by his trainer for £65,000 at the Goffs UK Premier Yearling Sale in Doncaster. He demonstrated precocity, a trait favoured by many breeders, but, in truth, was better in the late summer of his juvenile year than in the earlier months. He had been fourth at Newbury on his debut in mid-May, won easily on fast ground at Windsor next time and then finished a two-length fifth to Arizona in the Group 2 Coventry Stakes at Royal Ascot. He had an official rating of 103 after that but the figure soared after his fourth start.

The race was the Group 2 Qatar Richmond Stakes at Goodwood, the ground was good and, like all but one of his career outings, the Prix Maurice de Gheest of 2020, run over six furlongs. He got into a battle with Threat, who would take the Group 2 Gimcrack Stakes and Group 2 Champagne Stakes on his next two starts, but finally got the better of that opponent in the last quarter furlong and pulled clear for a three-quarter-length victory. The subsequent Group 2 Royal Lodge Stakes winner Royal Dornoch was another three lengths adrift in third. The latter rival was also among those behind when he finished a neck and two-and-a-half-length third to Earthlight and Raffle Prize in the Group 1 Darley Prix Morny on heavy ground at Deauville two and a half weeks later.

The underfoot conditions were markedly different at Newmarket in late September when Golden Horde and Earthlight met again, this time filling the top two placings in the Group 1 Juddmonte Middle Park Stakes. The André Fabre-trained colt broke the juvenile course record while beating his English rival by a neck, there was a further gap of one and three-quarter lengths to the third, Summer Sands, and another length and a quarter back to Threat, who had to settle for fifth. Golden Horde finished that year on an official mark of 114.

He raced prominently throughout the Group 1 Commonwealth Cup on his seasonal reappearance at the Royal Ascot meeting in June, leading the horses racing nearest to the stands' side of the track as Mums Tipple cut out the early running. That rival weakened with a quarter of a mile to go, Golden Horde moved to the front a furlong later and then kept on well to beat Kimari by a length and a half. That filly was not seen out again, but the Wesley Ward-trained bay, a fifteen-length debut winner over four and a half furlongs as a two-year-old, had won blacktype sprints at Saratoga, Keeneland and Oaklawn Park between her narrow defeat by Raffle Prize in 2019's Group 2 Queen Mary Stakes and her excellent effort at the venue twelve months later. Ventura Rebel, who was two and a half lengths farther back in third, would go on to take a Group 3 contest at the Curragh. Fifth-placed Millisle, although not the force she was at two, later won the Group 3 Ballyogan Stakes at Naas, whereas sixth-placed Royal Crusade beat Glen Shiel to win the Group 3 Qatar Prix de Ris-Orangis at Deauville on his only subsequent outing.

Golden Horde failed by margins of one and a quarter lengths and a neck to beat the four-year-old geldings Oxted and Sceptical in the Group 1 Darley July Cup Stakes. He had broken well, went to the front, moved to the rail and tried to make all, but he came under pressure a quarter of a mile from home, drifted towards the centre of the track and never looked like catching the winner. He also set off in front at Deauville the following month, disputing the lead with Hello Youmzain, but weakened in the final half-furlong of the Group 1 LARC Prix Maurice de Gheest and had to settle for fifth, beaten by a total of one and a half lengths. This was Space Blues's day and that colt caught Hello Youmzain in the final few yards to win by three-quarters of a length. Lope Y Fernandez and Earthlight came next, the Ballydoyle runner snatching third near the finish and being only a head away from a higher placing.

The Group 1 Betfair Sprint Cup Stakes on soft ground at Haydock in early September turned out to be his career finale. The field split into two groups and the chestnut was never headed in his one on the far side of the track. Unfortunately for his connections, both Dream of Dreams and Glen Shiel, racing on the near side, were ahead at the post and so he finished third. The margins were a length and a quarter and a neck, and both the fourth and fifth, Art Power and Hello Youmzain, had also been racing on the favoured near-side group. One can only speculate as to whether or not he would have won the race had he raced on their side of the track, but it seems likely that he would at least have finished second.

The Group 1 Qipco British Champions Sprint Stakes at Ascot in mid-October had been an intended target, but a tendon injury ruled out his chance to participate and, a few days after the race, his retirement was announced. He is now at Nurlan Bizakov's Haras de Montfort & Préaux in France where he will cover his first book of mares at a fee of €10,000. That Normandy-based farm has only two other stallions on its roster: leading sire Le Havre (by Noverre) and the intriguing Recorder (by Galileo). That former William Haggas-trained chestnut won the Group 3 Acomb Stakes on the last of just three starts, his dam, Memory (by Danehill Dancer), won the Group 2 Cherry Hinton Stakes, his fee for 2021 is advertised as €4,000, and his breeder and racing owner, Queen Elizabeth II, has been supporting him at stud. She bred two of the foals in his first crop, four from his second, and sent him another mare in 2020. His first juveniles will be in action this coming season.

Golden Horde's sire spent the 2020 season France having moved to Haras de Grandcamp after spending his first six seasons as Cheveley Park Stud in Newmarket, but he has since moved on to Italy. Lethal Force won both the Group 1 Diamond Jubilee Stakes and Group 1 July Cup as a four-year-old and was rated 128 by Timeform. However, like the other early stallion sons of Dark Angel (by Acclamation), he has been slow to make an impact at pattern level as a sire; at the time of writing, ten of his progeny have earned blacktype but only his Group 1 star is a stakes winner. Several members of his family were racehorses of note in France, so perhaps he will do well in his new home. Golden Horde, on the other hand, comes from a branch of a famous US family.

He is the best of five winners out of Entreat (by Pivotal), a Cheveley Park homebred who was trained by Sir Michael Stoute and made all to win an extended nine-and-a-half-furlong maiden on fast ground at Folkestone as a three-year-old. His half-sister Exhort (by Dutch Art) won over the extended ten furlongs at York at that same age but the best of her five wins came the following summer when she beat Billesdon Brook by three-quarters of a length in a one-mile listed contest on fast ground at Pontefract. She then joined her owner-breeder's broodmare band and was bred to their dual ten-furlong Group 1-winning stallion Ulysses (by Galileo) last year. Several of his yearlings fetched six-figure sums in 2020, headed by a 320,000-guinea Tattersalls Book 1 colt, and although his long-term potential is with three-year-olds and older horses, it would not be a surprise to see him come up with some talented first-crop juveniles this coming autumn.

He also has an interesting half-brother called Line of Departure, a first-crop son of the champion freshman sire Mehmas (by Acclamation). The colt is a £260,000 graduate of the Goffs UK Premier Yearling Sale, he ran seven times for the Roger Varian stable and reeled off a treble during the summer. He had been placed in two of his first three starts, won nurseries at Yarmouth and Ascot and then scooped a prize of £122,900 when winning the Weatherbys Racing Bank £200,000 2-Y-O Stakes over six and a half furlongs at Doncaster. He disappointed behind Alkumait in the Group 2 Mill Reef Stakes on his final start, which led to his official handicap mark being trimmed from 101 to 99, and although consigned at the Tattersalls Autumn Horses-in-Training Sale in late October, was a 120,000-guinea vendor buy-back.

Entreat had fillies in 2019 and 2020, by Zoffany (by Dansili) and Zoustar (by Northern Meteor) respectively, and she was bred to Blue Point (by Shamardal) last season. Producer (by Dutch Art) is the best of her siblings and he got off the mark as a freshman sire in 2020 from a handful of progeny in the USA. During his racing days he won the Group 3 Criterion Stakes and Group 3 Supreme Stakes over seven furlongs in England, landed a one-mile Group 2 contest in Turkey plus listed contests at Leicester and Epsom. River Saint (by Irish River), their dam, was only placed but she was out of Imagining (by Northfields), which made her a half-sister to the prolific Grade 1 star Serena's Song (by Rahy). That US champion went on to become a broodmare of note, getting Group 1 Coronation Stakes winner Sophisticat (by Storm Cat), graded scorers Grand Reward (by Storm Cat), Harlington (by Unbridled) and Schramsberg (by Storm Cat) and the listed winners Serene Melody (by Street Cry) and Serena's Tune (by Mr Prospector), and she is the ancestor of plenty of other of note. For example, she is the grandam of the European pattern winners Suphala (by Frankel) and Vocalised (by Vindication; sire of Group 1 winner Verbal Dexterity) and US Grade 2 scorer Made You Look (by More Than Ready), and she is the third dam of Noble Tune (by Unbridled's Song) and Honor Code (by A.P. Indy). Grade 2 winner Noble Tune was runner-up in the Grade 1 Breeders' Cup Juvenile Turf and has sired a couple of stakes winners in South Africa, whereas US champion older male Honor Code, who won the Grade 1 Metropolitan Handicap and Grade 1 Whitney Stakes and finished third in the Grade 1 Breeders' Cup Classic, stands at Lane's End Farm in Kentucky. The two stakes winners from his first crop are 2020's Grade 1 Santa Anita Derby winner and Grade 1 Kentucky Derby fourth Honor A.P. and the Grade 3 Withers Stakes scorer Max Player, who picked up third place in both the Grade 1 Belmont Stakes and Grade 1 Travers Stakes.

Serena's Sister, a full sister to Serena's Song and half-sister to River Saint, is also of considerable note even though she finished out of the frame on both her starts on the track, and that's because of the impact she has had at stud. Her son Doubles Partner (by Rock Hard Ten) was a dual Grade 1-placed Grade 2 scorer from eight to nine furlongs and has sired winners from a small number of runners, and her stakes-winning daughter Stormy Venus (by Stormy Atlantic) is the dam of Don Americo (by Mr Greeley), a twelve-furlong Grade 2 winner in Peru. However, two of her other daughters have also produced stakes winners and of those, one stands out.

Princess Serena (by Unbridled's Song), who got her sole win over a mile, has produced eight winners from eight runners, headlined by the Group 1 Prix d'Ispahan winner Zabeel Prince (by Shamardal), his Group 2-winning full brother Puissance de Lune, and Group 2-placed, stakes-winning full sister Queen Power. Puissance de Lune has sired the dual Oaks-placed Australian Group 2 winner Moonlight Maid in his first crop, whereas his half-sister Serena's Storm (by Statue of Liberty) has done her part for the family by coming up with two well-known daughters. Rizeena (by Iffraaj) won both the Group 1 Moyglare Stud Stakes and Group 2 Queen Mary Stakes as a juvenile, added the Group 1 Coronation Stakes at three, and her first foal is the Simon and Ed Crisford-trained Latest Generation (by Frankel). He won a one-mile Doncaster maiden on his second start, disappointed when out of the frame behind One Ruler in the Group 3 Emirates Autumn Stakes over the same trip at Newmarket next time and, at the time of writing, holds entries in both the Group 1 Tattersalls Irish 2,000 Guineas and Group 1 Investec Derby. Summer Romance (by Kingman) is the other daughter of note and that €800,000 Arqana breeze-up graduate, a pattern-placed stakes winner at two, won the Group 3 Princess Elizabeth Stakes over eight and a half furlongs at Epsom on the second of her three starts in 2020 (see Volume 2).

Many of those horses are remotely related to Golden Horde. However, it is encouraging for his prospects that there are other males in branches of his family that have achieved blacktype success as stallions. Being on a small roster that is headed by one of France's best and most popular stallions, he looks ideally placed to garner plenty of support, so don't be surprised if he is a leading freshman sire in France in 2024 and a source of talented sprinters and milers beyond then.

SUMMARY DETAILS
Bred: Cn Farm Ltd
Owned: AlMohamediya Racing
Trained: Clive Cox
Country: England
Race record: 410132-1303-

Career highlights: 3 wins inc Commonwealth Cup (Gr1), Qatar Richmond Stakes (Gr2), 2nd Juddmonte Middle Park Stakes (Gr1), 3rd Darley July Cup Stakes (Gr1), Betfair Sprint Cup Stakes (Gr1), Darley Prix Morny - Finale des Darley Series (Gr1)

GOLDEN HORDE (IRE) – 2017 chestnut colt

Lethal Force (IRE)	Dark Angel (IRE)	Acclamation (GB)
		Midnight Angel (GB)
	Land Army (IRE)	Desert Style (IRE)
		Family At War (USA)
Entreat (GB)	Pivotal (GB)	Polar Falcon (USA)
		Fearless Revival (GB)
	River Saint (USA)	Irish River (FR)
		Imagining (USA)

HELLO YOUMZAIN (FR)

Kodiac (by Danehill) was placed on his only start at two, had one win and two unplaced finishes from a three-race season at three, won only four of his twenty starts across his career and earned only one piece of blacktype, when runner-up to Fayr Jag in the Group 3 Hackwood Stakes at Newbury as a five-year-old. Those were not the racing credentials of a horse of whom one might expect great things at stud, but he is superbly bred, his Group 1-winning three-parts brother Invincible Spirit (by Green Desert) was then a young team member at the Irish National Stud and had an outstanding year as a freshman sire during what would be his relation's final year on the track. The timing was fortunate and Kodiac secured a berth at Tally-Ho Stud for 2007. His initial €5,000 fee dipped a little, as is quite common in the third and fourth seasons of a horse's career, but then started its rise as his offspring started winning. It has soared in recent seasons and now, having turned twenty years old, his €65,000 charge places him among the most expensive sires in Europe.

His stock is highly sought-after in the auction ring, many win as juveniles, and although his overall record still pales in comparison to that of Invincible Spirit, his tally of sixty-five stakes winners features five who have won at least once at the highest level. Four of those are sprinters, one a middle-distance horse, and two of them achieved the feat in 2020: juvenile filly Campanelle and four-year-old colt Hello Youmzain. Ten of his progeny have hit the target at Group 2 level, including Coventry Stakes winner Nando Parrado and Flying Childers Stakes scorer Ubettabelieveit in 2020, and his latest batch of two-year-olds also included Group 3 scorer Umm Kulthum and listed-race winners Bahrain Pride, Captain Magnum, Frenetic, and Zoetic.

Last season was also a notable one for him in another area, one that has significance for Hello Youmzain's future now that he has retired from racing to take up a stallion role in France and New Zealand. That is because it was the first year that sons of Kodiac had runners of their own. It is far too early to get carried away by anything that a freshman sire of 2020 achieved, but it is fair to say that Adaay, Coulsty, Kodi Bear, and Prince of Lir are among those who have shown potential.

Six- and seven-furlong Group 2 scorer Adaay stands at Whitsbury Manor Stud and has a profile that suggests his best results may come with his three-year-olds and older horses. He had a large number of runners, a double-digit tally of winners plus three who were blacktype-placed. Ballyhane Stud's Prince of Lir also had plenty of runners and, in addition to two who were placed in listed races, his first season was highlighted by The Lir Jet, the Group 2 Norfolk Stakes winner who was runner-up in the Group 1 Phoenix Stakes and Group 2 Prix Robert Papin.

Rathasker Stud's Coulsty was stakes-placed at two and a six-furlong pattern winner at three, and from a smaller number of runners than many of his cohorts had, he came up with the Group 3 Princess Margaret Stakes winner and Group 2 Duchess of Cambridge Stakes third Santosha, Italian listed scorers Sopran Aragorn and Suicide Squad, and two other blacktype earners. His latest crops are tiny, but his first-year results should provide him with a much-needed boost in support. Kodi Bear, on the other hand, stands at Rathbarry Stud. He was a listed winner and Group 1 Dewhurst Stakes runner-up at two, a Group 2-winning miler at three, and also off the mark as a blacktype sire. His double-digit tally of freshman-year winners includes the Listed Stonehenge Stakes winner and Group 2 Royal Lodge Stakes third Cobh, plus four others who made the frame at least once in pattern company.

Each of that quartet of Kodiac horses has shown the potential to become a prolific sire of winners with high-class handicappers, plus some stakes and pattern winners thrown in. It is entirely possible that one or more of them will get at least one Group 1 winner at some point. Hello Youmzain outperformed them on the track and it is likely that he will do the same at stud. His pedigree was reviewed in detail in *European Group 1 Winners of 2019*, and the key point here is that his third dam, Sandy Island (by Mill Reef), was a three-parts sister to 1985's runaway Group 1 Derby hero Slip Anchor (by Shirley Heights). His stallion career was not as successful as one might have hoped but he did get the triple classic heroine User Friendly plus the Italian Group 1 scorers Morshdi, Posidonas and Slicious, Group 1 Melbourne Cup runner-up Give

The Slip, plus Group 2 Great Voltigeur Stakes winner and Group 1 Champion Stakes fourth Stowaway who later achieved fame as a National Hunt stallion.

Hello Youmzain's closer relations include two siblings of note. Royal Youmzain (by Youmzain), a Group 2 winner over seven and a half furlongs in Italy as a two-year-old, went on to be a Group 1 Deutsches Derby-placed dual ten-furlong pattern winner in Germany. That one's full brother Saglawy was a stakes-placed winner on the flat in France before becoming a Grade 1-placed juvenile Grade 2-winning hurdler for the Willie Mullins stable. Sadly, he died last September. That pair are by a middle-distance horse but, like Hello Youmzain, their half-sister Zuhoor Baynoona is by a sprinter, Elnadim (by Danzig), so it's no surprise that she got her blacktype success over five furlongs. Their unraced dam, Spasha, is a Shamardal-sired (by Giant's Causeway) daughter of Spa (by Sadler's Wells), so there is both speed and stamina to be passed on there. Given his racing record, it seems that Hello Youmzain may have got the speed influence from both sides of his family.

Aside from his fourth-place finish to Mohaather in the Group 3 Greenham Stakes and runner-up spot to Space Blues in 2020's Group 1 LARC Prix Maurice de Gheest, every race he ran was over six furlongs. Victory in the Group 2 Critérium de Maisons-Laffitte headlined his three-race season as a juvenile, he won both the Group 1 Sprint Cup and Group 2 Sandy Lane Stakes and finished third in the Group 1 Commonwealth Cup at three, and he added the Group 1 Diamond Jubilee Stakes to his CV at the age of four. He was always prominent in that Royal Ascot feature and had to battle for victory, beating the subsequent Group 1 star Dream of Dreams and the sadly ill-fated Sceptical by a head and a neck. Khaadem was another length and a quarter behind in fourth, followed by Speak In Colours, One Master and The Tin Man.

That fine effort made his fifth-place finish in the Group 1 Darley July Cup Stakes a bit disappointing. He had every chance a quarter of a mile from home but weakened in the closing stages as Oxted went on to secure victory from Sceptical, Golden Horde and Khaadem. He was beaten by a total of four lengths, and had the popular veteran Brando not been so slowly away, he too would likely have finished ahead of him instead of a neck behind in sixth. His aforementioned Deauville second was a better effort. He and Golden Horde, racing wide apart, disputed the lead for much of the race, and while the three-year-old weakened in the final half furlong, Hello Youmzain kept on to the line, only losing out to the eye-catching turn of foot shown by Space Blues. That colt swept past near the finish to win by three-quarters of a length, the strong-finishing Lope Y Fernandez was a head back in third, with Earthlight and Golden Horde close up in fourth and fifth, followed by the subsequent Prix de l'Abbaye de Longchamp winner Wooded who never looked dangerous on this occasion.

He returned to Haydock to bid for a repeat Group 1 Betfair Sprint Cup Stakes win but despite racing on what seemed to be the favoured near side of the track, he had to settle for fifth. He stayed on well in the final furlong but never looked likely to win the race. The ground was soft, as it had been the year before and when he got his big win as a two-year-old, and he was beaten by a total of three and three-quarter lengths as Dream of Dreams led home Glen Shiel, Golden Horde and Art Power. The Group 1 Qipco British Champions Sprint Stakes at Ascot was the obvious next target and reportedly under consideration, but instead his retirement from racing was announced on October 9th along with confirmation that he was already settling in at Haras d'Etreham in France. He is also due to serve shuttle-stallion duties at Cambridge Stud in New Zealand from 2021.

Hello Youmzain, the best sprinter son of Kodiac, is a dual Group 1 star who won five of his dozen starts, was successful in pattern company as a juvenile, and earned just short of £580,000 in prize money. He should prove popular in his new role and, given his racing and pedigree profile, looks like a horse who will get plenty of winners in all age groups, his best being sprinters or milers and at least a few of them proving effective at ten furlongs.

SUMMARY DETAILS

Bred: Rabbah Bloodstock Ltd
Owned: Haras d'Etreham & Cambridge Stud
Trained: Kevin Ryan

Country: England
Race record: 121-41310-1020-
Career highlights: 5 wins inc Diamond Jubilee Stakes (Gr1), Betfair Sprint Cup Stakes (Gr1), Armstrong Aggregates Sandy Lane Stakes (Gr2), Criterium de Maisons-Laffitte (Gr2), 2nd LARC Prix Maurice de Gheest (Gr1) 3rd Commonwealth Cup (Gr1)

HELLO YOUMZAIN (FR) – 2016 bay colt

Kodiac (GB)	Danehill (USA)	Danzig (USA)
		Razyana (USA)
	Rafha	Kris
		Eljazzi
Spasha (GB)	Shamardal (USA)	Giant's Causeway (USA)
		Helsinki (GB)
	Spa (GB)	Sadler's Wells (USA)
		Sandy Island

IN SWOOP (IRE)

The Oppenheim/Ullman family's Gestüt Schlenderhan notched up a remarkable twentieth Deutsches Derby as breeder and nineteenth as owner when In Swoop landed the spoils at Hamburg in July. What made their latest star unusual is that he is not trained in Germany. They closed their private training centre in Bergheim in late 2019 and moved their horses to France, which is how In Swoop came to be trained by for them by Francis-Henri Graffard. Their main trainer had been Jean-Pierre Carvalho; he moved to Mülheim. Germany's loss is France's gain as the colt is one of the best horses in Europe, his end-of-year rating of 122 making him one of the top middle-distance three-year-old colts of 2020.

In Swoop did not begin his career until mid-May of 2020 when he won an eleven-furlong maiden on soft ground at Lyon Parilly. Three weeks later he finished third to Gold Trip and Influx in the Group 2 Prix Greffulhe over the same course and distance, beaten by a length and a head, again on soft. He had encountered minor traffic a furlong out but once he got clear he stayed on well; it was a promising performance from an inexperienced colt. The ground was described as good-to-soft at Hamburg the following month and again staying on strongly over the final furlong, he hit the front about half a furlong out and held off Torquator Tasso to take Germany's premier classic by three-quarters of a length. The runner-up would go on to establish himself as arguably the best of his age in that country, making the frame in three more Group 1s by the end of the year including victory in the Grosser Preis von Berlin.

The Deutsches Derby result was also notable from a breeding point of view as both of the first two home were sons of the somewhat underrated Adlerflug (by In The Wings). That Group 1 star comes from a branch of the famous stallion-producing family of Galileo (by Sadler's Wells), Sea The Stars (by Cape Cross), King's Best (by Kingmambo), Tertullian (by Miswaki) and Tamayuz (by Nayef) and he reportedly resides in Monsun's old box at Schlenderhan, staying there while his main owner's farm Gestüt Harzburg, is being renovated. The seventeen-year-old has sixteen stakes winners, five of whom have won at least once at Group 1 level. That elite quintet includes Ito, a full brother to In Swoop.

Ito was a four-length winner of the Group 1 Grosser Preis von Bayern, he was a dual Group 2 scorer, runner-up to Second Step in the Group 1 Grosser Preis von Berlin and to Silverwave in the Group 2 Prix Foy, stands at Gestüt Erftmühle and will have his first three-year-olds in action this coming season. But back to In Swoop whose two subsequent runs were excellent ones, both over twelve furlongs at ParisLongchamp although on contrasting ground. First, he got up on the line to pip his old rival Gold Trip in the Group 1 Juddmonte Grand Prix de Paris in mid-September, the pair finishing two and a half lengths behind the winner, Mogul, but a length and three-quarters ahead of that colt's Derby-winning stablemate Serpentine. Three weeks later, he almost won the Group 1 Qatar Prix de l'Arc de Triomphe.

Enable was the horse many hoped would win, the great mare making a second attempt to try to win the race for a record third time, but the ground was heavy and that ruined her chance. She finished sixth, half a length ahead of her stablemate Stradivarius, the great stayer also unsuited by such underfoot conditions. Persian King, fresh from impressive performance in the Group 1 Prix du Moulin de Longchamp over a mile, tried to make all. His stamina was uncertain, which made the tactic a bold move, but he kept on when passed, holding on by a head to deny Gold Trip a placing. However, Sottsass and In Swoop had powered past him, the chestnut having gone to the front a furlong out and the younger bay staying on strongly and closing all the way to the line. Sottsass rounded off the track phase of his career with a neck victory, with Persian King, also racing for the final time before commencing stallion duties, one and three-quarter lengths behind in third.

In Swoop remains in training and there is reason to hope that he will be at least as good in 2021 as he was last season. His star brother, Ito, got all of his big wins at four and five years of age, whereas their half-sister Igraine (by Galileo) was a ten-and-a-half-furlong Group 3 scorer in New Zealand as a five-year-old and both a listed scorer and short-headed in a Group 3 contest in

Australia at the age of six. She is now a broodmare and her first foal, a daughter of Fastnet Rock (by Danehill), arrived in September 2020. Their dam, Iota (by Tiger Hill), won the Group 1 Preis der Diana (German Oaks), which makes In Swoop a Derby winner sired by the same country's Derby winner and out of one of its Oaks winners, something we also saw in England in 2014 when Australia, the son of Galileo and Ouija Board, followed parents' example with a classic victory at Epsom.

There are many other stakes winners to be found in branches of the first four generations of the pedigree, including the Group 1-placed pattern-winning French miler Spectre (by Siyouni) and the Group 2 Mehl-Mülhens-Rennen (German 2000 Guineas) scorer Irian (by Tertullian). Both the latter and his half-brother Ibicenco (by Shirocco) provide further illustration of what older horses in the family can achieve. Irian was a prolific blacktype performer in Hong Kong from four to six, whereas Ibicenco, who was runner-up in the Group 1 Preis von Europa as a three-year-old, went to Australia where he was a pattern-placed stakes-winning stayer at four and a Group 3 Geelong Cup scorer at five. As for Iota, one of those special mares that have produced two individual Group 1 stars, there may be more to tell in the coming years. Her new three-year-old is a Gavin Hernon-trained filly named Iffy (by Australia), she returned to Adlerflug in 2018 and 2019 and was bred to Highland Reel (by Galileo) in 2020.

SUMMARY DETAILS

Bred: Stall Ullmann
Owned: Gestüt Schlenderhan
Trained: Francis-Henri Graffard
Country: France
Race record: -13122-
Career highlights: 2 wins inc IDEE 151st Deutsches Derby (Gr1), 2nd Qatar Prix de l'Arc de Triomphe (Gr1), Juddmonte Grand Prix de Paris (Gr1), 3rd Prix Greffulhe (Gr2)

IN SWOOP (IRE) – 2017 bay colt

Adlerflug (GER)	In The Wings	Sadler's Wells (USA)
		High Hawk
	Aiyana (GER)	Last Tycoon
		Alya (GER)
Iota (GER)	Tiger Hill (IRE)	Danehill (USA)
		The Filly (GER)
	Iora (GER)	Konigsstuhl (GER)
		Incitation (GER)

KAMEKO (USA)

Kameko created a piece of racing history as a two-year-old by becoming the first horse ever to win a Group 1 race in Europe on an artificial track. The Group 1 Vertem Futurity Trophy Stakes, usually over a mile on turf at Doncaster, had to be postponed due to the track being waterlogged. The race was moved to Newcastle, where it was run on November 1st, 2019, and Kameko advertised his classic potential with a three-and-a-quarter-length defeat of Innisfree on the Tapeta surface.

With the early weeks of the latest season cancelled due to the Covid-19 pandemic, England's mile classics were moved to the first weekend in June. That is usually Derby and Oaks weekend, but those Epsom classics were moved to the start of July, held on the traditional Eclipse Stakes weekend. This added an unusual dimension to the Guineas races in that for most candidates it had been impossible to have a prep race. However, the Group 1 Qipco 2000 Guineas placings went to colts most would have expected to see in the frame anyway, albeit perhaps not in the 'right' order.

The unbeaten juvenile champion Pinatubo was an odds-on favourite but could not show the final-furlong power he had done at the Curragh on his penultimate start of 2019 and he had to settle for third. One can never be sure when it's a horse's first run of the year, but it looked as though the mile may have stretched his stamina. The sadly ill-fated Wichita had gone to the front a quarter of a mile from home and was only headed a half furlong out when Kameko came to join him. The latter, ridden by Oisin Murphy, had encountered traffic problems, had to switch from an inner position to several 'lanes' to the right, and then he found himself waiting for a gap to emerge between Wichita and Military March. It did, the latter colt weakened slightly to finish fourth, while Kameko, still drifting a bit to his right, ran on well to take the classic by a neck. There was another length back to Pinatubo in third and a further gap of two and a half lengths and a neck to Military March and long-shot Juan Elcano.

The Group 1 Investec Derby was the obvious next step for him, despite doubts about his stamina. There are sons of the outstanding US stallion Kitten's Joy (by El Prado) who stay twelve furlongs, and Champion Hurdle star Alderbrook (by Ardross) appears among Kameko's distant relations. However, most of those sired by the stallion or produced from the family are typically effective around a mile to ten furlongs, and that suggested a possible scenario where he could be going well a quarter of a mile from home at Epsom only to run out stamina soon after.

The Epsom classics were, like so much of the 2020 racing calendar, run behind closed doors, but even if the stands had been filled on that first Saturday in July it is likely that there would still have been a somewhat muted response to the Derby result. In a performance reminiscent of that of Slip Anchor and Steve Cauthen in 1985, Serpentine and Emmet McNamara set off in front, slipped the field and never looked like being caught. The chestnut, who had been unplaced in two maidens before winning one by nine lengths just one week before, was a five-and-a-half-length winner at odds of 25/1, chased home by 50/1 listed scorer Khalifa Sat who was half a length in front of the 66/1 maiden Amhran Na Bhfiann. The winner would finish fourth in a pair of Group 1s on his only subsequent outings, the runner-up was fifth in his only other race, leaving the third to be the only horse in the frame that day who made the frame subsequently. And yet that colt fractured a fetlock while finishing as runner-up in a Naas maiden; he underwent surgery and was reported as being likely to return to action in 2021. Many of the runners in that classic turned out to be well below the required standard as the year progressed, but Kameko, who had been another nose back in fourth, sixth-placed Mogul and eleventh-placed Pyledriver went on to prove themselves to be among the leaders of their generation.

Kameko dropped back to a mile at Goodwood three and a half weeks later but found himself short of room at a key stage in the Group 1 Qatar Sussex Stakes and was eased near the line. He extended his margin of superiority over Wichita to two lengths but passed the post the same amount behind Siskin, Ireland's classic-winning miler who, in finishing third here, was losing his unbeaten record. It was the four-year-olds Mohaather and Circus Maximus who came out on top, the pair separated by three-quarters of a length and with the latter half a length in front of Siskin. In a year when some of the top races were dominated by geldings, it was good to see some fine stallion prospects in action. Each of the first four is now in his first season at stud and it is likely that the fifth would have been a popular recruit in 2021 or 2022 had he recovered from an unfortunate injury in Australia in late October.

York was the next stop on his agenda and it gave us another chance to assess his stamina range. He was one of two three-year-olds taking on a trio of excellent older horses in the Group 1 Juddmonte International Stakes over the extended ten furlongs on good ground. The likeable pattern winner Rose of Kildare was outclassed in fifth but picked up a cheque for almost £7,400 for her connections. Kameko raced beside the rail and got into a battle with Magical from under three out. He seemed to be getting the better of that standout mare at the two-furlong pole, going about a length in front of her. However, she fought back, he came under pressure, she headed him a furlong out and soon went past. Lord North, who lost a shoe in the race, also overtook the colt in the final furlong, relegating him to fourth. Of course, none of them had ever looked like catching Ghaiyyath that day, Godolphin's subsequently crowned Horse of the Year having made all towards the centre of the track, powering home to win by three lengths. The margins between Magical, Lord North and Kameko were one and a quarter lengths and three-quarters of a length.

Of the distances more commonly raced over in Europe, a mile was clearly Kameko's ideal trip and it was over that distance that he ran on his final two starts. The Group 2 Shadwell Joel Stakes over the Rowley Mile at Newmarket in late September promised to be a good test as he had conditions in his favour while having to give five pounds to each of his rivals. They included the top-class Benbatl, former Group 1 scorer Zabeel Prince and the capable pair Regal Reality and Tilsit, with the 111-rated recent pattern scorer Top Rank completing the line-up. Benbatl tried to make all but, on his first start for seven months, he couldn't raise his game in the closing stages and had to settle for third, beaten by half a length and the same as Kameko, who hit the front a furlong out, and then Regal Reality went past. There was a two-and-a-quarter-length gap back to Tilsit in fourth. The time was quick and the performance at least as good as his classic victory, if not a shade better.

The Grade 1 FanDuel Breeders' Cup Mile was to be his final race before taking up stallion duties, but although racing prominently in the early stages on the firm turf at Keeneland in early November, he never looked dangerous, weakening in the final furlong to finish seventh, albeit beaten by a total of three and a quarter lengths. This was the day that the Ballydoyle outsider Order of Australia, trying the distance for the first time since his two-year-old debut, sprang a 40/1 surprise, beating his stablemates Circus Maximus and Lope Y Fernandez by a neck and three-quarters of a length. Kameko, the Calumet Farm-bred $90,000 Keeneland September Yearling Sale graduate, would retire with a record of four wins and two second-place finishes from ten starts, a classic and juvenile Group 1-star who was among the best of his age in both of his seasons to race.

Kameko has joined the roster at his owner's Tweenhills Farm & Stud in Gloucestershire, the second son of Kitten's Joy to do so, and he looks sure to be very popular in his new role. His initial book will reportedly include around forty-five mares belong to his owners and their clients, and the Group 1 winners Con Te Partiro and Nymphea are among those confirmed as being on his list. Sadly, the stud's popular multiple Group 1 star Roaring Lion was lost after a battle with colic having completed just a single season, the grey leaving behind just a single crop of "cubs", as the adverts have called them. The latest supplement to Weatherbys' *Return of Mares* lists ninety-one registered foals by him and thirty "no returns"; it is remarkable how high the numbers of "no returns" have become in recent years.

It is too early to know how Kitten's Joy will fare as a sire of stallion sons given that of his small number to go to stud most are in early stages of their career. These include the now Japan-based Hawkbill, whose sole European crop of foals arrived in 2020; the Lanwades Stud-based sprinter-miler Bobby's Kitten, whose string of first-crop juvenile winners in 2020 include the Group 2 Beresford Stakes runner-up Monaasib; the high-class miler Taareef, who stands at Haras du Mezeray and had his first foals last year; and, of course, Roaring Lion. It is a branch of the Sadler's

Wells (by Northern Dancer) male line, so there would not appear to be any reason to doubt that one or more important sires will emerge from it.

Kameko is out of the capable miler Sweeter Still (by Rock of Gibraltar), an Anne-Marie O'Brien-bred mare who finished fourth in the Listed Flame of Tara Stakes over six furlongs at the Curragh on her only start for Aidan O'Brien before crossing the Atlantic where she switched between three different trainers over the next few seasons. She was a Grade 3 winner and dual listed scorer over a mile in California, was a nose runner-up in the Grade 2 Providencia Stakes at Santa Anita and finished third in the Grade 2 Honeymoon Handicap over nine furlongs at Hollywood Park. The mare's half-sister Belle Artiste (by Namid) won the Group 3 Derrinstown Stud 1,000 Guineas Trial at Leopardstown but, from the point of view of their relation's new career, their unlucky half-brother Kingsbarns (by Galileo) is more significant. He won the Group 1 Racing Post Trophy, was third in the Group 1 Queen Elizabeth II Stakes, sired a small crop while on the Coolmore roster in Ireland, went to Drakenstein Stud in South Africa, died due to colic three years later, but left behind some talented offspring. Gabor won the Grade 1 Thekwini Stakes over a mile at Greyville as a juvenile, whereas King of Gems won a Grade 2 over a mile at Kenilworth at three.

Their dam's pattern-placed, stakes-winning half-brother Kafhar (by In The Wings) sired winners in Italy from limited opportunities, and the notable racehorses who appear under the various branches of fourth generation include Rip Van Winkle (by Galileo). His connection to Kameko is remote—they share a fourth dam and represent the Sadler's Wells male line—but his record deserves comment. He was a champion on the track, winning the Group 1 Juddmonte International Stakes, Group 1 Sussex Stakes and Group 1 Queen Elizabeth II Stakes, and although his results as a member of the Coolmore stallion team were disappointing, he fared better from his seasons at Windsor Park Stud in New Zealand, where he died last August at the age of fourteen. His Group 1 Phoenix Stakes-winning son Dick Whittington stands as a private stallion in Ireland, sired nine foals in 2019 and 29 in 2020; whereas his other European progeny include 2019's Group 2 Derby Italiano scorer Keep On Fly, pattern-winning sprinter The Happy Prince, plus the popular and multiple blacktype-placed Irish filly Cribbs Causeway.

Rip Van Winkle's southern hemisphere crops include the late dual Group 1 star Te Akau Shark, Group 1 New Zealand Oaks winner and Group 1 New Zealand 1000 Guineas runner-up Jennifer Eccles, the mile group winners Capella and Kingsguard, seven-furlong Group 2 scorer Subpoena, and pattern-winning stayer Bizzwinkle. He has also had a mile classic winner in both India and Kazakhstan (neither country is listed in Part I of the International Cataloguing Standards) and an Eclipse Award-winning steeplechaser in the USA. His relations under this level of the family also include Grade 1 Queen Elizabeth II Challenge Cup Stakes winner Danish (by Danehill) and her Group 1 Dubai World Cup-winning grandson African Story (by Pivotal), plus, as noted above, the high-class ten-furlong horse turned Champion Hurdle hero and successful National Hunt stallion Alderbrook, but they are almost as distantly connected to Rip Van Winkle as they are to Kameko. Fifth dam Mesopotamia (by Zarathustra) was the classic-placed juvenile filly champion and daughter of 1955's Irish Oaks winner Agars Plough (by Combat).

Kameko, a top-class autumn two-year-old who became a classic-winning miler at three, is one of the brightest prospects among the latest intake of new sires and it will be fascinating to see how his stallion career turns out. There could be some high-class performers among his summer and autumn juveniles and you'd expect to see his best results coming with milers and middle-distance horses aged three and upwards.

SUMMARY DETAILS

Bred: Calumet Farm
Owned: Qatar Racing Ltd
Trained: Andrew Balding
Country: England
Race record: 1221-144410-
Career highlights: 4 wins inc Qipco 2000 Guineas (Gr1), Vertem Futurity Trophy Stakes (Gr1), Shadwell Joel Stakes

(Gr2), 2nd Juddmonte Royal Lodge Stakes (Gr2), Betway Solario Stakes (Gr3)

KAMEKO (USA) – 2017 bay/brown colt

Kitten's Joy (USA)	El Prado (IRE)	Sadler's Wells (USA)
		Lady Capulet (USA)
	Kitten's First (USA)	Lear Fan (USA)
		That's My Hon (USA)
Sweeter Still (IRE)	Rock of Gibraltar (IRE)	Danehill (USA)
		Offshore Boom
	Beltisaal (FR)	Belmez (USA)
		Ittisaal

LORD NORTH (IRE)

It is only since 1986, and thanks in part to the exploits of the talented pair Teleprompter and Bedtime, that geldings can run in most Group 1 races in Europe. They are still barred from the classics (a European classic, in its pure and traditional sense, is for three-year-olds only, with geldings excluded), from all of the top two-year-old races and from a variety of other top-level contests, including the Prix de l'Arc de Triomphe, but they proved a potent force in 2020 among the races in which they were permitted to compete. Lord North took high rank among them and he finished the year on rating of 123.

This was the sort of promise he had shown the previous autumn when an impressive winner of the prestigious Cambridgeshire Handicap over nine furlongs at Newmarket. He was runner-up in the even more valuable Balmoral Handicap over a mile on heavy ground after that, then easily won a ten-furlong listed contest in similar conditions at Newmarket, but in 2020 he ran only in pattern company and with just a single start not being at Group 1 level. That was the Group 3 Betway Brigadier Gerard Stakes over ten furlongs on good-to-soft ground at Haydock in early June where he short-headed Elarqam and left Telecaster a further length and a quarter behind.

Ten days later, he followed up with a top-class effort in the Group 1 Prince of Wales's Stakes over a few yards short of the full ten furlongs at Ascot. The ground was good, he hit the front a furlong out and stayed on well to beat Addeybb and Barney Roy in style. It was a one-two-three for geldings, the colts Japan and Bangkok and the filly Mehdaayih were the next ones across the line, and the margins were three and three-quarter lengths, one and a quarter lengths, a half-length, a nose and a neck.

He never looked like winning the Group 1 Juddmonte International Stakes at York two months later, staying on past a weakening Kameko to take third to Ghaiyyath and Magical. Godolphin's champion had made all the running and never looked in any danger, Magical had got the better of Kameko in a duel they'd had along the rails, and although Lord North may have finished closer had he not lost a shoe, it is debatable if he would have been able to deny Ballydoyle's mare the second-place prize. Ghaiyyath won by an easy three lengths, Magical was a length and a quarter in front of Lord North, and Kameko was three-quarters of a length behind him. The only other runner was the talented but, on this occasion, outclassed filly Rose of Kildare.

Lord North finished last of the ten runners in the Group 1 Qipco Champion Stakes at Ascot in mid-October. The ground was soft that day, quite different to what he'd been running on throughout the year, but it had been heavy on his final two starts of the previous season and soft when he made a winning debut as a two-year-old, so it's hard to see that as a reason for his poor performance. His final start of the year was much better as, on firm ground at Keeneland, he finished fourth Tarnawa, Magical and Channel Maker in the Grade 1 Longines Breeders' Cup Turf. It was still a little below his best yet not really disappointing. The margins were a length, a nose and one and three-quarter lengths, and he finished a head in front of the runner-up's Group 1-winning stablemate Mogul.

The gelding is the third foal of Najoum (by Giant's Causeway), a mare who won two of her four starts for the Godolphin team, namely a seven-furlong Redcar maiden on her second juvenile outing and a one-mile Kempton nursery a month later. Her first foal is an unraced broodmare called Peronism (by Street Cry), that one's full brother Chronicles won a ten-furlong maiden for the Jim Bolger stable, and her fourth is Divine Blessing (by Teofilo) who failed to make the frame in four starts in France in 2020, beaten by a total of just over fifty lengths. The mare had a first-crop son of Postponed (by Dubawi) in 2019, a New Approach (by Galileo) filly in 2020 and was then among the initial book of mares covered by Too Darn Hot (by Dubawi).

Najoum has three siblings of particular note, headed by Bandini (by Fusaichi Pegasus). He got the best of his five wins in the Grade 1 Blue Grass Stakes, spent a few years at stud in Kentucky but got only a handful of stakes winners and blacktype earners and he was exported to Saudi Arabia. His half-sister Discourse (by Street Cry) won the Group 3 Sweet Solera Stakes at Newmarket as a juvenile in 2011 and has produced three talented offspring at stud so far. The fillies Discursus (by Dubawi) and

Hadith (by New Approach) won listed races, whereas Blown By Wind (by Invincible Spirit) has won five times for the Mark Johnston stable, from five to seven furlongs, achieving a peak handicap mark of 107. That now five-year-old also ran twice for the Salem bin Ghadayer stable in January, shortly before this book went to print, and he was a four-length winner of the Group 3 Jebel Ali Mile on the second of those starts. My Mammy (by Came Home) is the third of Najoum's notable siblings and that is because she is the stakes-placed dam of Grade 1 Ashland Stakes winner Out For A Spin (by Hard Spun) and the listed scorers Sweet Victory (by Blame) and Ferdinanda (by Giant's Causeway), all fillies.

Divine Dixie (by Dixieland Band), a stakes-placed dual three-year-old winner, is the grandam of Lord North. She is a half-sister to the stakes winner Stormy Atlantic (by Storm Cat)—best known here as being the sire of the Ed Walker-trained Group 1-placed, Group 2-winning miler Stormy Antarctic—she is related to a string of other stakes and pattern winners, including the ill-fated Group 1-placed, Group 2-winning stayer Incanto Dream (by Galileo), and she is a daughter of 1990's Grade 1 Santa Anita Oaks heroine Hail Atlantis (by Seattle Slew). Lord North's fifth dam, therefore, is the US juvenile champion Moccasin (by Nantallah), a full sister to the classic-placed Florida Derby winner Ridan and dam of the classic-placed juvenile Group 1 winner and successful sire Apalachee (by Round Table). His sixth dam is Rough Shod (by Gold Bridge), who is also a direct ancestor of Nureyev (by Northern Dancer), Sadler's Wells (by Northern Dancer) and countless other top horses). The seventh dam is 1934's Yorkshire Oaks winner Dalmary (by Blandford).

Being a Group 1-winning son of Dubawi (by Dubai Millennium) and from this family, Lord North would have been an interesting stallion prospect. However, he was gelded shortly after losing his unbeaten record in late May of his three-year-old season when he finished last of eight in the Listed Heron Stakes over a mile at Sandown. In remarks made after the horse's Cambridgeshire victory later that year, trainer John Gosden mentioned that group potential had been evident earlier in the season but that "his mind was the problem"; perhaps Lord North would not have become the top-level performer he is without the operation. No doubt he will be back in action in 2021, and there is every reason to hope that he can continue to make his presence felt at the highest levels of competition.

SUMMARY DETAILS
Bred: Godolphin
Owned: HH Sheikh Zayed bin Mohammed Racing
Trained: John Gosden
Country: England
Race record: 1-102121-11304-
Career highlights: 6 wins inc Prince of Wales's Stakes (Gr1), Betway Brigadier Gerard Stakes (Gr3), Weatherbys TBA James Seymour Stakes (L), bet365 Cambridgeshire Handicap, 3rd Juddmonte International Stakes (Gr1)

LORD NORTH (IRE) – 2016 bay gelding

Dubawi (IRE)	Dubai Millennium (GB)	Seeking The Gold (USA)
		Colorado Dancer
	Zomaradah (GB)	Deploy
		Jawaher (IRE)
Najoum (USA)	Giant's Causeway (USA)	Storm Cat (USA)
		Mariah's Storm (USA)
	Divine Dixie (USA)	Dixieland Band (USA)
		Hail Atlantis (USA)

LOVE (IRE)

Love ran only three times last year but left nobody in any doubt as to her superiority among the three-year-old filly division. One can easily pick holes in the merits of those she beat, but the simple fact is that no other member of that class was in her league over twelve furlongs and the sole four-year-old that lined-up against her at York was the 110-rated (now 108-rated) Manuela de Vega. It is unfortunate that she did not have an opportunity to take on the colts, although such a target had been scheduled. However, with the ground at ParisLongchamp turning heavy at the start of October, she was taken out of the Arc. As it turned out, she would not have had the chance to run anyway. A contaminated feed issue ruled all of the Ballydoyle horses out of the race.

It is true that the conditions of the Prix de l'Arc de Triomphe are perceived as favouring three-year-old fillies, but it is not the race I would have targeted had I had the incredibly good fortune to own her. For me there was just one obvious target: the St Leger. Yes, it is possible that the extended fourteen furlongs may have stretched her stamina a bit more than ideal, but victory in that classic would have secured her place in the history books in a way that an Arc win would not have managed. In 1955, Meld swept the Fillies' Triple Crown—the 1000 Guineas, Oaks and St Leger—and we had to wait until 1985 to see the feat repeated, this time by Oh So Sharp. The utterly dominant manner in which Love won the first two legs, and the Yorkshire Oaks, painted her as the most likely candidate we have seen since. Is she a better horse than Galileo Chrome and Berkshire Rocco, the one-two from Doncaster? Yes. Would she have beaten them over that trip? Possibly. Of course, I have no association with Love: she is owned and bred by Coolmore and will eventually join their mighty broodmare band. First, she is due to return to action on the track in 2021 when, it is hoped, she can pick up where she left off.

Her first three runs as a two-year-old gave no hint of the stardom that awaited; her four subsequent outings showed her to be talented but in need of improvement to become a potential classic winner. She had won the Group 3 Silver Flash Stakes by three and a quarter lengths and beaten Daahyeh by three-quarters of a length in the Group 1 Moyglare Stud Stakes, but she had finished fifth to Alpine Star in the Group 2 Debutante Stakes and third to Quadrilateral in the Group 1 Fillies' Mile. My concluding remarks in her essay in *European Group 1 Winners of 2019* were as follows: "As a seven-furlong juvenile Group 1 winner with Group 1 form over a mile at two, there is a chance that a Galileo filly from this family may not only stay middle distances at three but show improved form in that range. However, there is also a chance that ten furlongs may be as far as Love will want to go, and we won't know for certain until she steps up in distance. It will be disappointing if she is not at least as good at three as she was in her first season, and if she can improve then this mid-April-born chestnut could become a leading member of the Ballydoyle classic-age fillies."

She made her seasonal reappearance in the Group 1 Qipco 1000 Guineas at Newmarket in early June—it will never seem anything but strange to speak of that classic being in that month—and was joint second-favourite, with Millisle, behind Quadrilateral. The standard of the field looked mixed, the top four in the market—Raffle Prize was the fourth—being fillies of proven quality but the rest an array of promise and varying ability at lower levels. It didn't look any better after the race, aside from the winner, and months later it still looks like a weak edition of the classic. Love ground her way to the front a furlong out but then pulled away from the field to score by four and a quarter lengths and a head from Cloak of Spirits and Quadrilateral. There were margins of a length and half a length back to Final Song and Romsey, and then a gap of over three lengths to the sixth, Under The Stars. Millisle (seventh) dropped back to sprinting, Summer Romance (eighth) beat Cloak of Spirits next time in the Group 3 Princess Elisabeth Stakes but then finished well-beaten in the Group 1 Prix Rothschild. Of the principals, Cloak of Spirits notched up a listed win and three pattern placings from seven additional starts, Quadrilateral's only subsequent outings showed her to have retained some ability but not quite be the force she was or promised to be, 100/1 Final Song had had the benefit of four prior outings in Asia and the best she could manage in five later starts was a second-place finish in a seven-furlong listed contest, 200/1 Romsey was out of the frame in all of her ensuing runs, whereas Under The Stars won a seven-furlong listed contest next time before finishing well-beaten twice in pattern company.

It is a similar story with the Group 1 Investec Oaks, although this time Love went to the front a quarter of a mile from home and completely outclassed her seven rivals, her nine-length winning margin just behind Sun Princess (1983), Noblesse (1963), and Jet Ski Lady (1991) who won their editions of the classic by twelve lengths, ten lengths and ten lengths respectively. The Group 2 Ribblesdale Stakes winner and second, Frankly Darling and Ennistymon, finished third and second this time. However, two listed-race placings were all the latter could manage in six subsequent outings, whereas Frankly Darling finished well-beaten in the Yorkshire Oaks and all but tailed off at Ascot in October. Fourth-placed Queen Daenerys finished first past the post in a listed race over fourteen furlongs at ParisLongchamp in September only to fail the post-race test. The tailed-off Gold Wand picked up a listed-race win later, but it was the Aidan O'Brien-trained Passion (fifth) who emerged as the best of the beaten horses in the race, going on to become a classic-placed pattern winner. She is reviewed in *Volume 2: Great Britain & Ireland's Group 2 & Group 3 Winners.*

Love could only beat what was put against her at Epsom and she did so with consummate ease and in race-record time. One of her five rivals in the Group 1 Darley Yorkshire Oaks finished tailed off the following month and none of the others ever looked like posing any danger, thereby giving the classic star another chance to shine. Having hit the front over three furlongs from home, she steadily pulled away from the field to pass the post five lengths clear of the staying-on Alpinista, with One Voice another two lengths behind in third. That pattern-winning filly had been a neck runner-up to Fancy Blue in the Group 1 Nassau Stakes on her previous start but disappointed later, whereas Alpinista, a listed scorer by over three lengths at ten furlongs on her previous outing, failed by only half a length to beat Antonia de Vega in the Group 3 Princess Royal Stakes a month later.

Love's pedigree was reviewed in detail in last year's annual, so a quick overview will suffice. The daughter of Galileo (by Sadler's

Wells) is the best of four stakes winners out of Pikaboo (by Pivotal). Her full sister Peach Tree won the Group 3 Stanerra Stakes over fourteen furlongs, a possible indication that Love may have stayed the St Leger distance, her full sister Flattering won the Group 3 Munster Oaks Stakes, and half-sister Lucky Kristale (by Lucky Story) won both the Group 2 Lowther Stakes and Group 2 Duchess of Cambridge Stakes over six furlong as a juvenile. Her dam's siblings include the triple seven-furlong Group 2 scorer Arabian Gleam (by Kyllachy) and stakes-winning sprinter Kimberella (by Kyllachy)—they can be described as being three-parts brothers to Pikaboo—and, in a 2020 update to the page, they also include the dam of Pogo (by Zebedee). That Charles Hills-trained grandson of Invincible Spirit (by Green Desert) finished third in the Royal Hunt Cup at Royal Ascot on his seasonal reappearance, ran away with a one-mile listed contest at Windsor eleven days later, then finished third to Persian King in the Group 1 Prix d'Ispahan over nine furlongs at Chantilly and chased home Happy Power in the Group 2 Challenge Stakes over seven furlongs at Newmarket. He is the star son of Cute (by Diktat), a mare who failed to win in four starts, all of them as a two-year-old.

The Group 3 Prix Fille de l'Air winner Skia (by Motivator) is the better of two stakes winners out of Pikaboo's winning half-sister Light Quest (by Quest For Fame), whereas their dam, Gleam of Light (by Danehill), is a winning half-sister to the dam of the Group 2-placed stakes winner Royal Alchemist (by Kingsinger). Gold Runner (by Runnett), the third dam of Love, was a half-sister to the dual 2000 Guineas star Don't Forget Me (by Ahonoora). He had also been a talented two-year-old, winning the Group 2 Champagne Stakes and Group 3 Vintage Stakes, and he sired a few Group/Grade 2 scorers from his Irish-conceived crops.

Love, a 110-rated Group 1 Moyglare Stud Stakes winner at two and 123-rated triple Group 1 star at three, is due to stay in training as a four-year-old. It is a pity that she did not get the chance to take on Enable over twelve furlongs on decent ground—I suspect the older mare would have had the edge in such an encounter—but if she's happy and well and trains on then she has the potential to take over from the now-retired Magical as one of her stable's star ten-to-twelve-furlong performers.

SUMMARY DETAILS

Bred: Coolmore
Owned: Michael Tabor & Derrick Smith & Mrs John Magnier
Trained: Aidan O'Brien
Country: Ireland
Race record: 4211013-111-
Career highlights: 5 wins inc Investec Oaks (Gr1), Qipco 1000 Guineas (Gr1), Darley Yorkshire Oaks (Gr1), Moyglare Stud Stakes (Gr1), Jockey Club of Turkey Silver Flash Stakes (Gr3), 3rd bet365 Fillies' Mile (Gr1)

LOVE (IRE) – 2017 chestnut filly

Galileo (IRE)	Sadler's Wells (USA)	Northern Dancer
		Fairy Bridge (USA)
	Urban Sea (USA)	Miswaki (USA)
		Allegretta
Pikaboo (GB)	Pivotal (GB)	Polar Falcon (USA)
		Fearless Revival
	Gleam of Light (IRE)	Danehill (USA)
		Gold Runner

LUCKY VEGA (IRE)

The juvenile class of 2020 was not as strong as in some previous years, creating the impression that the brightest stars among them may not be identified until this coming summer and autumn. However, for a few shining moments in August, Lucky Vega looked like a potential classic colt. He may still live up to that promise.

The Jessica Harrington-trained bay, yet another notable winner bred by Pat O'Kelly's famous Kilcarn Stud, is a €110,000 graduate of the Goffs November Foal Sale and joined his current connections after being sold on for €175,000 at the following autumn's Goffs Orby Sale. He made his debut at Naas in early June, beating the previously raced and subsequent stakes winner Lipizzaner by half a length. Battleground finished fifth and Laws of Indices ninth. The latter had been beaten by a total of six lengths by the winner, landed a Navan maiden on his next start and then caused quite a shock when meeting his old rival at the Curragh in mid-July. The race was the Group 2 GAIN Railway Stakes over six furlongs, the ground was yielding, and this time the margin between the pair was half a length, but in favour of the Ken Condon-trained colt. His supporters were rewarded with odds of 66/1, there were further gaps of two and three-quarter lengths and a head back to the third and fourth, Arctician and Merchants Quay, and it didn't seem like a fluke. Lucky Vega stayed on strongly in the closing stages, briefly looking as though he might get up, but his rival pulled out a bit more near the line to seal the verdict.

Then came that day in August. Surprisingly, the once-raced maiden St Mark's Basilica was sent off as favourite for the Group 1 Keeneland Phoenix Stakes, and although he would later go on to take the Group 1 Dewhurst Stakes at Newmarket, he was found wanting on this occasion, losing fourth in the final strides as Laws of Indices stayed on to beat him by a neck for that spot. But this was Lucky Vega's day and the way he pulled away from the field inside the final furlong, passing the post three and a half lengths and a short head in front of Aloha Star and The Lir Jet, was impressive. His old rival was another half a length behind, and the placings of the second and third were reversed following a stewards' enquiry. Harrington indicated in post-race interviews that the Group 1 Juddmonte Middle Park Stakes was a likely target but that she felt he'd stay seven furlongs too. He was runner-up in the former, keeping on well to the line but never quite looking like he would beat the half-length winner, Supremacy, who made all. The pair pulled two and a quarter lengths clear of Minzaal, with Tactical and The Lir Jet three-quarters of a length and a length behind in fourth and fifth. His unfortunate run in the seven-furlong Group 1 Goffs Vincent O'Brien National Stakes came between those two notable performances. He met with traffic problems at a key stage of the race and, in the circumstances, did well to finish fifth, two and a half lengths behind the impressive length-and-a-half winner, Thunder Moon. Wembley, St Mark's Basilica and Master of The Seas were the other three in front of him at the line, he and the latter pair finishing a short head, half a length and the same behind the runner-up.

Lucky Vega is a son of the dual French classic star Lope de Vega (by Shamardal), a Ballylinch Stud stallion who is well established among the best horses standing in Europe. Some of his seventy-seven stakes winners were conceived in Australia, as were three of his dozen Group 1 winners, and his overall tally includes horses who have excelled in all age groups, a few who have stayed twelve furlongs with ease, and, so far, one European Group 1 classic star. That is Phoenix of Spain, the Irish 2,000 Guineas-winning grey who covered 148 mares last year in his first season at the Irish National Stud.

Most of the best sired by Lope de Vega tend to be sprinters or milers, so the distaff side of the pedigree will be important in determining just how far Lucky Vega will stay. Here, however, there is mixed evidence. His dam, Queen of Carthage, is an unraced daughter of the Group 1-winning miler Cape Cross (by Green Desert), a stallion who got his best winners over a wide range of distances and did exceptionally well with his Epsom classic runners, for example, Golden Horn, Ouija Board, and Sea The Stars. The mare is a daughter of the Group 1 Prix de l'Opera and dual Group 2 Prix Jean Romanet winner Satwa Queen (by Muhtathir), a high-class mile-to-ten-furlong performer, and that late star—she died in 2015 at the age of thirteen—is the dam of the nine-furlong German listed scorer Important Time (by Oasis Dream). She was also a half-sister to Spadoun (by Kaldoun), who won the Group 1 Criterium de Saint-Cloud over ten furlongs a juvenile, was later successful over hurdles at Auteuil and went on to become a successful National Hunt sire. Her full brother Satwa King won a trio of two-mile handicap hurdles at Limerick and was runner-up in a similar contest over five furlongs farther at the same venue. There is clearly some stamina in the family. But has Lucky Vega inherited any of it?

Satwa Queen's siblings also include the lightly raced seven-furlong juvenile stakes winner Anbella (by Common Grounds), a mare whose progeny have tended more towards speed and whose daughter Masaya (by Dansili), a five-furlong winner who was also a twice stakes-placed winner over seven, is also producing horses who are best at under a mile, notably Gussy Mac (by Dark Angel). That now three-year-old won two of his six starts last season including a five-furlong listed contest at Sandown in July. Queen of Carthage, on the other hand, has produced two winning half-sisters to Lucky Vega, both of them sprinters. Lady Clair (by Canford Cliffs) won twice over five furlongs as a two-year-old, missed out on blacktype when fourth in the Group 2 Lowther Stakes over six, and later won a five-and-a-half-furlong contest as a three-year-old. Boston Beauties (by Zoffany) got her sole win over five furlongs on firm turf at Gulfstream Park in December of her two-year-old season.

So, a case can be made for each of three propositions: that he will be a sprinter, he will be a miler, and he will be a middle-distance horse. Lucky Vega, who finished his first season with a rating of 116 and so ranked just four pounds behind the divisional champion, St Mark's Basilica, holds entries in the Group 1 Tattersalls Irish 2,000 Guineas, Group 1 Emirates Poule d'Essai des Poulains and the Group 1 Derby Stakes. He may stay both distances and even improve for the increased amount of ground in the last-named classic, but it's not guaranteed, and it is even possible on pedigree that he may ultimately prove best at six and seven furlongs. Finding out will be an interesting journey.

SUMMARY DETAILS

Bred: Kilcarn Stud
Owned: Zhang Yuesheng
Trained: Jessica Harrington
Country: Ireland
Race record: 12102-
Career highlights: 2 wins inc Keeneland Phoenix Stakes (Gr1), 2nd Juddmonte Middle Park Stakes (Gr1), GAIN Railway Stakes (Gr2)

LUCKY VEGA (IRE) – 2018 bay colt

Lope de Vega (IRE)	Shamardal (USA)	Giant's Causeway (USA)
		Helsinki (GB)
	Lady Vettori (GB)	Vettori (IRE)
		Lady Golconda (FR)
Queen of Carthage (USA)	Cape Cross (IRE)	Green Desert (USA)
		Park Appeal
	Satwa Queen (FR)	Muhtathir (GB)
		Tolga (USA)

MAC SWINEY (IRE)

This is one of the most intriguing members of the new classic generation and it would be no surprise to see him win at the highest level again in 2021.

Yet another horse of note bred by the great Irish trainer Jim Bolger, the first indication that most of us had that he is regarded as the stable's Derby horse came after he won his maiden at the Curragh in mid-July. It was his second start—he had finished a four-length fifth to Hudson River over the same course and distance three weeks before—and he looked full of promise in beating Wembley by a length and a half. The runner-up had finished third in that prior Curragh race and went on to become one of the highest-rated juveniles in Europe. The pair appeared to have the race to themselves two out, the chestnut headed the front-running bay over half a furlong from home and went clear in the closing stages. Colour Sergeant stayed on strongly inside the final furlong to finish a closing half-length third and there was a gap of three and a half lengths back to the fourth, Hms Seahorse (it is registered this way with Weatherbys and not as you'd expect to see, HMS Seahorse). It was in post-race interviews that assistant trainer Una Manning mentioned that this was Bolger's Derby horse.

Two of the colt's next three runs were disappointing: ninth to Military Style in the Group 3 Japan Racing Association Tyros Stakes and eighth to Thunder Moon in the Group 1 Goffs Vincent O'Brien National Stakes. They are his only races so far on good ground—his winning form has been on yielding, soft and heavy—but in an interview published in *The Irish Field* at the end of October, Bolger told journalist Daragh Ó Conchúir that those defeats "would be my problem, not the horse's problem" and added: "I wasn't sure and I'm still not sure why but I do know that it has nothing to do with the ground". Words worth keeping in mind the next time we see the colt running on good ground; do not discount him because of the underfoot conditions.

The winning run between those two disappointments was in the Group 2 Galileo Irish EBF Futurity Stakes over seven furlongs on soft at the Curragh in August. Ontario tried to make all and still had his head in front about a quarter of a furlong to go when Cadillac, to his right, and Mac Swiney, to his left, moved past him. The margins were half a length and the same, Snapraeterea was another length and a half back in fourth and they were clear of the rest, who included the subsequent Group 1 scorer Van Gogh (sixth).

His final outing came on Saturday, October 24th, an afternoon that must be one of the most remarkable in Bolger's lengthy career. The Mark Johnston-trained Gear Up won the Group 1 Criterium de Saint-Cloud a few minutes before Mac Swiney won the Group 1 Vertem Futurity Trophy Stakes at Doncaster, and within the hour Flying Visit had taken the Group 3 Eyrefield Stakes. Both Gear Up and his sire, Teofilo (by Danehill), were bred by Bolger, who trained the stallion to be champion two-year-old. He also bred both of Mac Swiney's parents, his broodmare sire and maternal grandam, and not only bred and trains Flying Visit but bred and trained that colt's dam, Fionnuar, and broodmare sire, Teofilo, too.

Eight went to post for the Doncaster race, with Godolphin's One Ruler, who had beaten Van Gogh by nearly two lengths in the Group 3 Emirates Autumn Stakes over the trip at Newmarket a fortnight earlier, sent off favourite. Listed winner Cobh, who had finished third to New Mandate in the Group 2 Royal Lodge Stakes on his most recent start, set off in front and was not headed until about two out when Baradar, racing towards the centre of the track, took over. One Ruler, closest to the rails, and Mac Swiney, to that colt's left, were staying on. The long-time leader weakened inside the final furlong, Mac Swiney closed on Baradar and then moved past him with ease. One Ruler stayed on into second, with the final margins being three-quarters of a length and two and a quarter lengths. Cobh was one and three-quarter lengths behind in fourth and there was four-length gap back to others, headed by State of Rest.

That race has been the number-one trial for the 2000 Guineas in recent seasons with the 2017, 2018 and 2019 editions going to Saxon Warrior, Magna Grecia, and Kameko respectively. In the past it was always regarded as being a Derby trial. Kingston Hill, who won the race in 2013, went on to be runner-up at Epsom and won the St Leger, whereas Camelot, in 2011, is the most recent winner of this race to go on to add the Derby the following year. He also won the 2000 Guineas and was runner-up in the St Leger while bidding for the Triple Crown.

Mac Swiney is a son of New Approach (by Galileo), the unbeaten juvenile champion who was runner-up to Henrythenavigator in both the 2000 Guineas and Irish 2,000 Guineas but won the Derby and Irish Champion Stakes before trouncing ten rivals in the Champion Stakes at Newmarket by six lengths and more. He was trained by Bolger and is out of Park Express (by Ahonoora), whom Bolger trained to win the Phoenix Champion Stakes, but was bred by Lodge Park Stud. The Dalham Hall Stud stallion is now sixteen, he covered only forty-eight mares last season and has been listed as private for 2021. His fifty-five stakes winners include eight who have won at the highest level, notably the classic-winning miler Dawn Approach (bred and trained by Bolger; blacktype sire now at Redmondstown Stud), Derby hero Masar (covered 147 mares at Dalham Hall Stud; first foals in 2021) and Oaks winner Talent (dam of 2020's Group 1-placed French Group 2 scorer Ambition, by Dubawi).

Like Dawn Approach, last season's unrelated Group 1-placed dual Group 2 winner Magic Lily showed more speed than stamina, in her case despite being out of the dual Oaks heroine Dancing Rain (by Danehill Dancer). However, Mac Swiney is inbred 2x3 to Galileo (by Sadler's Wells) and you would imagine that must boost his prospects of being one of his sire's middle-distance horses. His eldest half-brother Slaney Street (by Intense Focus) is not in the same league but has won over eight and ten furlongs and been a one-length runner-up over an extended thirteen furlongs in Ireland. That said, it would not be a surprise to see the younger colt perform with credit over a mile before stepping up to the Derby distance.

He is the fourth foal of Halla Na Saoire (by Teofilo), his now two-year-old half-brother has been named Quavering (by Vocalised) and his dam was bred to young classic sire Make Believe (by Makfi) in 2020. The mare was unraced but her full brother Light Heavy won the Group 2 Derrinstown Stud Derby Trial Stakes and Group 3 Ballysax Stakes and finished third to

Camelot in the Group 1 Irish Derby in 2012. Their half-sister Halla Siamsa (by Montjeu) is the winning dam of three blacktype horses, most notably the Group 1 Dewhurst Stakes winner Parish Hall (by Teofilo), who is inbred 3x3 to Sadler's Wells (by Northern Dancer). He went on to add the Group 3 Meld Stakes, Group 3 Diamond Stakes and two editions of the Listed Alleged Stakes, he stands at Bolger's Redmondstown Stud, got off the mark as a freshman sire in 2020, had twenty-two foals last year and his 2021 crop will come from a book of thirty-two mares.

Third dam Amoura (by Northfields) was unraced, fourth dam Visala (by Labus) was unplaced in three starts and fifth dam Evisa (by Dan Cupid) was unraced, but the latter had two daughters of note. Visala was a half-sister to Demia (by Abdos), who won the Group 3 Prix de Flore and Group 3 Prix Penelope, and Ezana (by Ela-Mana-Mou), the winning dam of stakes winner and outstanding broodmare Ebaziya (by Darshaan). Ebaziya and her descendants are remote connections of Mac Swiney, but she won the Ballysax Stakes, Trigo Stakes and Oyster Stakes, was placed in the Group 2 Blandford Stakes and Group 3 Killavullan Stakes, and she is the dam of the Group 1-stars Ebadiyla (Irish Oaks, Prix Royal-Oak), Edabiya (Moyglare Stud Stakes), Enzeli (Gold Cup) and Estimate (Gold Cup).

Mac Swiney is named in honour of the Irish patriot Terence MacSwiney, who died 100 years almost to the day of the colt's Group 1 victory. He was rated 116 at two, four pounds below the divisional champion, St Mark's Basilica, and he is a horse of considerable potential. It will be fascinating to find out just how good he will be at his peak. The Group 1 Qipco 2000 Guineas on May 1st is his first big target, but if he misses race that then stable companion Poetic Flare will take his place at Newmarket and Mac Swiney will use the Derrinstown Stud Derby Trial at Leopardstown as his springboard to Epsom.

SUMMARY DETAILS
Bred: J S Bolger
Owned: Mrs J S Bolger
Trained: Jim Bolger
Country: Ireland

Race record: 010101-
Career highlights: 3 wins inc Vertem Futurity Trophy Stakes (Gr1), Galileo Irish EBF Futurity Stakes (Gr2)

MAC SWINEY (IRE) – 2018 chestnut colt

New Approach (IRE)	Galileo (IRE)	Sadler's Wells (USA)
		Urban Sea (USA)
	Park Express	Ahonoora
		Matcher
Halla Na Saoire (IRE)	Teofilo (IRE)	Galileo (IRE)
		Speirbhean (IRE)
	Siamsa (USA)	Quest For Fame
		Amoura (SA)

MAGICAL (IRE)

Magical has been retired to stud. The same was said last year after she rounded off an outstanding four-year-old season with defeat of Addeybb in the Group 1 Qipco Champion Stakes at Ascot. It was her third Group 1 triumph among five pattern wins in 2019, she had been a Group 1 winner at three and a Group 1-placed Group 2 scorer at two, and she was heading off to the paddocks and due for a rendezvous with rising-star stallion No Nay Never (by Scat Daddy) at Coolmore Stud. That was a proposed mating of intrigue, one that could have produced a son or daughter who would be effective at anywhere from six to twelve furlongs. However, not long after last year's annual went to print, her connections announced a change of plans. She had done so well over the winter that she would instead return to training as a five-year-old. It was a brave move given all she had achieved, but it was one rewarded in style as, from seven starts, all of them in Group/Grade 1 races, she added a further three wins and four placings to her already glittering CV. Magical's final tally stands at a dozen wins and ten placings from twenty-eight starts and a total of £4,875,498 in prize money.

Only four rivals lined up against her on her much-anticipated seasonal reappearance, the Group 1 Alwasmiyah Pretty Polly Stakes over ten furlongs at the Curragh in late June. She made all and won easily, and aside from confirmation that she was clearly happy, well and in top form for her fourth year on the track, the most important thing we learned from that race was that the Jessica Harrington-trained chestnut Cayenne Pepper had trained on from two to three and could be both a classic contender and a force within the middle-distance fillies' division. The subsequent classic-placed Group 2 scorer stayed on well in the final furlong without ever looking like a threat, finishing four and a half lengths adrift of Magical but clear of the older pair Fleeting and True Self.

A month later, Magical went for another ten-furlong spin at the Curragh, this time making all to beat Sir Dragonet and Search For A Song by two and a quarter lengths and two lengths in the rescheduled Group 1 Tattersalls Gold Cup, the race run over the even ten furlongs instead of its usual extra-half-furlong distance.

The talented three-year-old Armory finished half a length back in fourth, three-quarters of a length and a length and a quarter in front of Leo de Fury and Buckhurst. The runner-up would go on to take the Group 1 Cox Plate on his next start, chased home by Armory, whereas Search For A Song would record a repeat victory in the Group 1 Irish St Leger.

August's run was at York where, in the Group 1 Juddmonte International Stakes, she raced near the rail, settled in second as Ghaiyyath made the running a few horse-widths to her right. She came under pressure over two out, got into a battle with the 2000 Guineas winner Kameko, who moved up on her inside and briefly headed her, but she stayed on as his stamina became stretched to its apparent limit and eventually passed the post three lengths behind Godolphin's star, who made all. Lord North was a length and a quarter back in third, three-quarters of a length in front of Kameko. Rose of Kildare, the only other runner, was outclassed and yet this tough pattern winner was far from disgraced given that she crossed the line just under three lengths behind Kameko.

The Group 1 Irish Champion Stakes at Leopardstown the following month, the jewel of the opening day of Irish Champions Weekend, attracted a small but select field of four Group 1-stars plus two Group 2 winners, and it promised to be one of the races of the year. Leo de Fury was outclassed and trailed home a never-dangerous last. He was gelded soon afterwards having managed to beat only one rival in three races since his impressive three-length defeat of Fleeting in the Group 2 Mooresbridge Stakes in June. Japan also disappointed, the previous year's Derby third, Arc fourth and dual Group 1 star seemingly no longer the force of old. He was eased near the finish when his chance was gone. Up front, Ghaiyyath had again set out to make all but this time Magical did not give him as easy a time at the front as he had at York. There was only about a neck between them as they swung into the straight, both of them under pressure and with Japan still in with a chance on the inside. He weakened as Armory and Sottsass were running on strongly in a fight for third that the three-year-old ultimately won by a short-head, but Ghaiyyath and Magical likely didn't notice. They were locked together in a battle that would surely have had the crowds on their feet and roaring had this not been a behind-closed-doors Covid-year with empty stands. Magical finally started to get the better of her rival about half a furlong out, albeit with barely a fluctuating head advantage, until finally it became a neck, half a length and then, at the line, three-quarters of a length. Armory and Sottsass were a length and a quarter farther behind.

One can speculate as to why Ghaiyyath failed to run up to the peak he had shown previously, and with no disrespect to a talented colt who could improve to become a force in the older-horse division in 2021, that Armory could finish so close to him at the line that day was a clear reflection that the multiple Group 1-star had performed below his best. Horses are not machines, far from it, and to finish runner-up to Magical in Ireland takes nothing away from his own glittering record. This was her day, arguably her finest hour, and it put her name in the record books along with Dylan Thomas as the only dual winners of the Irish Champion Stakes.

Magical was sent off the favourite for each of her final three starts but had to settle for minor honours in them all. She had Derby winner Serpentine three and a half lengths behind in the Group 1 Qipco Champion Stakes on soft ground at Ascot in October but was two and a half lengths and half a length away from victory, beaten by Addeybb and Skalleti. The turf was firm at Keeneland in November and she ran another fine race, again keeping on to the line, but this was Tarnawa's day. The Dermot Weld-trained four-year-old won by a length to complete her top-level hat-trick. Channel Maker was a nose away in third, followed by Lord North and Mogul, who were one and three-quarter lengths and a head back in fourth and fifth. It was then on to Hong Kong where, in mid-December, she finished a staying-on third to the Japanese pair Normcore and Win Bright in the Group 1 Longines Hong Kong Cup over ten furlongs at Sha Tin. The margins were three-quarters of a length and a short head, with another Japanese runner, Danon Premium, a length and a quarter behind in fourth.

There were suggestions after that race that Magical might stay in training as a six-year-old, but it wasn't long before the decision was made. She would not race again.

Magical's pedigree was reviewed in detail in both the 2018 and 2019 editions of *European Group 1 Winners*, so just a quick recap will suffice. The daughter of Galileo (by Sadler's Wells) is a full sister to Rhododendron, who won the Group 1 Fillies' Mile at two, Group 1 Prix de l'Opera at three and Group 1 Lockinge Stakes as a four-year-old. Their dam, Halfway To Heaven (by Pivotal), was also a multiple Group 1 star, sweeping the Irish 1,000 Guineas, Nassau Stakes and Sun Chariot Stakes in 2008, and the mare is a half-sister to a pair of pattern-winning sprinters: Tickled Pink (by Invincible Spirit) and Theann (by Rock of Gibraltar). The latter is also notable as being the dam of the US mile Grade 1 winner Photo Call (by Galileo) and the Group 2 Richmond Stakes scorer Land Force (by No Nay Never), who covered 155 mares in his debut season at Highclere Stud in 2020. His sire, his precocity and speed, and his relationship to the classic-placed Group 3 Coventry Stakes winner and Group 1 sire Verglas (by Highest Honor) will have contributed to his popularity. Land Force's half-sister, the Group 2 King Stand Stakes and Group 2 Temple Stakes winner and Group 1 July Cup runner-up Cassandra Go (by Indian Ridge), is the grandam of Magical.

There are plenty more good horses to be found in the family, including the Group 1 Melbourne Cup winner Cross Counter (by Teofilo), but what's in the first two generations of it is more than enough to illustrate why Magical is one of the most exciting additions to the broodmare ranks in recent years. There have been racemares who have been better than her but few who can rival her blend of class, consistency, durability and toughness. Many stars of the track have failed to live up to hopes or expectations at stud, just as happens with the colts, but with her pedigree and connections it will be a huge disappointment if she fails to produce at least one son or daughter of note.

SUMMARY DETAILS
Bred: Orpendale, Chelston & Wynatt
Owned: Derrick Smith
Trained: Aidan O'Brien
Country: Ireland
Race record: 211244-414012-111222101-1121323-

Career highlights: 12 wins inc Qipco Champion Stakes (Gr1), Qipco Irish Champion Stakes (Gr1-twice), Tattersalls Gold Cup (Gr1-twice), Qipco British Champions Fillies & Mares Stakes (Gr1), Alwasmiyah Pretty Polly Stakes (Gr1), Coolmore Highland Reel Irish EBF Mooresbridge Stakes (Gr2), Kilboy Estate Stakes (Gr2), Breast Cancer Research Debutante Stakes (Gr2), Alleged Stakes (Gr3), 2nd Juddmonte International Stakes (Gr1), Longines Breeders' Cup Turf (Gr1-twice), Prince of Wales's Stakes (Gr1), Coral-Eclipse Stakes (Gr1), Darley Yorkshire Oaks (Gr1), Moyglare Stud Stakes (Gr1), 3rd Qipco Champion Stakes (Gr1), Longines Hong Kong Cup (Gr1)

MAGICAL (IRE) – 2015 bay mare

Galileo (IRE)	Sadler's Wells (USA)	Northern Dancer
		Fairy Bridge (USA)
	Urban Sea (USA)	Miswaki (USA)
		Allegretta
Halfway To Heaven (IRE)	Pivotal (GB)	Polar Falcon (USA)
		Fearless Revival
	Cassandra Go (IRE)	Indian Ridge
		Rahaam (USA)

MISHRIFF (IRE)

Mishriff was one of Europe's top three-year-olds last season and he looks sure to prove a popular stallion when the time comes for him to take up such a role. The John Gosden-trained bay comes from a family that already has a number of its sons at various stages of their stud careers, a list that ranges from a leading international sire of renown to a celebrity who will be covering his first book of mares in 2021.

All of his juvenile runs were on heavy ground, including the Nottingham maiden he won by ten lengths that November, but he has since proved that he can go on any type of turf. He has also tried dirt and was runner-up in the valuable Saudi Derby over a mile on a fast track at Riyadh on his seasonal reappearance at the end of February, chasing home the Japanese colt Full Flat and with the subsequent 1000 Guineas fourth Final Song almost two lengths behind in third. He ran four times after returning home, winning three in a row but going out on a disappointing note when, having run keenly, he finished down the field behind Addeybb in the Group 1 Qipco Champion Stakes at Ascot in mid-October.

The first leg of his hat-trick came in a ten-furlong contest at Newmarket in early June. He had the benefit of a prior run, albeit four months before, but the impression he gave in beating Volkan Star and Waldkonig by four lengths and a neck was that he won strictly on merit; he was simply the best horse on the day. He had been in front fully three furlongs from home and although he went left over a furlong out, he was already well clear of his closest pursuers. Both the runner-up and fifth, Al Aasy, who finished ten and a half lengths behind the winner, would go on to pattern success.

Rather than step to the full Derby distance, the colt was kept at ten furlongs with the exception of his next start, the Group 1 Prix du Jockey Club (French Derby) at Chantilly which is over an extra half furlong. The ground had been soft at Newmarket, it was good-to-soft here, and despite meeting with some traffic problems in the final quarter mile, he stayed on strongly in the closing stages, hitting the front about half a furlong to go and winning the classic by margins of one and three-quarter lengths and a neck from The Summit and Victor Ludorum. That pair had been the first two home in the Group 1 Poule d'Essai des Poulains (French 2000 Guineas) a month before, separated then by a length and a half although in reverse order.

The first three met again at Deauville the following month for what is often said to be the most prestigious Group 2 race in France, the Prix Guillaume d'Ornano. This time the ground was heavy, Mishriff hit the front over a quarter of a mile from home and stayed on well to score by four and a half lengths. The Summit, who had led in the early stage and raced separate from the others for part of the race, outstayed Victor Ludorum for second, beating him by a head this time around, whereas Dream Works, the only other runner, who had led after two furlongs until about three from home, weakened and was eased, trailing in a dozen lengths adrift.

The 120-rated colt is best judged on his two French wins and not his Ascot run. He is a first-crop son of Make Believe (by Dubawi), the Group 1 Poule d'Essai des Poulains and Group 1 Prix de la Foret star who also raced in the same colours though was trained by André Fabre. The young Ballylinch Stud stallion has been represented by five stakes winners so far and his quartet of pattern-race scorers include Rose of Kildare, who is reviewed in *Volume 2: Great Britain & Ireland's Group 2 & Group 3 Winners.*

Mishriff is the third foal and third blacktype horse out of Contradict (by Raven's Pass); an excellent start for the mare. Orbaan (by Invincible Spirit), his eldest sibling, won a one-mile listed contest in France, whereas Momkin (by Bated Breath) has come close to blacktype success a couple of times. He was a neck runner-up to Suedois in the Group 3 Supreme Stakes and to Skardu in the Group 3 Craven Stakes and has also been placed in the Group 3 Thoroughbred Stakes and Listed Sir Henry Cecil Stakes; both of those mile contests were won by Duke of Hazzard. The mare was bred to Invincible Spirit (by Green Desert) in 2018 and to Frankel (by Galileo) in 2019 but there are no returns listed from either covering. She returned to Frankel last year.

Contradict was also a likely candidate to produce at least one notable runner given that she is a winning daughter of Acts of

Grace (by Bahri), the Group 3 Princess Royal Stakes-winning half-sister to Invincible Spirit, Sadian (by Shirley Heights), Massarra (by Danehill) and Kodiac (by Danehill). The first-named of those is well-known as being a leading international sire and long-time flag bearer at the Irish National Stud, whereas the last-named on that list is the pattern-placed horse who Tally-Ho Stud developed into a multiple Group 1 and much-in-demand sire, especially among those seeking to breed two-year-old and sprint talent. Sadian won the Group 3 John Porter Stakes and Group 3 Ormonde Stakes, quite a contrast to the juvenile listed success and Group 2 Prix Robert Papin-second of Massarra, a filly who went on to become a broodmare of note. Her daughter Nayarra (by Cape Cross) won the Group 1 Gran Criterium and juvenile champion filly title in Italy, Gustav Klimt (by Galileo) was a classic-placed juvenile Group 2 scorer before joining the Coolmore stallion team—first yearlings will be on offer in 2021—and he has a trio of stakes-winning full sisters plus a Group 1-placed brother.

Just the above would be more than enough to highlight why Mishriff had the potential to become a high-class racehorse and that he could have a busy stallion career ahead of him someday, but there is plenty more of note on the page. Rafha (by Kris), his grandam, won the Group 1 Prix de Diane (French Oaks) and has five half-sisters of note. Chiang Mai (by Sadler's Wells) was the one who excelled on the track and that Group 3 Blandford Stakes winner is the dam of the Group 1 Pretty Polly Stakes heroine Chinese White (by Dalakhani). Stakes-placed Al Anood (by Danehill) is the dam of the Group 2-winning South African champion stayer Enaad (by High Chaparral) and the dual Australian juvenile Group 1-star Pride of Dubai (by Street Cry) whose global first crop included five juvenile stakes winners in Europe in 2020. Fayfa (by Slip Anchor) was also placed in a listed race and the New Zealand-bred Contessa Vanessa (by Bullbars) is the most notable of her descendants as that great-granddaughter is a classic-placed Group 2 winner in her native land.

Wosaita (by Generous) and El Jazirah (by Kris) are the other two sisters, the latter a full sister to Rafha. Wosaita's daughter Whazzis (by Desert Prince) won a pattern race in Italy, but her

Listed Chesham Stakes winner Whazzat (by Daylami) became the dam of the Group 1-placed juvenile Group 2 scorer and young Rathbarry Stud stallion James Garfield (by Exceed And Excel), who has his first yearlings in 2021. Wosaita is also the grandam of the multiple US Grade 1-star Uni (by More Than Ready) and of Nkosikazi (by Cape Cross), who won the Group 3 Hoppings Stakes last season and so is reviewed in *Volume 2*. El Jazirah is, of course, a full sister to Rafha. Her grandson Master Carpenter (by Mastercraftsman), who won over five furlongs in early April of his juvenile year and was later a pattern scorer over nine furlongs, stands at March Hare Stud and his small first crop are now yearlings. His dam's stakes-winning half-sister Mount Elbrus (by Barathea) is the dam of Lava Flow (by Dalakhani), the stakes-winning mare who gave us the Timeform 134-rated juvenile champion and subsequent classic-placed Group 1 winner Pinatubo (by Shamardal). That Dalham Hall Stud team member is arguably the most exciting new sire in 2021.

If you go back another step on the page then you will find that Eljazzi (by Artaius), the fourth dam of Mishriff, was out of the Yorkshire Oaks runner-up Border Bounty (by Bounteous) and so was a half-sister to the classic-placed Group 2 winner Valley Forge (by Petingo), to classic-placed pattern winner and champion sire Pitcairn (by Petingo) and to their full sister Dingle Bay, the dam of the Group 1-winning stayer and successful National Hunt sire Assessor (by Niniski).

It is a family with a long and rich history of producing talented racehorses and successful stallions. Mishriff is already well-established as the former and there is every reason to hope that he will eventually go on to a notable career in the latter role. He has been given an eye-catching entry in the US$20 million Saudi Cup due to be run over nine furlongs on dirt at Riyadh in late February. A good performance in that conditions race, with a first prize of about £7.3 million and likely to attract some top US dirt runners, would open all sorts of options for the colt and it will be fascinating to see how he gets on if taking his place in the line-up.

SUMMARY DETAILS
Bred: Nawara Stud Ltd

Owned: Prince A A Faisal
Trained: John Gosden
Country: England
Race record: 431-21110-
Career highlights: 4 wins inc Prix du Jockey Club (Gr1), Prix Guillaume d'Ornano - Haras du Logis Saint-Germain (Gr2), Betfair Exchange Free Bet Streak Newmarket Stakes (L)

MISHRIFF (IRE) – 2017 bay colt

Make Believe (GB)	Makfi (GB)	Dubawi (IRE)
		Dhelaal (GB)
	Rosie's Posy (IRE)	Suave Dancer (USA)
		My Branch (GB)
Contradict (GB)	Raven's Pass (USA)	Elusive Quality (USA)
		Ascutney (USA)
	Acts of Grace (USA)	Bahri (USA)
		Rafha

MISS YODA (GER)

Miss Yoda made headlines when sharing the top position at 2018's BBAG September Yearling Sale and the €280,000 filly, who was bred by Gestüt Etzean, made headlines again in Germany in 2020 when landing the Group 1 Henkel-Preis der Diana (German Oaks) at Dusseldorf in early August. The John Gosden-trained chestnut had won the Listed Oaks Trial at Lingfield on her seasonal reappearance in early June, disappointed when down the field behind Frankly Darling in the Group 2 Ribblesdale Stakes at Ascot eleven days later and was only fourth to Al Aasy in the Group 3 Bahrain Trophy Stakes at Newmarket a month before her first international trip. Frankie Dettori took the ride in Germany, as he did on her final run both last season and in 2019, and despite failing to steer a straight course at times in the final quarter mile, the pair made all to win the classic by three-quarters of a length and a nose from Zamrud and Virginia Joy, with the Irish-trained favourite Silence Please another length and a half back in fourth.

The ground was good that day, it had been good-to-firm at Lingfield and her two one-mile wins as a juvenile had been secured on good ground at Sandown and on the Polytrack at Kempton. Her disappointing performances during the summer were on good-to-soft, it was heavy when the finished among those who were tailed off behind Wonderful Tonight in the Group 1 Qatar Prix de Royallieu over fourteen furlongs at ParisLongchamp in early October, and this suggests that she may be better suited to racing on a sound surface. Her only other race has been the Group 3 Godolphin Flying Start Zetland Stakes at Newmarket, a ten-furlong juvenile contest that has become an important late-season test in recent years. The ground there was soft and although she lost her unbeaten record that day it was by no means a poor effort. Max Vega won by three lengths and Miss Yoda finished three-quarters of a length in front of the third, Berkshire Rocco. Volkan Star (sixth) and Subjectivist (seventh) were among those further behind, but both clearly improved considerably from two to three.

Miss Yoda is one of fourteen top-level winners among the seventy-three stakes winners by the Timeform 140-rated superstar and Gilltown Stud stallion Sea The Stars (by Cape Cross). Galileo's Arc and dual classic-winning half-brother is now fifteen years old, commands a fee of €150,000 and achieved another feat of note in 2020 when becoming the paternal grandsire of the Group 1-winning miler Alpine Star (by Sea The Moon). It's one thing being an outstanding sire of racehorses but another to become a stallion of long-term impact, and although that can be done via broodmare daughters of note—he is the broodmare sire of the Irish pattern winner Love Locket (by No Nay Never)—it is through developing a potent male line that ensures his legacy. Having a Group 1 and prolific blacktype-siring horse as his first stallion son makes for an eye-catching start.

Matchmaking (by Mastercraftsman), a half-brother to Miss Yoda, won four middle-distance handicaps for the Sir Mark Prescott yard in the space of a month during the summer of 2018. They are out of Monami (by Sholokhov), a mare born during her sire's days being aimed at the flat sector, and she was a talented performer at both two and three years of age. She was trained by Andreas Wöhler, won the Group 3 Preis der Winterkönigin easily as a juvenile, went on to add the Group 2 Diana-Trial over ten furlongs at Hoppegarten, and although disappointing when finishing down the field behind Salomina in the Group 1 Preis der Diana, she bounced back to take third place in the Group 1 Premio Vittorio di Capua over a mile. That race was won by Amaron (by Shamardal), he stands at her owner-breeder's Gestüt Etzean and is the sire of her 2018-born Mahanadi, a colt who made €49,000 in Baden-Baden as a yearling. Her 2019-born Kingman (by Invincible Spirit) colt made 340,000 guineas in Newmarket as a foal and there was a full sister to Miss Yoda born in Germany on May 17th last year.

Monami, a chestnut with more white colouring on her face than her star daughter has, is a half-sister to the Group 1 Oaks d'Italia and Grade 2 Orchid Handicap winner and blacktype producer Meridiana (by Lomitas) and she is out of Monbijou (by Dashing Blade), a dual stakes-placed winner whose siblings include a listed scorer and whose relations include a few who have won at pattern level. Her fourth dam, Meernymphe (by Imperial), was a star performer in East Germany as a three-year-old in 1970, so is another of note in the family, as is Centre Divider (by Giant's Causeway), a Grade 1 Man o'War Stakes runner-up and half-brother to two stakes winners out of Meridiana. He is a successful sire in Scandinavia where his early winners include 2019's Dansk St Leger scorer and Dansk Derby runner-up Good Fella.

This combination of racing record and pedigree makes Miss Yoda a fascinating addition to the broodmare ranks.

SUMMARY DETAILS

Bred: Gestüt Etzean
Owned: Westerberg
Trained: John Gosden
Country: England
Race record: 112-10410-
Career highlights: 4 wins inc 162nd Henkel-Preis der Diana - German Oaks (Gr1), Betsafe Top Price All Runners Oaks Trial Fillies' Stakes (L), 2nd Godolphin Flying Start Zetland Stakes (Gr3)

MISS YODA (GER) – 2017 chestnut filly

Sea The Stars (IRE)	Cape Cross (IRE)	Green Desert (USA)
		Park Appeal
	Urban Sea (USA)	Miswaki (USA)
		Allegretta
Monami (GER)	Sholokhov (IRE)	Sadler's Wells (USA)
		La Meilleure
	Monbijou (GER)	Dashing Blade
		Meerdunung (GDR)

MOGUL (GB)

Mogul (by Galileo) made headlines on his first public appearance, selling for 3,400,000 guineas from Book 1 of 2018's Tattersalls October Yearling Sale in Newmarket. It was no surprise that he made a seven-figure sum or that Coolmore had bought him. He had a top-class though unlucky full sister and two pattern-winning full brothers, the latter pair trained by Aidan O'Brien. One of them had won the Group 2 Beresford Stakes narrowly a few days before the sale and was being spoken of as a potential classic contender, so the timing was perfect. Now, more than two years later, we can say that Newsells Park Stud's stakes-placed broodmare Shastye (by Danehill) is the dam of two Group 1 winners and but for a somewhat unfortunate stewarding decision would instead be among those rare gems with three.

Shastye's daughter Secret Gesture (by Galileo) was trained by Ralph Beckett and the Group 2 Middleton Stakes is the best of the three blacktype wins on her record. Her Listed Oaks Trial success at Lingfield had been achieved by ten lengths, she chased home Talent in the Group 1 Oaks at Epsom and Penelopa in the Group 1 Preis der Diana (German Oaks) at Dusseldorf, was third to Ribbons in the Group 1 Prix Jean Romanet and to The Fugue in the Group 1 Yorkshire Oaks, and if you see her on a catalogue page then you will also see a third-place finish in the Grade 1 Beverly D Stakes at Arlington. However, she had passed the post a length and a quarter and a neck clear of Watsdachances and Stephanie's Kitten in that nine-and-a-half-furlong contest, edged to her right near the finish, the move was deemed to have cost Stephanie's Kitten second place and so Secret Gesture was disqualified and placed behind that rival. She was sold to Godolphin for $3,500,000 at 2016's Keeneland November Sale and her first foal, Silent Wave (by War Front), is a stakes-placed dual six-furlong winner, now aged four.

The year-younger Maurus (by Medicean), a pattern-placed stakes winner in Australia, was followed by Group 3 winner Sir Issac Newton (by Galileo) and then a winning filly named Secret Sense (by Street Cry) who arrived three years before Shastye's second major representative, the aforementioned Beresford

Stakes winner, Japan. That colt had a disappointing season in 2020 when third to Ghaiyyath in the Group 1 Coral-Eclipse was his best performance in five starts, but he was one of Europe's top three-year-olds in 2019. Third to Anthony Van Dyck in that blanket finish to the Group 1 Derby at Epsom on his second outing of the year, he easily won the Group 2 King Edward VII Stakes at Ascot next time, followed that with a half-length defeat of Slalom in the Group 1 Grand Prix de Paris and then got the better of Crystal Ocean in a battle for the Group 1 Juddmonte International Stakes at York, beating the star older horse by a head. His final run of that season was in the Group 1 Prix de l'Arc de Triomphe when he finished an honourable fourth to Waldgeist, Enable and Sottsass.

Mogul, the tenth foal of his dam, made his debut in a one-mile maiden on yielding-to-soft ground at Gowran Park in mid-August of his juvenile season, but although sent off favourite there he was no match for the front-running Geometrical, a Jim Bolger-trained colt who was having his third start and trying the distance for the first time. He made up for that five-and-a-half-length defeat by winning easily at the Curragh sixteen days later, followed that with defeat of Sinawann in the Group 2 KPMG Champions Juvenile Stakes (registered as the Golden Fleece Stakes) at Leopardstown on the opening day of Irish Champions Weekend and then closed out his campaign with a fourth-place finish in the rescheduled Group 1 Vertem Futurity Trophy Stakes on the Tapeta at Newcastle at the start of November, won by Kameko.

The colt looked like one of the Ballydoyle team's brightest Derby prospects, but his classic year started off with disappointment. He was odds-on when finishing only fourth to Pyledriver in the Group 2 King Edward VII Stakes at Ascot and could then manage only sixth behind his stablemate Serpentine at Epsom. As a result, he was only third in the market for the six-runner Group 3 John Pearce Racing Gordon Stakes at Goodwood next time, the list headed by Derby fifth English King and Group 3 Bahrain Trophy Stakes winner Al Aasy, the latter bidding for a hat-trick. If you paused the race a furlong out, you'd likely think that the front-running Subjectivist was going to hold on and that the under-pressure Mogul might pick up second or third. But the picture changed half a furlong later, the leader's gap under a length and with Highland Chief and Mogul staying on well. The Irish colt soon went to the front and he passed the post three-quarters of a length in front of Highland Chief, with the same margin back to future Group 1 scorer Subjectivist in third. English King was nearly two lengths farther back in fourth, a head in front of the Derby runner-up, Khalifa Sat.

It was widely expected that he would follow-up in the Group 2 Sky Bet Great Voltigeur Stakes at York three weeks later but this time, having again being under pressure two out, he did not pick up as he had done at Goodwood. Pyledriver, giving three pounds to all of his rivals, was in front at that point and the colt stayed on well to the line, taking the prize by a comfortable three and a half lengths from Highland Chief, who was half a length and a head in front of Mogul and Berkshire Rocco. It was a performance that made Group 1 success look unlikely but instead he went on to win two of his remaining three starts, all of them at the highest level.

The Group 1 Juddmonte Grand Prix de Paris, run two months later than usual due to the Covid-19-related restructuring of the calendar, was run on good ground at ParisLongchamp in mid-September. The line-up included the winners of the Derby (Serpentine) and Deutsches Derby (In Swoop), but this was Mogul's day. He hit the front a furlong and a half from home, soon went clear and never looked like being caught. In Swoop, who would fill the runners-up position in the Arc the following month, a race Mogul missed due to a much-publicised contaminated feed issue, stayed on strongly to short-head Gold Trip for second, with Serpentine one and three-quarter lengths back in fourth and Highland Chief another two lengths adrift in fifth.

Only fifth to Tarnawa in the Grade 1 Longines Breeders' Cup Turf on firm ground at Keeneland in early November, Mogul ended the year on a high with a three-length defeat of Exultant in the Grade 1 Longines Hong Kong Vase at Sha Tin in mid-December, again hitting the front a furlong and a half from home before staying on strongly for victory. The Tony Cruz-trained runner-up, an Irish-bred son of Teofilo (by Galileo) who was third to Churchill in 2017's Group 1 Irish 2000 Guineas—racing then as Irishcorrespondent and trained by Michael Halford—is among the best ten-to-twelve-furlong horses ever to have raced in Hong Kong; the five-time Group 1 star has accumulated career earnings of almost £7.7 million.

Shastye's now two-year-old full sister to Mogul, Japan and Secret Gesture is a 3,400,000-guinea Tattersalls Book 1 graduate also to be trained by Aidan O'Brien. The mare was bred to both Galileo and Dubawi (by Dubai Millennium) in 2020. Her success at stud is not really a surprise and although her produce record surpasses that of her dam, Saganeca (by Sagace), that mare is also the dam of two top-level winners. Sagamix (by Linamix) won the Group 1 Prix de l'Arc de Triomphe, Arc-placed Sagacity (by Highest Honor) landed the Group 1 Criterium de Saint-Cloud, and their sibling Sage Et Jolie (by Linamix) won the Group 2 Prix de Mallaret before going on to produce the Group 1 Prix d'Ispahan scorer Sageburg (by Johannesburg) at stud. Saganeca's offspring also include Sagalina (by Linamix), who is the non-winning dam of the Group 1 Prix Saint-Alary winner Sagawara (by Shamardal), and her own racing career featured Group 2 success in the Prix de Royallieu and a Group 1 placing in the Gran Premio di Milano. Third dam Haglette (by Hagley) was out of Sucrette (by Zucchero), a winning half-sister to the King George VI and Queen Elizabeth Stakes winner and classic sire Nasram (by Nasrullah) and Irish Derby scorer Tambourine (by Princequillo), and she was a granddaughter of the Arc-placed Prix Vermeille heroine La Mirambule (by Coaraze).

Mogul has the potential to be a leading middle-distance horse again in 2021. He is reportedly to be aimed at all the major ten- and twelve-furlong races, and with his year-older brother Japan also remaining in training for another year it is possible that the pair could meet on the track. Looking further ahead, one would presume that the brothers will both get a chance at stud, so it will be interesting to see which one will develop the better long-term profile.

SUMMARY DETAILS

Bred: Newsells Park Stud
Owned: Michael Tabor, Derrick Smith & Mrs John Magnier

Trained: Aidan O'Brien
Country: Ireland
Race record: 2114-4013101-
Career highlights: 5 wins inc Longines Hong Kong Vase (Gr1),
Juddmonte Grand Prix de Paris (Gr1), KPMG Champions
Juvenile Stakes (Gr2), John Pearce Racing Gordon Stakes (Gr3),
3rd Sky Bet Great Voltigeur Stakes (Gr2)

MOGUL (GB) – 2017 bay colt

Galileo (IRE)	Sadler's Wells (USA)	Northern Dancer
		Fairy Bridge (USA)
	Urban Sea (USA)	Miswaki (USA)
		Allegretta
Shastye (IRE)	Danehill (USA)	Danzig (USA)
		Razyana (USA)
	Saganeca (USA)	Sagace (FR)
		Haglette (USA)

MOHAATHER (GB)

When Showcasing was a racehorse an examination of his pedigree suggested that he represented an emerging speed-oriented branch of his family once largely middle distance in focus. What we have seen in the past few years, however, indicates that while there is plenty of speed there it is one that is proving capable of getting plenty of milers and ten-furlong horses too. The triple Australian Group 1 star Foreteller (by Dansili) is one example. There is, therefore, no surprise that this son of Oasis Dream (by Green Desert) has emerged not only as a source of speed and precocity but as one who for whom the descriptor classic sire may apply someday. There were early signs that he was going to get some talented milers, and now, in addition to his Group 1- and classic-placed Group 2 scorers over that distance, he has supplied his first one to hit the top over that trip.

Misfortune kept us from seeing more of Mohaather. His three-year-old season was cut short by a hairline condylar stress fracture and his career ended by what was described as "significant bone bruising to his near-hind fetlock" a few weeks after his finest hour, defeat of a top-class field in the Group 1 Qatar Sussex Stakes at Goodwood in late July. He has joined Shadwell's stallion team at Nunnery Stud, with a first-season fee of £20,000, and looks sure to prove popular in his new role.

The Marcus Tregoning-trained colt was runner-up in a six-furlong Newbury maiden in late September of his juvenile year, narrowly won a Nottingham maiden over the same trip a few weeks later and then took a big step-up in class in his stride by adding the Group 3 Horris Hill Stakes over seven furlongs at Newbury on his final start of the year. He kicked off his three-year-old season with victory in the Group 3 Greenham Stakes over that same course and distance and, on heavy ground, his fifth-place to finish to King of Change in the Group 1 Queen Elizabeth II Stakes was encouraging on his return from injury. He disappointed first time out at four, when only seventh to Circus Maximus in the Group 1 Queen Anne Stakes at Ascot in June, but then swept to the front a furlong from home before trouncing San Donato by almost four lengths in the Group 2 Betfred Summer

Mile Stakes on the round course at that venue. Duke of Hazzard was a neck back in third, three-quarters of a length in front of Lord Glitters.

San Donato re-opposed at Goodwood two and a half weeks later but having looked dangerous over a furlong out he weakened quickly and played no part in the finish, eventually passing the post eight and a half lengths behind Mohaather. Circus Maximus had tried to make all but the multiple Group 1 star was unable to repel Mohaather. The dark bay encountered traffic problems in the straight and had to switch to his left, moving from an inside position to the outside of the pack. Kameko, who was racing on the rails, also ran short of room but was unable to break free and had to settle for fourth. The undefeated classic star Siskin had a good position on the outside, beside a weakening San Donato and ahead of Mohaather as the field began its charge into the final furlong. The Irish three-year-old closed rapidly on the front-running Irish four-year-old, but Mohaather went after him, was quickly upsides and then swept past. The final margins were three-quarters of a length and half a length, with Siskin passing the post two lengths in front of the unlucky Kameko, who was the same margin clear of the ill-fated Wichita.

A 110,000-guinea Tattersalls October Book 2 graduate, Mohaather was bred by Gaie Johnson Houghton and has a string of winning siblings, two of whom are of particular note. His full sister Prize Exhibit is among those who provided an early indication of their sire's potential to get top-class milers. Her wins include the Grade 2 Monrovia Handicap over six and a half furlongs but also the Grade 2 San Clemente Handicap and two Grade 3 contests, all over a mile, and she was only beaten by a total of two and a quarter lengths when finishing third in the 2015 edition of the Grade 1 Del Mar Oaks over nine furlongs. She returned briefly to the country of her birth where she was sold for 775,000 guineas at the Tattersalls December Mare Sale in 2017 to the famous Irish farm Barronstown Stud. Both of her first two foals are by the phenomenal and prolific champion sire Galileo (by Sadler's Wells), a now two-year-old filly and a yearling colt. Coolmore bought the former for 2,800,000 guineas from Tattersalls' Book 1 Sale in October.

Roodle (by Xaar) is the other notable sibling. She only won twice on the track but then became the dam of the Group 1 Queen Anne Stakes winner Accidental Agent. A son of the speedy but short-lived classic-placed Group 2 scorer Delegator (by Dansili), he was also bred by Johnson Houghton and would have been an interesting stallion prospect. However, his form at five was mixed and generally disappointing, he was gelded at the end of that year and returned to action for a quartet of disappointing runs in 2020. Roodeye (by Inchinor), the dam of Mohaather, earned her blacktype when third in the Listed Dick Poole Fillies' Stakes as a two-year-old and she is one of four blacktype earners out of the Listed Firth of Clyde Stakes runner-up Roo (by Rudimentary). Gallagher (by Bahamian Bounty), who was placed in the Group 1 Prix Morny, Group 2 Mill Reef Stakes and Group 2 Richmond Stakes, is the best of them. Two of their other siblings have added to the page by producing a stakes-placed juvenile at stud.

Roo's is a half-sister to the Group 2 Gimcrack Stakes winner Bannister (by Inchinor)—he is very closely related to Roodeye—and to Runway Dancer (by Dansili), the mare who gave us the Group 1 Middle Park Stakes winner and Group 1 Diamond Jubilee Stakes third Astaire (by Intense Focus). Her dam, Shall We Run (by Hotfoot), was out of the three-time French winner Sirnelta (by Sir Tor) and that made her a half-sister to the Group 1 Cheveley Park Stakes heroine Dead Certain (by Absalom) and to Pounelta (by Tachypous), the winning dam of the Group 3 Jersey Stakes scorer Lots of Magic (by Magic Ring). If you go back farther on the page then you will find that Finelta (by Fine Top), the winning fifth dam of Mohaather, was a full sister to 1963's Prix du Jockey Club and Grand Prix de Paris star Sanctus, the sire of Prix Jacques le Marois winner Dictus and Prix de la Foret scorer Stratege.

Details of some of Mohaather's early bookings were revealed in mid-December and his initial roster of mares will include classic heroine Ghanaati (by Giant's Causeway), South African star Majmu (by Redoute's Choice), and last season's Group 1 Falmouth Stakes and Group 1 Sun Chariot Stakes winner Nazeef (by Invincible Spirit). The list also includes Asheerah (by Shamardal), who is the stakes-placed dam of the classic-winning miler and young Derrinstown Stud stallion Awtaad (by Cape Cross), a blacktype sire as a freshman in 2020. Mohaather will be an interesting member of the freshman class of 2024 and it would not be a surprise to see him come up with some smart late-season juveniles, but his long-term potential likely lies with his three-year-olds and older horses, most of them seen to best effect in the six-to-ten-furlong range.

SUMMARY DETAILS
Bred: Mrs R F Johnson Houghton
Owned: Hamdan Al Maktoum
Trained: Marcus Tregoning
Country: England
Race record: 211-10-011-
Career highlights: 5 wins inc Qatar Sussex Stakes (Gr1), Betfred Summer Mile Stakes (Gr2), Watership Down Stud Greenham Stakes (Gr3), Molson Coors (Horris Hill) Stakes (Gr3)

MOHAATHER (GB) – 2016 bay colt

Showcasing (GB)	Oasis Dream (GB)	Green Desert (USA)
		Hope (IRE)
	Arabesque (GB)	Zafonic (USA)
		Prophecy (IRE)
Roodeye (GB)	Inchinor (GB)	Ahonoora
		Inchmurrin
	Roo (GB)	Rudimentary (USA)
		Shall We Run (GB)

NAZEEF (GB)

History will remember Invincible Spirit (by Green Desert) as an influential sire. The Irish National Stud resident, now aged twenty-four, has sired twenty Group/Grade 1 scorers among an overall tally of 131 stakes winners, his growing band of sons at stud includes Kingman, Lawman and Mayson, each of whom sired a Group 1 winner in 2020, and his daughters have produced winners at all levels too. Hamdan Al Maktoum's Nazeef was the stallion's only top-level winner in Europe during the latest season, but she achieved the feat twice and, now a five-year-old, has joined her owner-breeder's powerful broodmare band.

Unlike most notable runners by her sire, Nazeef did not race as a two-year-old, instead making her debut in early June of her three-year-old season. She finished third that day, in a seven-furlong contest on the July Course in Newmarket but won a maiden over the course and distance almost three weeks later and followed that with clear-cut wins in four-runner contests over a mile at Chelmsford and the Rowley Mile course at Newmarket. Her pattern potential was evident when she beat classic and Group 1 heroine Billesdon Brook by three-quarters of a length in a listed race at Kempton last June, promise she fulfilled just thirteen days later.

The race was the Group 2 Duke of Cambridge Stakes over the straight mile at Royal Ascot, but it was not a strong one for the grade and it was weakened further with Magic Lily, Lavender's Blue and Jubiloso, all joint top-rated on 110, disappointing on the day. Nazeef had to fight for her victory, eventually getting her head in front on the line from the 100-rated stakes winner Agincourt who had made her bid for glory over a furlong out. The pair finished two and a half lengths in front of Queen Power, that filly was the same margin clear of the 125/1 Iconic Choice, with the next one across the line, almost three lengths farther adrift, being the 66/1 Posted. That quartet of beaten fillies would go on to notch up only two wins and four placings from nineteen starts, the better win being a one-mile listed success for Posted at Sandown in mid-September. Nazeef, on the other hand, recorded two Group 1 wins and a Group 1 placing from five subsequent outings, demonstrating that the best horse in the Ascot race was the one who won.

She extended her winning sequence to six when coming out on top in a blanket finish for the Group 1 Tattersalls Falmouth Stakes on soft ground. This time, Agincourt (fifth) was three and a half lengths adrift. Terebellum, who had failed by only a head to beat Circus Maximus in the Group 1 Queen Anne Stakes on her previous start, tried to make all. Nazeef looked the strongest challenger as they passed the furlong post, with former classic star Billesdon Brook staying on to the leader's left and One Master needing a gap just behind. That multiple Group 1-winning seven-furlong specialist was switched right about half a furlong out, coming wide of Nazeef, and all four ran on strongly to the line. Nazeef got there a neck in front of Billesdon Brook and with margins of a neck and half a length back to Terebellum and One Master.

Three weeks later, she tried ten furlongs for the first time and although unable to make it seven-in-a-row, it was a good effort. Seven fillies and mares lined up for the Group 1 Qatar Nassau Stakes at Goodwood, with the Japanese-trained Deirdre bidding for a repeat victory, but the Aidan O'Brien runner Magic Wand was sent off as favourite. That pair disappointed, finishing seventh and fifth respectively. Magic Wand had tried to make all but tired in the final furlong, although both the top prize and the runners-up one went to Ireland anyway. The Donnacha O'Brien-trained Fancy Blue, who went to the front a furlong out, held off the determined challenge of Jessica Harrington's representative One Voice, winning by a neck and so adding to her victory twenty-five days before in the Group 1 Prix de Diane (French Oaks). One Voice had taken a pattern contest at Leopardstown the previous month, and she is reviewed in *Volume 2: Great Britain & Ireland's Group 2 & Group 3 Winners*. That filly, who disappointed on her two runs post Goodwood, passed the post two and three-quarter lengths clear of the staying-on Nazeef. Queen Power and Magic Wand were a neck and a length farther back.

Nazeef tried the distance again the following month but this time, on soft ground at Deauville, she appeared not to stay. An odds-on favourite for the Group 1 Darley Prix Jean Romanet, she was under pressure from under two out, soon weakened and finished only ninth as the subsequent Breeders' Cup heroine Audarya beat the regally bred Ambition by a neck. It was no surprise to see her drop back to a mile for her final two starts, and although she finished in mid-field behind The Revenant in the Group 1 Queen Elizabeth II Stakes at Ascot on her final run, she won the Group 1 Kingdom of Bahrain Sun Chariot Stakes at Newmarket a fortnight before. The ground was heavy—the underfoot conditions were put forward as an explanation for the last-place finish of the classic scorer Peaceful—five of the dozen competitors had won at the highest level previously, and Nazeef's proven ability to stay a bit farther likely helped. The field had split into two groups but came back together about a quarter of a mile from home, Jim Crowley sent his mount to the front a furlong out and she stayed on well to beat Half Light by a length and a half. The pair had been racing on opposite sides of the field, Nazeef near the rails and the French filly in the centre of the course, but the latter moved left in the final furlong while making her challenge, passing the post a neck in front of Cloak of Spirits but a length and a half behind Nazeef. Champers Elysees ran on for fourth, another half-length back, with Terebellum fifth and Lady Bowthorpe running a big race to take sixth. Both the second (to Watch Me in the Prix Rothschild) and third (to Love in the 1000 Guineas) had been placed at the top level previously, whereas the fourth had won the Group 1 Matron Stakes on good ground at Leopardstown on her previous start.

Nazeef has now been retired to stud and it was announced in mid-December that she would be among the book of mares covered by Shadwell's Group 1-winning miler Mohaather (by Showcasing) in his first season at Nunnery Stud. The resulting foal will be inbred 4x3 to Green Desert (by Danzig) with additional duplications that include 5x5 to Doubly Sure (by Reliance II) and 5x5 to Warning (by Known Fact). We only count inbreeding that occurs within the first five generations, but it catches the eye that this foal will also carry crosses of 4x7 to Ahonoora (by Lorenzaccio) and 5x6 to Dancing Brave (by Lyphard). There is nothing particularly unusual in any of that, and no real evidence to suggest that there are any magical inbreeding formulae. It is what the various relations of the mare have achieved on the track and/or at stud that speak of their potential, and in her case, there is plenty there to suggest that she could become a broodmare of note.

She is the third foal of Handassa (by Dubawi), a mile stakes winner who had a Dark Angel (by Acclamation) colt last year before being bred to Frankel (by Galileo), and who has two talented 'uncles'. Desert Stone (by Fastnet Rock), who has been Grade 1-placed over a mile, won the Grade 2 San Gabriel Stakes over nine furlongs at Santa Anita last January, whereas his older full brother Euginio was first past the post in the Group 3 Darley Stakes over that same trip in 2018. Surprisingly, that horse has appeared on at least one 2020 catalogue page as a winner of that race despite having been disqualified after failing the post-race test; he is only a Group 3-placed winner and not a blacktype scorer.

Their dam, Starstone (by Diktat), died at the age of thirteen but was an unraced half-sister to the Group 1-winning sprinters Goodricke and Pastoral Pursuits. The full brothers are sons of Bahamian Bounty (by Cadeaux Genereux), won the Sprint Cup and July Cup respectively, but had had quite differing success at stud. Goodricke disappointed—he stood in England, Italy and Germany with only modest results—whereas long-time National Stud resident Pastoral Pursuits, now in his fourth season at Norton Grove Stud, has sired a long list of multiple and prolific winners of whom four have won at pattern level and nine in listed company. They include last season's Group 3 Renaissance Stakes scorer Ventura Rebel, a Richard Fahey-trained colt who is reviewed in *Volume 2*. Star (by Most Welcome), the third dam of Nazeef, died at the age of eleven but was a winning half-sister to the speedy pair Superstrike (by Superlative) and Four-Legged Friend (by Aragon) and to the dam of Sweet Lilly (by Tobougg), a dual mile stakes winner who also won a listed contest over the extended ten furlongs at York and was a neck runner-up to Passage of Time in the Group 3 Musidora Stakes over that course and distance.

All of this makes Nazeef a promising addition to the broodmare ranks, and although a dual Group 1 star over a mile, she has the potential to produce her best winners at anywhere from six to ten furlongs, and depending on their sire, possibly even a little farther.

SUMMARY DETAILS

Bred: Shadwell Estate Company Ltd
Owned: Hamdan Al Maktoum
Trained: John Gosden
Country: England
Race record: -3111-1113010-
Career highlights: 7 wins inc Kingdom of Bahrain Sun Chariot Stakes (Gr1), Tattersalls Falmouth Stakes (Gr1), Duke of Cambridge Stakes (Gr2), EBF/Unibet Snowdrop Fillies' Stakes (L), 3rd Qatar Nassau Stakes (Gr1)

NAZEEF (GB) – 2016 bay filly

Invincible Spirit (IRE)	Green Desert (USA)	Danzig (USA)
		Foreign Courier (USA)
	Rafha	Kris
		Eljazzi
Handassa (GB)	Dubawi (IRE)	Dubai Millennium (GB)
		Zomaradah (GB)
	Starstone (GB)	Diktat (GB)
		Star (GB)

ONE MASTER (GB)

One Master is effective from six furlongs to a mile but has excelled over seven and it is over that interim trip that she secured her place in the history books with a unique treble. On Sunday, October 4th, 2020, Lael Stables' homebred mare became the first horse ever to win the Group 1 Prix de la Foret for a third time. Much of the attention and focus during the build-up to that weekend had understandably been on Enable's hat-trick bid in the Arc, a target missed due to the heavy underfoot conditions. Luckily for the connections of One Master, she is one of those horses who can handle pretty much any turf conditions—she has never raced on an artificial or dirt track—and she fought her way to a neck victory over Earthlight to take the Qatar-sponsored test. In 2019, she had beaten City Light by half a length on very soft ground; in 2018, she short-headed Inns of Court on good ground. Her hat-trick is unique and may remain that way for a long time.

She ran seven times in 2020, finishing a half-length third to Glen Shiel in the Group 1 Qipco British Champions Sprint Stakes over six furlongs on soft ground at Ascot on her final start, just thirteen days after ParisLongchamp, and she made the frame in five.

She was only sixth to Hello Youmzain in the Group 1 Diamond Jubilee Stakes on her seasonal reappearance at the Royal Ascot meeting in June then met with some traffic problems before running on well to take fourth in the Group 1 Tattersalls Falmouth Stakes. That mile on soft ground was a test of her often-doubted stamina, but she was only beaten by margins of a neck, neck and half a length by Nazeef, Billesdon Brook and Terebellum and finished two and a half lengths clear of the fifth, Agincourt. She may have been best at seven, but she stayed a mile. The Group 3 Saint Clair Oak Tree Stakes was so close to being an unfortunate loss but, racing on the inside near the rail, she was finally able to edge left and find a gap, quickened up and just got there in the final stride. Short-head runner-up Valeria Messalina was a length in front of Althiqa—both of them three-year-olds—followed home by the talented five-year-olds Breathtaking Look and Anna Nerium.

Her performance in the Group 2 Sky Bet City of York Stakes next time was a shade disappointing. She only finished three-quarters of a length in front of Queen Jo Jo at level weights—a talented filly but some way below One Master's standard at their best—and was unable to catch Safe Voyage. He found a rich vein of form in 2020 and this day was one of his best as he made all and won going away by three and a half lengths. However, the pace he set was not a strong one, the race turned into a sprint and so the final margins were not necessarily an accurate reflection of the relative merits of eight runners.

Three weeks later, the mare almost won the Group 2 bet 265 Park Stakes at Doncaster. The Roger Varian-trained Molatham and the Aidan O'Brien-trained Wichita were fighting for the lead at the furlong pole, closely pursued to their right by Urban Icon and with One Master making her bid to their left. Within half a furlong the picture changed quickly as the Ballydoyle colt began to assert and looked briefly like he might be set for a clear-cut victory. However, the mare was staying on strongly, the pair drew level in the final few yards and the three-year-old was only a short-head in front as the pair hit the line. Molatham was another two lengths back in third, a neck ahead of Urban Icon. Former Group 1 star Limato was another two lengths behind in fifth on what was the final race of his long career. Sadly, it was also to be the final time we would see the winner in action as he failed to recover from surgery for an injury sustained shortly after he arrived in Australia where he had a few potential big-race targets; he would likely have made a popular stallion in Europe someday.

One Master would run twice more before retiring to the paddocks; her aforementioned record-breaking third victory in the Group 1 Prix de la Foret followed her third-place finish at Ascot. Her win in France required a further demonstration of her determination as Earthlight and old rival Safe Voyage proved worthy foes. Earthlight had gone to the front before they had gone a quarter of a mile and the dual Group 1 star, running for the final time before taking up stallion duties at Kildangan Stud, remained there until inside the final half furlong. He fought to the line but the mare was too strong and, with Pierre-Charles Boudot in the saddle, as he had been on six previous occasions, she won by a neck. The staying-on Safe Voyage was a short head back in third and finished a length and a half and a neck in front of the three-year-olds Tropbeau and Rubaiyat.

A trip to the Breeders' Cup was put forward after the race as being a potential seasonal finale for her but the Group 1 Qipco British Champions Sprint Stakes would come first. The ground was soft and she finished a staying-on half-length third as Glen Shiel and Brando hit the line only a nose apart. Art Power and Oxted were only half a length and a nose behind in fourth and fifth. She travelled to Keeneland for the Grade 1 Breeders' Cup Mile in early November but missed the engagement having shown signs of a muscle issue shortly after her arrival. A trip to Hong Kong in December was then reportedly under consideration as an alternative potential swansong but, in mid-November, that was ruled out and her retirement announced. The triple Group 1-star with seven wins and eight placings from twenty-three starts and almost £940,000 in prize money, a mare who did not make her debut until mid-August of her three-year-old season, is to reside at New England Stud.

One Master's pedigree was reviewed in detail in the 2018 and 2019 editions of *European Group 1 Winners*, so a brief recap will suffice now. She is by the Australian champion sire and long-time Coolmore Stud reverse-shuttler Fastnet Rock (by Danehill), a stallion whose daughters have produced Australian stars such as Gytrash (by Lope de Vega), Santa Ana Lane (by Lope de Vega) and Tivaci (by High Chaparral) and whose European pattern winners as a broodmare sire include the unbeaten Group 2 Beresford Stakes winner and potential 2021 classic star High Definition (by Galileo). Her dam, Enticing (by Pivotal), won the Group 3 King George Stakes and Group 3 Molecomb Stakes, she is a granddaughter of the Group 2 Flying Childers Stakes winner and Group 1 Prix de l'Abbaye runner-up Superstar Leo—Europe's juvenile filly champion of 2000—and comes from a branch of the prolific blacktype family whose Group 1 winners include the classic stars Footstepsinthesand (by Giant's Causeway) and Power (by Oasis Dream). It is going to be fascinating to see how she fares as a broodmare, and although there are no guarantees in this business, it will be disappointing if a mare of her pedigree and credentials fails to produce at least one son and/or daughter of note.

SUMMARY DETAILS
Bred: Lael Stable
Owned: Lael Stable
Trained: William Haggas
Country: England
Race record: -311-434110-432012-0412213-
Career highlights: 7 wins inc Qatar Prix de la Foret (Gr1-three times), Saint Clair Oak Tree Stakes (Gr3), Coolmore Stud Fairy Bridge Stakes (Gr3), totepool British EBF October Stakes (L), 2nd Qipco British Champions Sprint Stakes (Gr1), Tattersalls Falmouth Stakes (Gr1), Sky Bet City of York Stakes (Gr2), bet365 Park Stakes (Gr2), 3rd Qipco British Champions Sprint Stakes (Gr1), Queen Anne Stakes (Gr1), TRM Ballyogan Stakes (Gr3)

ONE MASTER (GB) – 2014 bay mare

Fastnet Rock (AUS)	Danehill (USA)	Danzig (USA)
		Razyana (USA)
	Piccadilly Circus (AUS)	Royal Academy (USA)
		Gatana (AUS)
Enticing (IRE)	Pivotal (GB)	Polar Falcon (USA)
		Fearless Revival
	Superstar Leo (IRE)	College Chapel (GB)
		Council Rock

ORDER OF AUSTRALIA (IRE)

There are many factors that come together to enable a horse to become a winner on the track and when the apparently successful formula has been found there is an obvious temptation to continue on that path. Class and distance are only two of them and sometimes a horse who has a lot of the former will perform well over trips that are within his compass but not ideal. But if he is winning or performing reasonably well in blacktype company then why change his path? I have often wondered how many individuals who were deemed to have failed to train on or to live up to their early potential were in fact horses who were instead merely running over the wrong trip. The number may be small, but for every Glen Shiel or Order of Australia we discover there are likely to be others who didn't get the chance to go a different flat route.

Both of those horses have pedigrees that could have seen them excel over middle distances, both are related to horses who hit the Group 1 target in that range more than once, and both started out on that path with some success before a change in direction. Both also have elements in their pedigree that could have produced a horse who is effective over shorter. The former dropped all the way down to sprinting, and although not quite in the same league as the brilliant Ajdal, the former juvenile star who went from an unplaced finish in the Derby to landing the Group 1 July Cup in the space of a few weeks and then added the Group 1 William Hill Sprint Championship (previously and since the Nunthorpe Stakes), he has won at the highest level over six furlongs. Order of Australia, on the other hand, has been fourth in the Irish Derby, won over that course and distance in late September, but then dropped to a mile and sprang one of the biggest top-level surprises of the year.

Given what he had achieved to that point his odds of 40/1 in the Grade 1 Breeders' Cup Mile at Keeneland in November were even a bit short, but this was his day, his trip, and there was no hint of fluke in how he went to the front in the final furlong and then held off the challenges of his stablemates Circus Maximus and Lope Y Fernandez to score by margins of a neck and three-quarters of a length. He was a four-and-three-quarter-length sixth behind the locally trained champion Golden Sixty in the Group 1 Longines Hong Kong Mile at Sha Tin the following month, which was disappointing but not a poor effort especially at a time of the year when most European horses are already on their winter break. He is a miler and it will be fascinating to see what he can achieve at the trip in 2021.

The only time he had tried that distance before his Grade 1 victory was on his sole start as a two-year-old. It was on heavy ground at Naas in early November and he finished a three-and-three-quarter-length fifth to Nobel Prize. He stepped up to ten furlongs for his three-year-old debut, wearing blinkers for the first time, and finished a two-length third to Tiger Moth in a Leopardstown maiden on fast ground. His performance in the Group 1 Dubai Duty Free Irish Derby eighteen days later appeared to confirm his status as a promising middle-distance prospect. He was under pressure a quarter of a mile from home, moved into third position but weakened in the final half furlong to pass the post a head, five lengths and a length and a quarter behind his stablemates Santiago, Tiger Moth and Dawn Patrol. Eight days later, he finished seventh to Mishriff in the Group 1 Prix du Jockey Club (French Derby) over ten and a half furlongs, beaten by a total of four and a half lengths.

He dropped to conditions level for his next two starts and won both of them by three-quarters of a length. The first was over ten and a half furlongs on the Polytrack at Dundalk and the second over twelve furlongs on good-to-yielding turf at the Curragh. They merely confirmed he had some ability while no doubt providing a confidence boost to the colt, but they were followed by a very disappointing effort on soft ground, this time in the ten-furlong Group 3 International Stakes at the Curragh. He had raced prominently in the early stages but came under pressure over three furlongs from home, weakened and was eased, finishing tailed off. That was the performance that immediately preceded his American win.

As his name suggests, this mid-February-born bay is a son of the dual Derby winner Australia (by Galileo). He represents the young Coolmore stallion's second crop and his top-level win arguably came at a crucial point in his sire's career. Many are quick to dismiss a stallion and given current fashions it is reasonable to assume that this regally bred horse may have had a challenging 2021 were it not for the results his offspring achieved on the track in the final few months of 2020. He has been represented by eleven pattern winners and five listed scorers, which is below what might have been expected of such a credentialed horse at this point of his career, and by the end of August he had two Group 2 winners, Beyond Reason and Leo de Fury, heading his roll of honour. Several of his progeny had been Group 1-placed, including Cayenne Pepper (a Group 2 winner in September) and Sir Ron Priestley in classics, but a stallion needs Group 1 winners to keep the dream alive. He now has two: Galileo Chrome won the St Leger at Doncaster almost two months before the Breeders' Cup meeting.

Order of Australia was bred by Aidan and Anne-Marie O'Brien's Whisperview Trading Ltd and he is out of Senta's Dream (by Danehill), an unraced daughter of the US Grade 1 star Starine (by Mendocino). That French-bred mare was a stakes winner over a mile in her native land before crossing the Atlantic to continue her career. She took a nine-furlong Grade 2 contest by five lengths at Saratoga, added a two-and-a-half-length score in the Grade 1 Matriarch Stakes over the same trip at Hollywood Park before going on to win the Grade 1 Breeders' Cup Filly & Mare Turf over a furlong farther at Arlington eleven months later. She beat Banks Hill by a length and a half that day; seventeen years later her granddaughter Iridessa (by Ruler of The World) would take the same race by a neck at Santa Anita.

The Breeders' Cup race was one of four that Joseph O'Brien-trained bay won at the highest level. She beat Magic Wand by two and a quarter lengths to take the Group 1 Pretty Polly Stakes, beat Hermosa by three-quarters of a length in the Group 1 Matron Stakes and defeated that same classic star by a length and a half when winning the Group 1 Fillies' Mile as a juvenile. She was well-beaten in the Group 1 Irish Oaks on her only attempt at twelve furlongs, had been fourth to Hermosa in the Group 1 Irish 1,000 Guineas and third to Billesdon Brook in the Group 1 Sun Chariot Stakes and retired to stud with over £1.56 million in prize money to her name. Iridessa, who can be described as being a three-parts sister to Order of Australia, changed hands after her retirement and her new owner, Katsumi Yoshida, sent her to No Nay Never (by Scat Daddy) in 2020.

Order of Australia has won over ten and a half and twelve furlongs, and it is possible that there could be some good prizes to be earned with him over middle-distances as a four-year-old. However, it seems that a mile on good ground or faster—it was firm at Keeneland—is what he needs to show his true ability. It will be very interesting to see how his career develops from this point and no surprise if he can make an impact in the milers' division this coming season.

SUMMARY DETAILS

Bred: Whisperview Trading Ltd
Owned: Derrick Smith, Mrs John Magnier, Michael Tabor &
      Mrs A M O'Brien
Trained: Aidan O'Brien
Country: Ireland
Race record: 0-34011010-
Career highlights: 3 wins inc FanDuel Breeders' Cup Mile presented by Permanently Disabled Jockey Fund (Gr1)

ORDER OF AUSTRALIA (IRE) – 2017 bay colt

		Sadler's Wells (USA)
Australia (GB)	Galileo (IRE)	Sadler's Wells (USA)
		Urban Sea (USA)
	Ouija Board (GB)	Cape Cross (IRE)
		Selection Board
Senta's Dream (GB)	Danehill (USA)	Danzig (USA)
		Razyana (USA)
	Starine (FR)	Mendocino (USA)
		Grisonnante (FR)

Invincible Spirit's (by Green Desert) position as one of Europe's leading sires is without question. He has also been strengthening his profile as a sire of stallion sons, some of whom have excelled and some who have disappointed. Kingman, Lawman and I Am Invincible wasted no time in establishing their merit, various others have sired stakes winners, and were it not for the emergence of Oxted, then Mayson would be on the list of those who have not lived up to expectations. Yes, he has just that Group 1 July Cup winner as a pattern scorer among only eight stakes-winning offspring so far, but when he has had one it raises the hope that there will be more to come. The now thirteen-year-old Cheveley Park Stud resident, also a July Cup star, gets a lot of multiple winners, his other blacktype earners include five who have been placed in pattern races, and he remains an interesting prospect. His top son comes from his fourth crop.

Oxted, who is trained by Roger Teal, was gelded before he ever ran and he was a well-beaten fifth in a six-furlong Doncaster maiden on soft ground in November of his juvenile year, his only start at two. He won a seven-furlong novice race on good-to-firm at Salisbury on his first run at three, dropped to six furlongs at Newbury the following month, where he was a half-length runner-up to Khaadem in the Listed Shalaa Carnarvon Stakes, and has remained sprinting ever since. He disappointed on his next two outings, was then partnered by Cieren Fallon for the first time in a Newmarket handicap, finishing a half-length second, and the partnership has remained intact since. They won the famous Portland Handicap over the extended five and a half furlongs at Doncaster next time, the gelding's only other run in 2019.

Oxted ran three times in 2020, kicking off the campaign with a promising one-length defeat of Breathtaking Look in the Group 3 Betway Abernant Stakes on good-to-firm at Newmarket in early June, the runner-up finishing three and three-quarter lengths clear of the third, Emaraaty Ana. He had been going well over two out, went clear about a furlong later and although the mare was closing in the final half furlong, he never looked like being caught. The following month, on good ground, the four-year-old staked his claim to be considered as the champion sprinter of the year with a length-and-a-quarter-length defeat of Sceptical in the Group 1 Darley July Cup Stakes. He had gone to the front over a quarter of a mile from home and although moving to his right over a furlong out and, once clear, moving across the recent Group 1 Commonwealth Cup scorer Golden Horde, he kept on well to the line. Golden Horde passed the post a neck behind Sceptical but a length and a half and a length in front of Khaadem and Hello Youmzain, with Brando another neck back in sixth. Sceptical, the lightly raced gelding who had been a listed winner and third in the Group 1 Diamond Jubilee Stakes on his previous two starts, was sadly lost the following month. The Denis Hogan-trained rising star for whom owner James McAuley had paid only £2,800 as an unraced three-year-old gelding who was sold in Doncaster by Godolphin, notched up four wins and three placings from seven starts but suffered a fatal injury on the gallops in early August.

Oxted had a wind procedure done shortly after this victory and was not seen in action again until mid-October. The ground was heavy when Mayson won the July Cup by five lengths but not all of his offspring appreciate such deep underfoot conditions, and Oxted may be one of them; almost all of his racing has been done on good ground or faster. He ran well in the Group 1 Qipco British Champions Sprint Stakes at Ascot on soft ground on his final start and was a narrow leader over a furlong out, racing in the centre of the track with Glen Shiel. If you froze the race at the furlong pole then you'd likely have selected him as the winner, but he had raced freely in the early stages and lacked the recent match-fitness-edge of many of his rivals, so when he was headed inside the final half furlong, he had nothing more to give. Glen Shiel and Brando flashed past the line together, closely followed by One Master, Art Power and Oxted, the final margins being a nose, half a length, half a length and a nose.

The gelding is the second-born foal of the five-furlong and triple six-furlong winner Charlotte Rosina (by Choisir)—her first one died—and his now three-year-old full brother, Chipstead, was fourth in a seven-furlong Lingfield maiden in mid-December, a third start for the Roger Teal-trained bay. The mare slipped to Lethal Force (by Dark Angel) from a 2018 covering, was barren to Adaay (by Kodiac) in 2019, was then sold for £45,000 at the Tattersalls Ascot November Sale and bred to Cable Bay (by Invincible Spirit). She is out of the six-time winner Intriguing Glimpse (by Piccolo), that mare is a daughter of the seven-time scorer Running Glimpse (by Runnett), and the latter's siblings feature Captain Horatius (by Taufan), the talented and prolific ten-to-twelve-furlong horse whose list of blacktype results featured wins in the Group 2 Premio Ellington and Group 2 Grosser Preis von Deutschland plus six listed races. He was also placed ten times at pattern level and he was trained by John Dunlop.

Oxted is an important first Group 1 winner for his sire. He was also the first winner at the highest level for his trainer and his jockey, and there is every reason to hope that the talented gelding can continue to do well at the top of the sprinters' division in 2021. It was revealed, shortly before this book went to print, that he was in preparation for a potential trip to Saudi Arabia for a $1.5 million six-furlong race on dirt, and that plans after that included a possible run at Meydan on Dubai World Cup night, followed by Royal Ascot and then another crack at the July Cup at Newmarket.

SUMMARY DETAILS

Bred: Homecroft Wealth Racing
Owned: S Piper, T Hirschfeld & D Fish
Trained: Roger Teal
Country: England
Race record: 0-120421-110-
Career highlights: 4 wins inc Darley July Cup Stakes (Gr1), Betway Abernant Stakes (Gr3), William Hill Portland Handicap, 2nd Shalaa Carnarvon Stakes (L)

OXTED (GB) – 2016 bay gelding

Mayson (GB)	Invincible Spirit (IRE)	Green Desert (USA)
		Rafha
	Mayleaf (GB)	Pivotal (GB)
		Bayleaf (GB)
Charlotte Rosina (GB)	Choisir (AUS)	Danehill Dancer (IRE)
		Great Selection (AUS)
	Intriguing Glimpse (GB)	Piccolo (GB)
		Running Glimpse (IRE)

PALACE PIER (GB)

Kingman (by Invincible Spirit) was an outstanding miler and he has already come up with a son who may be equally talented. His first-crop is headlined by the classic winner and Arc-placed mile Group 1 ace Persian King (new to Haras d'Etreham in 2021) but the John Gosden-trained Palace Pier represents his second one. Kingman's only defeat in an eight-race career came when he finished a half-length runner-up to Night of Thunder in a vintage edition of the 2000 Guineas, and the four-time Group 1 scorer stands at Banstead Manor Stud. His twenty-nine stakes winners also include last season's Grade 1 Hollywood Derby victor Domestic Spending: an excellent start to the stallion career of the classic-winning relation to leading sire Oasis Dream (by Green Desert). Palace Pier, on the other hand, has met with defeat once in six starts and the dual Group 1-star is due to return to action this coming season.

The 600,000-guinea Tattersalls Book 1 graduate was bred by Highclere Stud and Floors Farming and he had a more patient introduction to top-class racing than many similarly talented horses. We frequently see the best horses go into blacktype company after their maiden success but this colt's foray into stronger company did not happen until he was already an unbeaten three-time winner. Both of his outings as a two-year-old were over seven furlongs at Sandown, a maiden and a novice race which he won by an aggregate of eight and a quarter lengths. He hit the front a furlong from home on his debut and then drew clear, whereas he made all second time out, going clear inside the final furlong before being eased near the line.

Clearly a horse with a considerable amount of potential, he made his third start in a mile handicap on the Tapeta at Newcastle, a race in which he was giving weight to all bar one of his six rivals. If you had paused the race over a furlong out then you might have been ready to think of him as another flashy juvenile who wouldn't live up to expectations at three. Rob Havlin was asking him to go forward but the colt looked doubtful to catch Acquitted, the bay who had moved easily into the lead two out and gone a few lengths clear. As they passed the furlong pole it was clear the pair had the race to themselves but Palace Pier still had ground to make up. Then the penny dropped out half a furlong out, he was a length in front in a matter of strides and three and a quarter lengths clear at the line. The runner-up was in receipt of nine pounds; it was an eye-catching performance, one that confirmed the impression of Group 1 potential. It was also the only time that anyone other than Frankie Dettori rode him on the track.

With the Derby just a month away this obvious miler drew some speculation and quotes about him for that race, which seemed silly yet inevitable, and I was reminded of the moment more than twenty-five years before when a top Irish trainer was asked if his just-unsaddled six-furlong Naas juvenile conditions winner might be a Derby horse. Mental maturity was a reason put forward by his connections as to why he had made his reappearance in a handicap rather than being pitched straight into pattern company, and we saw the benefit of taking a patient approach when the colt won the Group 1 St James's Palace Stakes a fortnight later. He was slowly away but soon made up the ground and he raced keenly at the back, with Pinatubo, as Wichita cut out a steady pace up front. He raced widest of the seven-runner field as they were fanned out swinging around the final bend, but he was clearly going very well, as was Pinatubo. Royal Dornach, who had been between them, dropped back. Wichita still had a narrow lead over Threat as they passed the two pole, but Pinatubo and Palace Pier were almost to them. Then Threat gave way, Pinatubo got his head in front, Palace Pier was being asked for more while Wichita was keeping on well at the rail. Briefly it became a three-way battle, but at the half-furlong pole the Irish colt dropped to a narrow third as Palace Pier got his head in front. He went clear with some ease and passed the post a length in front, with a head separating Pinatubo and Wichita and a five-and-a-half-length gap back to the fourth, Positive.

The ground had been good-to-soft at Ascot but was described as *collant* on France-Galop's site the day of the Group 1 Prix du Haras de Fresnay-le-Buffard Jacques le Marois at Deauville in mid-August. That translates as holding, although it was reported on the *Racing Post*'s website as heavy, which is *lourd*. Regardless of which was the more accurate description, it would add to the challenge of this mile contest, as would taking on older rivals for the first time, but Palace Pier handled the situation with aplomb. He hit the front a furlong out and kept on well to the line, holding off the Jessica Harrington-trained Coronation Stakes heroine Alpine Star by three-quarters of a length. There was a five-length gap back to Circus Maximus in third, with Persian King (fourth) and Romanised (fifth) running below form, beaten by further margins of three lengths and two and a half lengths.

Despite the soft ground at Ascot two months later, Palace Pier was widely expected to extended his unbeaten record to six in the Group 1 Queen Elizabeth II Stakes. Punters saw only The Revenant and Circus Maximus as potential dangers in a fourteen-horse field, but the race did not turn out as hoped. He was slowly away but that was not what led to his defeat. Roseman set off in front and was only headed two out when The Revenant and Palace Pier made their challenge. However, while the French gelding and the Roger Varian-trained long-shot kept going and fought it out all the way to the line, only a head separating them at the end, Palace Pier did not pick up. He kept pace with them for a while but it was clear, as they passed the furlong pole, that he was not going to win. Dettori eased the pressure on his mount about half a furlong out and looked down at the colt's right side as if concerned that something was amiss. He passed the post three and a quarter lengths behind the front pair and only half a length ahead of the 66/1 Sir Busker. The rest, which included four prior Group 1 scorers, finished strung out, most of them performing well below their best. It emerged that the favourite had lost his left-fore shoe and Dettori, reporting that the colt had not changed legs, likened it to trying to drive a car on three wheels.

Palace Pier is the third foal of Beach Frolic (by Nayef), an unraced mare who has joined Coolmore's broodmare band having been bought by them for 2,200,000 guineas during the most recent edition of the Tattersalls December Mare Sale in Newmarket. She was offered in foal to the sprint star Blue Point (by Shamardal), due around April 20th, and that will be her seventh foal. Her Derby-entered son Tiger Beetle (by Camelot), a 300,000-guinea Tattersalls Book 2 graduate, is trained by Sir Michael Stoute for King Power Racing Co Ltd though finished down the field in a one-mile Kempton maiden in mid-November, his sole start to date. Her new two-year-old, a 320,000-guinea Book 1 graduate, has been named Highland Frolic (by Highland Reel), and she had a son of Almanzor (by Wootton Bassett) on April 1st last year. Her Shadwell-owned, winning daughter Tatweej (by Invincible Spirit) was bred to Awtaad (by Cape Cross) in 2020.

Beach Frolic's success as a broodmare is not a surprise. She is out of the well-related winner Night Frolic (by Night Shift) and so is a half-sister to the Group 2 Dante Stakes victor Bonfire (by Manduro) and Group 2 Windsor Forest Stakes scorer Joviality (by Cape Cross), both of whom were placed at the highest level. The latter is closely related to Palace Pier and in addition to her big mile win at Ascot, she landed the Group 3 Musidora Stakes over the extended ten furlongs at York and was third in the Grade 1 Beverly D Stakes over about a furlong less than that at Arlington.

Miss d'Ouilly (by Bikala), the third dam of Palace Pier and a half-sister to the Group 1 Prix Jacques le Marois heroine Miss Satamixa (by Linamix), was a listed-race winner in France whose Grade 3-winning daughter Miss Caerleona (by Caerleon) became a broodmare of note. That half-sister to Night Frolic is responsible for the Grade 2 winner Miss Coronado (by Coronado's Quest) and the Group 3 Nell Gwyn Stakes winner and Group 1 Coronation Stakes runner-up Karen's Caper (by War Chant), and her string of stakes-winning descendants include the Group/Grade 1-placed pair Comicas (by Distorted Humor) and Arethusa (by A.P. Indy). She is also grandam of Group 1 Irish Oaks runner-up Miss Jean Brodie (by Maria's Mon).

Palace Pier is a 125-rated dual Group 1-winning miler whose pedigree gives him a good chance of staying ten furlongs. He has won on everything from good-to-firm to heavy on turf, plus he has won on the artificial Tapeta surface, and his return to action is eagerly awaited. It will be disappointing if he fails to add further Group 1 success to his record, but regardless of how the 2021 season goes for him, he has already done more than enough to earn a good berth at stud whenever his racing days come to an end. His pedigree is free of Sadler's Wells (by Northern Dancer), Danehill (by Danzig) and Dubawi (by Dubai Millennium), he does of course carry Green Desert (by Danzig) and is inbred 5x4 to

Northern Dancer (by Nearctic) and to Dubawi's great-grandsire Mr Prospector (by Raise a Native).

SUMMARY DETAILS

Bred: Highclere Stud and Floors Farming
Owned: Sheikh Hamdan bin Mohammed Al Maktoum
Trained: John Gosden
Country: England
Race record: 11-1113-
Career highlights: 5 wins inc Prix du Haras de Fresnay-le-Buffard Jacques le Marois (Gr1), St James's Palace Stakes (Gr1), 3rd Queen Elizabeth II Stakes - sponsored by Qipco (Gr1)

PALACE PIER (GB) – 2017 bay colt

		Green Desert (USA)
	Invincible Spirit (USA)	Rafha
Kingman (GB)		Zamindar (USA)
	Zenda (GB)	Hope (IRE)
		Gulch (USA)
	Nayef (USA)	Height of Fashion (FR)
Beach Frolic (GB)		Night Shift (USA)
	Night Frolic (GB)	Miss d'Ouilly (FR)

PEACEFUL (IRE)

Peaceful—the name likely to remain as the required incorrect answer to the quiz question "which horse gave Galileo the outright world record number of individual Group 1 winners?"

The late multiple champion sire Danehill (by Danzig) sired a phenomenal 348 stakes winners of whom eighty-three won at least once at the highest level, figures clearly displayed anywhere that quotes Weatherbys' data, for example in the *Racing Post*'s pedigree charts supplied by that organisation. Yes, eighty-three Group 1 winners and not the eighty-four that has been quoted in so many places. Some lists/databases include Fairy King Prawn among his tally, others name Scintillation instead, but the fact is that neither of those horses belong there. Both got top-level wins in Hong Kong that were, at the time, only recognised as being Group 1s locally; they were not international Group 1s as per the International Cataloguing Standards and so count only as listed-race wins. The same is true of the edition of the one-mile Yasuda Kinen that Fairy King Prawn won in Japan at a time when only the Japan Cup, among that nation's entire racing calendar, carried international Group 1 status. Both of those horses are correctly counted as listed-race winners only.

In November 2019, the Aidan O'Brien-trained Magic Wand won the Group 1 Mackinnon Stakes over ten furlongs at Flemington in Australia thereby becoming the eighty-fourth Group 1 winner sired by Galileo (by Sadler's Wells); the new world record. When Peaceful won the Tattersalls Irish 1,000 Guineas at the Curragh in June, becoming her sire's eighty-fifth to succeed at Group 1 level, she merely extended his already-existing outright world record total by one more. The great stallion's tally currently stands at eighty-nine among a total of 332 stakes winners, and it looks odds-on that he will surpass Danehill's record stakes-winner total in 2021. There is a popular pedigree website that shows Galileo as already having 352 stakes winners, but National Hunt blacktype scorers, presumably the extra ones being counted there, are not included in a stallion's stakes-winner figures.

Galileo's blacktype tally does includes Peaceful's older sister Easter because she won the Listed Hurry Harriet Stakes at

Gowran Park. That was the better of her two wins on the track but she was also multiple blacktype-placed, notably in the Group 3 Dance Design Stakes, Group 3 Denny Cordell Lavarack & Lanwades Stud Stakes and Group 3 Give Thanks Stakes. Easter's first foal, Three Sided Story (by War Front), finished third in three starts in the USA, that filly was followed by an Irish-born son of Curlin (by Smart Strike) in 2018, named Rush Delivery, and the mare had a Muhaarar (by Oasis Dream) filly in 2019, followed by a son of Kingman (by Invincible Spirit).

As for Missvinski, their dam, she had a full sister to her classic heroine in early April of 2019 and she was bred back to Galileo last season. The mare is daughter of the classic-placed European sprint champion Stravinsky (by Nureyev), which means that her progeny, all of whom are full-siblings, are inbred 3x4 to Northern Dancer (by Nearctic) and 4x4 to Special (by Forli), along with two other duplications within the first five generations of their pedigree. She was a talented miler, a dual stakes winner who was runner-up in the Group 1 Prix d'Astarte at Deauville and in the Group 3 Prix de la Grotte at Longchamp. She is, aside from her daughters, the most notable horse to appear under both her dam and grandam, but if you go back to the next generation of the family then you will find a plethora of notable racehorses one of whom is in early stages a promising stallion career.

Careless Aly (by Alydar), the unraced third dam of Peaceful, produced only five winners from thirteen foals, so a similar strike-rate to that of her dam, Careless Notion (by Jester). That stakes-placed winner had fifteen foals but only six winners and yet became a broodmare of influence. Her son Cacoethes, a full brother to Careless Aly, disappointed at stud, as did most males by his famous sire, but he was a very talented racehorse for the Guy Harwood stable. He had finished a five-and-a-half-length third to Nashwan in the Listed Autumn Stakes on his only outing at two but when the pair met again at Epsom the following June, it was he who was seen as the big danger to the brilliant chestnut. He had made a winning return to at action at Brighton, followed that seven-length score with a four-length win in the Group 3 Derby Trial at Lingfield, and hit the front three furlongs from home in the Derby. Nashwan soon moved up to join him and it seemed briefly that the expected duel was about to materialise, but then Nashwan went on in style, eventually passing the post seven lengths clear of Cacoethes. The bay held on to third, by half a length from Ile de Nisky, but had no answer for the strong-finishing Terimon who reached the line two lengths in front of him. Cacoethes won the Group 2 King Edward VII Stakes at Ascot a few weeks later, made Nashwan fight hard for his neck victory in the Group 1 King George VI and Queen Elizabeth Stakes at the same venue a month later, chased home Ile de Chypre in the Group 1 Juddmonte International Stakes at York and, the following year, beat Alwuhush by a length and a half to take the Grade 1 Turf Classic over twelve furlongs on firm turf at Belmont Park.

Their Californian-bred half-sister Fabulous Notion (by Somethingfabulous) won nine races and over $700,000 in prize money, and the best of her blacktype wins came in the Grade 1 Santa Susana Stakes. She then went on to become the dam of Fabulously Fast (by Deputy Minister), who is a Grade 1 Test Stakes winner inbred 3x3 to Northern Dancer, and the grandam of City of Light (by Quality Road). That horse won the Grade 1 Malibu Stakes at three, the Grade 1 Breeders' Cup Dirt Mile and Grade 1 Triple Bed Stakes at four and the Grade 1 Pegasus World Cup Invitational Stakes at five and he retired to Lane's End Farm in Kentucky with career earnings of over $5.6 million. His first foals arrived in 2020.

Careless Notion's daughters also include Not So Careless (by Desert Wine) and Champagne Virgin (by Wing Out). The former is the winning dam of the dual US Grade 1 winner Subordination (by Mt Livermore), who sired plenty of winners in both North and South America, and grandam of Careless Jewel (by Tapit), who won the Grade 1 Alabama Stakes over ten furlongs in 2009. Champagne Virgin, on the other hand, was placed in three of her six starts, but her prolific daughter Island Jamboree (by Explodent) was a multiple stakes winner before going on to success at stud. That mare's son Capri (by Generous) won the Group 2 Grand Prix de Chantilly, but her daughter Fiji (by Rainbow Quest) was the Eclipse Award winner as US Champion Turf Female in 1998 after a season in which she won both the

Grade 1 Yellow Ribbon Stakes and Grade 1 Gamely Handicap. Island Jamboree's Grade 1 Blue Grass Stakes-winning grandson Java's War (by War Pass) will have his first three-year-olds in action in 2021.

These are the pedigree credentials that Peaceful will take to stud. Her classic victory and a seven-length maiden success at Thurles as a juvenile are the only wins on her record, but she had been a neck runner-up in a listed contest at Newmarket on the final of three starts at two—she was unplaced on her racecourse debut that August—and she put up two other good performances in 2020. The Group 1 Prix de Diane Longines (French Oaks) produced a bunched finish, with margins of a short neck, a head and a head separating the first four, but it was a strong edition of the ten-and-a-half-furlong Chantilly classic. Peaceful was perhaps a bit unlucky not to have won the race as she encountered some traffic problems over a quarter of a mile from home, but she had every chance to make up for that thereafter and stayed on well to finish third to Fancy Blue and Alpine Star. Raabihah was fourth and the subsequent US Grade 1 scorer Magic Attitude, another daughter of Galileo, was another two and a half lengths back in fifth.

She got her revenge on Fancy Blue at Leopardstown two months later, beating that Donnacha O'Brien-trained dual Group 1 star by a length and a half in the Group 1 Coolmore America 'Justify' Matron Stakes over a mile on good ground, but was the day that the Johnny Murtagh-trained Champers Elysees put up the best performance of her career to date, and so Peaceful had to settle for second, beaten by almost as far as she finished in front of her old rival. It had been a strongly run race.

It is hard to know what to make of her final two starts. The heavy ground was put forward as an excuse after her last-place finish behind Nazeef in the Group 1 Kingdom of Bahrain Sun Chariot Stakes over the Rowley Mile at Newmarket in early October, and while acknowledging that there is a considerable difference in standard between a juvenile listed contest and an all-aged Group 1 over the same trip, the ground was also heavy when she failed narrowly to beat Born With Pride in the Listed Montrose Fillies' Stakes over the same course and distance eleven months before. She was also eased when her chance was gone in the Grade 1 Maker's Mark Breeders' Cup Filly & Mare Turf over nine and a half furlongs on firm ground at Keeneland a month later, under pressure over three furlongs from home and dropping back soon after.

Peaceful has been retired to the paddocks. Had she raced again then it would have been interesting to see how she might have got on at ten or even twelve furlongs on good or good-to-soft/yielding ground. Not everything by Galileo stays the latter distance, but her aforementioned full sister, Easter, was Group 3-placed over it and she has a minor full brother who has been placed over further in France, so perhaps it could have been worth a try. It will be fun to see how her offspring turn out.

SUMMARY DETAILS

Bred: Coolmore
Owned: Michael Tabor, Derrick Smith & Mrs John Magnier
Trained: Aidan O'Brien
Country: Ireland
Race record: 012-13200-
Career highlights: 2 wins inc Tattersalls Irish 1,000 Guineas (Gr1), 2nd Coolmore America 'Justify' Matron Stakes (Gr1), British Stallion Studs EBF Montrose Fillies' Stakes (L), 3rd Prix de Diane Longines (Gr1)

PEACEFUL (IRE) – 2017 bay/brown filly

Galileo (IRE)	Sadler's Wells (USA)	Northern Dancer
		Fairy Bridge (USA)
	Urban Sea (USA)	Miswaki (USA)
		Allegretta
Missvinski (USA)	Stravinsky (USA)	Nureyev (USA)
		Fire The Groom (USA)
	Miss U Fran (USA)	Brocco (USA)
		Careless Aly (USA)

PERSIAN KING (IRE)

Persian King is now a stallion at Haras d'Etreham in France, a role in which he looks sure to be very popular. He was a top-class racehorse, a triple Group 1 star, and he will arguably be remembered as much for two races he lost as for his victories. That is not because there was anything wrong with those loses; they were top-class performances and the second one was remarkable. In all, he notched up eight wins and four placings from thirteen starts—fourth is 'out of the frame', not placed— and his earnings of over €1.4 million surpassed €1.7 million when French premiums were added in.

The first of those notable defeats was the one that ended his winning sequence, when the Group 1 Poule d'Essai des Poulains (French 2000 Guineas)-winner was a beaten odds-on favourite in the Group 1 Prix du Jockey Club (French Derby) on what turned out to be his final race for a few days past a full year. Sottsass, the colt who outstayed him and won the ten-and-a-half-furlong classic by two lengths would go on to finish third in that year's Group 1 Prix de l'Arc de Triomphe and to win that famous race in 2020. That son of Siyouni (by Pivotal) is also now at stud, in his case Coolmore in Ireland. And it is Sottsass's Arc that represents the second of Persian King's notable efforts in defeat. The colt proved himself to be one of the top milers in Europe, but on what was to be his career finale his connections not only decided to go for gold by tackling the Prix de l'Arc de Triomphe but to make all the running with their star colt on the heavy ground. Despite the conditions and the distance, Persian King was not headed until a furlong from home and he kept going to the line, holding off Gold Trip by a head for third place. Pierre Charles-Boudot was able to dictate the pace, ensuring it would not become a strong test of stamina, and so maximised his mount's ability to last the distance.

Persian King's season began in a one-mile listed race on good-to-soft at Chantilly in early June but the result was something of an upset. His stablemate Magny Cours set off in front, quickened the pace a quarter of a mile from out and kept on strongly to the end, holding on by a short neck. He was six lengths clear of the third, the multiple pattern-placed filly Queen, and while by no means a bad effort, it was a shade disappointing to see him beaten on his return to action. The winner went on to beat former Group 1 scorer Aspetar in a listed contest at Sandown next time, whereas Persian King landed the Group 2 Prix du Muguet at Saint-Cloud, taking the one-mile test by margins of a length and a quarter and three-quarters of a length from Pretreville and Skalleti. It was a highly encouraging effort; the classic star was back.

Three weeks later, he added the Group 1 Prix d'Ispahan at Chantilly, moving to the front two and a half furlongs from home, taking over from the front-running Pogo and fighting off a challenge from Stormy Antarctic before going on to score by two lengths from the latter, with the early leader another one and three-quarter lengths back in third. The ground was good, the time quick, and the nine-furlong trip clearly no problem.

It is disappointing when the ground comes up heavy, or close to it, on Group 1 days and mildly irritating to hear the often-stated one-liner "good horses go on any ground". It is not a 'truth'— horses are not all-terrain vehicles and many good, brilliant and even great ones have clear preferences for some underfoot conditions over others; it in no way lessens their merit if they can't produce their best on any surface. Seven talented horses lined-up for the Group 1 Prix du Haras de Fresnay-le-Buffard Jacques le Marois at Deauville in mid-August, the ground was described as *collant* (holding) on France-Galop's site but heavy (*lourd*) on the *Racing Post*'s one, and it was clear that the underfoot conditions affected the result. The winner would likely have won anyway, but the distances between the chief protagonists were exaggerated by the state of the ground. Palace Pier beat Alpine Star by three-quarters of a lengths but with further margins of five lengths, three lengths and two and a half lengths back to Circus Maximus, Persian King and Romanised.

Good ground at ParisLongchamp a few weeks later enabled Persian King to show his best, although seeing half of the experienced six-runner field not breaking as well as the others was something of a surprise. All were Group 1 stars, four of them classic winners, five of them are now at stud. Circus Maximus tried to make all but had little more to give when Persian King headed him a quarter of a mile out. The Irish colt got tired, the French one went clear, whereas the English star, Pinatubo, stormed home on his outside, finishing best of all but having had too much ground to make up. Persian King beat the three-year-old by one and three-quarter lengths, Circus Maximus was another six lengths behind, with gaps of a length, a head and five lengths back to Siskin, Victor Ludorum and Romanised, that trio never having looked dangerous.

Persian King, the standout member of his sire's first crop, is one of three top-level winners by the outstanding miler Kingman (by Invincible Spirit), a rising star on the Banstead Manor Stud team. The dual Group 1-winning miler Palace Pier—also reviewed in this volume—and Grade 1 Hollywood Derby scorer Domestic Spending (a gelding) are the other pair, both remaining in training in 2021 and with a future stallion career on the cards for the former. Group 2 scorers Headman (Figerro Breeding Farm, France) and Calyx (Coolmore Stud, Ireland) are also at stud, with the latter already a father: he covered 163 mares in 2020 and the first foals from them have arrived.

I reviewed his pedigree in detail in *European Group 1 Winners of 2019*, so a brief recap will suffice. Pretty Please (by Dylan Thomas), the winning dam of Persian King, is a half-sister to the classic-placed Group 1 winner Planteur (by Danehill Dancer) and that horse's star son Trueshan is reviewed in *Volume 2: Great Britain & Ireland's Group 2 & Group 3 Winners*. They are out of Plante Rare (by Giant's Causeway), who is an unraced half-sister to the Group 2 scorers and National Hunt sires Policy Maker (by Sadler's Wells) and Pushkin (by Caerleon) and to Group 3 Lancashire Oaks winner Place Rouge (by Desert King). Palmeraie (by Lear Fan), the third dam of Persian King, is a half-sister to Peinture Bleu (by Alydar), the Grade 2-winning dam of the brilliant middle-distance horse and notable sire Peintre Celebre (by Nureyev). That Timeform 137-rated champion won the Group 1 Prix du Jockey Club and Group 1 Grand Prix de Paris and ran away with the Group 1 Prix de l'Arc de Triomphe, he was a Coolmore Stud shuttle sire and got a dozen Group 1 winners among an overall total of sixty-seven blacktype scorers.

This is also a branch of the family from which the brilliant stayer Stradivarius (by Sea The Stars) comes and the most recent updates to the page come via the Grade 1-winning South African three-year-old Jet Dark (by Trippi) and the Saeed bin Suroor-trained Soft Whisper (by Dubawi), who ran away with the Listed UAE 1000 Guineas at Meydan shortly before this book went to print. The first-named of that pair is a Drakenstein Stud-bred grandson of Peintre Celebre's full sister Pine Chip and he won the Grade 1 L'Ormarins Queen's Plate over a mile at Kenilworth on January 9th, 2021. There are, of course, no guarantees in this business, but it will be disappointing if Persian King fails to come up with some notable sons and daughters. He looks a likely prospect to get some talented autumn juveniles to go along with three-year-olds and older horses who are effective across the full classic range.

SUMMARY DETAILS

Bred: Dayton Investments (Breeding) Ltd
Owned: Godolphin SNC & Ballymore Thoroughbred Ltd
Trained: André Fabre
Country: France
Race record: 2111-112-211413-
Career highlights: 8 wins inc Prix du Moulin de Longchamp (Gr1), Prix d'Ispahan (Gr1), The Emirates Poule d'Essai des Poulains (Gr1), Prix du Muguet (Gr2), Prix de Fontainebleau (Gr3), Masar Godolphin Autumn Stakes (Gr3), 2nd Qipco Prix du Jockey Club (Gr1), Prix de Montretout (L), 3rd Qatar Prix de l'Arc de Triomphe (Gr1)

PERSIAN KING (IRE) – 2016 bay colt

Kingman (GB)	Invincible Spirit (IRE)	Green Desert (USA)
		Rafha
	Zenda (GB)	Zamindar (USA)
		Hope (IRE)
Pretty Please (IRE)	Dylan Thomas (IRE)	Danehill (USA)
		Lagrion (USA)
	Plante Rare (IRE)	Giant's Causeway (USA)
		Palmeraie (USA)

PINATUBO (IRE)

Pinatubo was one of the most brilliant two-year-olds of the past century, he was a classic-placed Group 1 winner at three and is now embarking on a stud career that promises to be one of significance. He is by the sire of leading international sire Lope de Vega, comes from the family of leading international sire Invincible Spirit, and all of this, combined with the strength of support he is sure to receive, suggests that he is one of the most exciting prospective stallions to go to stud in recent years.

He was rated 128 at the end of his championship year—Timeform had him on 134—a six-race campaign that began with a three-and-a-quarter-length score over six furlongs on the Tapeta at Wolverhampton in early May and culminated in a two-length defeat of Arizona in the Group 1 Dewhurst Stakes. Between those races he landed the Woodcote Stakes at Epsom, beat Lope Y Fernandez by just over three lengths in the seven-furlong Listed Chesham Stakes, trounced Positive by five lengths in the Group 2 Vintage Stakes and then put up that remarkable performance at the Curragh when he beat Armory by nine lengths in the Group 1 Vincent O'Brien National Stakes. Both the details of those races plus an in-depth look at his pedigree were examined in *European Group 1 Winners of 2019* and the essay was reproduced in the April 25th, 2020 edition of *The Irish Field*. It also noted the cadence figures the colt had produced in three of his starts, said of his position within his family that "he looks likely to remembered as another of its two-year-old and mile stars rather than as one of its middle-distance horses" and concluded with the following observation: "With the way he won at the Curragh combined with his cadence and the speed in his pedigree, it would not be a surprise to see him drop back to seven furlongs for the Group 1 Prix Jean Prat and/or Group 1 Prix de la Foret." Pinatubo won the Qatar-sponsored Group 1 Prix Jean Prat on July 12th, 2020.

The delayed and compressed nature of the opening month of the 2020 flat season likely contributed to some pattern races results and line-ups that could have been different had the early season 'prep' races not been lost. Some may have bypassed the classics, while other top contenders may have emerged. There is no doubt that the best three colts in the race filled the first three positions in the Group 1 Qipco 2000 Guineas at Newmarket on the first Saturday in June. If they would have finished in the same order in a normal year, when trials would have preceded a race run on the first Saturday in May, is open to speculation. That said, the best three-year-old miler of the year won a handicap that same afternoon: Palace Pier, a horse who needed more time.

As the field passed the three-furlong marker in the Guineas, Persuasion and Juan Elcano led the field on the rails with Wichita and Mums Tipple still heading those racing more towards the centre and the previous year's Group 1 stars Pinatubo and Kameko poised to strike a few lengths behind. Persuasion was the first of them to crack and drop back, soon followed by Mums Tipple who was under pressure at the two pole where Wichita held a narrow lead over Pinatubo and Juan Elcano. Military March looked dangerous on the outside of the pack and Kameko was going well behind the leader but needing room. The Ballydoyle colt still held a narrow lead a furlong out, with Pinatubo on his inside, Kameko on his outside, Military March a close fourth and Juan Elcano trying to hold on to fifth. Kinross was staying on into sixth but everything else was well-beaten. It soon became apparent that neither of Godolphin's pair was going to win. The first three pulled clear of Military March, who held off Juan Elcano by a neck, but Pinatubo had to settle for third. Wichita was game in defeat, headed about half a furlong from home and beaten to the line by Kameko. The final margins were a neck and a length, with a gap of two and a half lengths back to the fourth.

Kameko stepped up in trip before returning to a mile and he is now a stallion at Tweenhills Farm & Stud in Gloucestershire. Wichita proved best at seven furlongs and would surely have made a popular stallion, but he sadly failed to recover from surgery to repair an injury he sustained in Australia in the fall. Military March ran a fine Derby trial that day but did not run again—he remains in training in 2021—but a few others in the field went on to blacktype success. Kinross (sixth) won a listed contest over a mile at Kempton in November, Royal Dornoch (tenth) landed the Group 3 Desmond Stakes over the trip, Cepheus (twelfth) stepped up to twelve furlongs and justified favouritism in a listed race in France in mid-December, whereas Al Suhail (fourteenth) was a runaway listed winner over a mile at the July Course in Newmarket a month after the classic but not seen out again after that.

Negative comments about Pinatubo were disappointing yet inevitable—how quick some are to try to write off a horse—even though he had finished a close third in a classic on his only run on ground described as good-to-firm, over a distance he had not previously tried and was a shade doubtful to stay. Receiving an order to pass a stalls test a day before his next start didn't help. So, he wasn't Frankel Mark Two, but of course, it's likely we won't see another in that superstar's league for many years to come, if ever.

He got his revenge on Wichita a fortnight later, beating that colt by a head in the Group 1 St James's Palace Stakes on good-to-soft at Ascot and with Positive and Threat five and a half lengths and a nose behind, but this was the day that Palace Pier made his first appearance in blacktype company. Pinatubo had looked set for victory when hitting the front a furlong out, but he came under pressure soon afterwards, was headed half a furlong from the line and was unable to fight off Palace Pier who won by a length. It looked like a mile was just a shade farther than ideal, so it was no surprise to see him drop back to seven the following month for the Group 1 Qatar Prix Jean Prat at Deauville. The André Fabre-trained pair Alson and Tropbeau, who had been seen as the main dangers, both ran poorly and finished well beaten, whereas a talented though seemingly over-priced pair chased him home. Pinatubo hit the front entering the final furlong and he kept on well to hold off the staying-on pair Lope Y Fernandez and Malotru, winning by margins of three-quarters of a length and two and a half lengths. The subsequent Group 1 Prix de l'Abbaye de Longchamp winner Wooded was another short neck back in fourth, a length and a quarter in front of the recent Group 3 Jersey Stakes scorer Molatham. The runner-up would go on to finish a close third in both the Group 1 Prix Maurice de Gheest and Grade 1 Breeders' Cup Mile; the now Hong Kong-based third had been a recent pattern-placed stakes winner coming into the race and a Group 3 scorer at two.

It was another Group 1 win on his record, albeit not a particularly strong race for the grade, and it arguably his next start that was his best of the year. All six runners in the 2020 edition of the Group 1 Prix du Moulin de Longchamp had at least two prior Group 1 wins to their name, two of them started slowly and were never dangerous, but the first two had it to themselves from over a furlong out. Circus Maximus had tried to make all but was headed by Persian King after six of the eight furlongs. That four-year-old went clear and never looked like being caught, an impressive performance on what was his penultimate start, but the manner in which Pinatubo made up ground in a sustained run over the final furlong and a half and the speed he showed in the closing stages were also eye-catching. The performance left a feeling that he may have been a shade unlucky not to have won, despite passing the post a length and three-quarters in second; he had been left with a lot of ground to make up in the final quarter mile. Circus Maximus was another six lengths adrift in third, a length and a head in front of the 2020 classic winners Siskin and Victor Ludorum, with 2018 classic star Romanised another five lengths behind. A September 8th sectional analysis article by Simon Rowlands on AtTheRaces.com showed that the colt should have won, summing up thus: "The conclusion in this instance is not borderline: it is stark. Pinatubo deserves to be upgraded by three to four lengths more than the horse who beat him by less than two. He was unlucky, and it is possible to estimate the degree to which he was unlucky. … Pinatubo was left with too much to do against a very smart rival who was not stopping …".

There had been talk of a potential Breeders' Cup bid, but it was announced on Fillies' Mile day that Pinatubo had been retired with immediate effect and would take up stallion duties at Dalham Hall Stud in 2021. His initial fee has been set at £35,000 and presuming good health for the season, he looks certain to be among the busiest stallions in England. I reviewed his pedigree in last year's annual with an emphasis on his racing potential. Assessing for stallion potential is slightly different and a horse who is bred to excel on the track is not necessarily one who is bred to succeed at stud. Pinatubo, however, has a stallion's pedigree and it will be quite a disappointment if he fails to sire pattern and Group 1 winners.

He is one of twenty-six top-level winners among an overall tally of over 150 blacktype scorers by the late and much-lamented Shamardal (by Giant's Causeway). That standout's record as a sire of stallions is less clear. His Group 1-winning sons Captain Sonador and Casamento sired a Group 1 winner apiece, but the former died young and the latter at the age of 12, neither having looked like being top-notch sires. Casamento had the longer career and so, unsurprisingly, the stronger record, but he had spent a year in Sweden and was covering National Hunt mares in Ireland at the time of his death. Amaron and Mukhadram were also Group 1 winners on the track. The first-named stands in Germany, now has four-year-olds but only one stakes winner, whereas the latter horse has three stakes winners from his first three racing-age crops and has been moved to Italy. Dual Australian Group 2 scorer Puissance de Lune, who missed a pair of Group 1 wins in photo finishes, has a Group 1-placed Group 2 scorer to his name. French Navy (exported to India in 2020), Shakespearean and Sommerabend have sired winners, and both Bow Creek and Dariyan got off the mark as a freshman sire in 2020, the latter's tally including two who were placed at Group 3 level. It will be interesting to see how they fare with their first three-year-olds and older horses.

But then there's Lope de Vega. He was a dual classic star, arguably the best and classiest son of his sire with runners to date. He was well supported from the outset of his career at Ballylinch Stud in Ireland, receiving backing by breeders that has strengthened as his Group 1 and other pattern winners have flowed. Lope de Vega is a leading international sire whose first stallion son, Belardo, was a standout freshman last season. And there's a lot of future potential too. Blue Point was one of Shamardal's most brilliant sons and that sprint star covered 198 mares in his maiden season at Kildangan Stud; he could be the next big hit for his sire. Earthlight, the dual six-furlong Group 1 star from a branch of the family of champion sire Be My Guest (by Northern Dancer), has joined Blue Point on Darley's roster in Ireland, and of course Pinatubo is on their team in Newmarket.

His race record will attract a lot of strong support—something that most of the early Shamardal stallions lacked—and, as noted above, he also has the considerable extra pull of being related to Invincible Spirit (by Green Desert). He is out of Lava Flow (by Dalakhani), who is a stakes-winning daughter of the stakes winner Mount Elbrus (by Barathea), and his third dam is El Jazirah (by Kris), an unraced sister to the Group 1 Prix de Diane (French Oaks) heroine Rafha (by Kris). That classic star's blacktype winners feature the Irish National Stud's flag bearer, who was a Group 1 winning sprinter before going on to fame at stud, and she is also responsible for Kodiac (by Danehill), a Group 3-placed sprinter who went one to become one of the most popular stallions in Ireland. His sixty-five stakes winners feature five who have won at the highest level—Campanelle and Hello Youmzain in 2020—and several of his sons were blacktype freshman sires last year. Invincible Spirit, on the other hand, has had twenty Group 1 winners among 131 blacktype scorers and his stallion sons feature I Am Invincible, Kingman, and Lawman.

Rafha's descendants also include the classic-placed Group 2 scorer and Castlehyde Stud stallion Gustav Klimt (by Galileo; first foals in 2020). Those who descend from her siblings include the dual Australian juvenile Group 1 star Pride of Dubai (by Street Cry), who had five juvenile stakes winners in 2020 from the European half of his global first crop (see *Volume 2: Great Britain & Ireland's Group 2 & Group 3 Winners*); Rathbarry Stud's Group 1-placed, Group 2-winning sprinter James Garfield (by Exceed And Excel) whose first foals arrived last year; and March Hare Stud's nine-furlong pattern winner Master Carpenter (by Mastercraftsman), another whose eldest progeny are now yearlings.

It is going to be fascinating to see how Pinatubo turns out as a stallion. Although he has the promise to be a leading freshman sire of 2024 and a likely source of talented two-year-olds beyond then, he has the potential to make a more meaningful long-term impact with sprinters and milers aged three and upwards, and even some middle-distance horses.

SUMMARY DETAILS

Bred: Godolphin
Owned: Godolphin
Trained: Charlie Appleby
Country: England
Race record: 111111-3212-
Career highlights: 7 wins inc Qatar Prix Jean Prat (Gr1), Darley Dewhurst Stakes (Gr1), Goffs Vincent O'Brien National Stakes (Gr1), Qatar Vintage Stakes (Gr2), Chesham Stakes (L), 2nd Prix du Moulin de Longchamp (Gr1), St James's Palace Stakes (Gr1), 3rd Qipco 2000 Guineas Stakes (Gr1)

PINATUBO (IRE) – 2017 bay colt

Shamardal (USA)	Giant's Causeway (USA)	Storm Cat (USA)
		Mariah's Storm (USA)
	Helsinki (GB)	Machiavellian (USA)
		Helen Street
Lava Flow (IRE)	Dalakhani (IRE)	Darshaan
		Daltawa (IRE)
	Mount Elbrus (GB)	Barathea (IRE)
		El Jazirah (GB)

PRETTY GORGEOUS (FR)

Prix du Jockey Club (French Derby) winner Lawman is among the eldest sire-sons of Invincible Spirit (by Green Desert) and the seventeen-year-old is now in his third season at Haras de Grandcamp having spent the previous eleven standing at Ballylinch Stud. His final Irish-conceived crop are juveniles of 2021 but his penultimate one features a filly who, like him, was born in the country in which he now resides, France. Pretty Gorgeous is his second pattern winner to carry the FR suffix— Rocques won the Group 3 Prix d'Aumale in 2018—she is the sixth of his offspring to become a top-level scorer and, in 2021, she may bid to give him a third Group 1 classic winner. Just The Judge won the 2013 edition of the Irish 1,000 Guineas shortly after being runner-up in the 1000 Guineas at Newmarket, whereas Harbour Law landed the St Leger at Doncaster three years later.

Pretty Gorgeous is a 525,000-guinea Tattersalls Book 1 graduate which noted agent Margaret O'Toole had secured for just €55,000 at the previous year's Arqana December Sale. She made a five-length winning debut in a mile maiden at Bellewstown in early July, a venue that has revealed some talented horses in recent seasons, and then spent the rest of the year running in pattern company, all of her races featuring rivalry with the same leading juvenile: Shale.

The pair first met in the Group 3 Frank Conroy Silver Flash Stakes over seven furlongs at Leopardstown in early August. The front-running Finest, one of the 50/1 outsiders, led the field around the final bend and was not headed until around a furlong and a half out when a somewhat green Shale, who had been close from the time they swung into the straight, took over and started to pull clear. Pretty Gorgeous was the obvious danger, but although she was closing throughout the final half furlong, her progress was not sufficient to catch her rival and so she passed the post a length and a half down. A Ma Chere and Snowfall hit the line together another three and a half lengths adrift, the former getting the valuable pattern-race placing by a short head.

Round two came at the Curragh sixteen days later, this time on soft ground in the Group 2 A.R.M. Holding Debutante Stakes, also over seven. It was clear from two out that the pair would play a major role in the finish, but it was the Joseph O'Brien-trained bay who was travelling better than the Donnacha O'Brien-trained one. Shale was being pushed along but went to the front over a furlong from home. Pretty Gorgeous moved up to draw level, still going strongly, and then pulled away steadily over the final half furlong. She won by two and a half lengths, the same margin that separated Shale and Mother Earth, with Meala three-quarters of a length back in fourth and Snowfall a well-beaten fifth.

The market painted a clear picture of how round three, the Group 1 Moyglare Stud Stakes, was expected to go. Pretty Gorgeous was a warm favourite ahead of Shale, Teresa Mendoza and Mother Earth, with everything else in the thirteen-runner line-up available at between 14/1 and 200/1. Pattern-placed winner Teresa Mendoza ran flat, whereas Mother Earth tried to make all but weakened and dropped back not long after being headed a quarter of a mile from home. It was there that the big two made their move. The pair battled throughout the final furlong but this time it was Shale who got the upper hand. She was always doing just enough to keep her rival at bay, passing the post three-quarters of a length in front. There was a one-and-three-quarter-length gap back to Ouduadatta in third with the Group 1 Phoenix Stakes sixth and now US-based Bubbles On Ice three-quarters of a length behind in fourth, her head just in front of once-raced maiden winner Thunder Beauty.

The ground had been good that day and also at Leopardstown, it had been yielding (akin to good-to-soft) on her debut and soft when she had won her Group 2 in such good style. The ground may be key to her prospects of hitting the top in 2021, a view that acquired further support when she won the Group 1 bet365 Fillies' Mile on soft at Newmarket on her final start. It was a race that made headlines for a somewhat bizarre reason that had nothing to do with the favourite's performance. She made steady progress in the final quarter mile, hit the front a furlong out and kept on well to the finish, holding off Indigo Girl by half a length. There was a similar gap back to the third, who was a neck in front of fourth-placed Dubai Fountain, and then a four-and-a-quarter-length gap back to Zabeel Queen in fifth. Shale failed to show her form that day and finished sixth, almost seven lengths behind her old rival.

It is the identity of the third-place finisher that made many headlines. Snowfall appeared to outrun her odds of 50/1 but a viewer spotted an error that had been missed by everyone, including the Ballydoyle representatives who had saddled her, led her up, and ridden her, and he raised the alarm. Aidan O'Brien—who was in Ireland due to Covid-related travel restrictions—had two runners in the race from among a small satellite group of horses he had based in England and the pair became mixed up. It was Mother Earth who passed the post in third, in the wrong colours and with the wrong number and wrong jockey. The inevitable enquiry deemed that there had been no intent behind the mix-up, that both carried the same weight and there was nothing in the rules that would require disqualification, so the result was merely amended to show Mother Earth as the third-place finisher and Snowfall eighth.

Pretty Gorgeous holds entries in both the Group 1 Tattersalls Irish 1,000 Guineas and Group 1 Juddmonte Irish Oaks, and while we already know she stays the former's distance well, she is not guaranteed to manage the latter's twelve furlongs. That is not to say that she won't stay. It is possible that she may be well-suited by the distances. That his best includes a Group 1 Gold Cup-placed, Group 1 St Leger winner proves that Lawman can get horses who have stamina, but his talented young daughter is out of a daughter of the Group 1 July Cup star Compton Place (by Indian Ridge) and the typical range in which the best in her family have excelled is seven to ten furlongs. Her broodmare sire may prove influential in determining her distance range, but it's also possible that this could come instead from female ancestors.

Her half-brother Alwaab (by Toronado) won a ten-furlong listed contest in France, her dam is the sprint winner and Listed Surrey Stakes-third (seven furlongs) Lady Gorgeous, and that mare is a half-sister to the dam of the classic-placed dual mile Group 1 star Qemah (by Danehill Dancer). That Jean-Claude Rouget-trained ace was third in the Group 1 Prix Marcel Boussac as a two-year-old, landed the Group 3 Prix de la Grotte over a mile on soft ground before taking third to La Cressonniere in the

Group 1 Poule d'Essai des Pouliches (French 1000 Guineas), and then completed her top-level double with victories in the Coronation Stakes at Ascot and Prix Rothschild at Deauville. She was also third to Alice Springs in the Group 1 Matron Stakes at Leopardstown, landed the Group 2 Duke of Cambridge Stakes as a four-year-old and came off worst in a four-way finish to that year's edition of the Rothschild, beaten by a total of half a length by the winner, Roly Poly. The only time she was asked to try beyond a mile was on her second start as a juvenile and it was only an extra half furlong at conditions level; she won by three lengths.

Qemah is out of a mile winner who was Group 3-placed over ten and a half furlongs: Karthica (by Rainbow Quest). That half-sister to Lady Gorgeous is a daughter of Cayman Sunset (by Night Shift), who won the Listed Dahlia Stakes over nine furlongs and failed to make the frame in four tries over farther. In fairness to her, one of those was a fourth-place finish behind Lailani in the Group 1 Nassau Stakes over ten furlongs and another was a similar placing in the Listed Middleton Stakes over the extended ten furlongs at York.

However, there is some encouragement with regard to the potential of Pretty Gorgeous to stay the Oaks distance if you look at her grandam's half brother I'm Supposin (by Posen). That grandson of Danzig (by Northern Dancer) won the non-blacktype Ulster Harp Derby over twelve and a half furlongs at Down Royal, was multiple blacktype-placed at up to fourteen furlongs and then posted a wide-margin success in the Grade 2 Kingwell Hurdle at Wincanton.

Pretty Gorgeous, who won the Cartier Award as the top juvenile filly last season, had an official end-of-year handicap mark of 113, so she shared the honours with Campanelle and Shale for the official title of champion two-year-old filly. She has obvious potential to play a leading role in the top fillies' races in 2021. In addition to her two Irish classic entries noted above, she is also engaged in the Group 1 Emirates Poule d'Essai des Pouliches, Group 1 Saxon Warrior Coolmore Prix Saint-Alary and Group 1 Prix de Diane Longines.

SUMMARY DETAILS
Bred: Ecurie Haras Du Cadran, E Ciampi, SAS I.E.I., Ecurie La
   Boetie
Owned: John Oxley
Trained: Joseph O'Brien
Country: Ireland
Race record: 12121-
Career highlights: 3 wins inc bet365 Fillies' Mile (Gr1), A.R.M.
Holding Debutante Stakes (Gr2), 2nd Moyglare Stud Stakes
(Gr1), Frank Conroy Silver Flash Stakes (Gr3)

PRETTY GORGEOUS (FR) – 2018 bay filly

Lawman (FR)	Invincible Spirit (IRE)	Green Desert (USA)
		Rafha
	Laramie (USA)	Gulch (USA)
		Light The Lights (FR)
Lady Gorgeous (GB)	Compton Place (GB)	Indian Ridge
		Nosey
	Cayman Sunset (IRE)	Night Shift (USA)
		Robinia (USA)

PRINCESS ZOE (GER)

The 2020 flat season for two star older mares revolved around getting them to ParisLongchamp in the first weekend in October where they would bid for further Group 1 glory and places in the record books. Two older mares did leave the venue with top-level victories to their name, as did a four-year-old filly who secured what would be the middle leg of a famous hat-trick, but it was not a pairing that anyone could have predicted when the delayed season finally got under way. One Master duly became the first horse ever to win the seven-furlong Prix de la Foret three times but fellow six-year-old Enable's bid for a record third Prix de l'Arc de Triomphe was ruined by underfoot conditions that were, for her, too deep.

Had anyone making predictions during the first lockdown suggested that a horse named Princess Zoe would be among the year's Group 1 winners then interested individuals may have scoured the lists of regally related two-year-olds and classic prospects based in the major yards. The more intrepid might have checked older sprinters across a wide range of stables. But the task would have generated some easily imaginable confusion. We can't find any such horse in training, so who are you talking about? She's a five-year-old German-bred daughter of an Irish-based National Hunt stallion, a dual winner from fifteen starts on the flat in her native land and, oh yeah, she's rated sixty-four, has had trouble with her feet, and has joined the Tony Mullins team as a potential Cheltenham Festival prospect. Are you having a laugh? No, and she could be heading to Paris for a crack at the 2021 edition of the Arc.

Her first run for her new connections was at Navan in late June when she finished runner-up in a sixteen-runner handicap over thirteen furlongs on soft ground and it was followed a few weeks later by her first win for them, in the Kildare Village Ladies Derby Handicap at the Curragh. She cruised forward to dispute the lead a quarter of a mile from home, Jody Townend asked her to go on a furlong out and the pair quickly went clear. It was an easy five-length win under a hands-and-heels ride and her trainer revealed in post-race interviews that the plan was now the big amateur race at the Galway Festival. She duly won that valuable Connacht Hotel Handicap by a length and a quarter, this time with Finian Maguire in the saddle, staying on strongly on the soft ground and proving that the near two-mile–one-furlong trip was comfortably in her range. She won that race off a mark of eighty-three, having been raised by thirteen pounds for her Curragh victory, and now Mullins was talking about a potential bid for the Cesarewitch Handicap at Newmarket in the fall.

Just five days later, she added her name to the list of horses who have won twice during a Galway Festival meeting, this time with the five-pound-claiming apprentice Joey Sheridan on board. It was another premier handicap, this time over twelve furlongs and with a seven-pound penalty, but neither the trip nor the weight made any apparent difference to her. The mare was travelling noticeably well a quarter of a mile from home, hit the front inside the final furlong and won a shade comfortably by half a length from Emperor of The Sun, that colt finishing five and a half lengths clear of the third, Lynwood Gold. Now Mullins had a more notable target in mind for his rising star: the Group 1 Qatar Prix du Cadran.

Raised to 101 and so still a long way short of the required standard for the top level, she made another visit to Galway on a foggy day in early September, this time for the Listed Ardilaun Hotel Oyster Stakes over a mile and a half. The ground was heavy, visibility poor, and the classic-placed Ennistymon again failed to show that level of form in finishing third, but the grey brought up her four-timer in style. Sheridan sent her to the front a furlong out and the pair kept on well for a comfortable win, this time beating Barrington Court by one and three-quarter lengths. That flat-bred Jessica Harrington-trained mare had come into the race as a hurdle and listed bumper winner who had run away with a Bellewstown maiden on her flat debut and would go on to boost the form with a Group 3 second and two listed wins on only subsequent outings.

Princess Zoe, on the other hand, made the journey to France. Heavy ground turned the two-and-a-half-mile Prix du Cadran into quite a slog, and the Frederic Rossi-trained Alkuin set off in front in a brave bid to make all. It was a good gallop in the conditions but not one that the pack chose to match, leaving the gelding to build up a substantial lead. One usually sees such leaders tire with a few furlongs to run and then drop back quickly as the rest of the field sweeps past, but that didn't happen here. He was getting tired in the final quarter mile but was still clear and there was only one horse making any inroads on his lead. There was a lot of ground to be made up and yet there was almost a sense of inevitability in the manner in which she was closing, triggering memories of the famous and almost slow-motion Grand National finish of 1973 when Red Rum eventually reeled in the game front-runner, Crisp. Alkuin kept going but the mare caught him near the line and was half a length up as they passed the post, with a fifteen-length gap to prior Cadran winner Call The Wind in third. It was a tremendous achievement for the mare, for her trainer and for the apprentice rider who had struck up such a good partnership with her.

Three weeks later she faced her toughest test to date, from a form perspective, when taking on seven rivals in the Group 1 Prix Royal-Oak over fifteen and a half furlongs. The ground was again heavy that day at ParisLongchamp, Seamie Heffernan was in the saddle, but although staying on in the closing stages she had had to settle for fourth. It would have been third in another few strides—she was only a neck behind the popular Group 1-winning veteran Holdthasigreen—and there was a fourteen-length gap back to the fifth. Three-year-olds dominated the finish, with Subjectivist beating Valia by two lengths. Holdthasigreen was another two and a half lengths behind.

There was still some speculation at this point about her going jumping and potentially lining up at Cheltenham in March but it soon seemed that those plans had been shelved; her trainer was talking about a potential Arc bid in 2021. He has also been quoted as saying she might have won it in 2020, but that's fanciful thinking. She is a 110-rated mare who is effective at twelve furlongs but needed every yard of the extra mile at ParisLongchamp to win the Group 1 Prix du Cadran and found the Royal-Oak trip just a bit too short to get another Group 1 placing on her record. Soft or heavy ground would aid her should that race, or other targets, come down to a test of stamina, but it is hard to imagine that she could find the extra ten-to-fourteen pounds that would likely be necessary to make the frame in an average Arc. That said, Princess Zoe could be a leading challenger for the various Cup races, the Group 1 Irish St Leger and potentially another attempt at the Prix Royal-Oak.

Bought out of Germany by Bernard Cullinane, the mare carries the well-known purple and yellow colours of Paddy Kehoe and his sister Philomena Crampton, ones carried to victory by another celebrity mare in the past. Grabel, whom Tony Mullins also trained, won four races on the flat and thirteen times under National Hunt rules, a career whose highlights included back-to-back wins in the Morgiana Hurdle at Punchestown, blacktype hurdle success at three consecutive Christmas festival meetings at Leopardstown, the Brown Lad Hurdle at Naas, and the ultra-valuable Duelling Grounds International over two miles, six furlongs at Kentucky Downs in the USA.

Princess Zoe was conceived when her sire, the Group 1 Preis von Europa and Group 1 Irish St Leger winner Jukebox Jury (by Montjeu), stood at Gestüt Etzean. He has since been covering triple-digit books of mares at Burgage Stud, the farm famously associated with the star National Hunt stallions Bob Back and Shantou, and his best winners before 2020 included the Grade 1 Triumph Hurdle scorer Farclas. She was bred by Gestüt Hony-Hof, is out of the well-related dual winner Palace Princess (by Tiger Hill) and has a half-brother who achieved a higher rating than she has done so far. The 115-rated Palace Prince (by Areion) won a Group 2 over a mile in Germany, three Group 3 contests over ten furlongs and two listed races, he chased home Nutan in the Group 1 Deutsches Derby and stood his first season as a stallion in France in 2020.

Their dam got her wins at around a mile and she is a daughter of 2003's Broodmare of the Year in Germany, Pasca (by Lagunas). That one-time winner is responsible for the juvenile champion Peppershot (by Big Shuffle), three-year-old mile champion Pepperstorm and the prolific Peppercorn, and the reason that those German full brothers did not win a Group 1 race is in part due to there being no races at that level in Germany at under ten furlongs. Padang (by Ile de Bourbon) heads the string of stakes winners who appear under the next generation of the pedigree and that Group 2 Preis der Diana (German Oaks) heroine can be described as being a three-parts sister to Pasca.

Princess Zoe has gone from being an obscure sixty-four-rated handicapper to one of the most popular horses in training in Ireland. It is possible that her Group 1 Prix du Cadran victory will remain her sole victory at the highest level on the flat, but her remarkable five-year-old season was all about achieving things that could scarcely have been dreamed about just months before, so who would want to rule out the possibility that she might hit the Group 1 target again? Looking further ahead, she has a pedigree that could see her make an impact at stud, hopefully with opportunities to breed flat horses rather than jumpers.

SUMMARY DETAILS

Bred: Gestüt Hony-Hof
Owned: Patrick F Kehoe & Mrs Philomena Crampton
Trained: Tony Mullins
Country: Ireland
Race record: -03121-0002323022-2111114-
Career highlights: 7 wins inc Qatar Prix du Cadran (Gr1), Ardilaun Hotel Oyster Stakes (L)

PRINCESS ZOE (GER) – 2015 grey mare

Jukebox Jury (IRE)	Montjeu (IRE)	Sadler's Wells (USA)
		Floripedes (FR)
	Mare Aux Fees (GB)	Kenmare (FR)
		Feerie Boreale (FR)
Palace Princess (GER)	Tiger Hill (IRE)	Danehill (USA)
		The Filly (GER)
	Pasca (GER)	Lagunas
		Palmas (GER)

SANTIAGO (IRE)

The delayed and compressed start to the 2020 season meant that most of the early classics were moved to later dates and that there was little to no time for any of their entrants to get in a prior run. It was strange to see some of the established trials being held after the classics with which they're typically associated and to see some of Royal Ascot's races taking on the role of pre-classic trial rather than post-classic compensation or progress. Aside from its opening day in March, the Irish season did not begin until early June but the Irish Derby did not move from its traditional position in the calendar. So rather than providing an opportunity for a classic champion to confirm his or her status as a leader of their generation, the line-up for the latest edition of the Dubai Duty Free-sponsored test consisted of a string of fourteen horses that we had little prior chance to know.

The sole filly, New York Girl, had won a Group 3 at two and been fourth in the Group 1 Irish 1,000 Guineas a fortnight before her Derby bid. Crossfirehurricane, a winner at Limerick on his only juvenile run, had won twice on the Polytrack at Dundalk in February and was still unbeaten having landed the Group 3 Gallinule Stakes on June 12th. Arthur's Kingdom had been runner-up to Mkfancy in the Group 1 Criterium de Saint-Cloud at two and chased home Pyledriver in the Group 2 King Edward VII Stakes at Royal Ascot, three days before Santiago landed the Group 2 Queen's Vase at the same meeting. The first three of those finished down the field at the Curragh and did nothing to advertise the form afterwards. New York Girl was unplaced in two more Group 1s before crossing the Atlantic to continue her career in the USA. She made a winning debut in a minor turf race at Gulfstream Park on New Year's Eve and has been placed in blacktype company since. Arthur's Kingdom was also exported, in his case to Hong Kong, but he wasn't seen in action until shortly before this book went to print, kicking off 2021 with two unplaced finishes. Crossfirehurricane also disappointed, beating only one home in a fourteen-runner race at Dundalk in the fall, and he has since moved to North America.

Santiago, on the other hand, won the Irish Derby. The big-race favourite hit the front a quarter of a mile from home, went clear and then had to battle to hold off the strong-finishing Tiger Moth who, despite looking a shade green, failed by just a head to give his rider, Emmet McNamara, what would have been the first leg of a remarkable Derby double. McNamara was on board Serpentine at Epsom the following week. Tiger Moth had won a ten-furlong Leopardstown maiden earlier in the month, beating Dawn Patrol by half a length, and it was that maiden who picked up third place in the classic, this time beaten by five lengths. It was hard to know what to make of the race on the day, the dubious nature of the form advertised by the fact that none of the third, fourth, fifth or sixth had ever won any sort of race before. However, by the end of the year it looked better.

Tiger Moth ran twice more, easily won a twelve-furlong Group 3 contest at Leopardstown on the opening day of Irish Champions Weekend before failing by only half a length to add the Group 1 Lexus Melbourne Cup over two miles at Flemington in early November. Dawn Patrol won a maiden and the Group 3 Loughbrown Stakes, finished third in a listed race and was unplaced twice, and the now gelded four-year-old could be a Cup horse in 2021. Fourth-placed Order of Australia was unplaced in the Group 1 Prix du Jockey Club (French Derby) next time but won three of his five subsequent runs, notably the Grade 1 Breeders' Cup Mile at Keeneland. Fiscal Rules was fifth, won a seven-furlong maiden three months later, was unplaced three times and has been gelded, whereas sixth-placed Gold Maze was unplaced at Epsom the following week, won a ten-furlong Curragh maiden and then finished fourth and third in blacktype races at Navan and Dundalk. It was not a strong edition of the Irish Derby, but the first two are high-class colts and the fourth found his forte when dropped down in trip.

Santiago also failed to win again but he was certainly not disgraced in either race. His prior two-and-three-quarter-length defeat of Berkshire Rocco over fourteen furlongs on soft ground at Ascot made it inevitable that he would be stepped back up in trip rather than be campaigned as a middle-distance horse, and while his St Leger bid was an obvious target, his Goodwood Cup one was a bold choice. He was the only horse backed to beat the odds-on favourite Stradivarius in the Al Shaqab-sponsored two-mile feature—it was 20/1 bar the pair in the seven-runner line up—and he finished an honourable third to the brilliant six-year-old. Four-year-old Nayef Road had tried to make all and kept on well to the line to take second. Santiago headed him briefly over a furlong out, with Stradivarius looking for room just behind and Eagles By Day making his move on the outside, but the three-year-old could not build on that. Nayef Road regained the lead and pulled a length and a quarter clear of his younger rival, but Stradivarius stormed past him in the final half furlong to win by a length. Eagles By Day was another three lengths adrift in fourth, followed home by Euchen Glen and Spanish Mission.

That was a month after the Curragh and six and a half weeks before the Group 1 Pertemps St Leger Stakes at Doncaster. He was sent off favourite to beat ten rivals in the fourteen-and-a-half-furlong classic, but although still with every chance of victory over a furlong out, he could not find anything extra and had to settle for fourth, flashing past the post level with but wide apart from Pyledriver. Galileo Chrome landed the spoils by a neck from Berkshire Rocco with Pyledriver and Santiago a length behind. They were another two and three-quarter lengths clear of Hukum, who was followed home by Dawn Patrol and subsequent Group 1 scorer Subjectivist. Galileo Chrome has been retired to stud, Berkshire Rocco won a listed contest shortly afterwards and is one to watch in 2021, Pyledriver looks set for a middle-distance campaign, whereas it seems likely that Santiago will continue in the stayers' division.

Santiago, whose maiden success was in a mile maiden on soft ground at Listowel as a two-year-old, comes from a branch of one of the most famous stallion-producing families of the modern era. However, having had his stamina talked up and run three times from fourteen furlongs to two miles, it seems likely that his future stud career will be in the National Hunt sector, which is a pity. He is a son of now Turkey-based Derby hero Authorized (by Montjeu), although the accolade of being the best son of his sire must go to the multiple Australian Group 1-star Hartnell. That £4 million-earner, a gelding, got his top-level wins at seven, eight, ten and twelve furlongs. Another of his leading sons, Mapperly Stud's Complacent, won the Group 1 Spring Champion Stakes over ten furlongs at Randwick, was runner-up in the Group 1 Victoria Derby and is off the mark with a dual winner from a handful of runners. Under National Hunt rules, Authorized is responsible for the ill-fated Grade 1 star Nichols Canyon and for the dual Grade 3 Grand National hero Tiger Roll.

Santiago's half-sister La Joconde (by Frankel) has been placed in two of her four starts to date but picked up blacktype in one of them, the Listed Staffordstown Stud Stakes in which she finished a two-and-a-half-length third to Fantasy Lady over a mile on soft ground at the Curragh in October. They are the first two foals of Wadyhatta (by Cape Cross), a half-sister to the classic-placed French stakes winner Motamarris (by Le Havre) and to Riqa (by Dubawi), the stakes-placed dam of the multiple Group 3-winning sprinter Tantheem (by Teofilo).

Their stakes-placed dam Thamarat (by Anabaa) is out of one-time scorer Al Ishq (by Nureyev) and that makes her a half-sister to the Group 1-winning miler and classic sire Tamayuz (by Nayef). That Derrinstown Stud resident has sired twenty-two stakes winners, four of them successful at the highest level—Blonde Me, G Force, Mustashry, and Precieuse—and he is also responsible for the juvenile Group 2 scorer and successful sire Sir Prancealot. Allez Les Trois (by Riverman), the fourth dam of Santiago, won the Group 3 Prix de Flore, and in addition to being the dam of the Group 1 Prix du Jockey Club winner and blacktype sire Anabaa Blue (by Anabaa), she is also the grandam of the dual Group 1-placed Group 3 winner Half Light (by Shamardal) and third dam of the classic-placed sprint Group 2 winner Mustajeeb (by Nayef).

Santiago's relationship to Tamayuz would make him an interesting flat-sire prospect but it is what appears under the fifth generation of his pedigree that will be the biggest pedigree selling point for him. That's because Allez Les Trois was out of the Group 3 Oaks Trial Stakes runner-up Allegretta (by Lombard) and so was a half-sister to Group 1 2000 Guineas winner and classic sire King's Best (by Kingmambo) and, of course, to the Group 1 Prix de l'Arc de Triomphe heroine and phenomenal broodmare

Urban Sea (by Miswaki). Santiago is a great-grandson of Sadler's Wells (by Northern Dancer), out of a Cape Cross (by Green Desert) mare and from the family of the dual Derby hero and great sire Galileo (by Sadler's Wells). That record-breaking prolific champion sire is a half-brother to the Timeform 140-rated superstar and outstanding sire Sea The Stars (by Cape Cross), and if you go through the various branches of the family you will also find Group 1 sire Tertullian (by Miswaki) and one that leads to the Group 1 winner and leading German sire Adlerflug (by In The Wings).

There are many other top-level winners who descend from Allegretta and her dam, Anatevka (by Espresso), including 2020 Group 1 scorers Sir Dragonet (by Camelot) and Torquator Tasso (by Adlerflug) and 2018's Derby winner Masar (by New Approach), now a young Dalham Hall Stud stallion whose first foals started to arrive just before this book went to print.

Santiago remains is a horse of considerable potential and it will be fascinating to see what he can achieve both as an older male on the track and eventually at stud. His dam's third foal is a Frankel filly for whom Haras d'Etreham paid €500,000 at Tattersalls' Book 1 sale in October—she has been named Wien and is to be trained by Francis-Henri Graffard—and the mare was bred to Galileo in 2020.

SUMMARY DETAILS

Bred: Lynch Bages Ltd
Owned: Michael Tabor, Derrick Smith & Mrs John Magnier
Trained: Aidan O'Brien
Country: Ireland
Race record: 221-1134-
Career highlights: 3 wins inc Dubai Duty Free Irish Derby (Gr1), Queen's Vase (Gr2), 3rd Al Shaqab Goodwood Cup Stakes (Gr1)

SANTIAGO (IRE) – 2017 bay colt

Authorized (IRE)	Montjeu (IRE)	Sadler's Wells (USA)
		Floripedes (FR)
	Funsie (FR)	Saumarez
		Vallee Dansante (USA)
Wadyhatta (GB)	Cape Cross (IRE)	Green Desert (USA)
		Park Appeal
	Thamarat (GB)	Anabaa (USA)
		Al Ishq (FR)

SEALIWAY (FR)

Heavy ground can exaggerate margins and the challenge for Sealiway in 2021 will be to prove that his impressive eight-length drubbing of Nando Parrado in the Group 1 Qatar Prix Jean-Luc Lagardere was a reasonable reflection of his talent. He had won three of his prior five starts, one of them a five-length score in a listed contest over the same trip, seven furlongs, on good-to-soft at Vichy, and he had been blacktype-placed in the other two. But his European finale represented a leap forward. Nando Parrado, who had won the Group 2 Coventry Stakes and been runner-up to Campanelle in the Group 1 Prix Morny, finished three-quarters of a length in front of the Group 2 Railway Stakes winner and Group 1 Phoenix Stakes fourth Laws of Indices, with the filly Libertine another neck back in fourth. Her only defeat in three prior outings had been when finishing a two-length fourth to King's Harlequin in the Group 3 Prix d'Aumale over a mile on good ground at ParisLongchamp.

Sealiway and Libertine both ran once more before the end of the year, both finishing fifth in their respective races but with those efforts representing a gulf in form. The filly was a beaten favourite in a nine-furlong listed contest, whereas the colt ran in the Grade 1 Breeders' Cup Juvenile Turf on good ground at Keeneland. Fire At Will won that one-mile test by three lengths from the Aidan O'Brien-trained Battleground, with margins of a neck, half a length and one length back to Outadore, Cadillac and Sealiway. He had gone to the front a quarter of a mile out when he won at Vichy, went clear over a furlong and a half from home at ParisLongchamp but never got closer than his final finishing position in America. Maybe it was being hampered early in the race, or the fastest surface and longest trip he had yet encountered, or the travelling, or even that he had been on the go since his winning debut at Saint-Cloud in mid-May. Perhaps it was a combination of factors. But he still remains a bright prospect and it would not be a surprise to see the Frederic Rossi-trained chestnut win again at the highest level in 2021.

The €62,000 Arqana Deauville August yearling sale graduate is a second-crop son of Galiway (by Galileo), a half-brother to the

Breeders' Cup-placed, Grade 2-winning miler and Canadian champion sire Silent Name (by Sunday Silence). The stallion's dam is a half-sister to the similarly talented Gold Away (by Goldneyev), the former Haras du Quesnay horse who gave us the multiple Group 1 star Alexander Goldrun, and although he showed some ability on the track it is fair to say that there have been plenty of more talented horses who have not been afforded a chance at stud. Galiway won a mile maiden and was runner-up in the Group 3 Horris Stakes from two starts at two, finished third in the Group 3 Prix de Fontainebleau first time out at three, was unplaced in both the Group 1 Poule d'Essai des Poulains (French 2000 Guineas) and Group 1 Prix du Jockey Club (French Derby) and then narrowly won a nine-furlong listed contest at Maisons-Laffitte on what turned out to be his last race. He covered his first four books at a fee of €3,000, that rose to €10,000 after his first juveniles featured the Group 3 Prix la Rochette scorer Kenway and it has been raised to €12,000 for 2021. Galiway has sired four stakes winners, three of them from his first crop, and he is an interesting prospect for the future.

Sealiway, a half-brother to a winner, is the third foal of the Listed Prix Herod winner Kensea (by Kendargent) and as she is out of Sea Island, a five-time winning daughter of Gold Away (by Goldneyev), that makes Sealiway inbred 3x4 to Blushing Away (by Blushing Groom). That the stakes-placed mare is the dam of the high-class miler Gold Away and of Galiway's Group 3 Prix Perth-winning dam, Danzigaway (by Danehill). His fourth dam, En Avant (by Kenmare), is a winning half-sister to the Group 2 Prix de Mallaret heroine Another Dancer (by Groom Dancer) and to On Air (by Chief Singer), who has had an eye-catching stud career. She won three times on the flat and once over hurdles, her lightly raced son Berenson (by Entrepreneur) was runner-up in the Group 1 National Stakes at the Curragh, her daughter Pollen (by Orpen) won the Group 3 Park Express Stakes and is a blacktype producer in Japan, and she is also the dam of the Listed Vintage Crop Stakes runner-up Swiss Roll (by Entrepreneur). That filly now has three sons of note, the eldest of them being the Group 2 Lonsdale Cup winner and Group 1 Irish St Leger second Ahzeemah (by Dubawi) and the youngest one being the Group 3-

placed Austrian School (by Teofilo). That capable flat stayer covered 26 mares in his first season at Clongiffen Stud in Ireland and has his first foals arriving this year. However, it is the middle brother who will be best remembered as the years roll on as he is none other than the dual Grade 3 Grand National hero Tiger Roll (by Authorized).

All of this makes Sealiway an intriguing prospect. It would be no surprise to see him run well in the Poule d'Essai des Poulains and/or Prix du Jockey Club or even to see him return to seven furlongs for the Prix Jean Prat and/or Prix de la Foret.

SUMMARY DETAILS
Bred: Guy Pariente Holding
Owned: La Haras De La Gousserie & Guy Pariente
Trained: Frederic Rossi
Country: France
Race record: 1131210-
Career highlights: 4 wins inc Qatar Prix Jean-Luc Lagardere (Grand Criterium) (Gr1), Prix des Jouvenceaux et des Jouvencelles (L), 2nd Prix la Rochette (Gr3), 3rd Prix Roland de Chambure (L)

SEALIWAY (FR) – 2018 chestnut colt

Galiway (GB)	Galileo (IRE)	Sadler's Wells (USA)
		Urban Sea (USA)
	Danzigaway (USA)	Danehill (USA)
		Blushing Away (USA)
Kensea (FR)	Kendargent (FR)	Kendor (FR)
		Pax Bella (FR)
	Sea Island (FR)	Gold Away (IRE)
		Equatoriale (FR)

SEARCH FOR A SONG (IRE)

Search For A Song was one of the leading three-year-old fillies of 2019, an Irish Oaks fourth who scored clear-cut victories in both the Listed Galtres Stakes and Group 1 Comer Group International Irish St Leger. The latter, achieved by a margin of two and a quarter lengths from Kew Gardens, identified her as an exciting prospect for 2020. The wisdom of the decision to keep her in training must have been subject to a shade of doubt after her seasonal reappearance at the Curragh in June. She was a joint-favourite for the Group 2 Coolmore Magna Grecia Irish EBF Mooresbridge Stakes over ten and a half furlongs, the ground was good-to-firm, as it had been for her big win the previous year, but although in front and going well three furlongs from home she was under pressure soon afterwards and weakened to finish a well-beaten sixth to Leo de Fury.

The Group 3 Munster Oaks Stakes at Cork the following month looked like an ideal opportunity for her to bounce back, however the twelve-furlong contest instead produced some minutes of deep concern for her wellbeing. She stumbled badly about quarter of a mile after the start, lost a considerable amount of ground and was soon pulled up. Jockey Oisin Orr, who would be in the saddle in all but one of her starts last season, later reported that she had slipped while rounding the first bend. The race was won by Kew Gardens' younger full sister, Snow. Thankfully, she was none the worse for the experience, but with such a disappointing start to her campaign it was not really a surprise to see her sent off at 50/1 for the rescheduled Group 1 Tattersalls Gold Cup over ten furlongs at the Curragh three weeks later. The ground was good-to-yielding, the trip short of her best, and if you paused the race three furlongs from home you might have been predicting imminent retirement. She was being pushed along in last place and seemingly booked to remain there. Two out, Magical was still going well in front while Orr was still hard at work on Search For A Song. The only difference in their relative positions at the furlong pole was that the Ballydoyle champion was further ahead of the pack, but then, half a furlong from the line, the chestnut began to stay on strongly. She passed three rivals in a matter of strides and secured third place, beaten by margins of two and a quarter lengths and two lengths as Magical led home a one-two for Ballydoyle. Sir Dragonet, the runner-up, was having his last outing for the stable before going on to Group 1 success for his new connections in Australia. Armory, Leo de Fury and Buckhurst were the fourth-, fifth- and sixth-place finishers.

The Group 1 Comer Group International Irish St Leger was the obvious next target and her performance there vindicated the decision to keep her in action as a four-year-old. Once again, she raced in rear and was being pushed along with three furlongs to race as the always-prominent recent Ebor Handicap winner Fujaira Prince made his bid for glory. That gelding led the field into the straight and kept going to the line, holding off the subsequent Group 1 Melbourne Cup star Twilight Payment by a neck, but Search For A Song had caught him half a furlong from home and stayed on strongly for a two-length win. Fifth-placed Passion was the only three-year-old in the line-up, the previous year's Irish Derby winner Sovereign disappointed in sixth, while the sponsors' own Raa Atoll (by Sea The Stars), a Group 2 winner who was one of the busiest new sires to stud in 2020—he covered 92 mares before his return to action in September—finished tailed off.

Search For A Song had one more run and again confirmed her superiority over Fujaira Prince, albeit by only half a length this time. The race was the Group 2 Qipco British Champions Long Distance Cup over a few yards short of two miles on soft ground at Ascot, Morando, Sovereign and Dawn Patrol were the next horses home, coming in at margins of a neck, half a length and one and a half lengths, but this was the day that Trueshan showed us what he could do as a stayer. A listed winner over twelve furlongs and an eighth-place finisher in the Ebor over fourteen, it was the Alan King-trained gelding's first attempt at two miles and, in the hands of Hollie Doyle, he hit the front over a furlong out and went clear for an impressive seven-and-a-half-length victory.

Search For A Song's pedigree was reviewed in detail in *European Group 1 Winners of 2019*, so a brief recap will suffice here. The daughter of prolific champion sire Galileo (by Sadler's Wells) is a Moyglare Stud homebred and the eighth foal of Polished Gem (by Danehill), a winning full sister to their Grade 1 Matriarch Stakes heroine Dress To Thrill. Her grandam, Trusted Partner (by Affirmed), won the Group 1 Irish 1,000 Guineas, third dam Talking Picture (by Speak John) was a Grade 1-star and juvenile filly champion in the USA in 1973, and Gallante (by Montjeu; Group 1 Grand Prix de Paris, Group 1 Sydney Cup), Vert de Grece (by Verglas; Group 1 Criterium International) and 2020 juvenile star Thunder Moon (by Zoffany; Group 1 National Stakes) are just three of the major winners who appear in branches of the family. One might have expected that it would be Dress To Thrill who would excel at stud rather than her lesser sister, but the former has been as disappointing as the latter has excelled.

Polished Gem has had ten racing-age progeny, all ten are winners and seven of them have scored in blacktype company. Sapphire (by Medicean) was her first-born, she won the Group 2 British Champions Fillies & Mares Stakes, was runner-up in the Group 1 Pretty Polly Stakes and is the dam of the Group 2-placed filly Kiss For A Jewel (by Kingman). Triple Group 2 scorer Custom Cut (by Notnowcato) was number two, and Group 1 Prince of Wales's Stakes star and young blacktype sire Free Eagle (by High Chaparral) was number four. He stands at the Irish National Stud and his first-crop son Khalifa Sat chased home Serpentine in the Derby at Epsom in July. Australian Group 3 scorer Valac (by Dark Angel) came next, pattern-placed stakes winner Falcon Eight (by Galileo) was born three years later, then came Search For A Song and her year-younger full sister Amma Grace, last year's Listed Trigo Stakes winner and Group 2 Blandford Stakes second. The mare's 2018 foal arrived on May 18th that year, is named Kyprios (by Galileo), made a winning debut for the Aidan O'Brien stable at Galway in September, finished down the field in the Group 3 Zetland Stakes and holds entries in both the Derby and Irish Derby. Polished Gem was bred to both Galileo and Sea The Stars (by Cape Cross) in 2020.

Dual Group 1 star Search For A Song will be a fascinating addition to the broodmare ranks, one with the potential to produce further Group 1 winners for her famous connections. However, first she has another season in front of her, one that is to be geared around bidding for a third victory in the Irish St Leger.

SUMMARY DETAILS
Bred: Moyglare Stud Farm Ltd
Owned: Moyglare Stud Farm
Trained: Dermot Weld
Country: Ireland
Race record: -12411-0P312-
Career highlights: 4 wins inc Comer Group International Irish St Leger (Gr1-twice), British EBF & Sir Henry Cecil Galtres Stakes (L), 2nd Qipco British Champions Long Distance Cup (Gr2), Irish Stallion Farms EBF Naas Oaks Trial (L), 3rd Tattersalls Gold Cup (Gr1)

SEARCH FOR A SONG (IRE) – 2016 chestnut filly

Galileo (IRE)	Sadler's Wells (USA)	Northern Dancer
		Fairy Bridge (USA)
	Urban Sea (USA)	Miswaki (USA)
		Allegretta
Polished Gem (IRE)	Danehill (USA)	Danzig (USA)
		Razyana (USA)
	Trusted Partner (USA)	Affirmed (USA)
		Talking Picture (USA)

SERPENTINE (IRE)

The world-famous Derby at Epsom was traditionally run on the first Wednesday in June and later moved to the first Saturday of that month. Had it been run on its usual day in 2020 then there would have been a very different result to what we actually got. In a topsy-turvy start to the season, delayed and rejigged due to the Covid-19 pandemic, classic trials were either cancelled or run after the classics for which they usually provide early tests, whereas Royal Ascot became a trial ground for the Epsom hopefuls rather than providing a shot at compensation for that classic festival's disappointments.

The Irish Derby did go ahead on its usual day, and three hours before the Aidan O'Brien-trained Santiago landed that classic by a head from his stablemate Tiger Moth, the team sent out a promising colt in a ten-furlong maiden. The regally related chestnut had been well-beaten at Galway on his only start as a two-year-old and had finished only fifth to Galileo Chrome in a ten-furlong Curragh maiden on fast ground on June 12th. He now wore cheekpieces for the first time, punters gave him another chance and the 5/2 favourite justified that support with a nine-length win. It was visually impressive, but it was only a maiden. One week later he lined up at Epsom, a 25/1 shot in a wide-open edition of the Group 1 Investec Derby.

The Group 1 2000 Guineas star Kameko was sent off favourite but his already doubtful stamina gave out and he had to settle for fourth, a nose away from making the frame. English King had looked good at Lingfield, beating Berkshire Rocco by almost three lengths, but he has not lived up to that promise yet and he finished a neck behind in fifth here, three-quarters of a length in front of Mogul, one of two subsequent middle-distance stars to emerge from the also-rans. Irish 2,000 Guineas runner-up Vatican City was not a guaranteed stayer on pedigree and he came home eighth, ahead of Gold Maze, Highland Chief and Pyledriver. Khalifa Sat had narrowly won the Listed Cocked Hat Stakes over eleven furlongs at Goodwood and outran his odds by holding off the Ballydoyle-trained maiden Amhran Na Bhfiann by half a length for second, but it was evident well before the end that nothing in the race had a chance of victory that day. Emmet McNamara pushed Serpentine to the front from the start, they slipped the field in Slip Anchor-style and came home unchallenged by five and a half lengths in a good time. A 25/1 shot beat colts priced at 50/1 and 66/1 in the world's most famous classic. Even if this had not been a behind-closed-doors running of the race it's doubtful there would have been much in the way of cheering and celebration among spectators. The result was more baffling than exciting and subsequent events did little to change its appearance.

Khalifa Sat was only fifth of six in the Group 3 Gordon Stakes on his only subsequent outing. Amhran Na Bhfiann's next start was in a ten-furlong Naas maiden at the start of August. Unfortunately, the 8/15 favourite, who passed the post a three-quarter-length runner-up to the Dermot Weld-trained filly Zawara, was lame pulling up. He had sustained a condylar fracture to a fetlock, which required surgery to insert two pins, but Aidan O'Brien expressed hope that the colt would be okay to return to action in 2021. Kameko dropped back in trip, finished fourth in the Sussex Stakes and Juddmonte International Stakes before putting up a top-class winning performance in the Group 2 Joel Stakes over the Rowley Mile at Newmarket. Pyledriver impressed with an easy victory over Highland Chief in the Group 2 Great Voltigeur Stakes next time and finished a close third in the Group 1 Pertemps St Leger Stakes, but Mogul was the best horse in the field. He beat Highland Chief in the Group 3 Gordon Stakes, was third in the Voltigeur, beat In Swop easily in the Group 1 Grand Prix de Paris, finished fifth to Tarnawa in the Grade 1 Breeders' Cup Turf and then trounced local star Exultant by three lengths in the Group 1 Longines Hong Kong Vase.

As for Serpentine, he was only fourth in the Grand Prix de Paris, finishing a total of four and a quarter lengths behind Mogul, this time ridden to settle behind the leaders. He was slow to break in the Group 1 Qipco Champion Stakes at Ascot in October but, now partnered by William Buick, was quickly urged forward to take up the running. He made a gallant effort in this considerably stronger race but was headed a quarter of a mile from home, and although he finished two and a half lengths and a neck in front of

Desert Encounter and Extra Elusive, he was only the fourth horse past the post. Addeybb won in great style from Skalleti and Magical, the margins two and a quarter lengths and half a length, and the star mare finished three and a half lengths clear of her Derby-winning stablemate. It was a good effort on the soft ground although not the race for which he had originally been an intended runner. Connections had paid €72,000 to supplement him for the Group 1 Qatar Prix de l'Arc de Triomphe which added considerably to the sting of his absence from the line-up at ParisLongchamp. The colt was one of a number of horses affected by a contaminated feed issue, all of whom were withdrawn from their Arc-day targets.

So here we are, looking at a Derby winner who remains something of an unknown quantity after six races. If he gets good ground and the chance to make the running in 2021 then he could be one of his team's top middle-distance horses of the year. Looking further ahead, it is likely going to be crucial to his future stallion prospects that he wins again at the highest level and perhaps also wins at least one good race over ten furlongs. He won a poor edition of the Derby and he is a Group 1-winning son of the phenomenal Galileo (by Sadler's Wells), the latter an accolade so common that a colt really needs to stand out in another way to be guaranteed a berth at stud. They are all from top families too—a mare doesn't get to visit Galileo unless she's equine royalty—but he does have it in his favour that he is out of a classic-placed half-sister to a juvenile filly champion and also to two classic stars, one of whom is also an Arc-winner who has sired Group 1 winners at stud.

Serpentine's dam, Remember When (by Danehill Dancer), was not a stakes winner but she was promoted to second place in the Oaks at Epsom, and she has produced four other stakes winners, all of them by Galileo. Wedding Vow, her first foal, won the Group 2 Kilboy Estate Stakes over nine furlongs at the Curragh, multiple pattern-placed Beacon Rock landed the Group 3 Gallinule Stakes at the same venue, Bound won the Listed Trigo Stakes over ten furlongs at Leopardstown, and Bye Bye Baby won the Group 3 Blue Wind Stakes there before finishing third to Forever Together in the Oaks at Epsom. Those were her first four foals. Her classic-entered son King of The Castle finished out of the frame on both of his starts in late-season mile maidens on somewhat heavy ground, and she had another Galileo colt on May 22nd, 2019.

Queen's Logic (by Grand Lodge), a Mick Channon-trainee who was undefeated in a five-race career, was the eldest of Remember When's three Group 1-winning siblings. She won the Group 3 Queen Mary Stakes, Group 2 Lowther Stakes and Group 1 Cheveley Park Stakes at two, chased home each time by the subsequent mile Group 1 scorer Sophisticat, and the last of those juvenile victories was by seven lengths on soft ground. She was an odds-on winner of the Group 3 Fred Darling Stakes the following April but didn't race again. Her son King's Advice (by Frankel) is a stakes-placed heritage handicap scorer with eleven wins to his name, mostly from twelve to fourteen furlongs, and he presents a striking contrast to her star daughter, Lady of The Desert (by Rahy). She won the Group 2 Diadem Stakes, Group 2 Lowther Stakes and Group 3 Princess Margaret Stakes over six furlongs, she was runner-up in the Group 1 Sprint Cup over the same trip and chased home Gilt Edge Girl in the Group 1 Prix de l'Abbaye de Longchamp over five before going on to become the dam of Queen Kindly (by Frankel). That three-parts sister to King's Advice followed in her dam's hoof-prints, winning the Group 2 Lowther Stakes at two and adding a listed sprint at three.

Homecoming Queen (by Holy Roman Emperor) is the youngest member of the Group 1-winning trio and she arrived two years after Remember When. She won a Group 3 over seven furlongs at Leopardstown and a mile listed contest at the Curragh but her nine-length demolition job in the Group 1 1000 Guineas at Newmarket was the standout performance of her career. Her Donnacha O'Brien-trained daughter Shale (by Galileo) was one of the top juvenile fillies in Europe in 2020 and the Group 1 Moyglare Stud Stakes heroine, who has two stakes-placed siblings, holds entries in both the Group 1 Tattersalls Irish 1,000 Guineas and Group 1 Juddmonte Irish Oaks.

However, Dylan Thomas (by Danehill) was the best of the siblings. He won the Irish Derby, King George VI and Queen Elizabeth Stakes, Prix de l'Arc de Triomphe, Prix Ganay, and back-to-back editions of the Irish Champion Stakes. He spent his stallion career under the Coolmore banner, initially as a flat sire but later finding support from National Hunt breeders. His tally of thirty-seven stakes winners is well below what would have been hoped but they feature nine who won at the highest level including Hong Kong champion Blazing Speed, Germany's former Horse of the Year and three-year-old filly champion Nightflower and former older filly champion Nymphea, Chilean champion Penn Rose, Italian champion Dylan Mouth, and Coronation Cup scorer Pether's Moon. There are two colts and five fillies in his most recent crop, now yearlings.

Hopefully, Serpentine will return to action in top form this coming season and give us the chance to find out how good he really is and if he can move past Dylan Thomas in his family's order of merit.

SUMMARY DETAILS

Bred: Coolmore
Owned: Mrs John Magnier, Michael Tabor & Derrick Smith
Trained: Aidan O'Brien
Country: Ireland
Race record: 0-01144-
Career highlights: 2 wins inc Investec Derby (Gr1)

SERPENTINE (IRE) – 2017 chestnut colt

Galileo (IRE)	Sadler's Wells (USA)	Northern Dancer
		Fairy Bridge (USA)
	Urban Sea (USA)	Miswaki (USA)
		Allegretta
Remember When (IRE)	Danehill Dancer (IRE)	Danehill (USA)
		Mira Adonde (USA)
	Lagrion (USA)	Diesis
		Wrap It Up

SHALE (IRE)

Shale, among the most regally related horses in training, is a live classic prospect for 2021. The Donnacha O'Brien-trained daughter of Galileo (by Sadler's Wells) is out of a classic-winning half-sister to two other Group 1 stars and she was one of the top fillies of her age in Europe last season, sharing the juvenile fillies' championship title with Campanelle and Pretty Gorgeous on a mark of 113. She was unplaced in a seven-furlong Leopardstown maiden on her debut in June and in the Group 1 bet365 Fillies' Mile at Newmarket on her final run of the year, but between those she notched up three wins and a second from four starts. Her rivalry with Pretty Gorgeous was among the highlights of the two-year-old scene, the final score standing at two-to-two, and it will be fascinating to see how they compare as three-year-olds.

Shale got off the mark at the second attempt, taking a one-mile maiden at Gowran Park in early July. The ground was described as soft-to-heavy, so neither the soft underfoot conditions nor the distance may be to blame for her end-of-year defeat in England, and she won that contest by three and a quarter lengths. Her other runs were all over seven furlongs, her wins on good ground and her second-place finish on soft; she is probably flexible with regard to going preference. Only a pair of 50/1 outsiders went off at longer odds than her in the eight-runner Group 3 Frank Conroy Silver Flash Stakes at Leopardstown in early August, but she hit the front over a furlong out and stayed on well to hold off the favourite, Pretty Gorgeous, by a length and a half. A Ma Chere and Snowfall were three and a half lengths and a short head back in third and fourth.

The front pair met again in the Group 2 A.R.M. Holding Debutante Stakes at the Curragh sixteen days later and this time it was Shale who headed the market. Again, she and Gavin Ryan went to the front over a furlong out. However, Pretty Gorgeous was travelling noticeably well to her left and Shane Crosse never had to get serious with that filly as she only had to be pushed out to take the race by two and a half lengths. Shale was the same margin clear of third-placed Mother Earth, with Meala three-quarters of a lengths back in fourth and a wide gap back to the rest, headed by Snowfall. Round three came in the Group 1 Moyglare Stud Stakes three weeks later. Only four of the thirteen runners were sent off at under 14/1, two of those finished well-beaten, and it was left to the established pair to fight it out again. They began their move forward a quarter of a mile from home, Shale taking up the running pursued by Pretty Gorgeous. The latter looked for a few strides like she might get there but Shale found more and stayed on for a three-quarter-length victory. There was a further gap of almost two lengths back to the third, Oodnadatta.

Her final run was disappointing, finishing sixth behind Pretty Gorgeous in the Fillies' Mile having never looked dangerous in the closing stages. As noted, she had already won over the trip and on softer ground, and you would expect a filly of her breeding to handle both with ease. It was on the soft side of good when her dam, Homecoming Queen, made all to beat Starscope by nine lengths in the Group 1 1000 Guineas at Newmarket in 2012, the runner-up followed home by Maybe, The Fugue and La Collina. It was by far the best performance of her career, but she also had a seven-furlong Group 3 win and a one-mile listed success to her name—the latter on yielding-to-soft at the Curragh—and she was a neck runner-up in a seven-furlong pattern race on heavy. Now owned by Katsumi Yoshida of Northern Farm, she produced a full brother to Shale in 2019, was bred to Saxon Warrior (by Deep Impact) and then sent to Japan where she had a filly on March 20th, 2020.

Homecoming Queen is a daughter of Lagrion (by Diesis) and that full sister to the Group 1 Middle Park Stakes runner-up Pure Genius is one of those prized and comparatively rare mares who have produced three Group 1 winners. Dylan Thomas (by Danehill) was her star son and that £2.2 million-earner won a string of Group 1s, notably the Irish Derby, King George VI and Queen Elizabeth Stakes, the Prix de l'Arc de Triomphe and back-to-back editions of the Irish Champion Stakes. He has sired nine top-level winners. Queen's Logic (by Grand Lodge), the eldest of the siblings, was an undefeated juvenile champion who ran away with the Group 1 Cheveley Park Stakes. She was a Group 3 scorer over seven furlongs on her only start at three, is the dam of the

Group 2-winning sprinter Lady of The Desert (by Rahy) and grandam of the Group 2 Lowther Stakes winner Queen Kindly (by Frankel). This augurs well for the eventual broodmare career of Shale, but so too does the produce record her dam's Oaks-placed half-sister Remember When (by Danehill Dancer). Five of her first six foals are stakes winners by Galileo, with the eldest of them being Group 2 scorer Wedding Vow and last season's Group 1 Derby star Serpentine the youngest; their details are discussed in his essay in this volume.

Shale holds entries in the Group 1 Tattersalls Irish 1,000 Guineas and Group 1 Juddmonte Irish Oaks, as you might expect, and she is also engaged in the Group 1 Prix de Diane Longines (French Oaks). She promises to be among Ireland leading three-year-old fillies of 2021. It remains to be seen, however, just how far she will stay. One might presume her an obvious middle-distance prospect, and it is entirely possibly that she will not only stay beyond ten furlongs but improve for it, but not every Galileo stays, and that includes her two blacktype siblings. Full brother Berkeley Square won over seven and a half furlongs at Tipperary, finished third to Rostropovich in the Group 2 Futurity Stakes over seven at the Curragh and then won over nine furlongs in Qatar the following spring. However, her sister, First of Spring, won over six furlongs on her first two starts at two, was unplaced in the Group 1 Prix Marcel Boussac over a mile, dropped back to six and a half furlongs at Deauville at three and was placed there, then went to North America where she won a six-furlong turf sprint at Aqueduct a few weeks before finishing third in a listed contest over that course and distance.

We won't know if Shale stays much beyond a mile until she tries it, and if she has some of her sister's speed then it is even possible that seven furlongs may be her ideal trip.

SUMMARY DETAILS

Bred: Coolmore
Owned: Derrick Smith, Mrs John Magnier & Michael Tabor
Trained: Donnacha O'Brien
Country: Ireland
Race record: 011210-

Career highlights: 3 wins inc Moyglare Stud Stakes (Gr1), Frank Conroy Silver Flash Stakes (Gr3), 2nd A.R.M. Holding Debutante Stakes (Gr2)

SHALE (IRE) – 2018 bay filly

		Northern Dancer
Galileo (IRE)	Sadler's Wells (USA)	Northern Dancer
		Fairy Bridge (USA)
	Urban Sea (USA)	Miswaki (USA)
		Allegretta
Homecoming Queen (IRE)	Holy Roman Emperor (IRE)	Danehill (USA)
		Razyana (USA)
	Lagrion (USA)	Diesis
		Wrap It Up

SISKIN (USA)

Siskin was an unbeaten Group 1 star as a two-year-old and although his three-year-old season was not as successful as hoped, it started in fine style with a near two-length victory in the Group 1 Tattersalls Irish 2,000 Guineas on fast ground at the Curragh in June. The delayed and compressed nature of the early part of the 2020 season meant that some of the classics were run much later than usual, with few to no chances for a prep race. That led to some slightly odd results, and while there was nothing surprising about the way in which Siskin showed a good turn of foot sweep past his rivals in the final furlong that day, the performance of runner-up Vatican City was followed by three unplaced runs from four starts. That chestnut has since been exported to Denmark. However, Lope Y Fernandez and Armory were the next two home, beaten by a further three-quarters of a length and a nose, and they did prove to be the high-class colts that their juvenile seasons suggested.

Shortly after his classic victory it was announced that breeding rights to the Juddmonte homebred had been sold. The identity of his future home was not revealed and although there was much speculation that it might be Coolmore Stud in Ireland, it turned out that the colt would actually be moving to Japan to begin his stallion career in 2021. This announcement came in late October, without naming the actual location, tied in with the news that he would make his final racecourse appearance at the Breeders' Cup. The famous Shadai Stallion Station was identified as being his new home shortly after that disappointing ninth-place finish at Keeneland, and he looks certain to be very popular in his new role.

The Group 1 Qatar Sussex Stakes is usually one of the most important mile races of the year in Europe and, in 2020, it lived up to that reputation. Three four-year-olds and four three-year-olds lined up, and although Son Donato weakened and dropped back in the final furlong having looked a big danger and Vatican City was found to be lame and having an irregular heartbeat after trailing home in rear, the other five made it a strong race. Circus Maximus made a gallant bid to lead from start to finish, only giving best near the finish as Mohaather produced an eye-catching turn of foot that swept him past everything in that final furlong. Siskin made Coolmore's horse fight to the line for second, the final margins three-quarters of a length and half a length, with an unlucky Kameko passing the post another two length adrift in fourth and Wichita fifth.

The Group 1 Prix du Moulin de Longchamp was an even stronger race with all six runners already having at least two top-level wins to their name. Circus Maximus again set off in front and Siskin was his closest pursuer at the line, a length down while passing the post a head in front of Victor Ludorum and with Romanised another five lengths adrift. However, they were all a long way behind the first two home. Persian King had taken over the lead a quarter of a mile from home and then shot clear. Were it not for Pinatubo, who had been set too much to do and flew home with a sustained run over the final furlong and a bit, he would have been a wide-margin winner. But Godolphin's juvenile champion and Prix Jean Prat scorer narrowed the gap to one and three-quarter lengths at the line while finishing six lengths clear of Circus Maximus.

Siskin is the star male among fourteen stakes winners by the top-class dirt horse First Defence (by Unbridled's Song), which would have made him a fascinating sire prospect in Ireland or Great Britain. He is free of Sadler's Wells (by Northern Dancer), Danehill (by Danzig), Sunday Silence (by Halo) and Kingmambo (by Mr Prospector) blood, which gives him an obvious appeal, but he is not an outcross. That word is so often misused by those who mean to say that a stallion represents a different sire line than Sadler's Wells or Danehill or whatever other one they are referencing, but what the term actually means is that the horse has no duplicated ancestors within the first five generations of its pedigree. Such horses are becoming rare given the obsession with inbreeding, and Siskin shows duplications of 5x5 Mr Prospector (by Raise a Native), 5x5 Northern Dancer (by Nearctic) and 5x4 Sir Ivor (by Sir Gaylord). He certainly provides plenty of opportunity for those who are trying to avoid close inbreeding. Danzig appears once in the fourth generation.

There is, of course, far more to a prospective stallion's pedigree credentials than the male line he represents, his level of inbreeding or the various sires that appear on his chart. If he can lay claim to being related to a successful stallion that has been produced by one of his direct female ancestors then that can be far more significant in determining his prospects. Siskin can do better than that. His third dam is Monroe (by Sir Ivor), which makes Best In Show (by Traffic Judge) his fourth dam, and so he comes from a famous international stallion-producing family. His grandam, Silver Star (by Zafonic), is a stakes-placed full sister to the juvenile champion and blacktype sire Xaar, Monroe's male descendants include the blacktype sires Bated Breath (by Dansili)—he got his first top-level winner in 2020—and Cityscape (by Selkirk), whereas Best In Show is a direct ancestor of Group 1 sires such as Aldebaran (by Mr Prospector), El Gran Senor (by Northern Dancer), Good Journey (by Nureyev), Hurricane Sky (by Star Watch), Manhattan Rain (by Encosta de Lago), Pathfork (by Distorted Humor), Redoute's Choice (by Danehill), Spinning World (by Nureyev), Try My Best (by Northern Dancer) and Umatilla (by Miswaki). Best In Show was a half-sister to the dam of Taufan (by Stop The Music). Many of those are remotely connection to him, but it will be a considerable disappointment if Siskin fails to add his name to his ancestor's roll of honour by siring at least one Group 1 star.

Looking at the pedigree from the perspective of Siskin as a racehorse rather than as a sire prospect, it is immediately noticeable that he is closely related to two others among his sire's small tally of stakes winners. His half-sister Talacre (by Flintshire) was a juvenile winner in 2020, their dam's fourth foal is a Noble Mission (by Galileo) filly who was born in late April 2019, and the mare, Bird Flown (by Oasis Dream), is booked to visit Frankel (by Galileo) for 2021. She is a winning half-sister to Barsanti (by Champs Elysees), who won the Listed Buckhounds Stakes and was runner-up in the Group 2 Hardwicke Stakes, and also to a mare named Rising Tornado (by Storm Cat). That one gave us the US champion and five-time Grade 1 star Close Hatches (by First Defence)—dam of the dual classic-placed multiple Grade 2 scorer Tacitus (by Tapit)—and her Grade 1 Kentucky Oaks-placed, stakes-winning full sister Lockdown. He was bred to be a high-class performer at around a mile, which is exactly what he was as a three-year-old, and as noted above, his grandam is a full sister to a juvenile champion.

It would have been good to see Siskin in action again as a four-year-old because there is every reason to believe that the Ger Lyons-trained colt could have added further European Group 1 success to his name. Instead, we can look forward to the arrival of his first foals in 2022. The two-year-old pattern program in Japan is strengthening though still with an emphasis mostly around a mile, so while he should get winners and potentially some blacktype horses as a freshman in 2024, it may be 2025 when we start to get a good idea of how his long-term future might pan out.

SUMMARY DETAILS

Bred: Juddmonte Farms Inc
Owned: Khalid Abdullah
Trained: Ger Lyons
Country: Ireland
Race record: 1111-1340-
Career highlights: 5 wins inc Tattersalls Irish 2,000 Guineas (Gr1), Keeneland Phoenix Stakes (Gr1), GAIN Railway Stakes (Gr2), Irish Stallion Farms EBF Marble Hill Stakes (L), 3rd Qatar Sussex Stakes (Gr1)

SISKIN (USA) – 2017 bay/brown colt

First Defence (USA)	Unbridled's Song (USA)	Unbridled (USA)
		Trolley Song (USA)
	Honest Lady (USA)	Seattle Slew (USA)
		Toussaud (USA)
Bird Flown (GB)	Oasis Dream (GB)	Green Desert (USA)
		Hope (IRE)
	Silver Star (GB)	Zafonic (USA)
		Monroe (USA)

"His brilliant half-sister has been a star as an older horse, and one of her dam's half-sisters almost beat Zenyatta as a five-year-old, so there is every reason to hope that this colt can be at least as good in 2020 as he was last season. If that proves to be the case, then he will surely be among the brightest stars of the year." So concluded the essay on Sottsass in *European Group 1 Winners of 2019* after a season in which he ran away with a listed race at Chantilly, beat Persian King by two lengths to win the Group 1 Prix du Jockey Club (French Derby) and added the Group 2 Prix Niel before finishing an honourable third to Waldgeist and Enable in the Group 1 Prix de l'Arc de Triomphe. He lived up to those expectations and has now joined the roster at Coolmore Stud in Ireland for what promises to be a busy stallion career.

His first run of the year was something of an upset. He went off the 2/5 favourite for the Group 2 Prix d'Harcourt over ten furlongs on very soft ground at ParisLongchamp in May but could only finish fourth, beaten by three-quarters of a length, a short neck and a length by Shaman, Way To Paris and Simona. It was an anti-climactic start to the year but he bounced back a month later, this time in the Group 1 Prix Ganay over a half furlong farther at Chantilly. Only five went to post, Shaman made a gallant bid to make all but got tired inside the final furlong as Sottsass and Way To Paris went on. The chestnut beat the grey by a head, with gaps of three lengths, a neck and two lengths back to Shaman, Palomba and Simona. The runner-up, who had easily won a Group 2 on his previous start, won the Group 1 Grand Prix de Saint-Cloud next time out and is now standing as a stallion at Coolagown Stud in Ireland.

Sottsass, however, was beaten next time out, although to be fair to him, he was giving the winner, Skalleti, six pounds, only lost by a neck, and had third-placed Motamarris four lengths behind. The race was the Group 3 Prix Gontaut-Biron Hong Kong Jockey Club over ten furlongs on heavy ground at Deauville in mid-August. He failed to make the frame in Ireland the following month but only in a short-head verdict that would have gone the other way in another stride. Magical won that Group 1 Irish

Champion Stakes by three-quarters of a length from Ghaiyyath, doubling-up on her victory in the same race twelve months before, and it is her three-year-old stablemate Armory who just lasted home in third, one and a quarter lengths behind Godolphin's outstanding five-year-old.

Everything he had done to this point showed that Sottsass was still a notably talented middle-distance horse but perhaps one who now needed a mile and a half to show his best, so when the ground came up heavy at ParisLongchamp on the first Sunday in October, ruining Enable's second attempt at an unprecedented Arc treble, it was no surprise to see him as the one who benefitted. Star miler Persian King tried to make all, his rider Pierre-Charles Boudot dictating the pace in a way that maximised the horse's chance of lasting the distance, and he was only headed a furlong out when Sottsass made his bid for glory. The classic-winning three-year-old In Swoop stormed home but the chestnut held off the bay by a neck at the line. There was a further gap of one and three-quarter lengths back to Persian King, with Gold Trip a head back in fourth, two lengths clear of the staying-on Raabihah.

The Arc had been his target all year, his task made easier by the effect of the conditions on Enable and Stradivarius plus the shock withdrawal of the Ballydoyle contenders—Japan, Mogul, Serpentine, and Sovereign—due to a contaminated feed issue. But a shade lucky or not, Sottsass accomplished his mission and goes to stud as a triple Group 1 winner who won at two and landed a classic at three.

He is the best son of the juvenile Group 1 victor and Haras de Bonneval stallion Siyouni (by Pivotal), a horse whosw five other top-level winners include four fillies, three of whom have won classics in France. His Group 1 Dewhurst Stakes-winning son St Mark's Basilica will likely bid for classic glory in 2021. The Group 1-placed Group 3 scorers City Light and Le Brivido are both at stud in France, the latter having spent his initial season at Overbury Stud in Gloucestershire, and they have their first foals arriving now, so some may look to them for an early indication of how the Siyouni stallions might fare in the long term. City Light was a top French sprinter, whereas Jersey Stakes winner Le Brivido was short-headed by Brametot in the Poule d'Essai des

Poulains (French 2000 Guineas). They will have had their first runners before Sottsass's early auction yearlings go through the ring, but while they are likely to have had winners by then, maybe plenty of them and even one or more blacktype horses, they are courting a different type of mare to what he will attract.

Sottsass is a middle-distance star who will likely be supported with classic-type mares and some speedier types, but with the aim of producing classic milers and middle-distance horses rather than sprinters and precocious types. His initial progeny will be two-year-olds in 2024 and some of them may indeed be blacktype horses at that age, but it seems likely that it will be 2025 and beyond when his best results as a sire begin to emerge. It's not just his own racing profile that suggests this but that of his closest relations. He is the third foal of the non-winning Galileo (by Sadler's Wells) mare Starlet's Sister, a full sister to the Group 3 Prix Cleopatre winner and Group 2 Prix de Mallaret runner-up Leo's Starlet. Their half-sister Anabaa's Creation is, as her name suggests, a daughter of the sprint champion Anabaa (by Danzig), and although she won a listed race late in her juvenile season, she was third in the Group 1 Prix Saint-Alary and later Grade 1 placed in the USA. Their dam, Premiere Creation (by Green Tune), was placed in both the Grade 1 Del Mar Oaks and Group 3 Prix Chloe.

As is widely known, Sottsass has two standout half-sisters, both of whom were sired by speed horses. My Sister Nat (by Acclamation) is the lesser of the pair yet won a Group 3 contest in France before going on to become a twelve-furlong Grade 3 winner for the Chad Brown stable and a head runner-up in the Grade 1 Flower Bowl Stakes over ten furlongs. She is by a sprint star who mostly gets sprinters plus some milers of note. Sistercharlie is the eldest of the siblings and that champion and classic-placed seven-time Grade 1 star is a daughter of the Group 1 Prix Morny winner Myboycharlie (by Danetime). However, despite his speed he has also been represented by Euro Charline (Beverly D Stakes) and Jameka (Caulfield Cup, The BMW, Crown Oaks), who got their top-level wins over nine and a half furlongs and twelve furlongs respectively. Sistercharlie's string of victories includes the Breeders' Cup Filly and Mare Turf plus two editions of both the Diana Stakes and Beverly D Stakes, her classic placing was when chasing home Senga in the Group 1 Prix de Diane (French Oaks) and her earnings total of over $3.78 million surpasses that of her Arc-winning half-brother.

It seems likely that Sottsass will have plenty of progeny who are inbred to Galileo, Sadler's Wells (by Northern Dancer), Danehill (by Danzig) and/or Pivotal (by Polar Falcon), and given his pedigree, race record and new connections, he is a fascinating stallion prospect.

SUMMARY DETAILS

Bred: Ecurie Des Monceaux
Owned: White Birch Farm
Trained: Jean-Claude Rouget
Country: France
Race record: 41-01113-41241-
Career highlights: 6 wins inc Qatar Prix de l'Arc de Triomphe (Gr1), Prix Ganay (Gr1), Qipco Prix du Jockey Club (Gr1), Qatar Prix Niel (Gr2), Prix de Suresnes (L), 2nd Prix Gontaut-Biron - Hong Kong Jockey Club (Gr3), 3rd Qatar Prix de l'Arc de Triomphe (Gr1)

SOTTSASS (FR) – 2016 chestnut colt

Siyouni (FR)	Pivotal (GB)	Polar Falcon (USA)
		Fearless Revival
	Sichilla (IRE)	Danehill (USA)
		Slipstream Queen (USA)
Starlet's Sister (IRE)	Galileo (IRE)	Sadler's Wells (USA)
		Urban Sea (USA)
	Premiere Creation (FR)	Green Tune (USA)
		Allwaki (USA)

SPACE BLUES (IRE)

Two of the Group 1-winning sprinters of 2020 are horses who started out heading towards a middle-distance route only to be brought back in trip. Glen Shiel spent considerably longer time than Space Blues going down that road and he was even blacktype placed at ten furlongs before changing stables and being tried in the shorter range. Space Blues, on the other hand, is a Godolphin homebred who won easily over an extended mile at Nottingham on his only start at two, was a disappointing favourite for a ten-furlong conditions race on soft ground at Newbury on his seasonal reappearance at three and then a head runner-up when sent off at odds of 1/3 for a novice contest over the course and distance of his juvenile run. The son of Dubawi (by Dubai Millennium) comes from a family that is full of milers and middle-distance horses, one whose branches include classic horses and a leading sire, but that was now clearly not his path.

He gave weight and a beating to a large field in a York handicap, followed that with a neck defeat of Urban Icon in the Listed Surrey Stakes at Epsom and then failed by only a head to beat Space Traveller in the Group 3 Jersey Stakes at Royal Ascot—all over seven furlongs. That is an awkward distance over which to excel in Europe given the few top-level events available to a top-notch performer. The Group 1 Prix de la Foret is the long-established one, he has not yet run in that, and it was the only one until the Group 1 Prix Jean Prat was reduced again in distance in 2019. It is now run over the distance at Deauville in early July and that inaugural shorter version gave us the first indication that this chestnut could be a top-class colt in the making. Too Darn Hot was in a league of his own, hitting the front a furlong and a half from home and winning easily by three lengths, but Space Blues beat everything else in the twelve-runner field by two lengths and more.

He returned to the venue a month later for the Group 1 LARC Prix Maurice de Gheest over six and a half furlongs, again running on well in the closing stages but not quite good enough to win. Fellow three-year-old Advertise landed the prize by a neck from the popular veteran Brando, with Space Blues three-quarters of a length back in third, a head in front of Spinning Memories and followed home by One Master, Pretty Pollyanna, Polydream and So Perfect. It would be seven months before he was seen in action again and although he finished down the field in a Group 3 sprint over six furlongs at Meydan in March, he won all four of his European starts in 2020, the first three of them over seven furlongs.

The sequence began at Haydock in the first week in June where, on ground described as good-to-soft, he hit the front inside the final furlong and beat Safe Voyage and Happy Power by a neck and one and a quarter lengths in the Listed Betway Spring Trophy Stakes. He beat his stablemate D'bai by a length and a quarter in the Group 3 Prix de la Porte Maillot in similar conditions at ParisLongchamp two weeks later and, a month after that, beat Duke of Hazzard by two lengths to add the Group 2 Qatar Lennox Stakes at Goodwood. He settled towards the rear in the early stages of that race, made noticeable progress on the outside of the pack over two out and then showed a fine turn of foot to hit the front over a furlong out and quickly put the result beyond any doubt. Escobar was a half-length back in third, with Safe Voyage, Sir Dancealot and D'bai the next three home, covered by a length. It was an impressive effort.

Space Blues ran only once more, overcoming traffic issues over two out, hitting the front well inside the final half-furlong and bringing up his four-timer with victory in the Group 1 LARC Prix Maurice de Gheest. The six-and-a-half-furlong trip may be a shade shorter than perfect for him but he handles it well and won this top test by three-quarters of a length from Hello Youmzain, with Lope Y Fernandez, Earthlight and Golden Horde following a head, short neck and half a length behind. It was arguably the best performance of his career and it likely guaranteed that he will attract plenty of attention at stud when his racing days come to an end.

He is, as noted above, by the classic-winning miler and Dalham Hall Stud flag bearer Dubawi, one of the all-time great English thoroughbred stallions. Forty-four of his offspring have won at least once at the highest level, so far, and have passed the 190-mark late in the year, he is on the verge of becoming one of the tiny handful of sires ever to notch up at least 200 individual stakes winners. Of course, none of the great sires of thirty-to-forty-plus years ago had any chance of reaching such a figure given the strict controls there used to be on book sizes and that shuttle sires were not yet a thing—the phenomenal Danzig (by Northern Dancer) came close with 198, forty-six of whom were Group/Grade 1 winners—but it is undoubtedly an exceptional achievement. Danehill (by Danzig) sired 348 including eighty-three (not eighty-four) Group 1 winners, Galileo (by Sadler's Wells) has a world record eighty-nine top-level winners among 332 stakes winners, Sadler's Wells (by Northern Dancer) had seventy-three Group 1 scorers among 294 stakes winners, whereas WinStar Farm stallion More Than Ready (by Southern Halo), who served some shuttle seasons in Australia, has hit 207 stakes winners, a total that features twenty-five who have won at least once at the highest level.

The Dubawi-sired stallions Al Kazeem, Makfi and Poet's Voice have sired at least one Group 1 winner apiece, Night of Thunder is a prolific blacktype sire with his first two crops though awaiting his first top-level winner, whereas New Bay did well as a freshman sire in 2020. There is also a string of his sons at earlier stages of their stud careers, so his profile as a sire of stallions looks sure to grow in the coming years.

Space Blues is a half-brother to the four-time pattern-winning miler Shuruq (by Elusive Quality), a former Saeed bin Suroor-trained filly who has already produced two blacktype daughters. Antoinette (by Hard Spun), a Bill Mott-trained stakes winner, was runner-up in last year's Grade 1 Belmont Oaks and third in the Grade 1 Coaching Club American Oaks, whereas the Eoin Harty-trained Javanica (by Medaglia d'Oro), now a three-year-old, was runner-up in three blacktype contests following her maiden win over a mile at Arlington in September. Like her star son, Miss Lucifer (by Noverre) was also best at seven furlongs, and although she was only a dual blacktype winner, the better of those two scored was in the Group 2 Challenge Stakes at Newmarket in which she beat Al Qasi and Roylsome by a length and a quarter and two lengths on ground described as being good-to-soft. One might have expected her to stay a mile given her sire excelled at that distance and her dam's siblings feature the middle-distance pattern winners Amfortas (by Caerleon) and Legend Maker (by Sadler's Wells), but she was unplaced on her only attempt at the trip.

Amfortas won the Group 2 King Edward VII Stakes and Group 2 Prix de Pomone-third Legend Maker landed the Group 3 Prix de Royaumont. The latter is also notable for her broodmare record because she is the dam of the Group 1 1000 Guineas heroine Virginia Waters (by Kingmambo) and Group 3 Gallinule Stakes winner and Group 1 Irish Derby runner-up Alexander of Hales (by Danehill) as well as being the direct ancestor of a string of blacktype winners. That list includes the Group 1 Irish Oaks-placed Group 3 Snow Fairy Stakes winner Rain Goddess (by Galileo) and Group 1 Matron Stakes scorer Chachamaidee (by Footstepsinthesand).

High Spirited (by Shirley Heights), the winning third dam of Space Blues, has several siblings of note, two for their produce record at stud and one for both her own racing talent and that of her offspring. High Tern (by High Line) won twice, her most prolific son Sooty Tern (by Wassl) won twenty times and six-time scorer Supremacy (by Vettori) was a stakes winner, but High-Rise (by High Estate) was her most notable representative, even if 1998's Group 1 Derby hero failed to make the grade at stud. Seriema (by Petingo) won only once on the track but her seven-time winning daughter Infamy (by Shirley Heights) landed the Grade 1 Rothmans International Stakes, Group 2 Sun Chariot Stakes and Group 3 Gordon Richards Stakes before going on to become the dam and ancestor of a string of stakes and pattern winners.

High Hawk, who was a full sister to High Spirited, was the most notable of all and she is the one who has perhaps the greatest significance with a view to assessing how Space Blues might fare as a stallion. She won the Group 1 Premio Roma, Group 2 Ribblesdale Stakes, Group 2 Park Hill Stakes and Group 3 Prix du Royaumont and later became the dam of several pattern-winning sons of whom In The Wings was the standout. He won the Grade 1 Breeders' Cup Turf, Group 1 Grand Prix de Saint-Cloud and Group 1 Coronation Cup, he finished fourth in the Group 1 Prix de l'Arc de Triomphe, stood at Kildangan Stud and was for a long time the number-one stallion son of Sadler's Wells (by Northern Dancer). He was only eighteen when he died but left behind sixty-four stakes winners of whom ten won at least once at the highest level. They included the Group 1 classic winners Central Park (Derby Italiano), Winged Love (Irish Derby) and Zanzibar (Oaks d'Italia) but also featured Adlerflug, Singspiel and Soldier Hollow. That latter trio won ten Group 1s between them, Adlerflug's pair included the Deutsches Derby, and all three went on to become significant sires.

Adlerflug, who stands at his owner-breeders' famous Gestüt Schlenderhan in Germany, has been represented by five top-level winners so far including 2020's Group 1 Deutsches Derby one-two, In Swoop and Torquator Tasso. The former went on to chase home Sottsass in the Group 1 Prix de l'Arc de Triomphe, whereas the classic second went on to win the Group 1 Grosser Preis von Berlin. Both colts are reviewed in detail elsewhere in this volume. Soldier Hollow stands at Gestüt Auenquelle and is established as one of Germany's top sires. His forty-six stakes winners include the Group 1 classic stars Pastorius (Deutsches Derby), Serienholde (Preis der Diana) and Weltstar (Deutsches Derby) plus the additional middle-distance Group 1 scorers Dschingis Secret (Haras de Saint Arnoult; yearlings in 2021) and Ivanhowe (Haras de Cercy; two-year-olds in 2021). The top-class international performer Singspiel, on the other hand, stood at Dalham Hall Stud, died at the age of 18 but sired 100 stakes winners of whom fourteen were successful at Group 1 level. They include Confidential Lady, Dar Re Mi, Moon Ballad, and Solow, and although none of his sons has made an impact as a stallion, he has become a notably successful broodmare sire.

Space Blues, a Group 1 winning Dubawi horse whose third dam is a full sister to the Group 1-winning dam of the influential stallion In The Wings, is a fascinating prospect both as a racehorse for this coming season and as a sire recruit of the future. He has been entered in the ultra-valuable stc 1351 Turf Sprint over seven furlongs at Riyadh in late February, so that conditions race may be where he starts his five-year-old campaign.

SUMMARY DETAILS

Bred: Godolphin
Owned: Godolphin
Trained: Charlie Appleby
Country: England
Race record: 1-4211223-01111-
Career highlights: 7 wins inc LARC Prix Maurice de Gheest (Gr1), Qatar Lennox Stakes (Gr2), Betway Spring Trophy Stakes (L), Investec Surrey Stakes (L), 2nd Qatar Prix Jean Prat (Gr1), Jersey Stakes (Gr3), 3rd LARC Prix Maurice de Gheest (Gr1)

SPACE BLUES (IRE) – 2016 chestnut colt

Dubawi (IRE)	Dubai Millennium (GB)	Seeking The Gold (USA)
		Colorado Dancer (IRE)
	Zomaradah (GB)	Deploy
		Jawaher (IRE)
Miss Lucifer (FR)	Noverre (USA)	Rahy (USA)
		Danseur Fabuleux (USA)
	Devil's Imp (IRE)	Cadeaux Genereux
		High Spirited

ST MARK'S BASILICA (FR)

The two-year-old class of 2020 was an unremarkable one, something that can result in a greater number of its subsequent three-year-old stars emerging from among the less exposed members or even from those who did not race by the end of that first season. Several showed potential but nothing among those who competed in multiple pattern events really did so with any consistency, and it was St Mark's Basilica who achieved the highest rating, a mark of 120 for his victory in the Group 1 Darley Dewhurst Stakes at Newmarket in October. Timeform also had him top of their listing, rated 121p, and while he is rightly called the champion two-year-old, the Cartier Award for the division bizarrely went instead to a colt several places down in the pecking order: Van Gogh, joint ninth-rated in the official figures on a mark of just 114. It has always been the case that the horse who tops the handicap earns the actual divisional title and so it is St Mark's Basilica who wears the crown.

The number of comments and reports that seem to attribute some of the 'blame' for the lower-than-average standard of the juvenile crop to the compressed nature of the early part of the season is also puzzling. That does not make sense given that all of the top juvenile contests ran as normal and only the first two months of the campaign were lost. It would have had an obvious effect on Royal Ascot's juvenile races, but in terms of judging the whole two-year-old season it is not a valid excuse. Weak years happen. Belardo was champion two-year-old in 2014 on a rating of just 119, the same mark shared by 2011's joint-champions, Camelot and Dabirsim; both Belardo and Camelot went on to further Group 1 success.

St Mark's Basilica looks certain to get a stallion berth when his racing days are over because not only is he a juvenile Group 1 scorer and divisional leader but he is a son of a rising star in the stallion ranks and out of a mare who has previously produced a classic winner. Magna Grecia (by Invincible Spirit) is that sibling and the Group 1 Vertem Futurity Trophy Stakes and Group 1 2000 Guineas star covered 180 mares in his maiden season at stud. He is a Coolmore sire, and if his younger brother fulfils his potential by adding further Group 1 success at anywhere from seven to ten furlongs this coming season, then it is a shade of odds-on that both sons of Cabaret (by Galileo) will be on that roster in 2022 and/or 2023.

He holds entries in both the Group 1 Tattersalls Irish 2,000 Guineas and Group 1 Dubai Duty Free Irish Derby, and while the former looks both a reasonable and likely target, there is no guarantee that he will stay he distance of the latter. There is some stamina in his family, although you have to go back to the fourth generation and its branches thereof to find it, and it may be that the ten and a half furlongs of the Group 1 Prix du Jockey Club (French Derby) may be more in his range than Epsom's or the Curragh's twelve. He is also engaged in the Group 1 Emirates Poule d'Essai des Poulains (French 2000 Guineas).

The mid-March-born bay is a 1,300,000-guinea graduate of Tattersalls' Book 1 sale and he was a beaten favourite on his first two starts, both over six furlongs at the Curragh. The ground was yielding when he finished a two-and-a-quarter-length runner-up in a maiden in late July, but the esteem in which he was held despite that loss was evident a fortnight later. How often do you see a maiden go off favourite for a Group 1 race? His performance in the Keeneland Phoenix Stakes was promising even though Lucky Vega won it easily by three and a half lengths from a bunch of five horses who finished close together. Aloha Star was second past the post, a short head in front of The Lir Jet and with margins half a length, a neck and half a length back to Laws of Indices, St Mark's Basilica and Bubbles On Ice, but she was dropped one place after a stewards' enquiry. He had looked a little green, which is hardly a surprise, but finished close to horses with prior winning pattern form, so that was encouraging.

St Mark's Basilica got off the mark at the third attempt, taking a maiden on soft ground, also over six at the Curragh, by a length and a quarter from Loch Lein. That previously once-raced Jessica Harrington-trained filly scored by six lengths at Cork on her only subsequent outing, whereas Duke of Mantua, stablemate of the winner, was a nose back in third on what was his debut, and that well-related and classic-entered son of No Nay Never (by Scat Daddy) won easily at Gowran Park shortly afterwards. As for the successful odds-on favourite, he ran twice more, both in Group 1 company.

Lucky Vega and Master of the Seas were sent off the joint-favourites for the Group 1 Goffs Vincent O'Brien National Stakes on the second day of Irish Champions Weekend, but the former encountered trouble in running and finished fifth, whereas the latter didn't settle as well as you'd hope and lost his unbeaten record, finishing fourth. This was Thunder Moon's big day. The Joseph O'Brien-trained bay had made an impressive winning debut over the course and distance a month before and so made it two-from-two when showing a fine turn of foot well inside the final furlong before going on to beat Wembley by a length and a half. Both that colt and his stablemate St Mark's Basilica stayed on well throughout the closing stages, the former pipping the latter on the line. There were margins of half a length and the same back to the two favourites.

The ground had been good there but was soft at Newmarket in October when the first three met again in the Dewhurst. Thunder Moon was widely expected to maintain his unbeaten record, something that would surely have guaranteed him the champion two-year-old title. He moved to his right to find an opening around two out and if you paused the race once he saw daylight you would likely have nominated him as the winner. The front-running 100/1 shot Devilwala, a pattern-placed colt having his first run for the Ralph Beckett stable, was still leading the field, holding the rails position. Fivethousandtoone was a few lengths wide of him but still there with a chance, and St Mark's Basilica was being pushed along between him and the favourite. Wembley was racing widest of all but also being driven along. The same five horses held the first five positions a furlong later but now Frankie Dettori had got St Mark's Basilica's head in front, Thunder Moon was beside him but with Declan McDonogh asking that colt for more, and Wembley, who had edged left to race closer to the principals, staying on under Ryan Moore. The favourite could find no more a half furlong out, which left the two Ballydoyle colts clear, and the final margin of victory was three-quarters of a length, with Wembley passing the post one and three-quarter lengths in front of Thunder Moon and Devilwala running a huge race to take fourth place, just a neck behind.

The Dewhurst looks like it was the strongest two-year-old race of the year and yet it had not been his intended next target after the National Stakes. He was supposed to run in the Group 1 Qatar Prix Jean-Luc Lagardere - Grand Criterium at ParisLongchamp on the first Sunday in October, and whether or not he would have beaten Sealiway that afternoon and in those conditions is open to debate. However, he was one of the Ballydoyle horses caught up in the contaminated feed problem that led to the team being withdrawn from all targets that day and, once cleared to run, was rerouted to Newmarket.

St Mark's Basilica is one of six top-level winners by Haras de Bonneval's juvenile Group 1 scorer and multiple classic sire Siyouni (by Pivotal) and he is the second male among them. The other one is, of course, the Group 1 Prix du Jockey Club and Group 1 Prix de l'Arc de Triomphe star Sottsass, now a stallion at Coolmore. His aforementioned dam, Cabaret, won the Group 3 Silver Flash Stakes, she has produced two other winners in addition to her pair of Group 1 sons, and she had another Siyouni colt in 2019. He has been named Paris Lights. The mare was bred to Kingman (by Invincible Spirit) in 2020. She is also notable as being a half-sister to the Group 3 Solario Stakes scorer Drumfire (by Danehill Dancer) and to the Group 2 Gimcrack Stakes-placed stakes winner Ho Choi (by Pivotal).

Witch of Fife (by Lear Fan), now the grandam of two Group 1 stars, earned her blacktype when finishing third in the Listed Sweet Solera Stakes as a juvenile. She is out of Fife (by Lomond), who was third in the Listed Lupe Stakes over ten furlongs, and she is a half-sister to Quiet Mouse (by Quiet American), the unraced dam of Ugo Fire (by Bluebird). That filly was among the better ones of her age in 2005 when she won the Group 3 C. L. Weld Park Stakes and finished third in the Group 1 Moyglare Stud Stakes. She was also fourth (not placed, no blacktype) in the Group 1 Phoenix Stakes that year and was twice Group 3-placed at around seven furlongs at three.

All of this paints a picture of a colt who could be best from seven to nine furlongs but might stay the extended ten furlongs of races such as the Prix du Jockey Club or Juddmonte International Stakes. If you go back another step on the page, however, then you will find that Fife's half-brother El Conquistador (by Shirley Heights) was runner-up in the Group 3 Goodwood Cup in the days when it was run over two miles and five furlongs. Also, his full sister Piffle did her part for the family by coming up with the Grade 1 Hollywood Turf Handicap scorer Frenchpark (by Fools Holme) and Group 1 Prix Vermeille heroine and blacktype producer Pearly Shells (by Efisio). Like the Vermeille, that Hollywood race is run over twelve furlongs. If some of that stamina has filtered down then perhaps St Mark's Basilica could stay the Derby distance, but the odds are stacked more in favour of him being most effective over shorter than that.

SUMMARY DETAILS

Bred: Robert Scarborough
Owned: Derrick Smith, Mrs John Mangier & Michael Tabor
Trained: Aidan O'Brien
Country: Ireland
Race record: 20131-
Career highlights: 2 wins inc Darley Dewhurst Stakes (Gr1), 3rd Goffs Vincent O'Brien National Stakes (Gr1)

ST MARK'S BASILICA (FR) – 2018 bay colt

Siyouni (FR)	Pivotal (GB)	Polar Falcon (USA)
		Fearless Revival
	Sichilla (IRE)	Danehill (USA)
		Slipstream Queen (USA)
Cabaret (IRE)	Galileo (IRE)	Sadler's Wells (USA)
		Urban Sea (USA)
	Witch of Fife (USA)	Lear Fan (USA)
		Fife (IRE)

STRADIVARIUS (IRE)

Although undefeated in five starts as a four-year-old and winner of five from six the following year, Stradivarius only managed to add two more races from six starts in 2020, with his final pair of runs resulting in unplaced finishes. The last time he had finished out of the frame was in his first two races as a two-year-old, back in 2016. One of his latest triumphs was only by a length and although it was in the Group 1 Al Shaqab Goodwood Cup, which he was winning for the fourth time, the effort was a shade below his best. That may seem like an odd remark to make in relation to such an occasion, but when he had met that race's principal rival, Nayef Road, almost six weeks before, in soft ground in the Group 1 Gold Cup at Ascot, he thrashed him by ten lengths. That was arguably the most brilliant performance of his glittering career, his third victory in the famous two-and-a-half-mile race, achieved on soft ground that wasn't thought ideal for him, and it secured his spot at the top of the stayers' division in the World's Best Racehorse Rankings. Topping that table was a feat he also achieved in both of the previous two seasons, albeit sharing the honours with Kew Gardens in 2018. But his new career-high figure of 125 put him in joint third overall in the world over any distance in 2020, equal to Addeybb, Bivouac, Classique Legend, Palace Pier, Persian King and Tiz The Law and behind only Ghaiyyath (130) and Authentic (126).

Before last season, the last time the popular chestnut ran over shorter than fourteen furlongs was in May of his three-year-old season, when he failed by only half a length to give thirteen pounds to Here And Now in a handicap over the extended twelve furlongs at Chester. It was the run that preceded his step-up into pattern company, a move that began with his neck defeat of Count Octave in the Group 2 Queen's Vase over fourteen furlongs at Royal Ascot. He beat Big Orange to land his first Group 1 Goodwood Cup shortly afterwards and was followed home by Rekindling and Coronet when finishing half a length and a short-head third to Capri and Crystal Ocean in a vintage edition of the Group 1 St Leger Stakes at Doncaster that September. His connections decided to try something a bit different in 2020, and although those three runs resulted in defeats, it would not be fair to say that the change was a failure. Indeed, it is to be hoped that he gets at least one more try at twelve furlongs in 2021.

He kicked off his six-year-old season in the Group 1 Hurworth Bloodstock Coronation Cup Stakes at Newmarket in early June. Ghaiyyath made all and broke the track record in taking the prize by two and a half lengths from the staying-on Anthony Van Dyck, with that ill-fated Derby winner finishing the same margin in front of Stradivarius. The rest of the field was well strung out behind. Stradivarius had been in second but not closing on the leader before the Ballydoyle colt edged past him a furlong out and Frankie Dettori eased up on him before the line. Given this was his first attempt at so short a distance for three years, it was an eye-catching performance. Thirteen days later, he put up that brilliant display in the Group 1 Gold Cup. Nayef Road made most of the running and was still at the head of affairs at the two-furlong pole, with most of the field under pressure or struggling. However, Stradivarius was absolutely cruising and it was only a matter of when Dettori would let him go. He waited for a few strides and then made his move, quickly going clear and then easing down a little near the line. A winning margin of ten lengths is rarely seen in Group 1 races, and the soft ground likely contributed despite it being a surface on which the favourite has not always been at his best. Cross Counter, who is best at up to two miles but was below his peak throughout 2021, picked up third, eight lengths adrift of Nayef Road.

As noted above, Stradivarius only beat Nayef Road by a length when winning his fourth Goodwood Cup, but that does not tell the whole story. The younger chestnut, a classic-placed dual pattern winner who will surely be a popular National Hunt stallion someday, set a steady pace, so an ability to excel at shorter than the advertised two miles became key. Most true stayers lack the necessary speed, but not Stradivarius. He encountered traffic problems from two out, finally got room a furlong later and only got to the front inside the final half furlong. The Group 1 Irish Derby winner Santiago, likely benefitting from the need for twelve-furlong pace rather than pure stamina, was a length and a quarter back in third, with a three-length gap back to Eagles By Day in fourth.

Anthony Van Dyck tried a similar tactic in the Group 2 Qatar Prix Foy in September, going to the front after a furlong, dictating a less than exacting pace and winning the twelve-furlong test, but only narrowly. Stradivarius was travelling well over two furlongs out and he kept on strongly to the line, failing by just a short neck to land the spoils. Nagano Gold was a length and a quarter back in third, the same margin in front of Skyward and followed closely by Way To Paris and Ziyad, the only other runners. The heavy ground ruined his chance in the Group 1 Qatar Prix de l'Arc de Triomphe the following month—finishing just under a seven-length seventh was a decent effort in the circumstances—but his final run of the year was a huge disappointment. The ground was soft, heavy in places, at Ascot on British Champions Day, he was in trouble a quarter of a mile from home, eased when his chance was clearly gone, and was one of three who finished tailed off: Dubious Affair and Broome were the other two. A vet examined him post-race but did not find any abnormalities. It had been announced, shortly after the Arc, that he would remain in training as a seven-year-old, and that plan did not change after Ascot.

Stradivarius's pedigree was reviewed in detail in *European Group 1 Winners of 2019*, so a brief overview will suffice. He is one of fourteen Group 1 winners among an overall tally of seventy-three stakes winners by Gilltown Stud's Timeform 140-rated superstar Sea The Stars (by Cape Cross). The first sire-son of that half-brother to Galileo (by Sadler's Wells) is the runaway Group 1 Deutsches Derby victor Sea The Moon, a Lanwades Stud stallion whose representatives in 2020 featured the classic-placed wide-margin Group 1 Coronation Stakes heroine Alpine Star and the Group 2 scorers Wonderful Moon and Quest The Moon, the latter a multiple Group 1-placed colt. Dual Derby star Harzand got off the mark as a freshman sire last season and had a couple of famously related Group 1 Irish Oaks entrants among his early winners, whereas Cloth of Stars (Haras du Logis; yearlings in 2021), Mekhtaal (Haras de Bouquetot; yearlings in 2021) and Zelzal (Haras de Bouquetot; freshman sire in 2021) are among his other flat-oriented sons at stud.

The chestnut is a half-brother to the dual ten-furlong pattern winner Persian Storm (by Monsun), out of the stakes-placed middle-distance scorer Private Life (by Bering) and so he is a great-grandson of the brilliant Pawneese (by Carvin II). That Timeform 131-rated filly won the Group 1 Oaks, Group 1 Prix de Diane (French Oaks) and Group 1 King George VI and Queen Elizabeth Stakes in 1976, and her siblings featured Petroleuse (by Habitat). That Group 3 Princess Elizabeth Stakes winner is the grandam of the Group 1 Prix du Jockey Club and Timeform 137-rated runaway Group 1 Prix de l'Arc de Triomphe star Peintre Celebre (by Nureyev)—sire of twelve Group 1 winners—and a direct and ancestor of the Grade/Group 1 winners Jet Dark (by Trippi), Planteur (by Danehill Dancer) and Persian King (by Kingman). If you go back farther on the page then you will find that his fifth dam, Petite Saguenay (by Nordiste), was a half-sister to Montaval (by Norseman). He won the King George VI and Queen Elizabeth Stakes, the Prix Dollar and Prix Gontaut-Biron, he was runner-up to Lavandin in the Derby at Epsom and although he died at the age of twelve, was a classic sire in Japan.

Stradivarius is one of the best stayers of recent decades but he has that key ingredient that most in the division lack: speed. It is that quality, plus his pedigree and his size that could make him a potential classic sire if given the chance. Many still hold a prejudice against stamina, and yet that ability and genetic tendency is needed if the breed is to continue to thrive. From where are we going to get the Derby, Oaks, Arc, St Leger and Cup horses of the future if all we breed from is sprinters, milers or flash-in-the-pan juveniles? He has been described by Timeform as being "smallish" and "no bigger than medium-sized", and he represents the Green Desert branch of Danzig's line, one whose success under National Hunt rules pales into insignificance compared to its achievements on the flat—Danehill is the branch of Danzig (by Northern Dancer) that excels in both sectors. It could potentially be a terrible waste were he to be consigned to covering hundreds of National Hunt-type mares instead of being given a proper chance by flat breeders, buyers and trainers.

SUMMARY DETAILS

Bred: Bjorn Nielsen
Owned: Bjorn Nielsen
Trained: John Gosden
Country: England
Race record: 041-121133-11111-111112-311200-
Career highlights: 16 wins inc Gold Cup (Gr1-three times), Al Shaqab (2020)/Qatar (2017-2019) Goodwood Cup Stakes (Gr1-four times), Qipco British Champions Long Distance Cup (Gr2), Weatherbys Hamilton Lonsdale Cup Stakes (Gr2-twice), Yorkshire Cup (Gr2-twice), Magners Rose Doncaster Cup Stakes (Gr2), Queen's Vase (Gr2), 2nd Qipco British Champions Long Distance Cup (Gr2), Qatar Prix Foy (Gr2), 3rd William Hill St Leger Stakes (Gr1), Qipco British Champions Long Distance Cup (Gr2)

STRADIVARIUS (IRE) – 2014 chestnut horse

Sea The Stars (IRE)	Cape Cross (IRE)	Green Desert (USA)
		Park Appeal
	Urban Sea (USA)	Miswaki (USA)
		Allegretta
Private Life (FR)	Bering	Arctic Tern (USA)
		Beaune (FR)
	Poughkeepsie (IRE)	Sadler's Wells (USA)
		Pawneese

SUBJECTIVIST (GB)

Subjectivist was a stakes-placed seven-length Chelmsford winner as a two-year-old but had his limitations exposed on several occasions. He's not a miler and he was well-beaten over ten furlongs on his final start. His rating dropped from a peak of ninety-eight down to ninety-four, so it was to be expected that he would take a handicap route at three. He finished third in a valuable twelve-furlong one first time out at three—the King George V Stakes at Royal Ascot—and then failed by only a length to take a similar contest over an extra quarter mile at Haydock, carrying twenty pounds more than the winner, Favorite Moon (sic), and despite encountering trouble in running. There was an eight-length gap back to the third. He returned to blacktype company, despite being rated only ninety-seven, and aside from two disappointing runs, he did enough in two other races to suggest that he could play a starring role in 2021.

He started in mid-July with a listed-race victory over eleven furlongs at Hamilton which he dictated from the start, setting a steady gallop before winding it up around halfway and winning easily by one and three-quarter lengths. He also tried to make all in the Group 3 John Pearce Racing Gordon Stakes over a furlong farther at Goodwood but had to give best to Mogul and Highland Chief who beat him by margins of three-quarters of a length and the same. Then he disappointed in the Group 2 Great Voltigeur Stakes, finishing only seventh to Pyledriver. That race is often seen as being a trial for the Group 1 St Leger Stakes, a classic in which his half-brother had been placed the year before, but Subjectivist was unable to match the feat, instead finishing only seventh.

Were those the only races he ran in 2020 then it's possible he would be on the shortlist for gelding, maybe even having some appeal as a potential hurdler, but what he did on his other two races not only propelled him to the fore but raised the likelihood of a stallion role in his future. Distance was the key. The first was the Group 3 Ladbrokes March Stakes over fourteen furlongs on soft ground at Goodwood at the end of August, a race his sibling had won en route to Doncaster, and although one of the four taking part was tailed off with an injury and the third appeared not to stay, the stakes-winning runner-up had chased home Enbihaar in the Group 2 Lillie Langtry Stakes on her previous start but was completely outclassed by the front-running Subjectivist. The underfoot conditions likely exaggerated his superiority, and all of Cabaletta's best form had been on a sounder surface, but it was hard not to be impressed with the way in which he went clear over the final quarter mile to win by fifteen lengths.

His second big win came two months later. He made all the running again, this time over fifteen and a half furlongs on heavy ground at ParisLongchamp, chased home by the three-year-old filly Valia plus the Group 1-winning older horses Holdthasigreen and Princess Zoe. The margins were two lengths, two and a half lengths and a neck, and the race was the Group 1 Prix Royal-Oak.

Two miles should be no problem to him given how he won in France. He wouldn't be guaranteed to get much further than that on pedigree—few would—but there is every reason to hope that he will stay the extra half mile of the Group 1 Gold Cup at Ascot. Good ground is not necessarily an inconvenience, which is an important consideration given the likelihood of sound underfoot conditions for many of the Cup races, and it may be that a greater worry will be one or more others determined to take him on in the early stages. It remains to be seen how he will fare at a high level if made to settle and come from behind. What we do know is that he is a better horse than his classic-placed, pattern-winning half-brother Sir Ron Priestley (by Australia), who is back in training with Mark Johnston—they could be described as three-parts brothers—and that his relationship to two horses in particular could make him very much in demand as a stallion someday.

The brothers are out of the multiple stakes-placed mare Reckoning (by Danehill Dancer), a half-sister to a blacktype earner and out of a half-sister to two other blacktype earners. These are the highlights of the first three generations of the pedigree. However, his third dam, Aspiration (by Sadler's Wells), is a winning full sister to the classic-placed juvenile Group 1 scorer Sholokhov and half-sister to Affianced (by Erins Isle), the pattern-placed, stakes-winning dam of the Group 1 Irish Derby and Group 1 Coronation Cup star Soldier of Fortune (by Galileo).

Sholokhov began stud life in Germany from where he sired the classic heroine Night Magic and eleven other stakes winners, but the now Glenview Stud resident is best known as being the sire of Grade 1 Cheltenham Gold Cup and Grade 1 Punchestown Gold Cup hero Don Cossack. His fifteen other National Hunt blacktype scorers include the Grade 1 Supreme Novices' Hurdle winner Shishkin and this season's talented novice hurdler Bob Olinger, both of those coming from their sire's Irish-bred crops. Soldier of Fortune shuttled to South America during his flat-sire days, he has had seven top-level winners from a mile to twelve furlongs among those Chilean- and Brazilian-born offspring, and he is in his sixth season as a National Hunt sire at Beeches Stud in Ireland, covering three-digit numbers of mares each year.

Subjectivist is a son of the unbeaten juvenile star and standout Kildangan Stud stallion Teofilo (by Galileo), a seventeen-year-old who is on the verge of becoming the first son of his sire to get 100 flat stakes winners. Twenty-one of them have won at least once at the highest level, his best representatives are typically effective at anywhere from seven furlongs to two miles, and in 2020 he was also the sire of the European-trained Group 1 winners Donjah, Gear Up, Tawkeel and Twilight Payment plus Hong Kong's top-level star Exultant, and his representatives as a broodmare sire featured the juvenile Group 1 scorer Mac Swiney (by New Approach).

The Mark Johnston-trained colt, who was bred by Mascalls Stud, is a 62,000-guinea graduate of Tattersalls' Book 2 yearling sale, and it will be fascinating to see what the future holds for him, on the track and at stud. Indeed, his pedigree will present something of a challenge for some National Hunt breeders given he is inbred 3x4 to Sadler's Wells (by Northern Dancer) and 3x3 to Danehill (by Danzig). He also shows duplications of 4x5 to Sharpen Up (by Atan) and 4x5x5x5 to Northern Dancer (by Nearctic), but most of that will drop off the page as inbreeding is only counted within the first five generations. Many of his future progeny will likely carry inbreeding to Sadler's Wells, Danehill, their sons Galileo and Danehill Dancer and others of their descendants. Luckily there will be plenty of good mares by other horses out there, ones representing stallions such as Beneficial (by

Top Ville), Flemensfirth (by Alleged), Presenting (by Mtoto), Saint des Saints (by Cadoudal) and Stowaway (by Slip Anchor), for example.

SUMMARY DETAILS
Bred: Mascalls Stud
Owned: Dr J Walker
Trained: Mark Johnston
Country: England
Race record: 2210240-32130101-
Career highlights: 4 wins inc Prix Royal-Oak (Gr1), Ladbrokes March Stakes (In Memory of John Dunlop) (Gr3), Irish Stallion Farms EBF Glasgow Stakes (L), 2nd Longines Irish Champions Weekend EBF Stonehenge Stakes (L), 3rd John Pearce Racing Gordon Stakes (Gr3)

SUBJECTIVIST (GB) – 2017 bay colt

Teofilo (IRE)	Galileo (IRE)	Sadler's Wells (USA)
		Urban Sea (USA)
	Speirbhean (IRE)	Danehill (USA)
		Saviour (USA)
Reckoning (IRE)	Danehill Dancer (IRE)	Danehill (USA)
		Mira Adonde (USA)
	Great Hope (IRE)	Halling (USA)
		Aspiration (IRE)

SUNNY QUEEN (GER)

Hyped-up horses come and go and many are soon forgotten. Fioravanti was one in the mid-1980s, a son of the phenomenal Northern Dancer (by Nearctic), out of the juvenile Group 1 star and subsequent Group 1-placed middle-distance Group 2 scorer Pitasia (by Pitskelly). The $2,300,000 Keeneland July purchase won a listed race at Phoenix Park as a two-year-old, but it was to remain his only blacktype despite racing on two continents. However, given the climate of the time, he got a chance at stud. He sired only a handful of foals, died young and seemed likely to be forgotten, but two of his daughters came to prominence on the track. One of them is the grandam of Sunny Queen.

Wixon was the better one, the top French juvenile filly of 1992. She made a winning debut in the Listed Prix Yacowlef, added the Group 3 Prix du Petit Couvert and Listed Prix Imprudence and was runner-up in each of the Group 2 Criterium de Maisons-Laffitte, Group 3 Prix d'Arenberg and Group 3 Prix Eclipse. The Allen Paulson homebred went on to become a blacktype producer and grandam at stud. Suivez, on the other hand, earned her blacktype when runner-up in a seven-furlong listed contest at two and another one over nine furlongs at three, both in Germany. Her third dam, Schönbrunn (by Pantheon), won the Preis der Diana (German Oaks) and Grand Prix de Deauville in 1969, sixth dam Schwarzgold (by Alchimist) won the Deutsches Derby and Preis der Diana in 1940 before going on to found a dynasty for her owner-breeders, Gestüt Schlenderhan, and so it was no surprise when Suivez went on to become a broodmare of note too.

She has produced the dual ten-and-a-half-furlong Group 2 winner Simoun (by Monsun), plus the listed scorers Shining (by Surumu), Soignee (by Dashing Blade) and Soudaine (by Monsun), the latter pair being fillies who have also gone on to success at stud. Soudaine's son Savoir Vivre (by Adlerflug) won the Group 2 Grand Prix de Deauville in 2016 and was runner-up in the Group 1 Deutsches Derby, and he is a half-brother to the eight- and nine-furlong stakes winner Sussudio (by Nayef). Soignee, on the other hand, is the dam of the Group 1 Prix de Diane (French

Oaks) heroine and Eclipse Award-winning champion Stacelita (by Monsun), the six-time top-level star whose daughter, Soul Stirring (by Frankel), landed the Group 1 Yushun Himba (Japanese Oaks) in 2017.

Suivez also had another daughter of note: Suivi (by Darshaan). She won four of her eight starts and missed out on blacktype when finishing fourth in a ten-and-a-half-furlong listed contest in Germany, but she is the dam of the lightly raced listed scorer Suestado (by Monsun) and last year's surprise Group 1 Allianz - Grosser Preis von Bayern heroine Sunny Queen. That Henk Grewe-trained bay cost Stefan Hahne just €35,000 at 2018's BBAG September yearling sale and raced in his colours until sold for a reported €500,000 before her Group 1 win. She is now in the ownership of the South African-owned Cayton Park Stud and is due to remain in training with Grewe in 2021.

Her big day came at the expense of the star three-year-old colt and market leader Torquator Tasso and having hit the front inside the final half furlong, she had to fight to hold him off for a neck victory. There was a two-length gap back to her better-fancied stablemate Dicaprio in third, the listed scorer whom the favourite had short-headed when gaining his Group 1 win a month before. The ground was heavy, which may have contributed to her improved form. She had been short-headed by Lucky Lycra in a Group 3 contest at Hanover on soft a fortnight before and had won listed races over ten and twelve furlongs at that same venue, one of them by eight and a half lengths on good ground. She had also finished three-quarters of a length behind the talented English filly Rose of Kildare when the pair finished third and fourth in the Group 2 T von Zastrow Stutenpreis over twelve furlongs at Baden-Baden—the ground there was good-to-soft— and her only other start was in a nine-furlong Hanover maiden in early May where she finished a close third.

Sunny Queen is German-bred by Anahita Stables and she comes from one of the most famous German distaff lines in the stud book. Sagace (by Luthier) and Slip Anchor (by Shirley Heights) are just two of the standouts in the family's roll of honour. However, her sire stands at Coolmore Stud in Ireland. Triple classic star Camelot (by Montjeu) has sired seven Group 1 scorers among his first thirty-three stakes winners, four of whom achieved the feat in 2020: Even So (Irish Oaks) and Sunny Queen in Europe, plus the Irish-bred pair Russian Camelot and Sir Dragonet in Australia. Irish Derby victor Latrobe is part of the earlier trio.

Whether or not she is up to winning at the highest level outside of Germany remains to be seen, and it is possible she will not be asked to do so, but Sunny Queen clearly has plenty of ability plus considerable potential for when she goes to stud.

SUMMARY DETAILS

Bred: Anahita Stables
Owned: Cayton Park Stud Ltd
Trained: Henk Grewe
Country: Germany
Race record: -314121-
Career highlights: 3 wins inc Allianz - Grosser Preis von Bayern (Gr1), pferdwetten.de - Gorilla Millions Cup (L), Goddert Sybrecht-Erinnerungsrennen (L), 2nd Grosser Preis der Mehl-Mülhens-Stiftung (Gr3)

SUNNY QUEEN (GER) – 2017 bay filly

Camelot (GB)	Montjeu (IRE)	Sadler's Wells (USA)
		Floripedes (FR)
	Tarfah (USA)	Kingmambo (USA)
		Fickle (GB)
Suivi (GER)	Darshaan	Shirley Heights
		Delsy (FR)
	Suivez (FR)	Fioravanti (USA)
		Sea Symphony

SUPREMACY (IRE)

The Middle Park Stakes has been one of England's top two-year-old races since the latter half of the nineteenth century. It was, for a long time, a classic pointer for the following season, but its recent history of winners is more frequently populated with those who proved best at up to seven furlongs, if they did go on to have a good three-year-old campaign at all. There are a few of its winners from the past thirty years who went on to add another Group 1 victory at three, but you have to go back to Rodrigo de Triano to find one who went on to classic success. He won the 2000 Guineas and Irish 2,000 Guineas in 1992, plus both the Juddmonte International Stakes and Champion Stakes. In contrast, Ten Sovereigns (2018 Middle Park Stakes), U S Navy Flag (2017), Dream Ahead (2010), and Oasis Dream (2002) went on to win the Group 1 July Cup, whereas Royal Applause (1995) landed the Group 1 Sprint Cup.

The juvenile class of 2020 was a substandard one, which raises the possibility that its big-race winners may be vulnerable against the best older horses or even be overtaken by less exposed members of their own cohort. However, there is reason to believe that such things may not be the fate of Supremacy. Whether or not he can win the July Cup remains to be seen, and he needs to improve to be up to that task, but right now he is arguably the leading candidate for the Group 1 Commonwealth Cup. The Clive Cox-trained bay won three of his four starts at two, his rating of 118 puts him just two pounds behind the juvenile champion, St Mark's Basilica, and he got his Group 1 win at the immediate expense of a colt who had already won at that level: Lucky Vega.

Supremacy is a £65,000 graduate of the Goffs UK Premier Yearling Sale and it looks odds-on that sprinting will be his game. He does have a relation who was a dual Group 1 winner at a mile, but the three other high-profile horses who appear under the first two generations of his pedigree were sprinters, one of whom landed the July Cup. Also, he represents the Tally-Ho Stud resident and champion freshman sire Mehmas (by Acclamation), a Group 2-winning sprinter who raced only as a two-year-old. That young stallion comes from a family famous for its milers and middle-distance horses, which suggests that he will get his best winners in the broad five-to-ten-furlong range, depending on the mares, but the odds are tilted in favour of his star first-crop son being effective in the shorter end.

The colt was unplaced in a six-furlong novice race at Windsor on his debut in mid-June but easily won a maiden over that course and distance three weeks later. He followed that with another eye-catching performance at Goodwood, making all to beat Yazaman and Lauded by four lengths and a neck in the Group 2 Qatar Richmond Stakes, but it was his final start of the year that secured his top rating. Group 1 Phoenix Stakes winner Lucky Vega was sent off favourite to make it a double in the eight-runner Juddmonte Middle Park Stakes at Newmarket in late September, and although he beat the Group 2 Gimcrack Stakes winner Minzaal by two and a quarter lengths, he failed by half a length to catch Supremacy who made all and battled well to hold off his rival by half a length, even pulling away slightly near the line. Tactical was another three-quarters of a length back in fourth, a length and three-quarters of a length in front of The Lir Jet and Lipizzaner.

Supremacy is the third foal and third sprint winner out of Triggers Broom. That mare is by the now Italy-based Group 1 Prix Morny winner Arcano (by Oasis Dream), who is related to the Group 1 Prix de l'Abbaye de Longchamp heroine Gilt Edge Girl (by Monsieur Bond); he mostly sires sprinters, as you might expect. It also looks certain that the mare's fourth foal will be a sprinter too, presuming he lives up to his pedigree and purchase price, as the 180,000-guinea Tattersalls Book 1 graduate is a first-crop son of another Tally-Ho Stud stallion: the Group 1-placed dual five-furlong Group 3 scorer Cotai Glory (by Exceed And Excel). Foal number five is an April 18th, 2020-born filly by that same stallion, and the mare was covered by him again last season.

Triggers Bloom was placed once in a five-race career but that was a ten-and-a-half-length third off a very low weight in a six-furlong Hamilton handicap, and her rating of forty-six going into that race dropped to thirty-six after her final start. Clearly, she had none of the family's talent. Her dam, Great Joy (by Grand Lodge), was stakes-placed in Germany, her stakes-placed half-sister A

Huge Dream (by Refuse To Bend) is the dam of the dual stakes-winning sprinter Mrs Gallagher (by Oasis Dream), but Xtension (by Xaar) and Beatrix Potter (by Cadeaux Genereux) are her most notable siblings. Xtension won the Group 2 Vintage Stakes over seven furlongs at two, he was runner-up in the Group 2 Coventry Stakes and third in the Group 1 Dewhurst Stakes, and went on to become a dual Group 1-winning miler in Hong Kong. Beatrix Potter, on the other hand, never won a race and her final handicap mark of sixty was a drop of twenty pounds on her career peak, but she is the dam of the Group 2 Mill Reef Stakes winner Pierre Lapin (by Cappella Sansevero) and his champion half-brother Harry Angel (by Dark Angel).

Like Harry Angel, Supremacy is by a son of Acclamation (by Royal Applause), which makes the younger colt a bit more closely related to that Group 1 July Cup and Group 1 Sprint Cup star than to others in his family. Europe's three-year-old sprint champion of 2017, Harry Angel was also trained by Cox. He won the Group 2 Mill Reef Stakes at two, his Group 1s plus the Group 2 Sandy Lane Stakes at three and the Group 2 Duke of York Stakes at four. He was runner-up to Caravaggio in the Group 1 Commonwealth Cup, to Blue Point in the Group 3 Pavilion Stakes and to Sands of Mali in the Group 1 British Champions Sprint Stakes, he has covered triple-digit books of mares in his first two seasons at Dalham Hall Stud and will have yearlings on offer this coming summer and autumn.

There will surely also be a stallion career in Supremacy's future, regardless how his three-year-old season turns out. He comes from a branch of the family of the US Grade 1 winner and Grade 1 sire Stephen Got Even (by A.P. Indy) although the connection is remote given that the blacktype scorer and prolific winner Avum (by Umbrella Fella) is their common ancestor; she's the third dam of Stephen Got Even and fourth dam of Supremacy. Of course, Harry Angel will have had runners before his 'nephew' has any foals born, whereas Xtension has sired several multiple winners from a handful of offspring. First, Supremacy has his three-year-old racing season ahead of him, and it will be disappointing if he fails to add further pattern success to his tally. All of his races so far have been on good ground or faster.

SUMMARY DETAILS

Bred: Kangyu International Racing
Owned: J Goddard
Trained: Clive Cox
Country: England
Race record: 0111-
Career highlights: 3 wins inc Juddmonte Middle Park Stakes (Gr1), Qatar Richmond Stakes (Gr2)

SUPREMACY (IRE) – 2018 bay colt

Mehmas (IRE)	Acclamation (GB)	Royal Applause (GB)
		Princess Athena
	Lucina (GB)	Machiavellian (USA)
		Lunda (IRE)
Triggers Broom (IRE)	Arcano (IRE)	Oasis Dream (GB)
		Tariysha (IRE)
	Great Joy (IRE)	Grand Lodge (USA)
		Cheese Soup (USA)

TARNAWA (IRE)

What a wonderful filly this is and what an exciting prospect she will be when she goes to the paddocks. It must have been tempting to retire her to stud following her top-level hat-trick in the autumn, but the Aga Khan homebred, who gave the great Irish trainer Dermot Weld a long-overdue first winner at the Breeders' Cup, is to return to action as a five-year-old. The plan is reportedly to build up to another autumn campaign, this time with the Group 1 Prix de l'Arc de Triomphe in mind.

Tarnawa had been stakes-placed at two and a triple pattern winner at three but took her form to a new level in 2020. She was not seen out until August 8th when the three-year-olds Cayenne Pepper and Passion were expected to beat her in the Group 3 Irish Stallion Farms EBF Give Thanks Stakes at Cork. It was a surprise to see her go off as long as 8/1 against that Irish Oaks-placed pair, because her three-year-old form was excellent, but not that she became the first dual winner of the race. Oisin Orr settled her towards the rear, began moving her forward steadily from three out, sent her to the front over a furlong and a half from home and never looked in any danger after that. Cayenne Pepper ran on well in the closing stages to put three and three-quarter lengths between herself and third-placed Passion, but Tarnawa won a shade comfortably by one and three-quarter lengths; she outclassed her rivals.

The Irish Oaks first- and fourth-place finishers, Even So and Laburnum, were among her nine rivals in the Group 1 Qatar Prix Vermeille at ParisLongchamp the following month, as were the Group 1-placed, Group 2 Princess of Wales's Stakes winner Dame Malliot, recent Group 3 scorer Wonderful Tonight and the highly regarded Raabihah. That Jean-Claude Rouget-trained chestnut had come off worst in the four-way photo finish for the Group 1 Prix de Diane Longines (French Oaks), beaten a short neck, head and head by Fancy Blue, Alpine Star, and Peaceful, but she had easily won a Group 3 contest at Deauville next time and was sent off favourite now on what was her first attempt at twelve furlongs. Dame Malliot tried to make all but was headed by Tarnawa with a furlong to go. The bay kept on well to the end but was no match for the Irish-trained chestnut who pulled three lengths clear by the finish. Raabihah stayed on to take second place on the line, with Laburnum another half a length behind in fourth and similar margins back to Wonderful Tonight and Even So. The fifth would go on to win back-to-back Group 1s on much different underfoot conditions.

The ground had been good at the Curragh and on her September visit to France but it was heavy at ParisLongchamp on the first Sunday in October. Fancy Blue and Laburnum were non-runners in the Group 1 Prix de l'Opera Longines due to a much-publicised contaminated feed issue, but it was still an Irish one-two in the ten-furlong test. The undefeated Group 1 Prix Saint-Alary scorer Tawkeel made the running until headed by the runaway Group 1 Coronation Stakes heroine Alpine Star over a quarter mile from home. That Jessica Harrington-trained chestnut, who had chased home Palace Pier in the Group 1 Prix Jacques le Marois on similar ground on her most recent outing, kept on well to the end but had to give best to Tarnawa who caught her around a quarter of a furlong out and won by a short neck. There were margins of three-quarters of a length and the same back to Audarya and Tawkeel, with Ambition another length and a quarter adrift in fifth. Both the first and third would go on to win on firm ground at the Breeders' Cup.

The James Fanshawe-trained Audarya, who had beaten Ambition by a neck to win the Group 1 Darley Prix Jean Romanet in August, rounded off her season with a neck defeat of Rushing Fall in the Grade 1 Maker's Mark Breeders' Cup Filly & Mare Turf over nine and a half furlongs at Keeneland. Tarnawa, on the other hand, took on the Grade 1 Longines Breeders' Cup Turf over twelve furlongs. Christophe Soumillion had been in the saddle for her first two top-level wins but a positive Covid-19 test ruled him this time, so Colin Keane got the ride. Channel Maker set a steady early pace, he went clear three out but came under pressure and was headed half a furlong from home as Tarnawa, who had been racing wide and staying on strongly, swept past. Magical stayed on to pip Channel Maker for second, with Lord North and Mogul another one and three-quarter lengths and a head behind in fourth and fifth, but Tarnawa won the race by a length. Her prolific

Group 1-winning Ballydoyle-based rival had been sent off favourite, but this, a first Breeders' Cup winner for Weld and also for Keane, was a very popular result. All three of the Irish runners plus both John Gosden-trained ones—Lord North and seventh-placed Mehdaayih—ran on Lasix.

Tarnawa is one of twenty-six Group 1 stars among over 150 stakes winners by the late and much-lamented Kildangan Stud flag bearer Shamardal (by Giant's Causeway). It will be 2022 before she goes to stud, but those of note now out of Shamardal mares include the Group 1 scorers Awtaad (by Cape Cross; Irish 2,000 Guineas), Hello Youmzain (by Kodiac; Diamond Jubilee Stakes, Sprint Cup), Latrobe (by Camelot; Irish Derby) and Pretty Pollyanna (by Oasis Dream; Prix Morny). There is also a Grade 1 winner in South Africa (Mighty High, by Pathfork) and a string of horses who have won other pattern races, all of which augurs well for her prospects of becoming a broodmare of note.

She is the first foal of Tarana (by Cape Cross), who had a Siyouni (by Pivotal) filly in 2020 before being bred to Frankel (by Galileo), and she is both a daughter and granddaughter of talented middle-distance fillies. Tarana won the Listed Oyster Stakes at Galway and Listed Martin Moloney Stakes at Limerick and the five blacktype races in which she was placed featured the Group 3 Curragh Cup. The mare's half-sister Tasalka (by Lope de Vega) won a ten-furlong Naas maiden for the Weld stable in July and was a neck runner-up in an eleven-furlong handicap at Killarney a few weeks later, and they are out of Tarakala (by Dr Fong) whom John Oxx trained to win four times including a four-length score in the Listed Galtres Stakes at York. Being effective on a wide range of underfoot conditions is also a valuable family trait. Tarakala got her wins on soft up to good-to-firm, Tarana won on good and yielding-to-soft, was listed placed on soft-to-heavy and Group 3-placed on good-to-firm, whereas third dam Tarakana (by Shahrastani) got her blacktype placings on heavy, good, and good-to-firm ground.

These are the highlights of the first three generations of the pedigree. If you look at the fifth dam then you will find a string of blacktype winners plus branches that lead to the contrasting Group 1 winners Damson (by Entrepreneur), Tiraaz (by Lear Fan) and Whisky Baron (by Manhattan Rain), but they are remotely connected to Tarnawa, as are her celebrity sixth and seventh dams. Tonnera (by Wild Risk) won the Prix Saint-Alary and was runner-up in the Poule d'Essai des Pouliches (French 1000 Guineas) in 1966, whereas Texana (by Relic) won the Prix de l'Abbaye de Longchamp.

Tarnawa, who has reportedly wintered well, promises to be a leading light of the European middle-distance scene again in 2021 before going on to what could be a very notable career at stud.

SUMMARY DETAILS
Bred: His Highness The Aga Khan's Studs SC
Owned: H H Aga Khan
Trained: Dermot Weld
Country: Ireland
Race record: 322-1310110-1111-
Career highlights: 8 wins inc Longines Breeders' Cup Turf (Gr1), Prix de l'Opera Longines (Gr1), Qatar Prix Vermeille (Gr1), Moyglare 'Jewels' Blandford Stakes (Gr2), Irish Stallion Farms EBF Give Thanks Stakes (Gr3-twice), Irish National Stud Racing Irish EBF Blue Wind Stakes (Gr3), 2nd Staffordstown Stud Stakes (L), 3rd Irish Stallion Farms EBF Salsabil Stakes (L)

TARNAWA (IRE) – 2016 chestnut filly

Shamardal (USA)	Giant's Causeway (USA)	Storm Cat (USA)
		Mariah's Storm (USA)
	Helsinki (GB)	Machiavellian (USA)
		Helen Street
Tarana (IRE)	Cape Cross (IRE)	Green Desert (USA)
		Park Appeal
	Tarakala (IRE)	Dr Fong (USA)
		Tarakana (USA)

TAWKEEL (GB)

This series of books has documented some of the increasing number of Group 1 winners who have had an initial or early win on one of the artificial tracks in Europe, a list that includes stars such as Anapurna, Billesdon Brook, Castle Lady, Covert Love, Cross Counter, Enable, Hawkbill, Holdthasigreen, Jack Hobbs, Lightning Spear, Mabs Cross, Nezwaah, Old Persian, Phoenix of Spain, Pinatubo, Seventh Heaven, Silverwave, Skitter Scatter, Stradivarius, Winter, and Zelzal. For most of them it was their debut or one or two early runs on such surfaces before moving on to turf, with one or more outings on the grass before going on to top-level success. Tawkeel did things a bit differently. When she stormed clear of her rivals in the Group 1 Saxon Warrior Coolmore Prix Saint-Alary at Chantilly in mid-June and went on to land the prize by five lengths, she did so on what was both the fourth race of her career and her debut on turf.

She kicked off her career at Pau on January 3rd, taking a newcomers' contest over a mile on CLOPF Fibresand by a length and a quarter. She followed-up with a four-and-a-half-length score over the same trip on the Polytrack at Cagnes-sur-Mer seven weeks later and then, after a three-month break, got home by a head in a nine-and-a-half-furlong conditions race on Deauville's Polytrack. She had been sent off as the favourite on each occasion.

The 2020 edition of the Prix Saint-Alary was one of those races moved to an alternate venue due to the Covid-19 pandemic, and the ground was described as good-to-soft for the ten-furlong test. She was in front as the field headed into their final furlong and pulled farther clear, crossing the line five lengths in front of the recent Group 3 Prix Vanteaux scorer Magic Attitude, with the maiden winner and race favourite Solsticia another head back in third. The latter went on to be a neck runner-up in a Group 3 contest in the autumn, but Magic Attitude, who was fifth in the Group 1 Prix de Diane (French Oaks) next time, moved to North America, joined the Arnaud Delacour stable, easily won the Grade 1 Belmont Oaks Invitational Stakes over ten furlongs on firm turf and finished third to Harvey's Lil Goil in the Grade 1 Queen

Elizabeth II Challenge Cup Stakes over a furlong less at Keeneland.

Tawkeel, on the other hand, was briefly touted as a candidate for the Group 1 Investec Oaks at Epsom. It would have been fascinating to see how she would have got on against Love, but instead she did not run again until the latter part of August. The ground was very soft at Deauville on the day of the Group 2 Shadwell Prix de la Nonette and this time the Jean-Claude Rouget-trained bay had to work harder to extend her unbeaten record. The English filly Frankel's Storm set a good gallop and soon went clear, followed by Tawkeel and Tickle Me Green, and the order remained the same until over a furlong out. The leader dropped back and eventually finished last of the seven, but Tawkeel and Tickle Me Green kept going and they secured the top two placings, separated by half a length at the line. Alkandora was three-quarters of a length back in third, with Solsticia another length and a half behind in fourth and a further four-and-a-half-length gap to the Group 2 Oaks d'Italia scorer, Auyantepui, in fifth.

Underfoot conditions were heavy at ParisLongchamp on the first Sunday in October when Tawkeel faced her toughest task to date. She was among a dozen fillies and mares who lined up for the Group 1 Prix de l'Opera Longines, she tried to make all, fought back when headed a quarter of a mile from home but had to settle for fourth place. Tarnawa and Alpine Star led home an Irish one-two, separated by a short neck, with the English runner Audarya three-quarters of a length back in third, the same distance in front of Tawkeel. Ambition and old rival Tickle Me Green filled the next two placings, beaten by further margins of one and a quarter lengths and three lengths.

Tawkeel is one of twenty-one Group 1 winners among ninety-four blacktype scorers by Kildangan Stud's excellent stallion Teofilo (by Galileo). She was among five of his European-trained progeny to strike at the top level during the year—the others were Donjah, Gear Up, Subjectivist and Twilight Payment—and he was also represented last year by Hong Kong's middle-distance star Exultant. That £7.7 million-earner, who was classic-placed in Ireland when named Irishcorrespondent, won Group 1s at ten and twelve furlongs at Sha Tin in the spring. The stallion's record as a broodmare sire is also relevant with regard to Tawkeel's long-term future and, in 2020, he struck in that sphere with the Group 1 scorer Mac Swiney (by New Approach) and Group 3 winner Flying Visit (by Pride of Dubai), both Jim Bolger-bred two-year-olds.

The Shadwell homebred is the first foal of Rafaadah (by Oasis Dream), who won a one-mile listed contest in France as a two-year-old, and she is a granddaughter of the talented Joanna (by High Chaparral). That mare's classic placing came about via the stewards as having finished fourth among the bunch of six fillies who were heads and necks apart in the Group 1 Poule d'Essai des Poulains (French 1000 Guineas) in 2010, she was moved up a spot following the relegation of first-past-the-post Liliside. However, she notched up six wins and four placings from eleven starts with the best victories coming in the Group 2 Prix de Sandringham, Group 3 Prix de la Porte Maillot, Group 3 Prix Imprudence and Group 3 Prix du Calvados. Her places featured a neck second to Regal Parade in the Group 1 Prix Maurice de Gheest and third in the Group 1 Prix Marcel Boussac. She is out of the stakes-placed six-time winner Secrete Marina, who is by the sprinter Mujadil (by Storm Bird), the likely source of her speed.

One might have expected that a son of the classic winning miler Aussie Rules (by Danehill) might also get a six-to-nine-furlong performer out of a Mujadil mare, but that's not how Joanna's half-brother turned out. He began his career in Italy where he easily won listed races over eight and ten furlongs and split Crackerjack King and Danedream in what was one of the best editions of the Group 2 Derby Italiano in recent years. A move to Hong Kong did not prove as successful as one would have hoped, although he did finish a half-length runner-up to Flintshire in the Group 1 Hong Kong Vase, so he moved to New Zealand and, for the Lance O'Sullivan and Andrew Scott stable, narrowly beat Humidor to win the Group 1 Livamol Spring Classic over ten furlongs on heavy ground at Hastings. He began his career under the name Cazals and finished it as Willie Cazals.

The contribution of Mujadil likely tempered Joanna's stamina but there is an established history of that trait in the family.

Amenity (by Luthier), the third dam of Joanna and fifth dam of Tawkeel, was a winning full sister to the French champion Ashmore, a Group 2 Prix Jean de Chaudenay and dual Group 2 Grand Prix de Deauville winner who was placed in the Group 1 Prix Royal-Oak, Group 1 Coronation Cup and two editions of the Group 1 Grand Prix de Saint-Cloud. A Teofilo out of an Oasis Dream (by Green Desert) daughter of a miler could easily excel in the six-to-nine-furlong range, but in addition to those pedigree attributes and a 4x4 to Danzig duplication on her chart, she is also inbred 3x4 to Sadler's Wells (by Northern Dancer), so it is not really a surprise that the middle-distance stamina came through instead. Tawkeel remains a fascinating prospect.

SUMMARY DETAILS

Bred: Shadwell Estate Co Ltd
Owned: Hamdan Al Maktoum
Trained: Jean-Claude Rouget
Country: France
Race record: -111114-
Career highlights: 5 wins inc Saxon Warrior Coolmore Prix Saint-Alary (Gr1), Shadwell Prix de la Nonette (Gr2)

TAWKEEL (GB) – 2017 bay filly

Teofilo (IRE)	Galileo (IRE)	Sadler's Wells (USA)
		Urban Sea (USA)
	Speirbhean (IRE)	Danehill (USA)
		Saviour (USA)
Rafaadah (GB)	Oasis Dream (GB)	Green Desert (USA)
		Hope (IRE)
	Joanna (IRE)	High Chaparral (IRE)
		Secrete Marina (IRE)

THE REVENANT (GB)

Dubawi (by Dubai Millennium) has done it all as a sire. The Dalham Hall Stud flag bearer can get two-year-old stars, classic horses, sprinters, milers, middle-distance performers, stayers, successful sire sons and good broodmare daughters. One of the striking aspects with his older horses is the number of them who excel at the age of five and upwards, often having been more than capable in their younger days too, and The Revenant, a top-class miler who is a direct descendant of a Sussex Stakes winner, is another fine example of that.

He began his career with the Hugo Palmer stable in England, winning a mile novice race at Haydock on his juvenile debut and then finishing third to the subsequent Derby runner-up Dee Ex Bee in a conditions race on heavy ground at Epsom. He moved to France the following year and has notched up nine wins and two second-place finishes from eleven starts for the Francis-Henri Graffard team. His three-year-old campaign did not begin until late that September and he ran four times in minor events, winning three. He was then gelded, easily won a listed race on heavy ground at Saint-Cloud in March of his four-year-old season and has run in nothing but pattern company since.

A narrow victory in the Group 3 Prix Edmond Blanc over the same course and distance, though good ground, three weeks later, was followed by a half-length defeat of Imaging in the Group 2 Badener Meile in Germany. It was just over four months before he was seen in action again, but that return to competition resulted in a four-and-a-half-length defeat of the classic scorer Olmedo in the Group 2 Prix Daniel Wildenstein on very soft ground at ParisLongchamp. He made the first of two trips to England a fortnight later and put up an excellent performance to chase home King of Change in the Group 1 Queen Elizabeth II Stakes on heavy ground.

It was reported in the fall that he could have had a spring campaign but his trainer decided to put him away for an autumn one instead as the Covid-19 restrictions delayed racing in the first part of the year. The chestnut has won on good ground but seems to be seen to best effect when there is plenty of ease in the underfoot conditions so bypassing the summer months was an understandable choice. It was for this reason and not due to any sort of problem that the gelding was not seen in action until the first Sunday in October. He hit the front with over a furlong to go in the Group 2 Qatar Prix Daniel Wildenstein and kept on well to beat Ziegfeld and Motamarris by a length and a quarter and the same, with Ancient Spirit another one and three-quarter lengths behind in fourth. It was not a particularly strong race for the grade but it did serve as an ideal warm-up for his second attempt at the race colloquially known as the QEII.

The ground was soft at Ascot, the dual Group 1 star Palace Pier was expected to extend his unbeaten record to six, but he lost a shoe, which had such an effect on his action that Frankie Dettori looked down to see if something was amiss inside the final furlong. The colt finished third, half a length and one and a quarter lengths in front of the long-shots Sir Busker and Veracious, but over three lengths behind the front pair. Listed scorer Roseman had tried to make all and almost pulled off a 28/1 surprise. The colt faced a strong challenge from The Revenant from a quarter of a mile out, that rival having visibly travelled smoothly for a while, but he fought all the way to the line. His older rival had inched his way to the front a furlong out and pulled about half a length clear at one point, but Roseman was closing again at the finish and the margin between them was only a head at the line. It will be fascinating to see what 2021 has in store for that pair, and also for Palace Pier.

The Revenant is a homebred son of Hazel Lavery, an €850,000 purchase at 2013's Goffs November Mare Sale. The Frankel (by Galileo) foal she was carrying that day was named Tsavo but doesn't share his younger sibling's talent; he was placed twice over ten and a half furlongs in France from just three starts. The mare's 2016 Kingman (by Invincible Spirit) filly Albanderi has shown little aptitude in a handful of middle-distance starts before and after a wind procedure, her now three-year-old daughter La Viette (by Oasis Dream) is in training with Francis-Henri Graffard but as yet unraced, and she had a daughter of Saxon Warrior (by Deep Impact) in 2020 before being bred back to Dubawi.

Hazel Lavery was trained by Charlies Hills and although she is by Excellent Art, a Group 1-winning miler son of Pivotal (by Polar Falcon), she is out of a daughter of Darshaan (by Shirley Heights) and was a talented middle-distance runner. All three of her runs at two had been over seven furlongs and she made the frame each time, beating debutante and future Breeders' Cup heroine Dank by two lengths at Newbury—Billesdon Brook's dam Coplow was third in that race—and then chasing home the subsequent Irish 1,000 Guineas winner Samitar in a valuable sales race at Newmarket. Although beaten by seven lengths when runner-up in a ten-furlong listed contest first time out at three, she was stepped up in trip, easily won a twelve-furlong listed contest at Newmarket, chased home Wild Coco in the Group 2 Park Hill Stakes over the St Leger course and distance at Doncaster and then beat Noble Mission by half a length to win the Group 3 St Simon Stakes on heavy ground at Newbury.

The mare's siblings include the pattern-placed middle-distance stakes winner Leo Gali (by Galileo) and also Duchess of Marmite (by Duke of Marmalade), a sixteen-time runner who notched up three wins and two placings over two miles on artificial tracks. Her dam, Reprise, was well-beaten on her only two starts, a mare who missed out on blacktype on the track but has several siblings who acquired some. They include the former Dermot Weld trainee Artema (by Common Grounds) who won the Group 3 Derrinstown Stud Derby Trial Stakes and was only beaten by a head and a head when third to Right Win and George Augustus in the Group 2 Gallinule Stakes in 1994. If you go farther back on the page then you will find that fourth dam Silver Echo (by Caerleon) was a half-sister to the Group 3 Gladness Stakes winner and Group 1 Irish 2,000 Guineas third Prince Echo (by Crowned Prince), whereas sixth dam Eastern Echo (by Colombo) won the Sussex Stakes in 1941, the race having been run at Newmarket that year.

The Revenant has never finished out of the first three, he is a top-class miler, a credit to his connections and one of many excellent advertisements for his sire. It would be good to see more of him in 2021 than we did last season and there would be little surprise if he wins again at the highest level.

SUMMARY DETAILS

Bred: Al Asayl Bloodstock Ltd
Owned: Al Asayl France
Trained: Francis-Henri Graffard
Country: France
Race record: 13-1211-11112-11-
Career highlights: 10 wins inc Queen Elizabeth II Stakes - sponsored by Qipco (Gr1), Qatar Prix Daniel Wildenstein (Gr2-twice), 41st Badener Meile powered by Geldermann Privatsetkellerei (Gr2), Prix Edmond Blanc (Gr3), Prix Altipan (L), 2nd Queen Elizabeth II Stakes - sponsored by Qipco (Gr1)

THE REVENANT (GB) – 2015 chestnut gelding

Dubawi (IRE)	Dubai Millennium (GB)	Seeking The Gold (USA)
		Colorado Dancer
	Zomaradah (GB)	Deploy
		Jawaher (IRE)
Hazel Lavery (IRE)	Excellent Art (GB)	Pivotal (GB)
		Obsessive (USA)
	Reprise (GB)	Darshaan
		Rapid Repeat (IRE)

THUNDER MOON (IRE)

Coolmore stallion Zoffany (by Dansili) died in early January, the just-turned 13-year-old lost due to liver failure. This was just a few months after his juvenile son Thunder Moon had established himself as one of the leading members of his age group in Europe. The 116-rated bay holds entries in the Group 1 Tattersalls Irish 2,000 Guineas, Group 1 Emirates Poule d'Essai des Poulains (French 2000 Guineas), Group 1 Prix du Jockey Club (French Derby) and Group 1 Dubai Duty Free Irish Derby, he is a May 1st-born colt, bred by Aidan and Anne-Marie O'Brien's Whisperview Trading Ltd and he is trained by their son, Joseph.

The colt carried Anne-Marie O'Brien's well-known orange and blue colours on his racecourse debut on ground described as good-to-yielding at the Curragh in early August, hitting the front over a furlong from home and staying on well to take that seven-furlong maiden by three and three-quarter lengths. He then switched to the ownership of Chantal Regalado-Gonzalez and so carried her equally well-known red and yellow colours to victory in the Group 1 Goffs Vincent O'Brien National Stakes over that same course and distance, this time on good ground. The Group 2 Superlative Stakes winner Master of The Seas and Group 1 Phoenix Stakes scorer Lucky Vega were sent off as joint favourites but had to settle for fourth and fifth, the latter having met with trouble in running. Thunder Moon also encountered traffic problems but unleashed an impressive turn of foot once he got a clear pathway, hitting the front inside the final half furlong and going away to beat Wembley and St Mark's Basilica by one and a half lengths and a short head, with half a length and the same back to the market leaders.

The Group 1 Darley Dewhurst Stakes often decides the title of Europe's juvenile champion and in what was a substandard year for two-year-olds, a good performance there would likely be the decider. It was—the winner took the crown—but although he had every chance a furlong from home, Thunder Moon could not produce the sort of burst on soft ground that he had shown at the Curragh and he finished only third, a neck in front of the front-running 100/1 shot Devilwala. The capable Cadillac was another length and a half back in fifth, but the finish was fought out by the Ballydoyle pair St Mark's Basilica and Wembley. They finished three-quarters of a length apart, with the runner-up another one and three-quarter lengths clear of Thunder Moon.

He remains a leading prospect for additional Group 1 success in 2021 and, looking further ahead, he has a pedigree that will likely make him a popular addition to the stallion ranks when his track days are over. You would expect him to be effective from seven to nine furlongs, on pedigree, and the turn of foot he showed at the Curragh suggests that he could be a top-class performer in that range on good ground or better, but it is also possible that he may stay beyond it. His half-brother Table Rock (by Fastnet Rock) won a ten-furlong maiden on soft ground at the Curragh but dropped back to a mile a month later, winning a premier handicap on good-to-firm at the same venue and then a Newmarket listed contest. He was renamed Anticipation when he went to Hong Kong but ran mostly from nine to twelve furlongs there, and although blacktype-placed once at the latter, his form was not as good as what he achieved when trained at Ballydoyle. His full brother Jaqen H'Ghar won over ten and twelve furlongs for the Joseph O'Brien stable.

Small Sacrifice (by Sadler's Wells), their dam, is a full sister to the dam of the six-furlong Group 3 Sirenia Stakes winner Love Lockdown (by Verglas) and half-sister to the dam of the juvenile mile Group 1 scorer Vert de Grece (by Verglas). She is also notable as being out of Trust In Luck (by Nashwan), a winning daughter of the Group 1 Irish 1,000 Guineas heroine Trusted Partner (by Affirmed) and so a representative of one of Moyglare Stud's most famous families. That classic-winning miler was a full sister to several stakes and pattern winners and out of the US juvenile filly champion Talking Picture (by Speak John). She produced eleven winners from fourteen foals and they featured the Grade 1 Matriarch Stakes scorer Dress To Thrill (by Danehill). You might expect, if told that a daughter of Trusted Partner became an outstanding success at stud, that it would be her track star who would achieve the feat, but sadly that one has disappointed. Instead, it is Dress To Thrill's full sister Polished Gem who has kept the family in the headlines.

A one-time winner as a two-year-old, she has produced seven stakes winners among ten successful runners, a feat that would be remarkable in itself. However, in addition to the pattern-placed stakes winners Falcon Eight (by Galileo) and Amma Grace (by Galileo), those blacktype horses are the dual Group 1 Irish St Leger star Search For A Song (by Galileo)—featured elsewhere in this volume—Group 1 Prince of Wales's Stakes winner and young Irish National Stud stallion Free Eagle (by High Chaparral), Group 1-placed Group 2 British Champions Fillies and Mares Stakes winner Sapphire (by Medicean), multiple Group 2-winning miler Custom Cut (by Notnowcato), and Australian Group 3 scorer Valac (by Dark Angel).

Zoffany won the Group 1 Phoenix Stakes at two and was runner-up in both the Group 1 St James's Palace Stakes and Group 1 Prix Jean Prat (then a mile) at three, losing the latter by only a head. He has sired a mixture of sprinters, milers and middle-distance horses, including some who have been placed in classics, so it may be whatever Thunder Moon has inherited from his dam that determines how far he will stay.

SUMMARY DETAILS

Bred: Whisperview Trading Ltd
Owned: Mrs C C Regalado-Gonzalez
Trained: Joseph O'Brien
Country: Ireland
Race record: 113-
Career highlights: 2 wins inc Goffs Vincent O'Brien National Stakes (Gr1), 3rd Darley Dewhurst Stakes (Gr1)

THUNDER MOON (IRE) – 2018 bay colt

Zoffany (IRE)	Dansili (GB)	Danehill (USA)
		Hasili (IRE)
	Tyranny (GB)	Machiavellian (USA)
		Dust Dancer (GB)
Small Sacrifice (IRE)	Sadler's Wells (USA)	Northern Dancer
		Fairy Bridge
	Trust In Luck (IRE)	Nashwan (USA)
		Trusted Partner (USA)

TIGER TANAKA (IRE)

Fortunes change hands at thoroughbred auction rings every year and plenty of top horses who graduate from those sales fetched a six-figure sum. Many cost in excess of €50,000 but every year there are also top-level performers whose start in life was at a humbler level. Of course, there are also a considerable number of top racehorses who never appeared in front of an auctioneer before becoming well-known, homebreds who, in some cases, represent generations of carefully planned breeding by their connections.

The story of Tiger Tanaka is remarkable, made more so by the fact that the €6,500 for which she changed hands at 2019's Tattersalls Ireland September Yearling Sale was not the direct route to her current connections. The Kellsgrange Stud-bred bay joined the Marc Pimbonnet stable in France, made her debut in the ownership of the partnership of Haras Du Ma and John Dwan, and then moved on. That debut was a six-furlong claimer on heavy ground at Lyon Parilly, a world away from Group 1 stardom, and she landed the spoils by a length.

It was then that she joined the Charley Rossi team and, now carrying the white and blue colours of Miguel Castro Megias, she justified favouritism with a four-length success in a seven-and-a-half furlong contest on the all-weather at Marseille Pont-de-Vivaux. Both this and her next two starts were also in claimers, each time an easy win and each time with Jessica Marcialis in the saddle. Their four-length victory was followed by a five-length score over the same course and distance, also in June, and then a two-and-a-half-length win over a mile on good ground at Marseille Borely on July 8th.

Four wins from four starts was an eye-catching record, one that demonstrated ability and precocity as well as more stamina than is typically associated with the first half of the year in juvenile racing, but it was all at a low level and so any suggestion that the filly could be a Group 1 winner in waiting would have seemed fanciful.

The Group 2 Prix Robert Papin was an interesting choice for her first foray into blacktype company. That race has long been run over five and a half furlongs, but now at Chantilly rather than at its old home of Maisons-Laffitte, the six-furlong contest attracted four runners. The Lir Jet was a short odds-on favourite having taken the Group 2 Norfolk Stakes at Royal Ascot on the second of his two winning starts. Axdavali, a seven-length winner at Deauville in late May, had been runner-up in the Group 3 Prix du Bois, Ventura Tormenta had been sixth in the Norfolk and fifth in the Group 2 Superlative Stakes from three starts, so the claimer looked likely to be the one who would struggle. But that's not how it turned out. Ventura Tormenta short-headed The Lir Jet, Tiger Tanaka was only a neck away in third, and Axdavali finished tailed off.

The bargain-basement filly was now a pattern-placed multiple winner and she resumed her winning streak a month later, this time landing the Group 3 Prix François Boutin by two lengths at Deauville. The seven-furlong contest was run on heavy ground and so was the Group 1 Qatar Prix Marcel Boussac - Criterium des Pouliches over a mile at ParisLongchamp on the first Sunday in October. This time it was the Richard Fahey-trained Fev Rover who was sent off favourite, the daughter of Gutaifan having won two of her four starts including the Group 2 Prix du Calvados at Deauville, but in what was a somewhat rough race in the straight, Marcialis and Tiger Tanaka avoided the trouble and galloped home to a three-quarter-length win from Tasmania, with one and a half lengths farther back to third-placed long-shot Rougir, and just over a length more to the favourite in fourth.

Tiger Tanaka had gone from being a €6,500 yearling to a horse claimed after a minor provincial win, to a multiple claiming-level scorer, to being a pattern winner and now successful at the highest level. She had also enabled her regular partner to become the first female rider ever to win a Group 1 race in France.

The horse who wins the Prix Marcel Boussac is traditionally viewed as being a leading classic contender for the following season and being the best of her age group in her adopted homeland, there remains every chance that Tiger Tanaka can follow that path too. However, it has to be said that the French juveniles of 2020 were somewhat underwhelming, and it was substandard year overall for two-year-olds, so it is possible that there are at least a few who will progress past her in 2021. She had one more run after her big win, and although not disgraced in finishing a two-length fourth in the Group 1 Criterium de Saint-Cloud, it is possible that the ten-furlong trip on heavy ground was a bit farther than ideal. The front-running Mark Johnston-trained colt Gear Up won the race by a short neck from Botanik, with the previously unbeaten Makaloun staying on strongly into third, a nose in front of the filly but one and three-quarter lengths behind the runner-up.

Tiger Tanaka is a daughter of the Rathasker Stud veteran Clodovil (by Danehill) and that Group 1 Poule d'Essai des Poulains (French 2000 Guineas) victor's tally of twenty-five stakes winners includes two others who have won at the highest level. Nahoodh, who was unlucky not to have been placed in or even won the Group 1 1000 Guineas, landed the Group 1 Falmouth Stakes at Newmarket. Moriarty, who was a runner-up in the Group 3 Gallinule Stakes when trained by Richard Hannon, excelled in Australia where he won a Group 1 contest over nine furlongs plus Group 2 races over ten, eleven and twelve furlongs. Clodovil's total also includes five whose best win has come in Group 2 company and two of those are stallions.

Es Que Love, who moved to France in 2019 after four seasons at Rathasker Stud, had a notable sprint daughter in 2020, Que Amoro, who was a listed winner before springing a mild surprise with her second-place finish to Battaash in the Group 1 Coolmore Nunthorpe Stakes at York. Gregorian, on the other hand, is now in his third season at Rathasker following four at the National Stud in Newmarket. He is already off the mark as a blacktype sire in 2021 because his son Gregorian Chant won a six-furlong listed contest on turf at Santa Anita in January, but in 2020 he had two daughters of note. Plainchant won the Group 2 Criterium de Maisons-Laffitte and Group 3 Prix Eclipse and was among the leading juvenile fillies in France, whereas the Kevin Ryan-trained Queen Jo Jo, who is reviewed in *Volume 2*, was a six-furlong Group 3 winner and seven-furlong Group 2 third, both at York, before being sold for 360,000 guineas at the Tattersalls December Mare Sale in Newmarket.

Tiger Tanaka is the first foal of Miss Phillyjinks (by Zoffany), a mare who notched up one win and three placings from sixteen starts. All of those times in the frame came about on artificial tracks—Tapeta at Wolverhampton and Polytrack at Dundalk and Lingfield—and her sole victory was in a dead-heat over six furlongs. She finished her career on a handicap mark of sixty-one, down from a career peak of sixty-eight, so she joins the growing list of well-bred but lowly rated fillies who have gone on to produce offspring of note at stud.

The mare has two siblings who are closely related to her star daughter, both of them sired by Clodovil. Bosstime won three times over a mile, whereas Refusetolisten won over seven furlongs and is now a successful young broodmare who has two noteworthy runners. Stormy Girl (by Night of Thunder) won a six-furlong listed sprint last year, and although her half-brother Dirty Rascal (by Acclamation) failed to make the frame in seven runs in 2020, his prior record includes a win over six furlongs plus two over seven furlongs and eight other placings that include the runners-up spot in a valuable sales race at Doncaster as a two-year-old.

Smoken Rosa (by Smoke Glacken), the grandam of Tiger Tanaka, did not win in a fourteen-race career but was placed three times. She is by a US sprint champion and out of Roses In The Snow (by Be My Guest), a three-time winner who was runner-up in a listed handicap over ten furlongs in England, and the prolific Snowdrops (by Gulch) is her best sibling. That mare raced mostly from eight to nine furlongs in North America, she won three Grade 3 races plus three at listed level, and she is the dam of Tawhid (by Invincible Spirit). He won the Group 3 Horris Hill Stakes as a two-year-old, added a listed contest over that same course and distance at three and was placed in the Group 2 Mehl-Mülhens-Rennen (German 2000 Guineas), Group 2 Hungerford Stakes and Group 3 Jersey Stakes.

Roses In The Snow is a half-sister to the pattern-placed stakes winner Distant Mirage (by Caerleon) and out of Desert Bluebell (by Kalaglow), and that makes her related to several horses of note. Shining Water, a full sister to Desert Bluebell, won the Group 3 Solario Stakes and finished third in the Group 2 Fillies' Mile as a two-year-old but went on to be runner-up in the Group 2 Park Hill Stakes—a race that her dam, Idle Waters (by Mill Reef) won—and then to become the dam of Tenby (by Caerleon). A juvenile star in 1992, when he won the Group 1 Grand Criterium, he went on to add the Group 2 Dante Stakes and to finish third in the Group 1 Eclipse Stakes. Like others by his classic-winning and dual champion sire, Tenby disappointed at stud.

Tiger Tanaka looks a likely contender for both the Group 1 Poule d'Essai des Pouliches (French 1000 Guineas) and Group 1 Prix de Diane (French Oaks). We already know that she stays a mile well, and although beaten over ten furlongs on her final start at two, she might fare better over that distance, and the extra half furlong, on a somewhat sounder surface at three. It will be interesting to see how she and the other leading French juveniles of 2020 get on in their classic season.

SUMMARY DETAILS
Bred: Kellsgrange Stud
Owned: Miguel Castro Megias
Trained: Charley Rossi
Country: France
Race record: 11113114-
Career highlights: 6 wins inc Qatar Prix Marcel Boussac - Criterium des Pouliches (Gr1), Prix François Boutin (Gr3), 3rd Darley Prix Robert Papin (Gr2)

TIGER TANAKA (IRE) – 2018 bay filly

Clodovil (IRE)	Danehill (USA)	Danzig (USA)
		Razyana (USA)
	Clodora (FR)	Linamix (FR)
		Cloche d'Or (GB)
Miss Phillyjinks (IRE)	Zoffany (IRE)	Dansili (GB)
		Tyranny (GB)
	Smoken Rosa (USA)	Smoke Glacken (USA)
		Roses In The Snow (IRE)

TORQUATOR TASSO (GER)

Gestüt Schlenderhan stallion Adlerflug (by In The Wings) comes from a branch of the famous family of Galileo (by Sadler's Wells) and Sea The Stars (by Cape Cross) and he was represented by two of the leading three-year-old middle-distance colts of 2020. The Irish-born but French-trained In Swoop won the Group 1 Deutsches Derby in July and later failed narrowly to beat Sottsass in the Group 1 Prix de l'Arc de Triomphe. Torquator Tasso, runner-up in the premier German classic, got his top-level win in the Group 1 Grosser Preis von Berlin, the day before the Arc. These two are among five top-level winners for their sire, with the other three being the Gestüt Ammerland stallion Iquitos (yearlings in 2021), Gestüt Erftmühle sire Ito (three-year-olds in 2021) and Preis der Diana (German Oaks) heroine Lacazar.

Torquator Tasso was unraced at two, he finished fourth in a ten-furlong Mülheim maiden on his debut in early May and gave first-season trainer Marcel Weiss an early winner when scoring over eleven furlongs at Cologne the following month. Both he and In Swoop stayed on well over the final furlong and a half of the Deutsches Derby but the French colt, who hit the front inside the final half furlong, got to the line with three-quarters of a length to spare. Grocer Jack passed the post an additional three-quarters of a length behind and the same margins separating him, Kaspar and Notre Ruler, the latter having short-headed the big-race favourite Wonderful Moon. However, Grocer Jack, who had chased home Wonderful Moon in a pair of pattern races in May and June, was later disqualified due to the presence of a banned substance in his post-race sample.

The ground was described there as being good-to-soft, as it was for both of his next two starts, twelve-furlong Group 1 contests at Baden-Baden and Hoppegarten. He was sent off favourite for the both of them but had to settle for third in the first, the Longines Grosser Preis von Baden. He moved into third place about half a furlong from home but was not able to improve on that, passing the post one and a quarter lengths and a neck behind Barney Roy and Communique. The fillies Donjah and Durance followed him home, a neck and a head behind, with

Quest The Moon three-quarters of a length back in sixth. Communique was again in opposition in the Group 1 Longines Grosser Preis von Berlin but ran no sort of race and finished tailed off. Torquator Tasso, on the other hand, showed a turn of foot to hit the front over a furlong from home and then had to battle all the way to the line to hold off a determined challenge from Dicaprio. Kaspar was a length and a quarter back in third with a further five-length gap to Grocer Jack in fourth.

The Henk Grewe-trained runner-up, another son of Adlerflug, had been a runaway listed winner at Munich in June and seventh in the Derby, and was again in the line-up for the Group 1 Allianz - Grosser Preis von Bayern at Munich in November. The ground was heavy that day, Torquator Tasso beat Dicaprio by two lengths this time, but the filly Sunny Queen had got her head in front inside the final half furlong and extended that to a neck at the line. It will be interesting to see how they run as four-year-olds and it is possible that renewed rivalry between the two colts could be a highlight of the German season.

Torquator Tasso was bred by Paul Vandeberg and he is a €24,000 graduate of the BBAG October yearling sale. He is the second foal of a non-winning mare named Tijuana (by Toylsome) and he will be a fascinating addition to the stallion ranks when the time comes. That's because he is inbred 4x5 to Anatevka (by Espresso). Who is she? She is the common ancestor shared by Adlerflug, Galileo and Sea The Stars. Her daughter Alya (by Lombard), the grandam of Adlerflug, is a full sister to Allegretta, the hugely influential broodmare who gave us the Group 1 Prix de l'Arc de Triomphe heroine Urban Sea (by Miswaki)—dam of Galileo and Sea The Stars—and Group 1 2000 Guineas star and classic sire King's Best (by Kingmambo), among others of note. Urban Sea's stakes-placed half-sister Turbaine (by Trempolino) is the dam of the Group 3 winner and German champion sire Tertullian (by Miswaki)—a three-parts brother to Urban Sea— plus several other blacktype horses, and also Tucana (by Acatenango), the winning grandam of Torquator Tasso.

This talented chestnut was rated 117 in the World's Best Racehorse Rankings for 2020; it would not be a surprise to see him improve on that figure in 2021.

SUMMARY DETAILS

Bred: Paul H Vandeberg
Owned: Gestüt Auenquelle
Trained: Marcel Weiss
Country: Germany
Race record: -412312-
Career highlights: 2 wins inc Longines 130th Grosser Preis von Berlin (Gr1), 2nd IDEE 151st Deutsches Derby (Gr1), Allianz - Grosser Preis von Bayern (Gr1), 3rd 148th Longines Grosser Preis von Baden (Gr1)

TORQUATOR TASSO (GER) – 2017 chestnut colt

Adlerflug (GER)	In The Wings	Sadler's Wells (USA)
		High Hawk
	Aiyana (GER)	Last Tycoon
		Alya (GER)
Tijuana (GER)	Toylsome (GB)	Cadeaux Genereux
		Treasure Trove (USA)
	Tucana (GER)	Acatenango (GER)
		Turbaine (USA)

TWILIGHT PAYMENT (IRE)

Durable, talented and, in 2020, a winner at the highest level, Twilight Payment is a credit to his connections, past and present. It will be good to see him back in action this coming season. A May 6th-born bay and one of three Group 1 winners who represented Jim Bolger as a breeder last year—Gear Up and Mac Swiney were the other two—he did not begin his career until mid-May of his three-year-old season. He finished fourth that day, over thirteen furlongs at Navan, and was a neck runner-up over ten at the same venue two weeks later, but the regard in which he was held by Bolger, who trained him up to the end of June 2019, was evident given that his next stop was Royal Ascot.

The twice-raced maiden finished third to Sword Fighter and Harbour Law in the Listed Queen's Vase over two miles, beaten by three-quarters of a length and the same and with fifteen rivals behind. The winner would go on to add the Group 2 Curragh Cup, whereas the runner-up landed the Group 1 St Leger at Doncaster that September. Twilight Payment, on the other hand, won a twelve-furlong maiden at the Curragh, chased home Order of St George in a Group 3 contest over fourteen furlongs at the same venue and then beat Forgotten Rules by half a length in a two-mile listed race on heavy ground, also at the Co Kildare venue. He made the frame in five out of six runs at four but failed to win any of them, and he was gelded before returning to action as a five-year-old.

He notched up one win and five placings from seven runs that year, the victory coming in the Listed Her Majesty's Plate over fourteen furlongs on fast ground at Down Royal in late July. Three of the placings came in pattern races and he missed out on making that four when finishing fourth to Flag of Honour in the Group 1 Irish St Leger. Although holding a triple-digit rating since after his Royal Ascot run at three, it was only as a five-year-old that he got his first pattern victory on the board. It was the Group 2 Curragh Cup at the Curragh, his final start for the Bolger yard, and he beat the Irish Derby winner Latrobe by a neck. Although unplaced on his first three runs for the Joseph O'Brien stable, those were the Group 1 Irish St leger, Group 1 Melbourne Cup and the ultra-valuable Longines Turf Handicap, the latter over fifteen furlongs on fast ground at Riyadh at the end of February 2020. Since then, however, he has been in outstanding form.

He had Falcon Eight five and a half lengths behind when chasing home Nickajack Cave in the Listed Saval Beg Levmoss Stakes over fourteen furlongs at Leopardstown in mid-June, having led a quarter of a mile from home but then caught and passed by the grey a furlong later. Thirteen days later he made all to beat Barbados and Sovereign by two and a half lengths and half a length in the Group 3 Comer Group International Vintage Crop Stakes over the same trip at the Curragh, the third—the previous year's surprise Irish Derby winner—passing the post two and a quarter lengths clear of Falcon Eight. He was a shade lucky next time, also over fourteen furlongs at the Curragh, because unless the Aidan O'Brien-trained maiden winner Memorabilis was going to be something, he really only had one potentially serious rival in the six-runner Group 2 Comer Group International Curragh Cup: his stablemate Master of Reality. The Ballydoyle colt tried to make all but didn't stay and finished a well-beaten fourth, Master of Reality finished a never-dangerous eight-length runner-up, and the ninety-six rated filly Camphor picked up some valuable blacktype in third, another seven lengths adrift.

Two months later, he finished a staying-on third to Search For A Song and Fujaira Prince in the Group 1 Comer Group International Irish St Leger, beaten by two lengths and a neck but three lengths clear of Barbados. Passion was another half a length back in fifth, one and three-quarter lengths in front of the favourite and disappointing classic winner Sovereign who had made most of the running. However, the performance for which Twilight Payment will be remembered for many years to come is his final one of 2020, when he made all to win the Group 1 Lexus Melbourne Cup at Flemington. Jye McNeil took the ride and the pair held off the Aidan O'Brien-trained Irish Derby runner-up Tiger Moth to win by half a length. The English gelding Prince of Arran ran another big race in the two-mile feature, again staying on strongly. He was a head away from splitting the Irish pair and one and three-quarter lengths clear of the fourth, New Zealand-bred and -trained The Chosen One. That horse short-headed

Persan, with Sir Dragonet, Verry Elleegant, Russian Camelot and Finche the next four home. Who would have thought, not so long ago, that the best an Australian-trained horse would do in a Melbourne Cup would be fifth place?

Twilight Payment is among twenty-one Group 1 winners that feature among over ninety stakes winners by Kildangan Stud's Teofilo (by Galileo), a horse whom Jim Bolger bred and trained. The top-level tally also includes the 2020 European-trained Group 1 scorers Donjah, Gear Up (bred by Bolger), Subjectivist, and Tawkeel, as well as the Hong Kong standout Exultant, who was originally a classic-placed runner for the Michael Halford stable in Ireland under the name Irishcorrespondent. His half-sister Bandiuc Eile (by New Approach) didn't win a race but was runner-up in the Group 2 Debutante Stakes, and they are out of the dual scorer Dream On Buddy (by Oasis Dream), a mare who comes from a famous family that has excelled for two other major breeders in the fairly recent past.

My Renee (by Kris S), the grandam of Twilight Payment, was bred by Pat O'Kelly's Kilcarn Stud and she won the Listed Give Thanks Stakes at Cork and Listed Harvest Stakes at Ascot before going on to become the dam of the high-class Banimpire (by Holy Roman Emperor). That seven-time winner was trained by Jim Bolger, she won the Group 2 Ribblesdale Stakes, Group 3 Ballysax Stakes, Group 3 Royal Whip Stakes, Group 3 Blue Wind Stakes and Group 3 Noblesse Stakes, was short-headed by Blue Bunting in the Group 1 Irish Oaks and finished third to Nahrain and Announce in the Group 1 Prix de l'Opera. My Renee's dam, Mayenne (by Nureyev), was unraced but always had the potential to leave behind some notable descendants.

She was bred by Robert Sangster's Swettenham Stud and in addition to being a daughter of one of the world's most influential stallions, she was out of the Group 1 Prix de l'Arc de Triomphe heroine Detroit (by Riverman). That prolific pattern winner landed the big one, and both the Horse of the Year and champion three-year-old filly titles in France, in 1980 and she made history fourteen years later when her son Carnegie (by Sadler's Wells) won the race too. She was the first Arc-winning filly to produce an Arc winner at stud, a feat that Urban Sea (dam of Sea The Stars) would later duplicate. Carnegie also won the Group 1 Grand Prix de Saint-Cloud, Group 2 Prix Niel and Group 2 Prix Eugene Adam, he was third in the Grade 1 Breeders' Cup Turf, and although never a major sire he did come up with a few New Zealand-bred Group 1 winners in Australia.

Detroit was also the dam of the Group 2 Prix Guillaume d'Ornano winner Antisaar (by Northern Dancer), who had been a $2,450,000 Keeneland July Yearling Sale graduate, plus the Group 3 St Simon Stakes winner Lake Erie (by Kings Lake) and listed scorer Honfleur (by Sadler's Wells), but she died in May 2001 following the birth of an Entrepreneur (by Sadler's Wells) filly. Named Mennetou but never raced, that filly became a successful broodmare. Her daughter Dawn Wall (by Fastnet Rock) won a one-mile Group 3 contest and nine-furlong listed race in Australia, Obama Rule (by Danehill Dancer) landed the Group 3 Dance Design Stakes over nine furlongs at the Curragh, whereas Osaila (by Danehill Dancer) was a Grade 1 Breeders' Cup Juvenile Fillies Turf Stakes third and Group 3 Princess Margaret Stakes winner at two who went on to add wins in the Group 3 Nell Gwyn Stakes and Listed Sandringham Handicap at three.

Twilight Payment has been a blacktype horse since his third start as a three-year-old and his career reached a new peak in 2020 at the age of seven. Although a shade below top class, he has been well placed throughout the years to make the most of the considerable talent he has. Presuming he's fit, happy and well again this coming season, there is every reason to hope he can add further gloss to his record.

SUMMARY DETAILS

Bred: J S Bolger
Owned: N C Williams, Mrs & Mrs L J Williams, et al
Trained: Joseph O'Brien
Country: Ireland
Race record: -423121-232230-2312423-241100-021131-
Career highlights: 8 wins inc Lexus Melbourne Cup (Gr1), Comer Group International Curragh Cup (Gr2-twice), Comer Group International Vintage Crop Stakes (Gr3), Saval Beg Levmoss Stakes (L), Her Majesty's Plate (L), Sycamore Lodge

Equine Hospital Loughbrown Stakes (L), 2nd Loughbrown Stakes (Gr3), Comer Group International Irish St Leger Trial Stakes (Gr3-twice), Saval Beg Levmoss Stakes (L-twice), 3rd Comer Group International Irish St Leger (Gr1), Comer Group International Curragh Cup (Gr2), Comer Group International Irish St Leger Trial Stakes (Gr3), Coolmore Vintage Crop Stakes (Gr3), Martin Molony Stakes (L), Queen's Vase (L)

TWILIGHT PAYMENT (IRE) – 2013 bay gelding

Teofilo (IRE)	Galileo (IRE)	Sadler's Wells (USA)
		Urban Sea (USA)
	Speirbhean (IRE)	Danehill (USA)
		Saviour (USA)
Dream On Buddy (IRE)	Oasis Dream (GB)	Green Desert (USA)
		Hope (IRE)
	My Renee (USA)	Kris S (USA)
		Mayenne (USA)

VAN GOGH (USA)

The champion two-year-old is the one who tops the end-of-year handicap for the division and, in 2020, that was St Mark's Basilica. His mark of 120 was one of the lowest for a juvenile champion in the modern era, but that will hardly matter when the time comes for him to go to stud. Bizarrely, Van Gogh was given the title at the Cartier Awards, even though he was only rated 114, enough to share ninth place in the order of merit on the official handicap. Aside from his four-length Group 1 victory on heavy ground on his final start, his only win in a seven-race season was a seven-furlong maiden at the Curragh in late September. He was runner-up in three pattern races, finished out of the frame in another one plus on his debut in July, and so he was a well-exposed member of his class, in a moderate year to boot.

That said, there are grounds to believe that Van Gogh may yet emerge as a leader within his age group. The Aidan O'Brien-trained colt, who was bred by Barronstown Stud, represents the second crop of the US Triple Crown winner American Pharoah (by Pioneerof The Nile) and he is out of Imagine (by Sadler's Wells), the classic-winning half-sister to the Timeform 139-rated wide-margin Derby, Irish Derby and King George superstar Generous (by Caerleon). Generous, as some may remember, was a 50/1 winner of the Group 1 Dewhurst Stakes as a two-year-old but took a huge leap forward when stepped up to middle distances as a three-year-old. It is not impossible that Van Gogh will follow in his hoof-prints by becoming a top ten- or twelve-furlong performer—the odds are slightly in favour of ten being his maximum—although it is harder to view him as one who might challenge his famous relation for the honour of being the best in the family.

Imagine won the Group 3 C.L. Weld Park Stakes over seven furlongs as a two-year-old plus a one-mile maiden at Gowran Park, she was runner-up in the Group 2 Rockfel Stakes and third in a listed contest, but out of the frame in her other two starts, one of those a fourth-place finish behind Crystal Music in the Group 1 Fillies' Mile. She was also comfortably beaten though placed in a pair of seven-furlong listed contests on her first two starts at three, but then she won the Group 1 Irish 1,000 Guineas by two lengths from Crystal Music, stepped up to twelve furlongs at Epsom and landed the Oaks by a length and a quarter from Flight of Fancy. She didn't run again.

Her first foal was the Aidan O'Brien-trained Horatio Nelson (by Danehill) and he excelled as a two-year-old, all his starts then over seven furlongs. He made a winning debut at the Curragh, was a clear-cut winner of the Group 3 Superlative Stakes, Group 2 Futurity Stakes and Group 1 Prix Jean-Luc Lagardere and lost his unbeaten record when a neck runner-up to Sir Percy in the Group 1 Dewhurst Stakes. He finished down the field behind George Washington in the 2000 Guineas the following spring and then suffered a fatal injury over a furlong out in the Derby at Epsom. The year-younger Red Rock Canyon (by Rock of Gibraltar) picked up third place in the Group 1 Irish Champion Stakes and Group 1 Tattersalls Gold Cup but managed only a ten-furlong Roscommon maiden win in a thirty-three-race career. That one's full sister Kitty Matcham notched up two narrow wins but no placings from ten starts, the better success coming in the Group 2 Rockfel Stakes over seven furlongs on her final juvenile run.

Viscount Nelson (by Giant's Causeway) was the next of Imagine's blacktype offspring. He won the Group 2 Al Fahidi Fort over a mile at Meydan and listed contests over seven and a half furlongs and ten furlongs at Tipperary and the Curragh respectively, plus his pattern placings featured third to Twice Over in the Group 1 Coral-Eclipse Stakes and to Canford Cliffs in the Group 1 Irish 2,000 Guineas. He went to stud in Chile. His full brother Point Piper was born two months before that classic third and he too showed talent at a mile, winning a Grade 3 handicap over the trip at Emerald Downs and a listed contest at Del Mar.

Van Gogh is the sixth blacktype horse for his dam. If he has inherited his parents' stamina then he could stay the Derby distance and even excel at it. However, it is striking that his siblings have tended to be better over eight to ten furlongs. Even the sadly ill-fated Horatio Nelson looked held just before his accident and may have finished unplaced had he not been injured. There are plenty of other notable horses in his family, going back over several generations, but if we look only at the other Group 1 winners who descend from his grandam, Doff The Derby (by Master Derby), then we find more horses who were best at ten furlongs and less.

Imagine's full sister Strawberry Roan was a classic-placed stakes-winning miler, and although full sister Shinko Hermes was not a blacktype horse, she produced two stakes winners and is the grandam of three top-level scorers. Sobetsu (by Dubawi) won the Group 1 Prix Saint-Alary, Dee Majesty (by Deep Impact) won the Group 1 Satsuki Sho (Japanese 2000 Guineas) over ten furlongs and was third in the Group 1 Tokyo Yushun (Japanese Derby), whereas Tower of London (by Raven's Pass), a pattern winner at a mile, was a Group 1-winning sprinter in Japan and is new to the Darley Japan stallion team for 2021. Then there's Wedding Bouquet (by Kings Lake), a half-sister to Imagine. She won the Group 3 C.L. Weld Stakes, was placed in the Group 1 National Stakes and Group 1 Phoenix Stakes before going on to Grade 3 success in the USA, and she is the grandam of the six-time Group 1 star Moonlight Cloud (by Invincible Spirit), winner of the Prix Jacques le Marois, the Prix du Moulin de Longchamp, the Prix la Foret and three editions of the Prix Maurice de Gheest.

As to the specifics of Van Gogh's first season on the track, having finished fourth in a maiden on his debut in mid-July, he was a neck runner-up to Military Style in the Group 3 Japan Racing Association Tyros Stakes over the same course and distance the following month but then only sixth of eight in the Group 2 Galileo Irish EBF Futurity Stakes on soft ground at the Curragh. That performance prompted a veterinary examination but he was found to be post-race normal. Cadillac had been the runner-up there and it was that colt who beat him by three and a half lengths when the pair were first and second in the Group 2 KPMG Champions Juvenile Stakes over a mile at Leopardstown on the opening day of Irish Champions Weekend. Van Gogh had tried to make all but had nothing more to give when the winner swept past him inside the final furlong. He also made most of the running at the Curragh two weeks later, this time winning a seven-furlong maiden by half a length on yielding ground.

He travelled abroad for his final two starts, valuable experience to get in at two for a potential classic colt. First stop was

Newmarket's Group 3 Emirates Autumn Stakes, run over the 2000 Guineas course and distance. The ground was soft, he was not as quickly away as some of his rivals, but Ryan Moore quickly moved him from his outside position to an inside one and settled him in about eighth of the ten runners. He was disputing last place in the well-bunched field passing halfway. Moore switched him to the right over a furlong out, found a gap to the outside of Dhahabi and beat that colt by a length and a half at the line, albeit while finishing one and three-quarter lengths behind the comfortable winner, One Ruler. It was a promising effort.

The merit of what he achieved on his final start is less clear because of the heavy underfoot conditions—such ground can make the form unreliable and can exaggerate or distort positions of relative merit—although his rating was raised to 114 on the strength of it. The Simon and Ed Crisford-trained Jadoomi was sent off favourite for that Group 1 Criterium International at Saint-Cloud in late October; the colt had won a Wolverhampton maiden on his third start and then run away with a one-mile sales race on heavy at ParisLongchamp. Godolphin's runner La Barrosa had won an Ascot maiden and the Group 3 Tattersalls Stakes over seven furlongs on good ground—he appeared not to handle the underfoot conditions in France and dead-headed for last place; he can do better than this. Darkness had finished fourth in the Group 3 Prix La Rochette before narrowly winning a one-mile listed contest on very soft ground at Lyon Parilly, Policy of Truth had taken the Group 3 Prix des Chenes over a mile on good at ParisLongchamp but was been unplaced first time out on good-to-soft, and the line-up was completed by Normandy Bridge, an unbeaten colt who had taken the Group 3 Prix Thomas Bryon over the course and distance and on heavy ground three weeks before. That last-named colt tried to make all but came under pressure three furlongs out. To his credit, he fought back after losing his position and got back up for second, beating Jadoomi and Policy of Truth by a neck and the same, but Van Gogh, who had hit the front a furlong and a half out, won comfortably by four lengths. It was impressive and full of promise for the future.

His famous sire, American Pharoah, stands at Ashford Stud in Kentucky. He was a champion at two and three, Horse of the

Year, crowned his Triple Crown-winning season with a wide-margin success in the Grade 1 Breeders' Cup Classic and, of course, raced only on dirt. However, there have been hopes from the start of his stallion career that he could sire turf horses in addition to the inevitable dirt stakes winners, and, so far, that aim is coming to fruition. Harveys Lil Goil, who won a mile maiden easily on dirt on her second of two starts at two, raced mostly on turf in 2020 and she gave her sire a first Grade 1 winner from his first crop when landing the Queen Elizabeth II Challenge Cup Stakes over nine furlongs at Keeneland in October, a month before she finished a close third to Audarya in the Grade 1 Breeders' Cup Filly & Mare Turf. Four Wheel Drive won the Group 2 Breeders' Cup Juvenile Turf Sprint at Santa Anita in 2019, his stablemate Maven landed the Group 3 Prix du Bois that same season, Sweet Melania was a Breeders' Cup-placed Grade 2 winner on turf as a juvenile and a Grade 3 winner over a mile on grass at Belmont Park in 2020 and, of course, Pista won the Group 2 Park Hill Stakes over the St Leger course and distance at Doncaster in September before taking second place in the Group 1 Prix de Royallieu at ParisLongchamp.

So, Van Gogh is a second top-level winner among the fourteen blacktype scorers that have emerged so far from his sire's first two crops. His pedigree gives him prospects of being a miler, of being effective at ten furlongs or possibly staying the Derby distance, and maybe even improving over the latter. It is also an outcross pedigree, which means that he has no duplicated ancestors within the first five generations. That variety could be a valuable attribute when the time comes for him to go to stud. Given the slight shade of doubt over his ability to go much beyond ten furlongs, we will have to wait to see how he gets on when he tries the trip to know if it suits him or not. He holds an entries in the Tattersalls Irish 2,000 Guineas, the Derby and Dubai Duty Free Irish Derby plus the Emirates Poule d'Essai des Poulains (French 2000 Guineas) and the Prix du Jockey Club (French Derby), so he could make multiple appearances on the classic scene. He is also engaged in the Group 1 Grand Prix de Paris.

Van Gogh is a fascinating prospect, both because of that final start and his pedigree, and it would not be a surprise to see him emerge as one of his stable's best three-year-olds of the new season.

SUMMARY DETAILS

Bred: Barronstown Stud
Owned: Michael Tabor, Derrick Smith, Mrs John Magnier & Mrs David Nagle
Trained: Aidan O'Brien
Country: Ireland
Race record: 4202121-
Career highlights: 2 wins inc Criterium International (Gr1), 2nd KPMG Champions Juvenile Stakes (Gr2), Emirates Autumn Stakes (Gr3), Japan Racing Association Tyros Stakes (Gr3)

VAN GOGH (USA) – 2018 bay colt

American Pharoah (USA)	Pioneerof The Nile (USA)	Empire Maker (USA)
		Star of Goshen (USA)
	Littleprincessemma (USA)	Yankee Gentleman (USA)
		Exclusive Rosette (USA)
Imagine (IRE)	Sadler's Wells (USA)	Northern Dancer
		Fairy Bridge (USA)
	Doff The Derby (USA)	Master Derby (USA)
		Margarethen (USA)

VICTOR LUDORUM (GB)

Godolphin had three homebred and undefeated juvenile Group 1 stars in 2019, all sons of the late and much-lamented Shamardal (by Giant's Causeway). Each went on to become a leading performer again as a three-year-old. Earthlight, who had been champion two-year-old in France, won the Group 3 Prix du Pin over seven furlongs and a listed contest over six, he was a neck runner-up to One Master in the Group 1 Prix de la Foret and finished a close fourth to Space Blues in the Group 1 Prix Maurice de Gheest. He is now a stallion at Kildangan Stud in Ireland, the farm where his sire held court for so long. Pinatubo was the overall European champion at two, one of the most brilliant performers in that age group in recent times. He added the Group 1 Prix Jean Prat at three, was placed in the Group 1 2000 Guineas, Group 1 St James's Palace Stakes and Group 1 Prix du Moulin de Longchamp and is now on the team at Dalham Hall Stud in England. Victor Ludorum was the third one, he will go to stud with the added attraction of being a classic winner, but that time has not yet come. He is listed on Godolphin's website as returning to training in 2021.

The early April born bay ran three times as a juvenile, winning easily over a mile on good ground at ParisLongchamp and Chantilly before beating Alson by three-quarters of a length to take the Group 1 Prix Jean-Luc Lagardere on very soft ground. The Group 1 Poule d'Essai des Poulains (French 2000 Guineas) was an obvious classic target for him, and although inbred 3x3 to the Irish Oaks winner Helen Street (by Troy), I explained in his entry in *European Group 1 Winners of 2019*, where his pedigree was reviewed in detail, why there was a chance that the ten-and-a-half-furlong trip of the Prix du Jockey Club (French Derby) could be as far as he might want to go at three. The essay concluded that "like his most famous male relations, we could see him in the best mile and ten-furlong contests after his classic bids".

He lost his unbeaten record on his seasonal debut. Sent off at odds-on for the Group 3 Prix de Fontainebleau over a mile on very soft ground at ParisLongchamp in May, he was asked for his effort over a furlong and a half out but was unable to peg back the front-running long-shot who made all for a one-and-three-quarter-length victory. That was The Summit, a seemingly exposed colt who had the benefit of a prior run—second in a listed contest at Saint-Cloud in March—and who would play a prominent role on the French three-year-old scene before later moving to Hong Kong where, as yet, he has failed to fire. Ecrivain moved past Victor Ludorum inside the final half furlong and was three-quarters of a length in front of him at the line, although the favourite did manage to hold off the staying-on Kenway by a short head.

The first four met again in the Group 1 Emirates Poule d'Essai des Poulains three weeks later. This time the ground was good-to-soft, recent conditions winner Reshabar tried to make all and he was not headed until Victor Ludorum took over a furlong out. The André Fabre-trained colt was ridden out to the line for a length-and-a-half score, chased home by The Summit. Alson was a neck back in third, three-quarters of a length and a short head in front of Celestin and Kenway. Ecrivain was beaten over a quarter of a mile from home and finished last of the nine. That colt, a juvenile pattern winner who had finished a close fourth in the Prix Jean-Luc Lagardere on his final run at two, disappointed next time too, in the Group 1 Prix du Jockey Club, but ran better when runner-up in a listed contest at Chantilly in the autumn. Victor Ludorum, on the other hand, was slowly away in that classic but had every chance a furlong out and looked briefly like he might be about to emulate his sire by winning both colts' classics. However, The Summit, who had gone to the front shortly before that point, held him off and was a neck in front at the line, that colt having been passed easily in the final half furlong by the John Gosden-trained Mishriff who landed the classic by one and three-quarter lengths. The ground was good-to-soft, subsequent mile star Order of Australia had set a good gallop until over two out, and the time was quick, but it looked as though that final half furlong was testing the outer limit of the favourite's stamina.

The first three met again in the Group 2 Prix Guillaume d'Ornano in mid-August, that ten-furlong contest arguably the most prestigious non-Group 1 race for three-year-olds in France. The Summit set off in front but was taken on by Dream Works after a quarter of a mile and that colt remained at the head of affairs until Mishriff made his move two out. Frankie Dettori sent the classic winner clear and he won easily by four and a half lengths, with The Summit holding off Victor Ludorum by a head and Dream Works, the only other runner, eased to finish another twelve lengths adrift. Once again, Victor Ludorum had been going well over a furlong out only to give the impression that the trip was not quite ideal, especially with the heavy ground making it more testing.

Everything looked to be in his favour on what turned out to be his final race of the year, the Group 1 Prix du Moulin de Longchamp on good ground in early September. Each of the six runners had won at least twice at the highest level, so it promised to be an informative race, but instead it was a bit odd. Half of them fluffed the start, especially Victor Ludorum, while Circus Maximus set a strong gallop and was not headed until Persian King took over two out, soon stormed clear and looked set for a wide-margin win. The early leader got tired, the three who were awkward leaving the stalls still had prospects of making the frame but could not capitalise on that, and that left only Pinatubo, who had been left with far too much to do to win, to chase after his older rival. The speed he showed in the final furlong was impressive but he passed the post a reducing one and three-quarter lengths behind Persian King, six lengths clear of Circus Maximus. Siskin was a length back in fourth, a head in front of Victor Ludorum and with Romanised another five lengths behind.

Victor Ludorum's pedigree was reviewed in detail in last year's essay so a brief outline will suffice this time around. He is, as noted above, inbred 3x3 to Helen Street and, as some will recognise, this makes him a Shamardal colt from the family of Shamardal. That is intriguing in a stallion prospect. He is a half-brother to the ill-fated stakes winner and Group 1 Irish Oaks third Mary Tudor (by Dawn Approach), his dam is the Group 3 Prix Cleopatre runner-up Antiquities (by Kaldounevees) and his grandam is Historian (by Pennekamp), a stakes-winning half-sister to Street Cry (by Machiavellian) and Helsinki (by Machiavellian). The latter is the stakes-placed dam of Shamardal, whereas Street Cry was, of course, a leading international sire too. Forever to be remembered as the stallion who gave us the great racemares Winx and Zenyatta, he won the Group 1 Dubai World Cup and Grade 1 Stephen Foster Handicap, got a Kentucky Derby winner in Street Sense, was a dual champion sire in Australia and sired over 130 stakes winners around the world of whom twenty-three were successful at the highest level. He has also made an impact with his stallion sons and broodmare daughters. Helen Street is also the fourth dam of the classic-placed mile Group 1 winner Territories (by Invincible Spirit), a young Dalham Hall Stud stallion who made a promising start as a freshman sire in 2020, his seven blacktype earners headed by the Group 1-placed pattern winner Rougir.

Hopefully, the 2021 season will give Victor Ludorum further opportunities to enhance his already notable CV. Races such as the Group 1 Prix Jacques le Marois and Group 1 Prix du Moulin de Longchamp look like ideal targets.

SUMMARY DETAILS

Bred: Godolphin
Owned: Godolphin SNC
Trained: André Fabre
Country: France
Race record: 111-31330-
Career highlights: 4 wins inc Emirates Poule d'Essai des Poulains (Gr1), Qatar Prix Jean-Luc Lagardere sponsorise par Manateq (Gr1), 3rd Prix du Jockey Club (Gr1), Prix Guillaume d'Ornano - Haras du Logis Saint-Germain (Gr2), Prix de Fontainebleau (Gr3)

VICTOR LUDORUM (GB) – 2017 bay colt

Shamardal (USA)	Giant's Causeway (USA)	Storm Cat (USA)
		Mariah's Storm (USA)
	Helsinki (GB)	Machiavellian (USA)
		Helen Street
Antiquities (GB)	Kaldounevees (FR)	Kaldoun (FR)
		Safaroa (FR)
	Historian (IRE)	Pennekamp (USA)
		Helen Street

WATCH ME (FR)

Watch Me sprang a 20/1 surprise in the Group 1 Coronation Stakes at Royal Ascot in 2019 but was an odds-on winner of both of her starts last year. She kicked off the summer with a two-and-a-half-length win against Norma in a one-mile listed contest on good ground at Deauville in July and then beat Half Light and Know It All by three-quarters of a length and a short head to add the Group 1 Prix Rothschild over the same course and distance three weeks later. Speak of The Devil, who had been a nose runner-up in the Group 1 Poule d'Essai des Pouliches (French 1000 Guineas), was two lengths back in fourth with old rival Norma another eight lengths adrift. This augured well for her season but instead it proved to be a final run; her retirement was announced five days later.

She is now embarking on stud career and she goes to the paddocks as the headline act for the top-class miler Olympic Glory (by Choisir). The grandson of Danehill Dancer (by Danehill) stands at Haras de Bouquetot in France and his six stakes winners include the classic-placed pattern scorer Grand Glory, plus Quick, who landed a Grade 3 handicap over twelve furlongs at Santa Anita shortly before this book went to print, both of those also representing his first crop. He also has nine others who have been blacktype placed, among them the Group 1 Australian Derby third Eric The Eel, so he is getting milers and middle-distance horses.

Watch Me 's pedigree and prior racing record were reviewed in detail in *European Group 1 Winners of 2019*. She is the best among a trio of winners out of Watchful (by Galileo) and she has three-year-old and two-year-old half-brothers by Elvstroem (by Danehill), named Watch Him and Watch It, in training in France. It is obvious, given the identity of her broodmare sire, that she comes from a notable family because only the best-bred mares get the chance to visit Galileo (by Sadler's Wells). Sharaya (by Youth), her third dam, won the Group 1 Prix Vermeille and has some speedy descendants of note. Her prolific grandson Hamish McGonagall (by Namid) was placed in the Group 1 Prix de l'Abbaye de Longchamp, Group 2 Prix du Gros-Chene, Group 3

Sapphire Stakes, Group 3 Prix du Petit Couvert, and two editions of the Group 1 Nunthorpe Stakes. Her granddaughter Sans Adieu (by French Deputy), on the other hand, won the Grade 2 Centaur Stakes and was runner-up in the Grade 1 Sprinters Stakes, both over six furlongs in Japan. Sharaya had a pair of talented half-sisters in Shannkara (by Akarad), a Grade 3 winner and blacktype producer in the USA, and Sharaniya (by Alleged), a high-class performer in France. That filly won the Group 2 Grand Prix d'Evry, Group 3 Prix de Royallieu and Group 3 Prix Minerve.

If you go back further then you will find that this is a branch of the family of the Timeform 131-rated classic star and influential stallion Blushing Groom (by Red God) and of the Japanese classic star and leading sire King Kamehameha (by Kingmambo). Their common ancestor is Aimee (by Tudor Minstrel)—grandam of Blushing Groom, fifth dam of King Kamehameha, seventh dam of Watch Me—so their connection is remote.

Watch Me, who is inbred 4x4 to Shirley Heights (by Mill Reef), is a dual Group 1-winning daughter of a top-class miler from the Danehill (by Danzig) sire line and she is out of a Galileo mare from a Group 1-producing family. This makes her a notable addition to the broodmare ranks and it would be no surprise to see her produce at least one son or daughter who is as talented as she is. Presuming all goes well for her over the coming year, Siyouni (by Pivotal) will be the sire of her first-born, a colt or filly who will be inbred 3x5 to Danehill and bred on somewhat similar lines to Sottsass.

SUMMARY DETAILS

Bred: Mme A Tamagni & Cocheese Bloodstock Anstait
Owned: Alexander Tamagni-Badmer & Mme Regula Vannod
Trained: Francis-Henri Graffard
Country: France
Race record: 31-10143-11-
Career highlights: 5 wins inc Prix Rothschild (Gr1), Coronation Stakes (Gr1), Prix Imprudence (Gr3), Qatar Prix de la Calonne - Fonds Européen de l'Elevage (L), Criterium du Languedoc - Prix Bernard de Marmiesse (L), 3rd Prix de l'Opera Longines (Gr1)

WATCH ME (FR) – 2016 bay filly

Olympic Glory (IRE)	Choisir (AUS)	Danehill Dancer (IRE)
		Great Selection (AUS)
	Acidanthera (GB)	Alzao (USA)
		Amaranthus
Watchful (IRE)	Galileo (IRE)	Sadler's Wells (USA)
		Urban Sea (USA)
	Sharakawa (IRE)	Darshaan
		Sharaya (USA)

WAY TO PARIS (GB)

Champs Elysees (by Danehill) was a somewhat underrated stallion and he spent his final two seasons covering National Hunt mares in a dual-purpose role at Castlehyde Stud in Ireland. His previous eight years had been served at his breeder's Banstead Manor Stud in England and his thirty stakes-winning offspring include the classic-winning miler Billesdon Brook, Australian Group 1 scorer Harlem, Group 1 Gold Cup victor Way To Paris, the classic-placed pattern-winning fillies Durance, Jack Naylor and Xcellence, and others such as Dame Malliot, Elysea's World, and Suffused who are Group/Grade 2 winners that have been placed at the highest level. He died at the age of fifteen and his youngest offspring are now two-year-olds.

At the time of his death his blacktype winners also included a horse who had been placed in a string of Group 2 and Group 3 contests in France and Italy and even ran in Enable's second Arc. When the grey beat Marmelo by a nose in the Group 2 Prix Maurice de Nieuil at ParisLongchamp in the summer of 2019 it became odds-on that he would earn a place at stud someday. The only question was when and where. Now we know and following an outstanding season in 2020, he looks sure to prove very popular in his new role at Coolagown Stud in Ireland. Way To Paris became the fourth Group 1 star for his late sire when he beat Nagano Gold and Ziyad by a neck and a head to take the Grand Prix de Saint-Cloud over twelve furlongs on good ground at the end of June, and the win came just a fortnight after he failed by only a head to beat Sottsass in the Group 1 Prix Ganay over a furlong and a half less at Chantilly.

He had finished unplaced in the Group 3 Prix Exbury over ten furlongs on heavy ground at Saint-Cloud on his seasonal debut in mid-March but put up a much better effort two months later, chasing home Shaman in the Group 2 Grand Prix de Chantilly, run this time over twelve and a half furlongs on good ground at Deauville. Following his Group 1 success, he was only beaten by a total of three and a quarter lengths when fifth to the ill-fated Derby winner Anthony Van Dyck in the Group 2 Prix Foy before then finishing down the field in both the Group 1 Prix de l'Arc de

Triomphe on heavy ground at ParisLongchamp and Group 1 Japan Cup over the same trip on firm ground at Tokyo.

Way To Paris, who comes from the family of a successful sire, promises to have a notably successful career as a National Hunt stallion. The Danehill branch of the Danzig (by Northern Dancer) sire line has a phenomenal record on the flat, of course, but it has also supplied many leading hurdlers and chasers too. Grey Way (by Cozzene), his dam, won the Group 2 Premio Lydia Tesio, she was Grade 2-placed in the USA and she is also responsible for the dual Italian ten-furlong Group 1 scorer Distant Way (by Distant View), who has sired winners and blacktype earners on the flat in Italy. His grandam, Northern Naiad (by Nureyev) was placed a few times but is a half-sister to the stakes-placed five-time winner U Win I Won (by Explodent), who went to stud in Ecuador, and also to Political Intrigue (by Deputy Minister), the unraced dam of Brazilian-bred standout Redattore (by Roi Normand). He was a Grade 1 winner in his native land before moving north to add the Grade 1 Eddie Read Handicap, Grade 1 Shoemaker Breeders' Cup Mile, Grade 2 San Francisco Breeders' Cup Mile Handicap, Grade 2 Citation Handicap, Grade 2 San Gabriel Handicap and Grade 2 Frank E Kilroe Mile Handicap. He later returned to Brazil as a stallion and has sired a string of Grade 1 winners from a mile and upwards. Redattore's Grade 3-placed full sister Brave Lady also did her part for the family by coming up with the Grade 1-winning miler Joe Bravo (by Vettori). He followed in the hoof-prints of his 'uncle' by moving to North America to continue his career but, sadly, suffered a fatal accident during training at Belmont Park.

Glamour (by Nasrullah), the fifth dam of Way To Paris, won the Test Stakes in 1956, a seven-furlong contest that carries Grade 1 status now, and in addition to being the dam of the St Leger winner Boucher (by Ribot) and his Bowling Green Handicap-winning half-brother and leading broodmare sire Poker (by Round Table), she was also responsible for the stakes-placed winner and influential mare Intriguing (by Swaps). The fourth dam of Way To Paris was the dam of champion filly Numbered Account (by Buckpasser), grandam of the leading sires Polish Numbers (by Danzig), Private Account (by Damascus) and Woodman (by Mr

Prospector), and ancestor of a long list of others whose were champions, Grade 1 stars and/or standouts at stud.

Way To Paris thoroughly earned his place at stud and with such a strong pedigree to back him up there is every reason to hope that he will become a sire of note.

SUMMARY DETAILS

Bred: Grundy Bloodstock Srl
Owned: Paolo Ferrario
Trained: Andrea Marcialis
Country: France
Race record: 4-14121-3132023-24230400-00221200-02121000-
Career highlights: 7 wins inc Grand Prix de Saint-Cloud (Gr1), Grand Prix de Chantilly (Gr2), Prix Maurice de Nieuil (Gr2), Premio Conte Felice Scheibler (L), Premio Merano - Tattersalls (L), 2nd Prix Ganay (Gr1), Prix d'Harcourt (Gr2), Qatar Prix Foy (Gr2), Prix Vicomtesse Vigier (Gr2), Premio Federico Tesio (Gr2), Gran Premio di Milano (Gr2), Prix de Barbeville (Gr3), Prix d'Hedouville (Gr3), Prix Exbury (Gr3), Gran Premio d'Italia (L), 3rd Grand Prix de Chantilly (Gr2), Gran Premio del Jockey Club (Gr2), Prix d'Hedouville (Gr3)

WAY TO PARIS (GB) – 2013 grey horse

Champs Elysees (GB)	Danehill (USA)	Danzig (USA)
		Razyana (USA)
	Hasili (IRE)	Kahyasi
		Kerali
Grey Way (USA)	Cozzene (USA)	Caro
		Ride The Trails (USA)
	Northern Naiad (FR)	Nureyev (USA)
		Fascinating Trick (USA)

WONDERFUL TONIGHT (FR)

Wonderful Tonight was one of the top three-year-old fillies in Europe in 2020 and yet by the time the Guineas and Oaks races had come and gone she had just one win, two places and a fourth to her name from four starts, barely on the radar for most race-watchers. The win had been in a ten-furlong maiden on heavy ground at Saint-Cloud in November, that short-head success coming a month after she had finished third in a one-mile maiden on similar ground at Doncaster. She was beaten by more than seven lengths when fourth to Franconia in a ten-furlong listed contest on good at Newbury on her reappearance in June and then chased home Valia over twelve furlongs at ParisLongchamp, picking up valuable blacktype. But then she made a leap forward.

She had been beaten by two and a half lengths in that French race but turned the tables to two and a half lengths in her favour when she met Valia again in the Group 3 Prix Minerve over an extra half furlong at Deauville in August. The ground was heavy and she made all, pulling away from the field at the finish. The subsequent Group 3 scorer Paix was another length back in third, a neck in front of Irish Oaks fourth Laburnum. The David Menuisier stable had a rising star in its midst. The ground was good at ParisLongchamp the following month, it was Dame Malliot who made the running but the Dermot Weld-trained Tarnawa who won the Group 1 Qatar Prix Vermeille. That chestnut, notching up what would be the first leg of a top-level treble, beat Raabihah and Dame Malliot by three lengths and a short head, with Laburnum another half a length back in fourth. Wonderful Tonight, who was unable to make an impact, was the same amount farther behind in fifth.

The ground was heavy when she returned to that venue three weeks later and soft at Ascot a fortnight after that, and these conditions suited her well. The twelve runners in the Qatar Prix de Royallieu, its second edition as a Group 1 contest over fourteen furlongs, finished well strung out, several of them tailed off, but two fillies had the race to themselves in the closing stages: Wonderful Tonight and Pista. The English filly had gone to the front fully three furlongs from home and although not steering a straight course in the final furlong, she never looked in danger of being caught. Pista, representing the Joseph O'Brien stable, had won the Group 2 Park Hill Stakes on her previous start. She too hung in the closing stages, but she only narrowed the gap to a length and a quarter at the line. Ebaiyra was another five lengths back in third. It was not a strong race for the grade but that hardly mattered to the connections of the newly crowned Group 1 winner.

The following month's Group 1 Qipco British Champions Fillies & Mares Stakes was a stronger race but Wonderful Tonight was even more impressive. She was travelling like a winner with under half a mile to run, soon moved into the lead and then stayed on strongly to the end to beat Dame Malliot by two and a half lengths. Passion, who had been fifth in Paris, was a length back in third, followed home by Mehdaayih and Irish Oaks winner Even So. It was soon revealed that she would remain in training as a four-year-old with a view to taking on the best middle-distance races. Whether she will be as effective on good ground remains to be seen, but there is no doubt that this filly has a considerable amount of ability and it will be fascinating to see how she gets on in the best open company in 2021.

Looking to her future broodmare career, this dual Group 1 star has the potential to excel in that role, and should she produce a top-class son someday then he would have prospects of becoming another notable stallion for the family.

Wonderful Tonight, one of five Group 1 stars among forty-three stakes winners by the leading French stallion Le Havre (by Noverre)—he stands at Montfort et Préaux—is a half-sister to the eight-and-a-half-furlong Aqueduct listed scorer Penjade (by Air Chief Marshal). Her dam, three-time winner Salvation (by Montjeu), is a half-sister to the US nine-furlong Grade 3 winner Hostess (by Iffraaj) and out of the Listed Oaks Trial Stakes winner Birdie (by Alhaarth). That mare is a half-sister to Fading Light (by King's Best)—the Group 3-placed dam of the multiple pattern-placed triple listed scorer Fireglow (by Teofilo)—and to the prolific middle-distance listed-race winner Faru (by Mtoto), but it is another of her siblings who provides the pointer to what a future top-class son in the family might achieve.

Fickle (by Danehill), a half-sister to Wonderful Tonight's grandam Birdie, sprang a 20/1 surprise off just seven-stone-thirteen in a listed ten-furlong handicap on turf at Newcastle on her final of five starts, but her daughter Tarfah (by Kingmambo) won two one-mile listed races plus the Group 3 Dahlia Stakes over nine furlongs before going on to become the dam of Camelot (by Montjeu).

That former Ballydoyle trainee was an unbeaten winner the Group 1 Racing Post Trophy in 2011 and lit up the following season's classic scene with victories in the 2000 Guineas, Derby and Irish Derby. He was a 2/5 favourite for the Group 1 St Leger Stakes at Doncaster, bidding to become the first Triple Crown champion since Nijinsky in 1970, but finished a three-quarter-length runner-up to the controversial and unfortunate Encke. Camelot was a Group 1-placed Group 2 scorer at four, joined the team at Coolmore Stud and wasted no time in establishing himself as a leading classic sire. His eldest progeny are now six years old, seven of his thirty-three stakes winners have won at the highest level, and those wins include European classics for Latrobe (Irish Derby) and Even So (Irish Oaks).

Wonderful Tonight, a €40,000 private purchase at 2018's Arqana Deauville August yearling sale, was bred by Sylvain Vidal and Mathieu Alex of Haras de Montfort et Préaux, under the banner of Ecurie Taos. She carries the well-known yellow and blue of Christopher Wright, colours that the champion juvenile filly Culture Vulture carried to classic victory in 1992. There is every reason to hope that she can add further Group 1 success to her record in 2021, either against her own sex or, if she can improve further and get suitable underfoot conditions, in open company.

SUMMARY DETAILS
Bred: Ecurie Taos
Owned: Christopher Wright
Trained: David Menuisier
Country: England
Race record: 31-421011-

Career highlights: 3 wins inc Qipco British Champions Fillies & Mares Stakes (Gr1), Qatar Prix de Royallieu (Gr1), Prix Minerve (Gr3), 2nd Prix de Thiberville (L)

WONDERFUL TONIGHT (FR) – 2017 bay filly

Le Havre (IRE)	Noverre (USA)	Rahy (USA)
		Danseur Fabuleux (USA)
	Marie Rheinberg (GER)	Surako (GER)
		Marie d'Argonne (FR)
Salvation (GB)	Montjeu (IRE)	Sadler's Wells (USA)
		Floripedes (FR)
	Birdie (GB)	Alhaarth (IRE)
		Fade (GB)

WOODED (IRE)

Wooded is a son of the juvenile Group 1 winner and established classic sire Wootton Bassett (by Iffraaj) and he spent the first twelve months of his career running mostly over seven furlongs. But it was when he dropped to five furlongs that he showed what he could really do and, after just two runs over that distance, he retired to take up stallion duties at Haras de Bouquetot where he will cover his first book of mares at a fee of €15,000.

Runner-up first time out at two, he won a Deauville maiden before finishing a short-neck second to Kenway in the Group 3 Prix La Rochette and then third to King's Command in the Group 3 Prix Thomas Bryon, beaten by almost four lengths on the very soft ground at Saint-Cloud. His performance first time out at three provided the first indication of the route that might lead to stardom for him, when he ran out a three-and-a-half-length winner of the Group 3 Prix Texanita over six furlongs at Chantilly in mid-May. He had hit the front over a furlong and a half from home and never looked like being caught once he went clear. Two months later he returned to seven furlongs and finished a three-and-a-half-length fourth to Pinatubo in the Group 1 Prix Jean Prat. That was a good performance and he only lost third in the final strides. His sixth-place finish in the following month's Group 1 LARC Prix Maurice de Gheest was a shade disappointing. The five who finished ahead of him are all top-class colts—Space Blues, Hello Youmzain, Lope Y Fernandez, Earthlight, and Golden Horde—and they finished fairly close together. However, Wooded passed the post almost two lengths adrift of the fifth having never looked dangerous.

A month later, he made his five-furlong debut in the Group 3 Qatar Prix du Petit Couvert at ParisLongchamp. The ground was good, Air de Valse made all to win by three-quarters of a length, but second place was not a bad effort for his first try at the distance. Both the winner and Lady In France, who had been three-quarters of a length back in third, re-opposed in the Group 1 Prix de l'Abbaye de Longchamp Longines on the first Sunday in October. This time the underfoot conditions were heavy and having hit the front a furlong and a half from home, Wooded stayed on well to the line to hold off the previous year's winner, Glass Slippers, by a neck. Liberty Beach was short neck behind in third, with another length, half a length and neck back to Lady In France, Keep Busy and Air de Valse. This was an eye-catching result given that fillies filled all the spots from second to sixth.

Wooded is the third Group 1 winner among seventeen stakes winners for his now Coolmore Stud-based sire. The other pair are the middle-distance standouts Audarya and Almanzor, the latter a popular member of the team at their sire's former home, Haras d'Etreham. The Timeform 133-rated classic star is a freshman sire in 2021, his first European yearlings made up to 250,000 guineas at auction and his New Zealand-born ones have been a big hit in the sales ring too.

Wooded's full brother Beat Le Bon is a pattern-placed miler but their dam, Frida La Blonde (by Elusive City), is a full sister to the pattern-placed dual stakes-winning sprinter Fred Lalloupet and half-sister to the speedy pattern-placed listed scorer Mon Pote Le Gitan. Feld Marechale (by Deputy Minister), another of her siblings, is the dam of the pattern-placed multiple mile stakes winner Maximum Aurelius (by Showcasing). Their dam, Firm Friend (by Affirmed), a stakes winner at two, also stayed a mile, taking second place in the Group 2 Premio Regina Elena (Italian 1000 Guineas), and if you go back further on the page you will a branch that leads to Magic Ring, one of the early notable sons of Green Desert (by Danzig). He won the Group 3 Norfolk Stakes and Group 3 Cornwallis Stakes, was third in the Group 1 Prix de l'Abbaye de Longchamp and sired a few stakes and pattern winners in Europe, North America and the southern hemisphere.

SUMMARY DETAILS

Bred: Gestüt Zur Kuste Ag
Owned: Al Shaqab Racing
Trained: Francis-Henri Graffard
Country: France
Race record: 2123-14021-
Career highlights: 3 wins inc Prix de l'Abbaye de Longchamp Longines (Gr1), Prix Texanita (Gr3), 2nd Qatar Prix du Petit

Couvert (Gr3), Prix la Rochette (Gr3), 3rd Prix Thomas Bryon Jockey Club de Turquie (Gr3)

WOODED (IRE) – 2017 bay colt

	Iffraaj (GB)	Zafonic (USA)
Wootton Bassett (GB)		Pastorale (GB)
	Balladonia (GB)	Primo Dominie
		Susquehanna Days (USA)
Frida La Blonde (FR)	Elusive City (USA)	Elusive Quality (USA)
		Star of Paris (USA)
	Firm Friend (IRE)	Affirmed (USA)
		Chere Amie (FR)

GROUP 1 WINNERS OF 2020
BY SIRE
(* freshman sire of 2020)

Adlerflug (GER) – In Swoop (IRE)
Adlerflug (GER) – Torquator Tasso (GER)

American Pharoah (USA) – Van Gogh (USA)

Australia (GB) – Galileo Chrome (IRE)
Australia (GB) – Order of Australia (IRE)

Authorized (IRE) – Santiago (IRE)

Camelot (GB) – Even So (IRE)
Camelot (GB) – Sunny Queen (GER)

Champs Elysees (GB) – Way To Paris (GB)

Clodovil (IRE) – Tiger Tanaka (IRE)

Dark Angel (IRE) – Battaash (IRE)

Deep Impact (JPN) – Fancy Blue (IRE)

Dream Ahead (USA) – Dream of Dreams (IRE)
Dream Ahead (USA) – Glass Slippers (GB)

Dubawi (IRE) – Ghaiyyath (IRE)
Dubawi (IRE) – Lord North (IRE)
Dubawi (IRE) – Space Blues (IRE)
Dubawi (IRE) – The Revenant (GB)

Elzaam (AUS) – Champers Elysees (IRE)

Excelebration (IRE) – Barney Roy (GB)

Fastnet Rock (AUS) – One Master (GB)

First Defence (USA) – Siskin (USA)

Galileo (IRE) – Circus Maximus (IRE)
Galileo (IRE) – Love (IRE)
Galileo (IRE) – Magical (IRE)
Galileo (IRE) – Mogul (GB)
Galileo (IRE) – Peaceful (IRE)
Galileo (IRE) – Search For A Song (IRE)
Galileo (IRE) – Serpentine (IRE)
Galileo (IRE) – Shale (IRE)

Galiway (GB) – Sealiway (FR)

Invincible Spirit (IRE) – Nazeef (GB)

Jukebox Jury (IRE) – Princess Zoe (GER)

Kingman (GB) – Palace Pier (GB)
Kingman (GB) – Persian King (IRE)

Kitten's Joy (USA) – Kameko (USA)

Kodiac (GB) – Campanelle (IRE)
Kodiac (GB) – Hello Youmzain (FR)

Lawman (FR) – Pretty Gorgeous (FR)

Le Havre (IRE) – Wonderful Tonight (FR)

Lethal Force (IRE) – Golden Horde (IRE)

Lope de Vega (IRE) – Lucky Vega (IRE)

Make Believe (GB) – Mishriff (IRE)

Mayson (GB) – Oxted (GB)

*Mehmas (IRE) – Supremacy (IRE)

Nathaniel (IRE) – Enable (GB)

New Approach (IRE) – Mac Swiney (IRE)

No Nay Never (USA) – Alcohol Free (IRE)

Olympic Glory (IRE) – Watch Me (FR)

Pivotal (GB) – Addeybb (IRE)
Pivotal (GB) – Glen Shiel (GB)

Sea The Moon (GER) – Alpine Star (IRE)

Sea The Stars (IRE) – Miss Yoda (GER)
Sea The Stars (IRE) – Stradivarius (IRE)

Shamardal (USA) – Pinatubo (IRE)
Shamardal (USA) – Tarnawa (IRE)
Shamardal (USA) – Victor Ludorum (GB)

Showcasing (GB) – Mohaather (GB)

Siyouni (FR) – Dream And Do (IRE)
Siyouni (FR) – Sottsass (FR)
Siyouni (FR) – St Mark's Basilica (FR)

Teofilo (IRE) – Donjah (GER)
Teofilo (IRE) – Gear Up (IRE)
Teofilo (IRE) – Subjectivist (GB)
Teofilo (IRE) – Tawkeel (GB)
Teofilo (IRE) – Twilight Payment (IRE)

Wootton Bassett (GB) – Audarya (FR)
Wootton Bassett (GB) – Wooded (IRE)

Zoffany (IRE) – Thunder Moon (IRE)

Acclamation (GB) – Battaash (IRE), by Dark Angel (IRE)
Acclamation (GB) – Supremacy (IRE), by Mehmas (IRE)

Cape Cross (IRE) – Miss Yoda (GER), by Sea The Stars (IRE)
Cape Cross (IRE) – Stradivarius (IRE), by Sea The Stars (IRE)

Choisir (AUS) – Watch Me (FR), by Olympic Glory (IRE)

Danehill (USA) – Campanelle (IRE), by Kodiac (GB)
Danehill (USA) – Hello Youmzain (FR), by Kodiac (GB)
Danehill (USA) – One Master (GB), by Fastnet Rock (AUS)
Danehill (USA) – Tiger Tanaka (IRE), by Clodovil (IRE)
Danehill (USA) – Way To Paris (GB), by Champs Elysees (GB)

Dansili (GB) – Thunder Moon (IRE), by Zoffany (IRE)

Dark Angel (IRE) – Golden Horde (IRE), by Lethal Force (IRE)

Diktat (GB) – Dream of Dreams (IRE), by Dream Ahead (USA)
Diktat (GB) – Glass Slippers (GB), by Dream Ahead (USA)

Dubai Millennium (GB) – Ghaiyyath (IRE), by Dubawi (IRE)
Dubai Millennium (GB) – Lord North (IRE), by Dubawi (IRE)
Dubai Millennium (GB) – Space Blues (IRE), by Dubawi (IRE)
Dubai Millennium (GB) – The Revenant (GB), by Dubawi (IRE)

El Prado (IRE) – Kameko (USA), by Kitten's Joy (USA)

Exceed And Excel (AUS) – Barney Roy (GB), by Excelebration
    (IRE)

Galileo (IRE) – Donjah (GER), by Teofilo (IRE)
Galileo (IRE) – Enable (GB), by Nathaniel (IRE)
Galileo (IRE) – Galileo Chrome (IRE), by Australia (GB)
Galileo (IRE) – Gear Up (IRE), by Teofilo (IRE)

Galileo (IRE) – Mac Swiney (IRE), by New Approach (IRE)
Galileo (IRE) – Order of Australia (IRE), by Australia (GB)
Galileo (IRE) – Sealiway (FR), by Galiway (GB)
Galileo (IRE) – Subjectivist (GB), by Teofilo (IRE)
Galileo (IRE) – Tawkeel (GB), by Teofilo (IRE)
Galileo (IRE) – Twilight Payment (IRE), by Teofilo (IRE)

Giant's Causeway (USA) – Pinatubo (IRE), by Shamardal (USA)
Giant's Causeway (USA) – Tarnawa (IRE), by Shamardal (USA)
Giant's Causeway (USA) – Victor Ludorum (GB), by Shamardal (USA)

Green Desert (USA) – Nazeef (GB), by Invincible Spirit (IRE)

Iffraaj (GB) – Audarya (FR), by Wootton Bassett (GB)
Iffraaj (GB) – Wooded (IRE), by Wootton Bassett (GB)

In The Wings – In Swoop (IRE), by Adlerflug (GER)
In The Wings – Torquator Tasso (GER), by Adlerflug (GER)

Invincible Spirit (IRE) – Oxted (GB), by Mayson (GB)
Invincible Spirit (IRE) – Palace Pier (GB), by Kingman (GB)
Invincible Spirit (IRE) – Persian King (IRE), by Kingman (GB)
Invincible Spirit (IRE) – Pretty Gorgeous (FR), by Lawman (FR)

Makfi (GB) – Mishriff (IRE), by Make Believe (GB)

Montjeu (IRE) – Even So (IRE), by Camelot (GB)
Montjeu (IRE) – Princess Zoe (GER), by Jukebox Jury (IRE)
Montjeu (IRE) – Santiago (IRE), by Authorized (IRE)
Montjeu (IRE) – Sunny Queen (GER), by Camelot (GB)

Noverre (USA) – Wonderful Tonight (FR), by Le Havre (IRE)

Oasis Dream (GB) – Mohaather (GB), by Showcasing (GB)

Pioneerof The Nile (USA) – Van Gogh (USA), by American
    Pharoah (USA)

Pivotal (GB) – Dream And Do (IRE), by Siyouni (FR)
Pivotal (GB) – Sottsass (FR), by Siyouni (FR)
Pivotal (GB) – St Mark's Basilica (FR), by Siyouni (FR)

Polar Falcon (USA) – Addeybb (IRE), by Pivotal (GB)
Polar Falcon (USA) – Glen Shiel (GB), by Pivotal (GB)

Redoute's Choice (AUS) – Champers Elysees (IRE), by Elzaam (AUS)

Sadler's Wells (USA) – Circus Maximus (IRE), by Galileo (IRE)
Sadler's Wells (USA) – Love (IRE), by Galileo (IRE)
Sadler's Wells (USA) – Magical (IRE), by Galileo (IRE)
Sadler's Wells (USA) – Mogul (GB), by Galileo (IRE)
Sadler's Wells (USA) – Peaceful (IRE), by Galileo (IRE)
Sadler's Wells (USA) – Search For A Song (IRE), by Galileo (IRE)
Sadler's Wells (USA) – Serpentine (IRE), by Galileo (IRE)
Sadler's Wells (USA) – Shale (IRE), by Galileo (IRE)

Scat Daddy (USA) – Alcohol Free (IRE), by No Nay Never (USA)

Sea The Stars (IRE) – Alpine Star (IRE), by Sea The Moon (GER)

Shamardal (USA) – Lucky Vega (IRE), by Lope de Vega (IRE)

Sunday Silence (USA) – Fancy Blue (IRE), by Deep Impact (JPN)

Unbridled's Song (USA) – Siskin (USA), by First Defence (USA)

GROUP 1 WINNERS OF 2020
BY GREAT-GRANDSIRE

Acclamation (GB) – Golden Horde (IRE), by Lethal Force (IRE), by Dark Angel (IRE)

Cape Cross (IRE) – Alpine Star (IRE), by Sea The Moon (GER), by Sea The Stars (IRE)

Danehill (USA) – Barney Roy (GB), by Excelebration (IRE), by Exceed And Excel (AUS)

Danehill (USA) – Champers Elysees (IRE), by Elzaam (AUS), by Redoute's Choice (AUS)

Danehill (USA) – Thunder Moon (IRE), by Zoffany (IRE), by Dansili (GB)

Danehill Dancer (IRE) – Watch Me (FR), by Olympic Glory (IRE), by Choisir (AUS)

Danzig (USA) – Campanelle (IRE), by Kodiac (GB), by Danehill (USA)

Danzig (USA) – Hello Youmzain (FR), by Kodiac (GB), by Danehill (USA)

Danzig (USA) – One Master (GB), by Fastnet Rock (AUS), by Danehill (USA)

Danzig (USA) – Nazeef (GB), by Invincible Spirit (IRE), by Green Desert (USA)

Danzig (USA) – Tiger Tanaka (IRE), by Clodovil (IRE), by Danehill (USA)

Danzig (USA) – Way To Paris (GB), by Champs Elysees (GB), by Danehill (USA)

Dubawi (IRE) – Mishriff (IRE), by Make Believe (GB), by Makfi (GB)

Empire Maker (USA) – Van Gogh (USA), by American Pharoah (USA), by Pioneerof The Nile (USA)

Giant's Causeway (USA) – Lucky Vega (IRE), by Lope de Vega (IRE), by Shamardal (USA)

Green Desert (USA) – Miss Yoda (GER), by Sea The Stars (IRE), by Cape Cross (IRE)

Green Desert (USA) – Mohaather (GB), by Showcasing (GB), by Oasis Dream (GB)

Green Desert (USA) – Oxted (GB), by Mayson (GB), by Invincible Spirit (IRE)

Green Desert (USA) – Palace Pier (GB), by Kingman (GB), by Invincible Spirit (IRE)

Green Desert (USA) – Persian King (IRE), by Kingman (GB), by Invincible Spirit (IRE)

Green Desert (USA) – Pretty Gorgeous (FR), by Lawman (FR), by Invincible Spirit (IRE)

Green Desert (USA) – Stradivarius (IRE), by Sea The Stars (IRE), by Cape Cross (IRE)

Halo (USA) – Fancy Blue (IRE), by Deep Impact (JPN), by Sunday Silence (USA)

Johannesburg (USA) – Alcohol Free (IRE), by No Nay Never (USA), by Scat Daddy (USA)

Northern Dancer – Circus Maximus (IRE), by Galileo (IRE), by Sadler's Wells (USA)

Northern Dancer – Love (IRE), by Galileo (IRE), by Sadler's Wells (USA)

Northern Dancer – Magical (IRE), by Galileo (IRE), by Sadler's Wells (USA)

Northern Dancer – Mogul (GB), by Galileo (IRE), by Sadler's Wells (USA)

Northern Dancer – Peaceful (IRE), by Galileo (IRE), by Sadler's Wells (USA)

Northern Dancer – Search For A Song (IRE), by Galileo (IRE), by Sadler's Wells (USA)

Northern Dancer – Serpentine (IRE), by Galileo (IRE), by Sadler's Wells (USA)

Northern Dancer – Shale (IRE), by Galileo (IRE), by Sadler's Wells (USA)

Nureyev (USA) – Addeybb (IRE), by Pivotal (GB), by Polar Falcon (USA)

Nureyev (USA) – Glen Shiel (GB), by Pivotal (GB), by Polar Falcon (USA)

Polar Falcon (USA) – Dream And Do (IRE), by Siyouni (FR), by Pivotal (GB)

Polar Falcon (USA) – Sottsass (FR), by Siyouni (FR), by Pivotal (GB)

Polar Falcon (USA) – St Mark's Basilica (FR), by Siyouni (FR), by Pivotal (GB)

Rahy (USA) – Wonderful Tonight (FR), by Le Havre (IRE), by Noverre (USA)

Royal Applause (GB) – Battaash (IRE), by Dark Angel (IRE), by Acclamation (GB)

Royal Applause (GB) – Supremacy (IRE), by Mehmas (IRE), by Acclamation (GB)

Sadler's Wells (USA) – Donjah (GER), by Teofilo (IRE), by Galileo (IRE)

Sadler's Wells (USA) – Enable (GB), by Nathaniel (IRE), by Galileo (IRE)

Sadler's Wells (USA) – Even So (IRE), by Camelot (GB), by Montjeu (IRE)

Sadler's Wells (USA) – Galileo Chrome (IRE), by Australia (GB), by Galileo (IRE)

Sadler's Wells (USA) – Gear Up (IRE), by Teofilo (IRE), by Galileo (IRE)

Sadler's Wells (USA) – In Swoop (IRE), by Adlerflug (GER), by In The Wings

Sadler's Wells (USA) – Kameko (USA), by Kitten's Joy (USA), by El Prado (IRE)

Sadler's Wells (USA) – Mac Swiney (IRE), by New Approach
(IRE), by Galileo (IRE)
Sadler's Wells (USA) – Order of Australia (IRE), by Australia
(GB), by Galileo (IRE)
Sadler's Wells (USA) – Princess Zoe (GER), by Jukebox Jury
(IRE), by Montjeu (IRE)
Sadler's Wells (USA) – Santiago (IRE), by Authorized (IRE), by
Montjeu (IRE)
Sadler's Wells (USA) – Sealiway (FR), by Galiway (GB), by
Galileo (IRE)
Sadler's Wells (USA) – Subjectivist (GB), by Teofilo (IRE), by
Galileo (IRE)
Sadler's Wells (USA) – Sunny Queen (GER), by Camelot (GB),
by Montjeu (IRE)
Sadler's Wells (USA) – Tawkeel (GB), by Teofilo (IRE), by
Galileo (IRE)
Sadler's Wells (USA) – Torquator Tasso (GER), by Adlerflug
(GER), by In The Wings
Sadler's Wells (USA) – Twilight Payment (IRE), by Teofilo
(IRE), by Galileo (IRE)

Seeking The Gold (USA) – Ghaiyyath (IRE), by Dubawi (IRE),
by Dubai Millennium (GB)
Seeking The Gold (USA) – Lord North (IRE), by Dubawi (IRE),
by Dubai Millennium (GB)
Seeking The Gold (USA) – Space Blues (IRE), by Dubawi (IRE),
by Dubai Millennium (GB)
Seeking The Gold (USA) – The Revenant (GB), by Dubawi
(IRE), by Dubai Millennium (GB)

Storm Cat (USA) – Pinatubo (IRE), by Shamardal (USA), by
Giant's Causeway (USA)
Storm Cat (USA) – Tarnawa (IRE), by Shamardal (USA), by
Giant's Causeway (USA)
Storm Cat (USA) – Victor Ludorum (GB), by Shamardal (USA),
by Giant's Causeway (USA)

Unbridled (USA) – Siskin (USA), by First Defence (USA), by
    Unbridled's Song (USA)

Warning – Dream of Dreams (IRE), by Dream Ahead (USA), by
    Diktat (GB)
Warning – Glass Slippers (GB), by Dream Ahead (USA), by
    Diktat (GB)

Zafonic (USA) – Audarya (FR), by Wootton Bassett (GB), by
    Iffraaj (GB)
Zafonic (USA) – Wooded (IRE), by Wootton Bassett (GB), by
    Iffraaj (GB)

GROUP 1 WINNERS OF 2020
BY DAM

Alina (IRE) – Barney Roy (GB), by Excelebration (IRE)

Alpha Lupi (IRE) – Alpine Star (IRE), by Sea The Moon (GER)

Anna Law (IRE) – Battaash (IRE), by Dark Angel (IRE)

Antiquities (GB) – Victor Ludorum (GB), by Shamardal (USA)

Beach Frolic (GB) – Palace Pier (GB), by Kingman (GB)

Bird Flown (GB) – Siskin (USA), by First Defence (USA)

Breeze Hill (IRE) – Even So (IRE), by Camelot (GB)

Bush Cat (USA) – Addeybb (IRE), by Pivotal (GB)

Cabaret (IRE) – St Mark's Basilica (FR), by Siyouni (FR)

Charlotte Rosina (GB) – Oxted (GB), by Mayson (GB)

Chenchikova (IRE) – Fancy Blue (IRE), by Deep Impact (JPN)

Concentric (GB) – Enable (GB), by Nathaniel (IRE)

Contradict (GB) – Mishriff (IRE), by Make Believe (GB)

Curious Mind (GB) – Galileo Chrome (IRE), by Australia (GB)

Dream On Buddy (IRE) – Twilight Payment (IRE), by Teofilo (IRE)

Duntle (IRE) – Circus Maximus (IRE), by Galileo (IRE)

Dyanamore (USA) – Donjah (GER), by Teofilo (IRE)

Enticing (IRE) – One Master (GB), by Fastnet Rock (AUS)

Entreat (GB) – Golden Horde (IRE), by Lethal Force (IRE)

Frida La Blonde (FR) – Wooded (IRE), by Wootton Bassett (GB)

Gearanai (USA) – Gear Up (IRE), by Teofilo (IRE)

Gonfilia (GER) – Glen Shiel (GB), by Pivotal (GB)

Green Bananas (FR) – Audarya (FR), by Wootton Bassett (GB)

Grey Way (USA) – Way To Paris (GB), by Champs Elysees (GB)

Halfway To Heaven (IRE) – Magical (IRE), by Galileo (IRE)

Halla Na Saoire (IRE) – Mac Swiney (IRE), by New Approach (IRE)

Handassa (GB) – Nazeef (GB), by Invincible Spirit (IRE)

Hazel Lavery (IRE) – The Revenant (GB), by Dubawi (IRE)

Homecoming Queen (IRE) – Shale (IRE), by Galileo (IRE)

Imagine (IRE) – Van Gogh (USA), by American Pharoah (USA)

Iota (GER) – In Swoop (IRE), by Adlerflug (GER)

Janina (GB) – Campanelle (IRE), by Kodiac (GB)

Kensea (FR) – Sealiway (FR), by Galiway (GB)

La Cuvee (GB) – Champers Elysees (IRE), by Elzaam (AUS)

Lady Gorgeous (GB) – Pretty Gorgeous (FR), by Lawman (FR)

Lava Flow (IRE) – Pinatubo (IRE), by Shamardal (USA)

Miss Lucifer (FR) – Space Blues (IRE), by Dubawi (IRE)

Miss Phillyjinks (IRE) – Tiger Tanaka (IRE), by Clodovil (IRE)

Missvinski (USA) – Peaceful (IRE), by Galileo (IRE)

Monami (GER) – Miss Yoda (GER), by Sea The Stars (IRE)

Najoum (USA) – Lord North (IRE), by Dubawi (IRE)

Night Gypsy (GB) – Glass Slippers (GB), by Dream Ahead
    (USA)

Nightime (IRE) – Ghaiyyath (IRE), by Dubawi (IRE)

Palace Princess (GER) – Princess Zoe (GER), by Jukebox Jury
    (IRE)

Pikaboo (GB) – Love (IRE), by Galileo (IRE)

Plying (USA) – Alcohol Free (IRE), by No Nay Never (USA)

Polished Gem (IRE) – Search For A Song (IRE), by Galileo
    (IRE)

Pretty Please (IRE) – Persian King (IRE), by Kingman (GB)

Private Life (FR) – Stradivarius (IRE), by Sea The Stars (IRE)

Queen of Carthage (USA) – Lucky Vega (IRE), by Lope de Vega
    (IRE)

Rafaadah (GB) – Tawkeel (GB), by Teofilo (IRE)

Reckoning (IRE) – Subjectivist (GB), by Teofilo (IRE)

Remember When (IRE) – Serpentine (IRE), by Galileo (IRE)

Roodeye (GB) – Mohaather (GB), by Showcasing (GB)

Salvation (GB) – Wonderful Tonight (FR), by Le Havre (IRE)

Senta's Dream (GB) – Order of Australia (IRE), by Australia (GB)

Shastye (IRE) – Mogul (GB), by Galileo (IRE)

Small Sacrifice (IRE) – Thunder Moon (IRE), by Zoffany (IRE)

Spasha (GB) – Hello Youmzain (FR), by Kodiac (GB)

Starlet's Sister (IRE) – Sottsass (FR), by Siyouni (FR)

Suivi (GER) – Sunny Queen (GER), by Camelot (GB)

Sweeter Still (IRE) – Kameko (USA), by Kitten's Joy (USA)

Tarana (IRE) – Tarnawa (IRE), by Shamardal (USA)

Tijuana (GER) – Torquator Tasso (GER), by Adlerflug (GER)

Triggers Broom (IRE) – Supremacy (IRE), by Mehmas (IRE)

Vasilia (GB) – Dream of Dreams (IRE), by Dream Ahead (USA)

Venetias Dream (IRE) – Dream And Do (IRE), by Siyouni (FR)

Wadyhatta (GB) – Santiago (IRE), by Authorized (IRE)

Watchful (IRE) – Watch Me (FR), by Olympic Glory (IRE)

GROUP 1 WINNERS OF 2020
BY BROODMARE SIRE

Arcano (IRE) – Supremacy (IRE), by Mehmas (IRE)

Bering – Stradivarius (IRE), by Sea The Stars (IRE)

Big Shuffle (USA) – Glen Shiel (GB), by Pivotal (GB)

Cape Cross (IRE) – Lucky Vega (IRE), by Lope de Vega (IRE)
Cape Cross (IRE) – Santiago (IRE), by Authorized (IRE)
Cape Cross (IRE) – Tarnawa (IRE), by Shamardal (USA)

Choisir (AUS) – Oxted (GB), by Mayson (GB)

Compton Place (GB) – Pretty Gorgeous (FR), by Lawman (FR)

Cozzene (USA) – Way To Paris (GB), by Champs Elysees (GB)

Dalakhani (IRE) – Pinatubo (IRE), by Shamardal (USA)

Danehill (USA) – Even So (IRE), by Camelot (GB)
Danehill (USA) – Mogul (GB), by Galileo (IRE)
Danehill (USA) – Order of Australia (IRE), by Australia (GB)
Danehill (USA) – Search For A Song (IRE), by Galileo (IRE)

Danehill Dancer (IRE) – Circus Maximus (IRE), by Galileo
   (IRE)
Danehill Dancer (IRE) – Serpentine (IRE), by Galileo (IRE)
Danehill Dancer (IRE) – Subjectivist (GB), by Teofilo (IRE)

Dansili (GB) – Dream of Dreams (IRE), by Dream Ahead
   (USA)
Dansili (GB) – Galileo Chrome (IRE), by Australia (GB)

Darshaan – Sunny Queen (GER), by Camelot (GB)

Dubawi (IRE) – Nazeef (GB), by Invincible Spirit (IRE)

Dylan Thomas (IRE) – Persian King (IRE), by Kingman (GB)

Elusive City (USA) – Wooded (IRE), by Wootton Bassett (GB)

Excellent Art (GB) – The Revenant (GB), by Dubawi (IRE)

Galileo (IRE) – Barney Roy (GB), by Excelebration (IRE)
Galileo (IRE) – Ghaiyyath (IRE), by Dubawi (IRE)
Galileo (IRE) – Sottsass (FR), by Siyouni (FR)
Galileo (IRE) – St Mark's Basilica (FR), by Siyouni (FR)
Galileo (IRE) – Watch Me (FR), by Olympic Glory (IRE)

Giant's Causeway (USA) – Lord North (IRE), by Dubawi (IRE)

Green Tune (USA) – Audarya (FR), by Wootton Bassett (GB)

Hard Spun (USA) – Alcohol Free (IRE), by No Nay Never
    (USA)

Holy Roman Emperor (IRE) – Shale (IRE), by Galileo (IRE)

Inchinor (GB) – Mohaather (GB), by Showcasing (GB)

Kaldounevees (FR) – Victor Ludorum (GB), by Shamardal
    (USA)

Kendargent (FR) – Sealiway (FR), by Galiway (GB)

Kingmambo (USA) – Addeybb (IRE), by Pivotal (GB)

Lawman (FR) – Battaash (IRE), by Dark Angel (IRE)

Librettist (USA) – Dream And Do (IRE), by Siyouni (FR)

Mark of Esteem (IRE) – Champers Elysees (IRE), by Elzaam
    (AUS)

Mind Games (GB) – Glass Slippers (GB), by Dream Ahead
(USA)

Montjeu (IRE) – Wonderful Tonight (FR), by Le Havre (IRE)

Mt. Livermore (USA) – Donjah (GER), by Teofilo (IRE)

Namid (GB) – Campanelle (IRE), by Kodiac (GB)

Nayef (USA) – Palace Pier (GB), by Kingman (GB)

Noverre (USA) – Space Blues (IRE), by Dubawi (IRE)

Oasis Dream (GB) – Siskin (USA), by First Defence (USA)
Oasis Dream (GB) – Tawkeel (GB), by Teofilo (IRE)
Oasis Dream (GB) – Twilight Payment (IRE), by Teofilo (IRE)

Pivotal (GB) – Golden Horde (IRE), by Lethal Force (IRE)
Pivotal (GB) – Love (IRE), by Galileo (IRE)
Pivotal (GB) – Magical (IRE), by Galileo (IRE)
Pivotal (GB) – One Master (GB), by Fastnet Rock (AUS)

Rahy (USA) – Alpine Star (IRE), by Sea The Moon (GER)

Raven's Pass (USA) – Mishriff (IRE), by Make Believe (GB)

Rock of Gibraltar (IRE) – Kameko (USA), by Kitten's Joy
(USA)

Sadler's Wells (USA) – Enable (GB), by Nathaniel (IRE)
Sadler's Wells (USA) – Fancy Blue (IRE), by Deep Impact (JPN)
Sadler's Wells (USA) – Thunder Moon (IRE), by Zoffany (IRE)
Sadler's Wells (USA) – Van Gogh (USA), by American Pharoah
(USA)

Shamardal (USA) – Hello Youmzain (FR), by Kodiac (GB)

Sholokhov (IRE) – Miss Yoda (GER), by Sea The Stars (IRE)

Stravinsky (USA) – Peaceful (IRE), by Galileo (IRE)

Teofilo (IRE) – Mac Swiney (IRE), by New Approach (IRE)

Toccet (USA) – Gear Up (IRE), by Teofilo (IRE)

Tiger Hill (IRE) – In Swoop (IRE), by Adlerflug (GER)
Tiger Hill (IRE) – Princess Zoe (GER), by Jukebox Jury (IRE)

Toylsome (GB) – Torquator Tasso (GER), by Adlerflug (GER)

Zoffany (IRE) – Tiger Tanaka (IRE), by Clodovil (IRE)

GROUP 1 WINNERS OF 2020
BY MATERNAL GRANDSIRE
(Sire of the broodmare sire)

Ahonoora – Mohaather (GB), by Showcasing (GB), dam by Inchinor (GB)

Arctic Tern (USA) – Stradivarius (IRE), by Sea The Stars (IRE), dam by Bering

Awesome Again (CAN) – Gear Up (IRE), by Teofilo (IRE), dam by Toccet (USA)

Blushing Groom (FR) – Alpine Star (IRE), by Sea The Moon (GER), dam by Rahy (USA)
Blushing Groom (FR) – Donjah (GER), by Teofilo (IRE), dam by Mt. Livermore (USA)

Cadeaux Genereux – Torquator Tasso (GER), by Adlerflug (GER), dam by Toylsome (GB)

Caro – Way To Paris (GB), by Champs Elysees (GB), dam by Cozzene (USA)

Danehill (USA) – Circus Maximus (IRE), by Galileo (IRE), dam by Danehill Dancer (IRE)
Danehill (USA) – Dream of Dreams (IRE), by Dream Ahead (USA), dam by Dansili (GB)
Danehill (USA) – Galileo Chrome (IRE), by Australia (GB), dam by Dansili (GB)
Danehill (USA) – In Swoop (IRE), by Adlerflug (GER), dam by Tiger Hill (IRE)
Danehill (USA) – Kameko (USA), by Kitten's Joy (USA), dam by Rock of Gibraltar (IRE)
Danehill (USA) – Persian King (IRE), by Kingman (GB), dam by Dylan Thomas (IRE)
Danehill (USA) – Princess Zoe (GER), by Jukebox Jury (IRE), dam by Tiger Hill (IRE)

Danehill (USA) – Serpentine (IRE), by Galileo (IRE), dam by
    Danehill Dancer (IRE)
Danehill (USA) – Shale (IRE), by Galileo (IRE), dam by Holy
    Roman Emperor (IRE)
Danehill (USA) – Subjectivist (GB), by Teofilo (IRE), dam by
    Danehill Dancer (IRE)

Danehill Dancer (IRE) – Oxted (GB), by Mayson (GB), dam by
    Choisir (AUS)

Dansili (GB) – Tiger Tanaka (IRE), by Clodovil (IRE), dam by
    Zoffany (IRE)

Danzig (USA) – Alcohol Free (IRE), by No Nay Never (USA),
    dam by Hard Spun (USA)
Danzig (USA) – Dream And Do (IRE), by Siyouni (FR), dam by
    Librettist (USA)
Danzig (USA) – Even So (IRE), by Camelot (GB), dam by
    Danehill (USA)
Danzig (USA) – Mogul (GB), by Galileo (IRE), dam by Danehill
    (USA)
Danzig (USA) – Order of Australia (IRE), by Australia (GB),
    dam by Danehill (USA)
Danzig (USA) – Search For A Song (IRE), by Galileo (IRE),
    dam by Danehill (USA)

Darshaan – Champers Elysees (IRE), by Elzaam (AUS), dam by
    Mark of Esteem (IRE)
Darshaan – Pinatubo (IRE), by Shamardal (USA), dam by
    Dalakhani (IRE)

Dubai Millennium (GB) – Nazeef (GB), by Invincible Spirit
    (IRE), dam by Dubawi (IRE)

Elusive Quality (USA) – Mishriff (IRE), by Make Believe (GB),
    dam by Raven's Pass (USA)
Elusive Quality (USA) – Wooded (IRE), by Wootton Bassett
    (GB), dam by Elusive City (USA)

Galileo (IRE) – Mac Swiney (IRE), by New Approach (IRE),
    dam by Teofilo (IRE)

Giant's Causeway (USA) – Hello Youmzain (FR), by Kodiac
    (GB), dam by Shamardal (USA)

Green Dancer (USA) – Audarya (FR), by Wootton Bassett (GB),
    dam by Green Tune (USA)

Green Desert (USA) – Lucky Vega (IRE), by Lope de Vega
    (IRE), dam by Cape Cross (IRE)
Green Desert (USA) – Santiago (IRE), by Authorized (IRE),
    dam by Cape Cross (IRE)
Green Desert (USA) – Siskin (USA), by First Defence (USA),
    dam by Oasis Dream (GB)
Green Desert (USA) – Tarnawa (IRE), by Shamardal (USA),
    dam by Cape Cross (IRE)
Green Desert (USA) – Tawkeel (GB), by Teofilo (IRE), dam by
    Oasis Dream (GB)
Green Desert (USA) – Twilight Payment (IRE), by Teofilo
    (IRE), dam by Oasis Dream (GB)

Gulch (USA) – Palace Pier (GB), by Kingman (GB), dam by
    Nayef (USA)

Indian Ridge – Campanelle (IRE), by Kodiac (GB), dam by
    Namid (GB)
Indian Ridge – Pretty Gorgeous (FR), by Lawman (FR), dam by
    Compton Place (GB)

Invincible Spirit (IRE) – Battaash (IRE), by Dark Angel (IRE),
    dam by Lawman (FR)

Kaldoun (FR) – Victor Ludorum (GB), by Shamardal (USA),
    dam by Kaldounevees (FR)

Kendor (FR) – Sealiway (FR), by Galiway (GB), dam by
 Kendargent (FR)

Mr Prospector (USA) – Addeybb (IRE), by Pivotal (GB), dam
 by Kingmambo (USA)

Northern Dancer – Enable (GB), by Nathaniel (IRE), dam by
 Sadler's Wells (USA)
Northern Dancer – Fancy Blue (IRE), by Deep Impact (JPN),
 dam by Sadler's Wells (USA)
Northern Dancer – Thunder Moon (IRE), by Zoffany (IRE),
 dam by Sadler's Wells (USA)
Northern Dancer – Van Gogh (USA), by American Pharoah
 (USA), dam by Sadler's Wells (USA)

Nureyev (USA) – Peaceful (IRE), by Galileo (IRE), dam by
 Stravinsky (USA)

Oasis Dream (GB) – Supremacy (IRE), by Mehmas (IRE), dam
 by Arcano (IRE)

Pivotal (GB) – The Revenant (GB), by Dubawi (IRE), dam by
 Excellent Art (GB)

Polar Falcon (USA) – Golden Horde (IRE), by Lethal Force
 (IRE), by Pivotal (GB)
Polar Falcon (USA) – Love (IRE), by Galileo (IRE), dam by
 Pivotal (GB)
Polar Falcon (USA) – Magical (IRE), by Galileo (IRE), dam by
 Pivotal (GB)
Polar Falcon (USA) – One Master (GB), by Fastnet Rock (AUS),
 dam by Pivotal (GB)

Puissance – Glass Slippers (GB), by Dream Ahead (USA), dam
 by Mind Games (GB)

Rahy (USA) – Space Blues (IRE), by Dubawi (IRE), dam by
 Noverre (USA)

Sadler's Wells (USA) – Barney Roy (GB), by Excelebration
(IRE), dam by Galileo (IRE)
Sadler's Wells (USA) – Ghaiyyath (IRE), by Dubawi (IRE), dam
by Galileo (IRE)
Sadler's Wells (USA) – Miss Yoda (GER), by Sea The Stars
(IRE), dam by Sholokhov (IRE)
Sadler's Wells (USA) – Sottsass (FR), by Siyouni (FR), dam by
Galileo (IRE)
Sadler's Wells (USA) – St Mark's Basilica (FR), by Siyouni (FR),
dam by Galileo (IRE)
Sadler's Wells (USA) – Watch Me (FR), by Olympic Glory
(IRE), dam by Galileo (IRE)
Sadler's Wells (USA) – Wonderful Tonight (FR), by Le Havre
(IRE), dam by Montjeu (IRE)

Shirley Heights – Sunny Queen (GER), by Camelot (GB), dam
by Darshaan

Storm Cat (USA) – Lord North (IRE), by Dubawi (IRE), dam by
Giant's Causeway (USA)

Super Concorde (USA) – Glen Shiel (GB), by Pivotal (GB), dam
by Big Shuffle (USA)

GROUP 1 WINNERS OF 2020
BY GRANDAM

Acts of Grace (USA) – Mishriff (IRE), by Make Believe (GB), out of Contradict (GB)

Anabaa Republic (FR) – Audarya (FR), by Wootton Bassett (GB), out of Green Bananas (FR)

Apogee (GB) – Enable (GB), by Nathaniel (IRE), out of Concentric (GB)

Arbusha (USA) – Addeybb (IRE), by Pivotal (GB), out of Bush Cat (USA)

Beltisaal (FR) – Kameko (USA), by Kitten's Joy (USA), out of Sweeter Still (IRE)

Birdie (GB) – Wonderful Tonight (FR), by Le Havre (IRE), out of Salvation (GB)

Cassandra Go (IRE) – Magical (IRE), by Galileo (IRE), out of Halfway To Heaven (IRE)

Caumshinaun (IRE) – Ghaiyyath (IRE), by Dubawi (IRE), out of Nightime (IRE)

Cayman Sunset (IRE) – Pretty Gorgeous (FR), by Lawman (FR), out of Lady Gorgeous (GB)

Cheyenne Star (IRE) – Barney Roy (GB), by Excelebration (IRE), out of Alina (IRE)

Devil's Imp (IRE) – Space Blues (IRE), by Dubawi (IRE), out of Miss Lucifer (FR)

Divine Dixie (USA) – Lord North (IRE), by Dubawi (IRE), out of Najoum (USA)

Doff The Derby (USA) – Van Gogh (USA), by American Pharoah (USA), out of Imagine (IRE)

Dynatrol (USA) – Donjah (GER), by Teofilo (IRE), out of Dyanamore (USA)

East of The Moon (USA) – Alpine Star (IRE), by Sea The Moon (GER), out of Alpha Lupi (IRE)

Firm Friend (IRE) – Wooded (IRE), by Wootton Bassett (GB), out of Frida La Blonde (FR)

Gleam of Light (IRE) – Love (IRE), by Galileo (IRE), out of Pikaboo (GB)

Gonfalon (GB) – Glen Shiel (GB), by Pivotal (GB), out of Gonfilia (GER)

Great Hope (IRE) – Subjectivist (GB), by Teofilo (IRE), out of Reckoning (IRE)

Great Joy (IRE) – Supremacy (IRE), by Mehmas (IRE), out of Triggers Broom (IRE)

Historian (IRE) – Victor Ludorum (GB), by Shamardal (USA), out of Antiquities (GB)

Intrigued (GB) – Galileo Chrome (IRE), by Australia (GB), out of Curious Mind (GB)

Intriguing Glimpse (GB) – Oxted (GB), by Mayson (GB), out of Charlotte Rosina (GB)

Iora (GER) – In Swoop (IRE), by Adlerflug (GER), out of Iota (GER)

Joanna (IRE) – Tawkeel (GB), by Teofilo (IRE), out of Rafaadah (GB)

Kangra Valley (GB) – Dream of Dreams (IRE), by Dream Ahead (USA), out of Vasilia (GB)

Kasora (IRE) – Fancy Blue (IRE), by Deep Impact (JPN), out of Chenchikova (IRE)

Lady Angola (USA) – Circus Maximus (IRE), by Galileo (IRE), out of Duntle (IRE)

Lady Dominatrix (IRE) – Campanelle (IRE), by Kodiac (GB), out of Janina (GB)

Lagrion (USA) – Serpentine (IRE), by Galileo (IRE), out of Remember When (IRE)
Lagrion (USA) – Shale (IRE), by Galileo (IRE), out of Homecoming Queen (IRE)

Machaera (GB) – Dream And Do (IRE), by Siyouni (FR), out of Venetias Dream (IRE)

Miss U Fran (USA) – Peaceful (IRE), by Galileo (IRE), out of Missvinski (USA)

Monbijou (GER) – Miss Yoda (GER), by Sea The Stars (IRE), out of Monami (GER)

Mount Elbrus (GB) – Pinatubo (IRE), by Shamardal (USA), out of Lava Flow (IRE)

My Renee (USA) – Twilight Payment (IRE), by Teofilo (IRE), out of Dream On Buddy (IRE)

Nasaieb (IRE) – Alcohol Free (IRE), by No Nay Never (USA), out of Plying (USA)

Night Frolic (GB) – Palace Pier (GB), by Kingman (GB), out of
Beach Frolic (GB)

Northern Naiad (FR) – Way To Paris (GB), by Champs Elysees
(GB), out of Grey Way (USA)

Ocean Grove (IRE) – Glass Slippers (GB), by Dream Ahead
(USA), out of Night Gypsy (GB)

Pasca (GER) – Princess Zoe (GER), by Jukebox Jury (IRE), out
of Palace Princess (GER)

Plaintiff (USA) – Gear Up (IRE), by Teofilo (IRE), out of
Gearanai (USA)

Plante Rare (IRE) – Persian King (IRE), by Kingman (GB), out
of Pretty Please (IRE)

Portelet (GB) – Battaash (IRE), by Dark Angel (IRE), out of
Anna Law (IRE)

Poughkeepsie (IRE) – Stradivarius (IRE), by Sea The Stars
(IRE), out of Private Life (FR)

Premiere Creation (FR) – Sottsass (FR), by Siyouni (FR), out of
Starlet's Sister (IRE)

Premiere Cuvee – Champers Elysees (IRE), by Elzaam (AUS),
out of La Cuvee (GB)

Reprise (GB) – The Revenant (GB), by Dubawi (IRE), out of
Hazel Lavery (IRE)

River Saint (USA) – Golden Horde (IRE), by Lethal Force
(IRE), out of Entreat (GB)

Roo (GB) – Mohaather (GB), by Showcasing (GB), out of
Roodeye (GB)

Rose of Jericho (USA) – Even So (IRE), by Camelot (GB), out
of Breeze Hill (IRE)

Saganeca (USA) – Mogul (GB), by Galileo (IRE), out of Shastye
(IRE)

Satwa Queen (FR) – Lucky Vega (IRE), by Lope de Vega (IRE),
out of Queen of Carthage (USA)

Sea Island (FR) – Sealiway (FR), by Galiway (GB), out of Kensea
(FR)

Sharakawa (IRE) – Watch Me (FR), by Olympic Glory (IRE),
out of Watchful (IRE)

Siamsa (USA) – Mac Swiney (IRE), by New Approach (IRE),
out of Halla Na Saoire (IRE)

Silver Star (GB) – Siskin (USA), by First Defence (USA), out of
Bird Flown (GB)

Smoken Rosa (USA) – Tiger Tanaka (IRE), by Clodovil (IRE),
out of Miss Phillyjinks (IRE)

Spa (GB) – Hello Youmzain (FR), by Kodiac (GB), out of
Spasha (GB)

Starine (FR) – Order of Australia (IRE), by Australia (GB), out
of Senta's Dream (GB)

Starstone (GB) – Nazeef (GB), by Invincible Spirit (IRE), out of
Handassa (GB)

Suivez (FR) – Sunny Queen (GER), by Camelot (GB), out of
Suivi (GER)

Superstar Leo (IRE) – One Master (GB), by Fastnet Rock
(AUS), out of Enticing (IRE)

Tarakala (IRE) – Tarnawa (IRE), by Shamardal (USA), out of
Tarana (IRE)

Thamarat (GB) – Santiago (IRE), by Authorized (IRE), out of
Wadyhatta (GB)

Trust In Luck (IRE) – Thunder Moon (IRE), by Zoffany (IRE),
out of Small Sacrifice (IRE)

Trusted Partner (USA) – Search For A Song (IRE), by Galileo
(IRE), out of Polished Gem (IRE)

Tucana (GER) – Torquator Tasso (GER), by Adlerflug (GER),
out of Tijuana (GER)

Witch of Fife (USA) – St Mark's Basilica (FR), by Siyouni (FR),
out of Cabaret (IRE)

GROUP 1 WINNERS OF 2020
BY THIRD DAM

Al Ishq (FR) – Santiago (IRE), by Authorized (IRE), out of
Wadyhatta (GB), out of Thamarat (GB)

Allwaki (USA) – Sottsass (FR), by Siyouni (FR), out of Starlet's
Sister (IRE), out of Premiere Creation (FR)

Amoura (USA) – Mac Swiney (IRE), by New Approach (IRE),
out of Halla Na Saoire (IRE), out of Siamsa (USA)

Aspiration (IRE) – Subjectivist (GB), by Teofilo (IRE), out of
Reckoning (IRE), out of Great Hope (IRE)

Atyaaf (USA) – Alcohol Free (IRE), by No Nay Never (USA),
out of Plying (USA), out of Nasaieb (IRE)

Benguela (USA) – Circus Maximus (IRE), by Galileo (IRE), out
of Duntle (IRE), out of Lady Angola (USA)

Bourbon Girl – Enable (GB), by Nathaniel (IRE), out of
Concentric (GB), out of Apogee (GB)

Careless Aly (USA) – Peaceful (IRE), by Galileo (IRE), out of
Missvinski (USA), out of Miss U Fran (USA)

Charita (IRE) – Barney Roy (GB), by Excelebration (IRE), out
of Alina (IRE), out of Cheyenne Star (IRE)

Cheese Soup (USA) – Supremacy (IRE), by Mehmas (IRE), out
of Triggers Broom (IRE), out of Great Joy (IRE)

Chere Amie (FR) – Wooded (IRE), by Wootton Bassett (GB),
out of Frida La Blonde (FR), out of Firm Friend (IRE)

Clicquot – Champers Elysees (IRE), by Elzaam (AUS), out of La
Cuvee (GB), out of Premiere Cuvee

Coast Patrol (USA) – Donjah (GER), by Teofilo (IRE), out of Dyanamore (USA), out of Dynatrol (USA)

Council Rock – One Master (GB), by Fastnet Rock (AUS), out of Enticing (IRE), out of Superstar Leo (IRE)

Dispute (USA) – Gear Up (IRE), by Teofilo (IRE), out of Gearanai (USA), out of Plaintiff (USA)

El Jazirah (GB) – Pinatubo (IRE), by Shamardal (USA), out of Lava Flow (IRE), out of Mount Elbrus (GB)

Equatoriale (FR) – Sealiway (FR), by Galiway (GB), out of Kensea (FR), out of Sea Island (FR)

Fade (GB) – Wonderful Tonight (FR), by Le Havre (IRE), out of Salvation (GB), out of Birdie (GB)

Fascinating Trick (USA) – Way To Paris (GB), by Champs Elysees (GB), out of Grey Way (USA), out of Northern Naiad (FR)

Fife (IRE) – St Mark's Basilica (FR), by Siyouni (FR), out of Cabaret (IRE), out of Witch of Fife (USA)

Gigawatt (FR) – Audarya (FR), by Wootton Bassett (GB), out of Green Bananas (FR), out of Anabaa Republic (FR)

Gold Runner – Love (IRE), by Galileo (IRE), out of Pikaboo (GB), out of Gleam of Light (IRE)

Grimpola (GER) – Glen Shiel (GB), by Pivotal (GB), out of Gonfilia (GER), out of Gonfalon (GB)

Grisonnante (FR) – Order of Australia (IRE), by Australia (GB), out of Senta's Dream (GB), out of Starine (FR)

Haglette – Mogul (GB), by Galileo (IRE), out of Shastye (IRE), out of Saganeca (USA)

Hail Atlantis (USA) – Lord North (IRE), by Dubawi (IRE), out of Najoum (USA), out of Divine Dixie (USA)

Helen Street – Victor Ludorum (GB), by Shamardal (USA), out of Antiquities (GB), out of Historian (IRE)

High Spirited – Space Blues (IRE), by Dubawi (IRE), out of Miss Lucifer (FR), out of Devil's Imp (IRE)

Imagining (USA) – Golden Horde (IRE), by Lethal Force (IRE), out of Entreat (GB), out of River Saint (USA)

Incitation (GER) – In Swoop (IRE), by Adlerflug (GER), out of Iota (GER), out of Iora (GER)

Ittisaal – Kameko (USA), by Kitten's Joy (USA), out of Sweeter Still (IRE), out of Beltisaal (FR)

Kozana – Fancy Blue (IRE), by Deep Impact (JPN), out of Chenchikova (IRE), out of Kasora (IRE)

Last Second (IRE) – Galileo Chrome (IRE), by Australia (GB), out of Curious Mind (GB), out of Intrigued (GB)

Leyete Gulf (IRE) – Glass Slippers (GB), by Dream Ahead (USA), out of Night Gypsy (GB), out of Ocean Grove (IRE)

Lulu Mon Amour (USA) – Addeybb (IRE), by Pivotal (GB), out of Bush Cat (USA), out of Arbusha (USA)

Margarethen – Van Gogh (USA), by American Pharoah (USA), out of Imagine (IRE), out of Doff The Derby (USA)

Mayenne (USA) – Twilight Payment (IRE), by Teofilo (IRE), out of Dream On Buddy (IRE), out of My Renee (USA)

Meerdunung (GDR) – Miss Yoda (GER), by Sea The Stars (IRE), out of Monami (GER), out of Monbijou (GER)

Miesque (USA) – Alpine Star (IRE), by Sea The Moon (GER), out of Alpha Lupi (IRE), out of East of The Moon (USA)

Miss d'Ouilly (FR) – Palace Pier (GB), by Kingman (GB), out of Beach Frolic (GB), out of Night Frolic (GB)

Monroe (USA) – Siskin (USA), by First Defence (USA), out of Bird Flown (GB), out of Silver Star (GB)

Noirmant – Battaash (IRE), by Dark Angel (IRE), out of Anna Law (IRE), out of Portelet (GB)

Palmas (GER) – Princess Zoe (GER), by Jukebox Jury (IRE), out of Palace Princess (GER), out of Pasca (GER)

Palmeraie (USA) – Persian King (IRE), by Kingman (GB), out of Pretty Please (IRE), out of Plante Rare (IRE)

Pawneese – Stradivarius (IRE), by Sea The Stars (IRE), out Private Life (FR), out of Poughkeepsie (IRE)

Rafha – Mishriff (IRE), by Make Believe (GB), out of Contradict (GB), out of Acts of Grace (USA)

Rahaam (USA) – Magical (IRE), by Galileo (IRE), out of Halfway To Heaven (IRE), out of Cassandra Go (IRE)

Rapid Repeat (IRE) – The Revenant (GB), by Dubawi (IRE), out of Hazel Lavery (IRE), out of Reprise (GB)

Ridge Pool (IRE) – Ghaiyyath (IRE), by Dubawi (IRE), out of Nightime (IRE), out of Caumshinaun (IRE)

Robinia (USA) – Pretty Gorgeous (FR), by Lawman (FR), out of Lady Gorgeous (GB), out of Cayman Sunset (IRE)

Rose Red (USA) – Even So (IRE), by Camelot (GB), out of Breeze Hill (IRE), out of Rose of Jericho (USA)

Roses In The Snow (IRE) – Tiger Tanaka (IRE), by Clodovil (IRE), out of Miss Phillyjinks (IRE), out of Smoken Rosa (USA)

Running Glimpse (IRE) – Oxted (GB), by Mayson (GB), out of Charlotte Rosina (GB), out of Intriguing Glimpse (GB)

Sandy Island – Hello Youmzain (FR), by Kodiac (GB), out of Spasha (GB), out of Spa (GB)

Sea Symphony – Sunny Queen (GER), by Camelot (GB), out of Suivi (GER), out of Suivez (FR)

Secrete Marina (IRE) – Tawkeel (GB), by Teofilo (IRE), out of Rafaadah (GB), out of Joanna (IRE)

Shall We Run (GB) – Mohaather (GB), by Showcasing (GB), out of Roodeye (GB), by Roo (GB)

Sharaya (USA) – Watch Me (FR), by Olympic Glory (IRE), out of Watchful (IRE), out of Sharakawa (IRE)

Somfas (USA) – Dream And Do (IRE), by Siyouni (FR), out of Venetias Dream (IRE), out of Machaera (GB)

Spout House (IRE) – Campanelle (IRE), by Kodiac (GB), out of Janina (GB), out of Lady Dominatrix (IRE)

Star (GB) – Nazeef (GB), by Invincible Spirit (IRE), out of Handassa (GB), out of Starstone (GB)

Talking Picture (USA) – Search For A Song (IRE), by Galileo (IRE), out of Polished Gem (IRE), out of Trusted Partner (USA)

Tarakana (USA) – Tarnawa (IRE), by Shamardal (USA), out of Tarana (IRE), out of Tarakala (IRE)

Thorner Lane – Dream of Dreams (IRE), by Dream Ahead (USA), out of Vasilia (GB), out of Kangra Valley (GB)

Tolga (USA) – Lucky Vega (IRE), by Lope de Vega (IRE), out of Queen of Carthage (USA), out of Satwa Queen (FR)

Trusted Partner (USA) – Thunder Moon (IRE), by Zoffany (IRE), out of Small Sacrifice (IRE), out of Trust In Luck (IRE)

Turbaine (USA) – Torquator Tasso (GER), by Adlerflug (GER), out of Tijuana (GER), out of Tucana (GER)

Wrap It Up – Serpentine (IRE), by Galileo (IRE), out of Remember When (IRE), out of Lagrion (USA)
Wrap It Up – Shale (IRE), by Galileo (IRE), out of Homecoming Queen (IRE), out of Lagrion (USA)

GROUP 1 WINNERS OF 2020
BY BREEDER

Al Asayl Bloodstock Ltd – The Revenant (GB)

Ali Meddeb, Mohamed – Galileo Chrome (IRE)

Anahita Stables – Sunny Queen (GER)

Ballyphilip Stud – Battaash (IRE)

Barronstown Stud – Van Gogh (USA)

Bearstone Stud Ltd – Glass Slippers (GB)

Bolger, J S – Gear Up (IRE)
Bolger, J S – Mac Swiney (IRE)
Bolger, J S – Twilight Payment (IRE)

Bowen, Karl – Champers Elysees (IRE)

Calumet Farm – Kameko (USA)

Churchtown House Stud – Alcohol Free (IRE)

Coolmore – Fancy Blue (IRE)
Coolmore – Love (IRE)
Coolmore – Peaceful (IRE)
Coolmore – Serpentine (IRE)
Coolmore – Shale (IRE)

Cn Farm Ltd – Golden Horde (IRE)

Darley – Glen Shiel (GB)

Dayton Investments (Breeding) Ltd – Persian King (IRE)

Ecurie Des Monceaux – Sottsass (FR)

Ecurie Haras Du Cadran, E Ciampi, SAS I.E.I., Ecurie La Boetie
    – Pretty Gorgeous (FR)

Ecurie Taos – Wonderful Tonight (FR)

Eliza Park International Pty Ltd – Barney Roy (GB)

Flaxman Stables Ireland Ltd – Circus Maximus (IRE)

Gestüt Etzean – Miss Yoda (GER)

Gestüt Hony-Hof – Princess Zoe (GER)

Gestüt Karlshof – Donjah (GER)

Gestüt Zur Küste Ag – Wooded (IRE)

Godolphin – Lord North (IRE)
Godolphin – Pinatubo (IRE)
Godolphin – Space Blues (IRE)
Godolphin – Victor Ludorum (GB)

Grundy Bloodstock Srl – Way To Paris (GB)

Guy Pariente Holding – Sealiway (FR)

Haras D'Ecouves – Audarya (FR)

Haras Du Logis Saint Germain – Dream And Do (IRE)

Highclere Stud and Floors Farming – Palace Pier (GB)

His Highness The Aga Khan's Studs SC – Tarnawa (IRE)

Homecroft Wealth Racing – Oxted (GB)

Johnson Houghton, Mrs R F – Mohaather (GB)

Juddmonte Farms Ltd – Enable (GB)
Juddmonte Farms Inc – Siskin (USA)

Kangyu International Racing – Supremacy (IRE)

Kellsgrange Stud – Tiger Tanaka (IRE)

Kilcarn Stud – Lucky Vega (IRE)

Lael Stables – One Master (GB)

Lynch Bages Ltd – Even So (IRE)
Lynch Bages Ltd – Santiago (IRE)

Mascalls Stud – Subjectivist (GB)

Moyglare Stud Farm Ltd – Search For A Song (IRE)

Nawara Stud Ltd – Mishriff (IRE)

Newsells Park Stud – Mogul (GB)

Niarchos Family – Alpine Star (IRE)

Nielsen, Bjorn – Stradivarius (IRE)

Orpendale, Chelston & Wynatt – Magical (IRE)

Prostock Ltd – Dream of Dreams (IRE)

Rabbah Bloodstock Ltd – Addeybb (IRE)
Rabbah Bloodstock Ltd – Hello Youmzain (FR)

Scarborough, Robert – St Mark's Basilica (FR)

Shadwell Estate Company Ltd – Nazeef (GB)
Shadwell Estate Company Ltd – Tawkeel (GB)

Springbank Way Stud – Ghaiyyath (IRE)

Stall Ullmann – In Swoop (IRE)

Tally-Ho Stud – Campanelle (IRE)

Tamagni, Mme A & Cocheese Bloodstock Anstalt – Watch Me (FR)

Vandeberg, Paul H – Torquator Tasso (GER)

Whisperview Trading Ltd – Order of Australia (IRE)
Whisperview Trading Ltd – Thunder Moon (IRE)

GROUP 1 WINNERS OF 2020
BY OWNER

Abdullah, Khalid – Enable (GB)
Abdullah, Khalid – Siskin (USA)

Aga Khan, H H – Tarnawa (IRE)

Al Asayl France – The Revenant (GB)

Al Maktoum, Sheikh Ahmed – Addeybb (IRE)

Al Maktoum, Hamdan – Battaash (IRE)
Al Maktoum, Hamdan – Mohaather (GB)
Al Maktoum, Hamdan – Nazeef (GB)
Al Maktoum, Hamdan – Tawkeel (GB)

Al Shaqab Racing – Wooded (IRE)

AlMohamediya Racing – Golden Horde (IRE)

Bearstone Stud Ltd – Glass Slippers (GB)

Bin Mohammed Al Maktoum, Sheikh Hamdan – Palace Pier
   (GB)

Bolger, Mrs J S – Mac Swiney (IRE)

Castro Megias, Miguel – Tiger Tanaka (IRE)

Cayton Park Stud Ltd – Sunny Queen (GER)

Darius Racing – Donjah (GER)

Faisal, Prince A A – Mishriff (IRE)

Ferrario, Paolo – Way To Paris (GB)

Fitzwilliam Racing – Champers Elysees (IRE)

Flaxman Stables, Mrs J Magnier, Michael Tabor & Derrick Smith
    – Circus Maximus (IRE)

Galileo Chrome Partnership – Galileo Chrome (IRE)

Gestüt Auenquelle – Torquator Tasso (GER)

Gestüt Schlenderhan – In Swoop (IRE)

Goddard, J – Supremacy (IRE)

Godolphin – Barney Roy (GB)
Godolphin – Ghaiyyath (IRE)
Godolphin – Pinatubo (IRE)
Godolphin – Space Blues (IRE)
Godolphin SNC – Victor Ludorum (GB)

Godolphin SNC & Ballymore Thoroughbred Ltd – Persian King
    (IRE)

Hambleton Racing XXXVI & Partner – Glen Shiel (GB)

Haras d'Etreham & Cambridge Stud – Hello Youmzain (FR)

Haras du Logis Saint Germain – Dream And Do (IRE)

HH Sheikh Zayed bin Mohammed Racing – Lord North (IRE)

Kehoe, Patrick F & Mrs P Crampton – Princess Zoe (GER)

Lael Stables – One Master (GB)

Le Haras De La Gousserie & Guy Pariente – Sealiway (FR)

Magnier, Mrs J & Mrs Paul Shanahan – Even So (IRE)

Tabor, Michael, Derrick Smith & Mrs J Magnier – Peaceful
    (IRE)
Tabor, Michael, Derrick Smith & Mrs J Magnier – Santiago
    (IRE)

Tabor, Michael, Derrick Smith, Mrs J Magnier & Mrs David
    Nagle – Van Gogh (USA)

Tamagni-Badmer, Alexander & Mme Regula Vannod – Watch
    Me (FR)

Teme Valley 2 – Gear Up (IRE)

Walker, Dr J – Subjectivist (GB)

Westerberg – Miss Yoda (GER)

White Birch Farm – Sottsass (FR)

Williams, N C, Mr & Mrs L J Williams, et al – Twilight Payment
    (IRE)

Wright, Christopher – Wonderful Tonight (FR)

Yuesheng, Zhang – Lucky Vega (IRE)

Ireland
Bolger, Jim – Mac Swiney (IRE)

Harrington, Jessica – Alpine Star (IRE)
Harrington, Jessica – Lucky Vega (IRE)

Lyons, Ger – Even So (IRE)
Lyons, Ger – Siskin (USA)

Mullins, Tony – Princess Zoe (GER)

Murtagh, Johnny – Champers Elysees (IRE)

O'Brien, Aidan – Circus Maximus (IRE)
O'Brien, Aidan – Love (IRE)
O'Brien, Aidan – Magical (IRE)
O'Brien, Aidan – Mogul (GB)
O'Brien, Aidan – Order of Australia (IRE)
O'Brien, Aidan – Peaceful (IRE)
O'Brien, Aidan – Santiago (IRE)
O'Brien, Aidan – Serpentine (IRE)
O'Brien, Aidan – St Mark's Basilica (FR)
O'Brien, Aidan – Van Gogh (USA)

O'Brien, Donnacha – Fancy Blue (IRE)
O'Brien, Donnacha – Shale (IRE)

O'Brien, Joseph – Galileo Chrome (IRE)
O'Brien, Joseph – Pretty Gorgeous (FR)
O'Brien, Joseph – Thunder Moon (IRE)
O'Brien, Joseph – Twilight Payment (IRE)

Weld, Dermot – Search For A Song (IRE)
Weld, Dermot – Tarnawa (IRE)

Great Britain
Appleby, Charlie – Barney Roy (GB)
Appleby, Charlie – Ghaiyyath (IRE)
Appleby, Charlie – Pinatubo (IRE)
Appleby, Charlie – Space Blues (IRE)

Balding, Andrew – Alcohol Free (IRE)
Balding, Andrew – Kameko (USA)

Cox, Clive – Golden Horde (IRE)
Cox, Clive – Supremacy (IRE)

Fanshawe, James – Audarya (FR)

Gosden, John – Enable (GB)
Gosden, John – Lord North (IRE)
Gosden, John – Mishriff (IRE)
Gosden, John – Miss Yoda (GER)
Gosden, John – Nazeef (GB)
Gosden, John – Palace Pier (GB)
Gosden, John – Stradivarius (IRE)

Haggas, William – Addeybb (IRE)
Haggas, William – One Master (GB)

Hills, Charles – Battaash (IRE)

Johnston, Mark – Gear Up (IRE)
Johnston, Mark – Subjectivist (GB)

Menuisier, David – Wonderful Tonight (FR)

Ryan, Kevin – Glass Slippers (GB)
Ryan, Kevin – Hello Youmzain (FR)

Stoute, Sir Michael – Dream of Dreams (IRE)

Teal, Roger – Oxted (GB)

Tregoning, Marcus – Mohaather (GB)

Watson, Archie – Glen Shiel (GB)

France
Fabre, André – Persian King (IRE)
Fabre, André – Victor Ludorum (GB)

Graffard, Francis-Henri – In Swoop (IRE)
Graffard, Francis-Henri – The Revenant (GB)
Graffard, Francis-Henri – Watch Me (FR)
Graffard, Francis-Henri – Wooded (IRE)

Marcialis, Andrea – Way To Paris (GB)

Rossi, Charley – Tiger Tanaka (IRE)

Rossi, Frederic – Dream And Do (IRE)
Rossi, Frederic – Sealiway (FR)

Rouget, Jean-Claude – Sottsass (FR)
Rouget, Jean-Claude – Tawkeel (GB)

Germany
Grewe, Henk – Donjah (GER)
Grewe, Henk – Sunny Queen (GER)

Weiss, Marcel – Torquator Tasso (GER)

United States of America
Ward, Wesley – Campanelle (IRE)

GROUP 1 WINNERS OF 2020
BY AUCTIONS
(where relevant; excluding vendor buy-backs)

Ireland
Goffs
Alcohol Free (IRE) – 2018 November Foal Sale – €40,000 –
Vendor: Churchtown House Stud – Purchaser: Littleton Stud
Gear Up (IRE) – 2019 Orby – €52,000 – Vendor:
Redmondstown Stud – Purchaser: Johnston Racing
Ghaiyyath (IRE) – 2015 November Foal Sale – €1,100,000 –
Vendor: The Castlebridge Consignment – Purchaser: John
Ferguson
Lucky Vega (IRE) – 2018 November Foal Sale – €110,000 –
Vendor: Kilcarn Stud – Purchaser: Michael Roy
Lucky Vega (IRE) – 2019 Orby Sale – €175,000 – Vendor:
Baroda Stud – Purchaser: BBA Ireland/Yulong Investments
Twilight Payment (IRE) – 2018 Horses-In-Training – €200,000 –
Vendor: Glebe House Stables – Purchaser: Kerr & Co Ltd,
Agent

Tattersalls Ireland
Champers Elysees (IRE) – 2017 November Flat Sale – €12,500 –
Vendor: Archway Stud from Mantlehill Stud – Purchaser:
Aughamore Stud
Champers Elysees (IRE) – 2018 September Yearlings Part 2 –
€28,000 – Vendor: Aughamore Stud – Purchaser: Johnny
Murtagh
Tiger Tanaka (IRE) – 2019 September Yearlings – €6,500 –
Vendor: Ballyreddin & Kellsgrange Studs – Purchaser:
Pascale Menard

Great Britain
DBS
Barney Roy (IRE) – 2015 Premier Yearling Sale – £70,000 –
Vendor: Castletown Quarry Stud, Ireland – Purchaser: Peter
& Ross Doyle Bloodstock

Goffs UK

Glen Shiel (GB) – 2019 Spring Horses-in-Training – £45,000 –
Vendor: Godolphin – Purchaser: Blandford Bloodstock

Golden Horde (IRE) – 2018 Premier Yearling Sale – £65,000 –
Vendor: Highclere Stud – Purchaser: Clive Cox Racing

Supremacy (IRE) – 2019 Premier Yearling Sale – £65,000 –
Vendor: Owenstown Stud, Ireland – Purchaser: Clive Cox
Racing

Tattersalls

Addeybb (IRE) – 2015 October Book 2 – 200,000gns – Vendor:
Genesis Green Stud – Purchaser: Shadwell Estate Company

Barney Roy (IRE) – 2014 December Foal Sale – 30,000gns –
Vendor: Irish National Stud – Purchaser: A T Bloodstock

Battaash (IRE) – 2015 October Book 2 – 200,000gns – Vendor:
Ballyphilip Stud, Ireland – Purchaser: Shadwell Estate
Company

Campanelle (IRE) – 2019 October Book 1 – 190,000gns –
Vendor: Tally-Ho Stud – Purchaser: Ben McElroy Agent

Dream of Dreams (IRE) – 2014 December Foal Sale –
37,000gns – Vendor: Bumble Mitchell – Purchaser: Mick
Flanagan, Agent

Mogul (GB) – 2018 October Book 1 – 3,400,000gns – Vendor:
Newsells Park Stud Ltd – Purchaser: M V Magnier

Mohaather (GB) – 2017 October Book 2 - 110,000gns – Vendor:
Hillwood Stud – Purchaser: Shadwell Estate Company

Palace Pier (GB) – 2018 October Book 1 – 600,000gns –
Vendor: Highclere Stud – Purchaser John Gosden Racing
LLP

Pretty Gorgeous (FR) – 2019 October Book 1 – 525,000gns –
Vendor: Glenvale Stud, Ireland – Purchaser: Joseph O'Brien

St Mark's Basilica (FR) – 2019 October Book 1 – 1,300,000gns –
Vendor: Norelands Stud, Ireland – Purchaser: M.V. Magnier

Subjectivist (GB) – 2018 October Book 2 – 62,000gns – Vendor:
New England Stud – Purchaser: Mark Johnston Racing

Way To Paris (GB) – 2014 October Book 2 – 50,000gns –
Vendor: Highclere Stud – Purchaser: Ambition Stud
Partnership

France
Arqana

Audarya (FR) – 2017 Deauville October (Yearlings) – €125,000 – Vendor: Capucines – Purchaser: Stroud Coleman Bloodstock Ltd

Pretty Gorgeous (FR) – 2018 December Sale – €55,000 – Vendor: Haras du Cadran – Purchaser: Margaret O'Toole

Sealiway (FR) – 2019 Deauville August (Yearlings) – €62,000 – Vendor: Colleville – Purchaser: Paul Nataf

Sottsass (FR) – 2017 Arqana Deauville August (Yearlings) – €340,000 – Vendor: Monceaux – Purchaser: Oceanic Bloodstock Inc

Wonderful Tonight (FR) – 2018 Deauville August (Yearlings) – €40,000 – Vendor: Coulances Sales – Purchaser: Private Sale

Wooded (IRE) – 2018 Deauville October (Yearlings) – €90,000 – Vendor: Etreham – Purchaser: Al Shaqab Racing

Germany
BBAG

Donjah (GER) – 2017 Baden-Baden September (Yearlings) – €100,000 – Vendor: Gestüt Karlshof – Purchaser: HFTB Racing Agency

Miss Yoda (GER) – 2018 Baden-Baden September (Yearlings) – €280,000 – Vendor: Gestüt Etzean – Purchaser: Blandford Bloodstock UK

Sunny Queen (GER) – 2018 Baden-Baden September (Yearlings) – €35,000 – Vendor: Gestüt Ohlerweiherhof (Agent) – Purchaser: Stefan Hahne

Torquator Tasso (GER) – 2018 Baden-Baden October (Yearlings) – €24,000 – Vendor: Gestüt Erftmühle – Purchaser: Gestüt Auenquelle

USA
Keeneland

Kameko (USA) – 2018 September Yearling Sale – $90,000 – Vendor: Paramount Sales – Purchaser: David Redvers

GROUP 1 WINNERS OF 2020
BY MONTH OF BIRTH

January
20 – Tiger Tanaka (IRE)
22 – Peaceful (IRE)
29 – Barney Roy (GB)
29 – Tawkeel (GB)

February
02 – Fancy Blue (IRE)
07 – Dream of Dreams (IRE)
08 – Circus Maximus (IRE)
09 – Addeybb (IRE)
09 – Lord North (IRE)
09 – Tarnawa (IRE)
10 – Battaash (IRE)
11 – Golden Horde (IRE)
11 – Van Gogh (USA)
12 – Enable (GB)
12 – Space Blues (IRE)
18 – Order of Australia (IRE)
18 – Persian King (IRE)
19 – Dream And Do (IRE)
23 – Mac Swiney (IRE)
24 – Pretty Gorgeous (FR)
24 – Sealiway (FR)
24 – Sunny Queen (GER)
25 – Siskin (USA)
27 – Lucky Vega (IRE)
28 – Stradivarius (IRE)

March
06 – Oxted (GB)
07 – Donjah (GER)
07 – In Swoop (IRE)
07 – Wonderful Tonight (FR)
08 – Gear Up (IRE)
11 – Pinatubo (IRE)

11 – Princess Zoe (GER)
11 – Santiago (IRE)
18 – St Mark's Basilica (FR)
18 – Watch Me (FR)
20 – Champers Elysees (IRE)
20 – Miss Yoda (GER)
20 – Palace Pier (GB)
20 – Serpentine (IRE)
23 – Alcohol Free (IRE)
24 – Alpine Star (IRE)
24 – Sottsass (FR)
25 – Glass Slippers (GB)
26 – Shale (IRE)
27 – Wooded (IRE)
28 – Supremacy (IRE)
30 – Search For A Song (IRE)
30 – Subjectivist (GB)

April
01 – Mishriff (IRE)
01 – One Master (GB)
03 – Mogul (GB)
03 – Victor Ludorum (GB)
07 – Kameko (USA)
13 – Love (IRE)
13 – Nazeef (GB)
13 – Way To Paris (GB)
16 – Campanelle (IRE)
19 – Ghaiyyath (IRE)
20 – The Revenant (GB)
21 – Audarya (FR)
21 – Torquator Tasso (GER)
22 – Hello Youmzain (FR)
25 – Even So (IRE)
26 – Mohaather (GB)
28 – Galileo Chrome (IRE)

May
01 – Thunder Moon (IRE)
06 – Twilight Payment (IRE)
07 – Glen Shiel (GB)
18 – Magical (IRE)

GROUP 1 WINNERS OF 2020
BY DATE OF EARLIEST CAREER WIN

January

03 – Tawkeel (GB) – 1m newcomers on standard at Pau, France
– 3yo

March

20 – Way To Paris (GB) – 1m2f maiden at San Siro, Italy – 3yo

April

03 – Tarnawa (IRE) – 10f maiden on good-to-yielding at
Leopardstown, Ireland – 3yo

28 – Oxted (GB) – 7f novice on good-to-firm at Salisbury,
England – 3yo

May

10 – Pinatubo (IRE) – 6f novice on standard at Wolverhampton,
England – 2yo

11 – Siskin (USA) – 6f conditions on good at Naas, Ireland –
2yo

12 – Sealiway (FR) – 6f newcomers on soft at Saint-Cloud,
France – 2yo

15 – In Swoop (IRE) – 1m3f maiden on soft at Lyon Parilly,
France – 3yo

18 – Battaash (IRE) – 5f novice on good at Bath, England – 2yo

21 – Sunny Queen (GER) – 1m2f listed on good at Hanover,
Germany – 3yo

27 – Dream of Dreams (IRE) – 6f novice on good-to-soft at
Haydock, England – 2yo

30 – Search For A Song (IRE) – 10f maiden on good-to-firm at
Fairyhouse, Ireland – 3yo

31 – Campanelle (IRE) – 5f maiden special weight on firm at
Gulfstream Park, USA – 2yo

June

03 – Golden Horde (IRE) – 6f maiden on good at Newbury,
England – 2yo

04 – Tiger Tanaka (IRE) – 6f claimer on heavy at Lyon Parilly, France – 2yo

08 – Lucky Vega (IRE) – 6f maiden on good-to-firm at Naas, Ireland – 2yo

12 – Galileo Chrome (IRE) – 10f maiden on good-to-firm at Curragh, Ireland – 3yo

14 – Addeybb (IRE) – 1m maiden on good-to-soft at Haydock, England – 3yo

14 – Torquator Tasso (GER) – 11f conditions on good at Cologne, Germany – 3yo

21 – Audarya (FR) – 10f novice on good-to-soft at Redcar, England – 3yo

27 – Nazeef (GB) – 7f maiden on good at Newmarket (July), England – 3yo

27 – Serpentine (IRE) – 10f maiden on good at Curragh, Ireland – 3yo

July

02 – Pretty Gorgeous (FR) – 1m maiden at Bellewstown, Ireland – 2yo

05 – Subjectivist (GB) – 7f novice on standard at Chelmsford, England – 2yo

06 – Supremacy (IRE) – 6f maiden on good-to-firm at Windsor, England – 2yo

08 – Shale (IRE) – 1m maiden on soft-to-heavy at Gowran Park, Ireland – 2yo

11 – Love (IRE) – 7f maiden on good-to-firm at Leopardstown, Ireland – 2yo

16 – Twilight Payment (IRE) – 1m4f maiden on good at Curragh, Ireland – 3yo

18 – Mac Swiney (IRE) – 7f maiden on yielding at Curragh, Ireland – 2yo

25 – Gear Up (IRE) – 7f novice auction at York, England – 2yo

25 – Kameko (USA) – 7f maiden on good at Sandown, England – 2yo

August

02 – Alpine Star (IRE) – 7f maiden on good at Galway, Ireland – 2yo

05 – Miss Yoda (GER) – 1m maiden on slow-to-standard at Kempton, England – 2yo

08 – Magical (IRE) – 1m maiden on good-to-yielding at Cork, Ireland – 2yo

09 – Thunder Moon (IRE) – 7f maiden on good-to-yielding at Curragh, Ireland – 2yo

13 – Wooded (IRE) – 7f maiden on good-to-soft at Deauville, France – 2yo

15 – Alcohol Free (IRE) – 6f novice on good-to-soft at Newbury, England – 2yo

16 – Glass Slippers (GB) – 5f novice on good-to-firm at Beverley, England – 2yo

22 – Hello Youmzain (FR) – 6f maiden on good-to-soft at Carlisle, England – 2yo

22 – St Mark's Basilica (FR) – 6f maiden on soft at Curragh, Ireland – 2yo

30 – Mogul (GB) – 1m maiden on good-to-yielding at Curragh, Ireland – 2yo

30 – Palace Pier (GB) – 7f maiden on good-to-firm at Sandown, England – 2yo

September

01 – Persian King (IRE) – 1m maiden on good-to-soft at Chantilly, France – 2yo

01 – Victor Ludorum (GB) – 1m newcomers on good at ParisLongchamp, France – 2yo

07 – The Revenant (GB) – 1m novice on good-to-soft at Haydock, England – 2yo

09 – Dream And Do (IRE) – 1m maiden on good-to-firm at Marseille Borely, France – 2yo

09 – Princess Zoe (GER) – 10f on soft at Munich, Germany – 3yo

12 – Santiago (IRE) – 1m maiden on soft at Listowel, Ireland – 2yo

18 – Fancy Blue (IRE) – 7f maiden on good at Naas, Ireland – 2yo

18 – Order of Australia (IRE) – 1m2f150y conditions on standard at Dundalk, Ireland – 3yo

19 – One Master (GB) – 6f maiden on soft at Yarmouth, England – 2yo

22 – Circus Maximus (IRE) – 1m maiden on heavy at Gowran Park, Ireland – 2yo

24 – Barney Roy (GB) – 1m maiden on good at Haydock, England – 2yo

26 – Even So (IRE) – 1m maiden on soft at Gowran Park, Ireland – 2yo

27 – Van Gogh (USA) – 7f maiden on yielding at Curragh, Ireland – 2yo

28 – Ghaiyyath (IRE) – 1m maiden on good-to-soft at Newmarket, England – 2yo

29 – Champers Elysees (IRE) – 6f auction race on heavy at Curragh, Ireland – 2yo

October

10 – Peaceful (IRE) – 1m maiden on yielding-to-soft at Thurles, Ireland – 2yo

14 – Donjah (GER) – 1m maiden on good at Cologne, Germany – 2yo

18 – Mohaather (GB) – 6f novice on good at Nottingham, England – 2yo

19 – Lord North (IRE) – 1m novice on soft at Redcar, England – 2yo

26 – Sottsass (FR) – 1m maiden on soft at Clairefontaine, France – 2yo

November

06 – Mishriff (IRE) – 1m 75y maiden on heavy at Nottingham, England – 2yo

07 – Space Blues (IRE) – 1m 75y maiden on good-to-soft at Nottingham, England – 2yo

07 – Stradivarius (IRE) – 1m maiden on standard at Newcastle, England – 2yo

10 – Watch Me (FR) – 1m listed on heavy at Toulouse, France – 2yo

12 – Glen Shiel (GB) – 7f 110y newcomers on heavy at Saint-Cloud, France – 2yo

22 – Wonderful Tonight (FR) – 10f maiden on heavy at Saint-Cloud, France – 2yo

28 – Enable (GB) – 1m maiden on standard at Newcastle, England – 2yo

GROUP 1 WINNERS OF 2020
BY DISTANCE OF THE GROUP 1 WINS

5f
Battaash (IRE)
Glass Slippers (GB)
Wooded (IRE)

6f
Alcohol Free (IRE)
Campanelle (IRE)
Dream of Dreams (IRE)
Glen Shiel (GB)
Golden Horde (IRE)
Hello Youmzain (FR)
Lucky Vega (IRE)
Oxted (GB)
Supremacy (IRE)

6.5f
Space Blues (IRE)

7f
One Master (GB)
Pinatubo (IRE)
Sealiway (FR)
Shale (IRE)
St Mark's Basilica (FR)
Thunder Moon (IRE)

1m
Alpine Star (IRE)
Champers Elysees (IRE)
Circus Maximus (IRE)
Dream And Do (IRE)
Kameko (USA)
Love (IRE)
Mac Swiney (IRE)

Mohaather (GB)
Nazeef (GB)
Order of Australia (IRE)
Palace Pier (GB)
Peaceful (IRE)
Persian King (IRE)
Pretty Gorgeous (FR)
Siskin (USA)
The Revenant (GB)
Tiger Tanaka (IRE)
Van Gogh (USA)
Victor Ludorum (GB)
Watch Me (FR)

1m1f
Barney Roy (GB)
Persian King (IRE)

1m1.5f
Audarya (FR)

1m2f
Addeybb (IRE)
Audarya (FR)
Barney Roy (GB)
Fancy Blue (IRE)
Gear Up (IRE)
Ghaiyyath (IRE)
Lord North (IRE)
Magical (IRE)
Tarnawa (IRE)
Tawkeel (GB)

1m 2.25f
Ghaiyyath (IRE)

1m2.5f
Fancy Blue (IRE)
Mishriff (IRE)
Sottsass (FR)

1m3f
Miss Yoda (GER)

1m4f
Barney Roy (GB)
Donjah (GER)
Enable (GB)
Even So (IRE)
Ghaiyyath (IRE)
In Swoop (IRE)
Love (IRE)
Mogul (GB)
Santiago (IRE)
Serpentine (IRE)
Sottsass (FR)
Sunny Queen (GER)

Tarnawa (IRE)
Torquator Tasso (GER)
Way To Paris (GB)

1m6f
Search For A Song (IRE)
Wonderful Tonight (FR)

1m6.5f
Galileo Chrome (IRE)

1m7.5f
Subjectivist (GB)

2m
Stradivarius (IRE)
Twilight Payment (IRE)

2m4f
Princess Zoe (GER)
Stradivarius (IRE)

**GROUP 1 WINNERS OF 2020
BY GOING DESCRIPTION FOR THE
GROUP 1 WINS**

TURF
Firm
Audarya (FR)
Order of Australia (IRE)

Good-to-firm
Enable (GB)
Ghaiyyath (IRE)
Kameko (USA)
Peaceful (IRE)
Siskin (USA)

Good
Alcohol Free (IRE)
Barney Roy (GB)
Battaash (IRE)
Champers Elysees (IRE)
Fancy Blue (IRE)
Galileo Chrome (IRE)
Ghaiyyath (IRE)
Glass Slippers (GB)
Hello Youmzain (FR)
Lord North (IRE)
Love (IRE)
Magical (IRE)
Miss Yoda (GER)
Mogul (GB)
Mohaather (GB)
Oxted (GB)
Persian King (IRE)
Pinatubo (IRE)
Santiago (IRE)
Search For A Song (IRE)
Serpentine (IRE)

Shale (IRE)
Space Blues (IRE)
Stradivarius (IRE)
Supremacy (IRE)
Tarnawa (IRE)
Thunder Moon (IRE)
Twilight Payment (IRE)
Watch Me (FR)
Way To Paris (GB)

Good-to-yielding
Lucky Vega (IRE)

Good-to-soft
Addeybb (IRE)
Alpine Star (IRE)
Barney Roy (GB)
Battaash (IRE)
Circus Maximus (IRE)
Dream And Do (IRE)
Fancy Blue (IRE)
Golden Horde (IRE)
In Swoop (IRE)
Love (IRE)
Mishriff (IRE)
Palace Pier (GB)
Sottsass (FR)
Tawkeel (GB)
Torquator Tasso (GER)
Victor Ludorum (GB)

Yielding
Even So (IRE)
Magical (IRE)

Soft
Audarya (FR)
Campanelle (IRE)
Donjah (GER)
Dream of Dreams (IRE)
Glen Shiel (GB)
Nazeef (GB)
Pretty Gorgeous (FR)
St Mark's Basilica (FR)
Stradivarius (IRE)
The Revenant (GB)

Soft-to-heavy
Palace Pier (GB)

Heavy
Gear Up (IRE)
Mac Swiney (IRE)
One Master (GB)
Princess Zoe (GER)
Sealiway (FR)
Sottsass (FR)
Subjectivist (GB)
Sunny Queen (GER)
Tarnawa (IRE)
Tiger Tanaka (IRE)
Van Gogh (USA)
Wonderful Tonight (FR)
Wooded (IRE)

**GROUP 1 WINNERS OF 2020
BY WINNERS OF TWO OR MORE
GROUP/GRADE 1 RACES**

Winners of three
Addeybb (IRE)
Barney Roy (GB)
Ghaiyyath (IRE)
Love (IRE)
Magical (IRE)
Tarnawa (IRE)

Winners of two
Audarya (FR)
Battaash (IRE)
Fancy Blue (IRE)
Glass Slippers (GB)
Mogul (GB)
Nazeef (GB)
Palace Pier (GB)
Persian King (IRE)
Sottsass (FR)
Stradivarius (IRE)
Wonderful Tonight (FR)

Ireland

Tattersalls Irish 2,000 Guineas (1m, Curragh, 3yo, no geldings) - Siskin (USA)

Tattersalls Irish 1,000 Guineas (1m, Curragh, 3yo fillies) - Peaceful (IRE)

Dubai Duty Free Irish Derby (1m4f, Curragh, 3yo, no geldings) - Santiago (IRE)

Alwasmiyah Pretty Polly Stakes (1m2f, Curragh, 3yo+ fillies) - Magical (IRE)

Juddmonte Irish Oaks (1m4f, Curragh, 3yo fillies) - Even So (IRE)

Tattersalls Gold Cup (1m2f, Curragh, 4yo+) - Magical (IRE)

Keeneland Phoenix Stakes (6f, Curragh, 2yo, no geldings) - Lucky Vega (IRE)

Coolmore America 'Justify' Matron Stakes (1m, Leopardstown, 3yo+ fillies) - Champers Elysees (IRE)

Irish Champion Stakes (1m2f Leopardstown, 3yo+) - Magical (IRE)

Derrinstown Stud Flying Five Stakes (5f, Curragh, 3yo+) - Glass Slippers (GB)

Moyglare Stud Stakes (7f, Curragh, 2yo fillies) - Shale (IRE)

Goffs Vincent O'Brien National Stakes (7f, Curragh, 2yo, no geldings) - Thunder Moon (IRE)

Comer Group International Irish St Leger (1m6f, Curragh, 3yo+) - Search For A Song (IRE)

Great Britain

Hurworth Bloodstock Coronation Cup Stakes (1m4f, Newmarket, 4yo+) - Ghaiyyath (IRE)

Qipco 2000 Guineas (1m, Newmarket, 3yo, no geldings) - Kameko (USA)

Qipco 1000 Guineas (1m, Newmarket, 3yo fillies) - Love (IRE)

Queen Anne Stakes (1m, Ascot, 4yo+) - Circus Maximus (IRE)

King's Stand Stakes (5f, Ascot, 3yo+) - Battaash (IRE)

Prince of Wales's Stakes (1m2f, Ascot, 4yo+) - Lord North (IRE)

Gold Cup (2m4f, Ascot, 4yo+) - Stradivarius (IRE)

Commonwealth Cup (6f, Ascot, 3yo) - Golden Horde (IRE)

Coronation Stakes (1m, Ascot, 3yo fillies) - Alpine Star (IRE)

St James's Palace Stakes (1m, Ascot, 3yo colts) - Palace Pier (GB)

Diamond Jubilee Stakes (6f, Ascot, 4yo+) - Hello Youmzain (FR)

Investec Oaks (1m4f, Epsom, 3yo fillies) - Love (IRE)

Investec Derby (1m4f, Epsom, 3yo, no geldings) - Serpentine (IRE)

Coral-Eclipse (1m2f, Sandown, 3yo+) - Ghaiyyath (IRE)

Tattersalls Falmouth Stakes (1m, Newmarket, 3yo+ fillies & mares) - Nazeef (GB)

Darley July Cup Stakes (6f, Newmarket, 3yo+) - Oxted (GB)

King George VI and Queen Elizabeth Qipco Stakes (1m4f, Ascot, 3yo+) - Enable (GB)

Al Shaqab Goodwood Cup Stakes (2m, Goodwood, 3yo+) - Stradivarius (IRE)

Qatar Sussex Stakes (1m, Goodwood, 3yo+) - Mohaather (GB)

Qatar Nassau Stakes (1m2f, Goodwood, 3yo+ fillies & mares) - Fancy Blue (IRE)

Juddmonte International Stakes (1m2f 56yds, York, 3yo+) - Ghaiyyath (IRE)

Darley Yorkshire Oaks (1m4f, York, 3yo+ fillies & mares) - Love (IRE)

Coolmore Nunthorpe Stakes (5f, York, 2yo+) - Battaash (IRE)

Betfair Sprint Cup Stakes (6f, Haydock, 3yo+) - Dream of Dreams (IRE)

Pertemps St Leger Stakes (1m6f 115y, Doncaster, 3yo, no geldings) - Galileo Chrome (IRE)

Juddmonte Cheveley Park Stakes (6f, Newmarket, 2yo fillies) - Alcohol Free (IRE)

Juddmonte Middle Park Stakes (6f, Newmarket, 2yo colts) - Supremacy (IRE)

Kingdom of Bahrain Sun Chariot Stakes (1m, Newmarket, 3yo+ fillies & mares) - Nazeef (GB)

Bet365 Fillies' Mile (1m, Newmarket, 2yo fillies) - Pretty
  Gorgeous (FR)
Darley Dewhurst Stakes (7f, Newmarket, 2yo, no geldings) - St
  Mark's Basilica (FR)
Qipco British Champions Sprint Stakes (6f, Ascot, 3yo+) - Glen
  Shiel (GB)
Qipco British Champions Fillies & Mares Stakes (1m3f 211y,
  Ascot, 3yo+ fillies & mares) - Wonderful Tonight (FR)
Queen Elizabeth II Stakes (sponsored by Qipco) (1m, Ascot,
  3yo+) - The Revenant (GB)
Qipco Champion Stakes (1m2f, Ascot, 3yo+) - Addeybb (GB)
Vertem Futurity Trophy Stakes (1m, Doncaster, 2yo, no
  geldings) - Mac Swiney (IRE)

France (distances in metres)
Emirates Poule d'Essai des Poulains (1600m, Deauville, 3yo
  colts) - Victor Ludorum (GB)
Emirates Poule d'Essai des Pouliches (1600m, Deauville, 3yo
  fillies) - Dream And Do (IRE)
Prix Ganay (2100m, Chantilly, 4yo+) - Sottsass (FR)
Saxon Warrior Coolmore Prix Saint-Alary (2000m, Chantilly, 3yo
  fillies) - Tawkeel (GB)
Grand Prix de Saint-Cloud (2400m, Saint-Cloud, 4yo+) - Way
  To Paris (GB)
Prix du Jockey Club (2100m, Chantilly, 3yo, no geldings) -
  Mishriff (IRE)
Prix de Diane Longines (2100m, Chantilly, 3yo fillies) - Fancy
  Blue (IRE)
Qatar Prix Jean Prat (1400m, Deauville, 3yo, no geldings) -
  Pinatubo (IRE)
Prix d'Ispahan (1800m, Chantilly, 3yo) - Persian King (IRE)
Prix Rothschild (1600m, Deauville, 3yo+ fillies & mares) -
  Watch Me (FR)
LARC Prix Maurice de Gheest (1300m, Deauville, 3yo+) - Space
  Blues (IRE)
Prix du Haras de Fresnay-le-Buffard Jacques le Marois (1m,
  Deauville, 3yo+, no geldings) - Palace Pier (GB)

Darley Prix Morny - Finale des Darley Series (1200m, Deauville, 2yo, no geldings) - Campanelle (IRE)

Darley Prix Jean Romanet (2000m, Deauville, 4yo+ fillies & mares) - Audarya (FR)

Prix du Moulin de Longchamp (1600m, ParisLongchamp, 3yo+, no geldings) - Persian King (IRE)

Juddmonte Grand Prix de Paris (2400m, ParisLongchamp, 3yo, no geldings) - Mogul (GB)

Qatar Prix Vermeille (2400m, ParisLongchamp, 3yo+ fillies & mares) - Tarnawa (IRE)

Qatar Prix de Royallieu (2800m, ParisLongchamp, 3yo+ fillies & mares) - Wonderful Tonight (FR)

Qatar Prix du Cadran (4000m, ParisLongchamp, 4yo+) - Princess Zoe (GER)

Qatar Prix Jean-Luc Lagardere (1400m, ParisLongchamp, 2yo, no geldings) - Sealiway (FR)

Qatar Prix Marcel Boussac - Criterium des Pouliches (1600m, ParisLongchamp, 2yo fillies) - Tiger Tanaka (IRE)

Qatar Prix de l'Arc de Triomphe (2400m, ParisLongchamp, 3yo+, no geldings) - Sottsass (FR)

Prix de l'Opera Longines (2000m, ParisLongchamp, 3yo+ fillies & mares) - Tarnawa (IRE)

Prix de l'Abbaye de Longchamp Longines (1000m, ParisLongchamp, 2yo+) - Wooded (IRE)

Qatar Prix de le Foret (1400m, ParisLongchamp, 3yo+) - One Master (GB)

Criterium International (1600m, Saint-Cloud, 2yo, no geldings) - Van Gogh (USA)

Criterium de Saint-Cloud (2000m, Saint-Cloud, 2yo, no geldings) - Gear Up (IRE)

Prix Royal-Oak (3100m, ParisLongchamp, 3yo+) - Subjectivist (GB)

Germany

IDEE 151st Deutsches Derby (1m4f, Hamburg, 3yo, no geldings) - In Swoop (IRE)

Grosser Dallmayr-Preis - Bayerisches Zuchtrennen (1m2f, Munich, 3yo+) - Barney Roy (GB)

162nd Henkel-Preis der Diana - German Oaks (1m3f,
    Dusseldorf, 3yo fillies) - Miss Yoda (GER)
58th Preis von Europa (1m4f, Cologne, 3yo+) - Donjah (GER)
130th Longines Grosser Preis von Berlin (1m4f, Hoppegarten,
    1m 4f, 3yo+) - Barney Roy (GB)
148th Longines Grosser Preis von Baden (1m4f, Baden-Baden,
    3yo+) - Torquator Tasso (GER)
Grosser Preis von Bayern (1m4f, Munich, 3yo+) - Sunny Queen
    (GER)

EUROPEAN-TRAINED
GROUP/GRADE 1 WINNERS OF 2020
OUTSIDE OF EUROPE

Australia
Ranvet Stakes (1m2f, Rosehill, 3yo+) – Addeybb (IRE)

Longines Queen Elizabeth Stakes (1m2f, Randwick, 3yo+) – Addeybb (IRE)

Lexus Melbourne Cup (2m, Flemington, 3yo+) - Twilight Payment (IRE)

Hong Kong
Longines Hong Kong Vase (1m4f, Sha Tin, 3yo+) - Mogul (GB)

United Arab Emirates
Jebel Hatta sponsored by Emirates Airline (1m1f, Meydan, 3yo+) – Barney Roy (GB)

United States of America
Breeders' Cup Turf Sprint (5f 110y, Keeneland, 3yo+) - Glass Slippers (GB)

Maker's Mark Breeders' Cup Filly & Mare Turf (1m1f 110y, Keeneland, 3yo+ fillies & mares) - Audarya (FR)

FanDuel Breeders' Cup Mile presented by Permanently Disabled Jockey Fund (1m, Keeneland, 3yo+) - Order of Australia (IRE)

Longines Breeders' Cup Turf (1m4f, Keeneland, 3yo+) - Tarnawa (IRE)

Aspetar, 72, 210
Aspiration, 277, 279, 368
Assatis, 35
Assessor, 169
Astaire, 181
Atan, 59, 278
Atyaaf, 35-6, 368
Aube Indienne, 77
Audarya, 6, 13, 40, 44-7, 185, 288, 292, 319, 336, 340, 342, 348, 350, 354, 359, 362, 369, 375, 380, 383, 387-8, 391, 395, 397-9, 403, 405
Aunt Pearl, 58
Aussie Rules, 99, 293
Australia, 7-9, 11, 13, 17-9, 81, 100-2, 118, 134, 193, 195, 277, 338, 341-2, 346-7, 349, 352-3, 357-8, 363, 366, 369-70
Austrian School, 238
Authentic, 271
Authorized, 7-8, 11, 18, 232-3, 235, 238, 338, 342, 347, 352-3, 359, 367-8
Auyantepui, 292
Awesome Again, 105, 357
Awtaad, 182, 202, 289

Bahamian Bounty, 181, 186
Bahri, 73, 168, 170
Balladonia, 47, 337
Bandini, 144
Bangkok, 27, 49, 143
Banks Hill, 194
Barathea, 169, 218-9
Barney Roy, 5, 9, 11, 18-9, 21, 26-7, 48-52, 72, 143, 307, 338, 341, 344, 349, 354, 361-2, 368, 375, 379, 383, 385-6, 388, 393, 395-7, 399, 403-5
Baron Samedi, 61
Barrington Court, 226
Barshiba, 33
Bated Breath, 167, 254
Batshoof, 64

Incitation, 135, 370
Indian Ridge, 14, 17, 52, 59-60, 83, 91, 97, 109-10, 164-5, 222, 224, 359
Indigo Girl, 221
Infamy, 263
Inns of Court, 188
Intense Focus, 158, 181
Intikhab, 50, 54
Intrigued, 100, 102, 363, 370
Intriguing Glimpse, 198, 363, 372
Invincible Spirit, 6-8, 11, 13, 18, 46, 55-6, 59, 76, 86, 110 127, 145, 150, 164, 167-8, 172, 181, 183, 187, 196, 198-9, 202-3, 205, 211-3, 218, 220, 224, 266, 269, 296, 305, 317, 324, 339, 342, 344-5, 350, 353, 358-9, 366, 372
Inzar, 77
Iora, 16, 135, 363, 370
Iota, 13, 16-7, 134-5, 350, 363, 370
Iquitos, 307
Iridessa, 194-5
Irish River, 35, 124, 126
Itu, 307
Ittisaal, 142, 370
Ivanhowe, 264

Jack Hobbs, 291
Jameka, 258
James Garfield, 169, 218
Janina, 59-60, 350, 364, 372
Japan, 27-8, 49, 108, 143, 162, 175, 177, 257
Java's War, 207
Jawaher, 110, 146, 265, 298
Jennifer Eccles, 141
Jester, 205
Jet Dark, 212, 274
Jet Ski Lady, 149
Jim And Tonic, 46
Joanna, 293-4, 364, 372
Joe Bravo, 329

Quarter Moon, 99
Que Amoro, 54, 112, 304
Queen Jo Jo, 189, 304
Queen Kindly, 14, 246, 250
Queen of Carthage, 153-5, 351, 366, 373
Queen's Logic, 14, 246, 249
Quest For Fame, 150, 160
Quiet American, 269

Raa Atoll, 240
Raabihah, 39, 85, 207, 257, 287-8, 331
Rafaadah, 293-4, 351, 364, 372
Raffle Prize, 120-1, 148
Rafha, 59-60, 131, 168-70, 187, 198, 203, 212, 218, 224, 371
Rahaam, 165, 371
Rahy, 14, 41, 43, 124, 246, 250, 265, 334, 346, 355, 357, 360
Rain Flower, 91
Rainbow Quest, 16, 23, 206, 223
Raise A Grand, 35
Raise a Native, 98, 203, 253
Raise Your Skirts, 119
Raja Baba, 31
Ransom O'War, 77
Rapid Repeat, 298, 371
Raven's Pass, 46, 109, 167, 170, 317, 355, 358
Razyana, 60, 93, 131, 178, 191, 195, 242, 251, 306, 330
Real Steel, 42
Reckless Abandon, 48
Reckoning, 277, 279, 351, 363, 368
Recorder, 122
Red God, 326
Red Ransom, 31, 77
Red Rum, 227
Redattore, 329
Redoute's Choice, 63, 66, 181, 254, 343-4
Redwood, 96
Refuse To Bend, 285
Regal Parade, 293

SOURCES

Many sources were consulted during the writing of this book.
The main ones were:

arion.co.nz
attheraces.com
bloodhorse.com/stallion-register/
bloodstockreports.co.uk
European Group 1 Winners of 2018
European Group 1 Winners of 2019
france-galop.com
ifhaonline.org
irishfield.ie
pedigreequery.com
racenet.com.au
racingpost.com
racingtv.com
timeform.com
Timeform's *Racehorses* annuals
Twitter
Weatherbys/BloodHorse Global Stallions app
Weatherbys' *Return of Mares 2019* & supplement
Weatherbys' *Return of Mares 2020* & supplement
wikipedia.org

Thank you for reading *Best Racehorses of 2020 – Volume 1:
European Group 1 Winners.*

If you enjoyed this book, please spread the word
and perhaps leave a review on Amazon, Goodreads or another
book-review site.

Even a single line will do.

Reviews help authors!